D0857811

Springer Texts in Business and Economics

For further volumes:
http://www.springer.com/series/10099

Springer Texts in Business and Economics

Marko Sarstedt • Erik Mooi

A Concise Guide to Market Research

The Process, Data, and Methods Using IBM SPSS Statistics

Second Edition

 Springer

Marko Sarstedt
Faculty of Economics and Management
Otto-von-Guericke-Universität
Magdeburg
Germany
and

Faculty of Business and Law
University of Newcastle
Callaghan
Australia

Erik Mooi
Faculty of Business and Economics
University of Melbourne
Parkville, Victoria
Australia
and

Aston Business School
University of Aston
Birmingham
The United Kingdom

1st Edition ISBN 978-3-642-12540-9
1st Edition ISBN 978-3-642-12541-6 (eBook)
1st Edition DOI 10.1007/978-3-642-12541-6
Springer Heidelberg Dordrecht London New York

ISSN 2192-4333   ISSN 2192-4341 (electronic)
ISBN 978-3-642-53964-0   ISBN 978-3-642-53965-7 (eBook)
DOI 10.1007/978-3-642-53965-7
Springer Heidelberg New York Dordrecht London

Library of Congress Control Number: 2014943446

Printed on acid-free paper

Springer is part of Springer Science+Business Media (www.springer.com)

To Alexandra, Charlotte, and Maximilian
- Marko Sarstedt -

To Irma
- Erik Mooi -

Preface

Charmin is a 70-year-old brand of toilet paper that made Procter & Gamble a key player in the US toilet paper market. In Germany, however, Charmin was unknown to consumers, something Procter & Gamble decided to change in the early 2000s. Acknowledging that European consumers have different needs and wants than their US counterparts, the company conducted massive market research efforts with hundreds of potential customers. The research included focus group interviews, observational studies, and large-scale surveys. These revealed considerable differences in usage habits. For example, 60% of Germans also use toilet paper to clean their noses, 8% to remove make-up, 7% to clean mirrors, and 3% to clean their childrens' faces. Further research led Procter & Gamble to believe that the optimal tissue color is blue/yellow and that the package needed to be cubic. Advertising tests showed that the Charmin bear worked well, giving the product an emotional appeal. In the end, Procter & Gamble launched Charmin successfully in an already saturated market.

In order to gain useful consumer insights, which allowed the company to optimize the product and position it successfully in the market, Procter & Gamble had to plan a market research process. This process included asking market research question(s), collecting data, and analyzing these using quantitative methods.

This book provides an introduction to the skills necessary for conducting or commissioning such market research projects. It is written for two audiences:
- Undergraduate as well as postgraduate students in business and market research, and
- Practitioners wishing to know more about market research, or those who need a practical, yet theoretically sound, reference.

If you search for market(ing) research books on Google or Amazon, you will find that there is no shortage of such books. However, this book differs in many important ways:
- This book is a bridge between the theory of conducting quantitative research and its execution, using the market research process as a framework. We discuss market research, starting with identifying the research question, designing the data collection process, collecting, and describing data. We also introduce essential data analysis techniques, and the basics of communicating the results, including a discussion on ethics. Each chapter on quantitative methods describes

key theoretical choices and how these are executed in IBM SPSS Statistics. Unlike most other books, we do not discuss theory *or* SPSS, but link the two.

– This is a book for non-technical readers! All chapters are written in an accessible and comprehensive way so that non-technical readers can also easily grasp the data analysis methods that are introduced. Each chapter on research methods includes examples to help the reader get a hands-on feel for the technique. Each chapter concludes with an illustrated real-life case, demonstrating the application of a quantitative method. We also provide additional real-life cases, including datasets, thus allowing readers to practice what they have learnt. Other pedagogical features such as key words, examples, and end-of-chapter questions support the contents.

– This book is concise, focusing on the most important aspects that a market researcher, or manager interpreting market research, should know.

– Many chapters provide links to further readings and other websites. Mobile tags in the text allow readers to quickly browse related web content using a mobile device (see section *How to Use Mobile Tags*). This unique merger of offline and online content offers readers a broad spectrum of additional and readily accessible information. A comprehensive Web Appendix with further analysis techniques, datasets, video files, and case studies is included.

A CONCISE GUIDE TO MARKET RESEARCH
The Process, Data, and Methods Using IBM SPSS Statistics

| Start | Chapters | Service | Downloads |

Chapter 9 - Cluster Analysis

Grouping similar customers and products is a fundamental marketing concept. It is used, for example, in market segmentation. As companies cannot connect with all their customers, they have to divide markets into groups of consumers, customers, or clients (called segments) with similar needs and wants. Each of these segments can then be targeted by firms who can position themselves in a unique segment (such as Ferrari in the high-end sports car market). While market researchers often form market segments based on theoretical or practical grounds, cluster analysis allows segments to be formed on the basis of data. The segmentation of customers constitutes a standard application of cluster analysis, but it may also be used in different, sometimes rather exotic contexts such as evaluating typical supermarket shopping paths or deriving employer branding strategies.

This chapter introduces the basic principles of and steps associated with cluster analysis. Special emphasis is paid to hierarchical and k-means clustering but the chapter also introduces the more recent two-step clustering approach.

Clustering variables _ hierarchical methods _ partitioning methods _ k-means _ two-step clustering _ agglomerative clustering _ divisive clustering _ distance matrix _ Euclidean distance _ city-block distance _ Chebychev distance _ matching coefficients _ dendrogram _ profiling clusters _ icicle diagram

– Lastly, we have set up a Facebook community page called *A Concise Guide to Market Research*. This page provides a platform for discussions and the exchange of market research ideas. Just look for our book in the Facebook groups and join.

How to Use Mobile Tags

In this book, you will find numerous two-dimensional barcodes (so-called mobile tags) which enable you to gather digital information immediately. Using your mobile phone's integrated camera plus a mobile tag reader, you can call up a website directly on your mobile phone without having to enter it via the keypad. For example, the following mobile tag links to this book's website at http://www. guide-market-research.com.

Several mobile phones have a mobile tag reader readily installed but you can also download a reader for free. In this book, we use QR (quick response) codes which can be accessed by means of the readers below. Simply visit one of the following webpages or download the App from the iPhone App store or from Google play:
- Kaywa: http://reader.kaywa.com/
- i-Nigma: http://www.i-nigma.com/
- Upcode: http://www.upcodeworld.com

Once you have a reader installed, just start it and point your camera at the mobile tag and take a picture (with some readers, you don't even have to take a picture). This will open your mobile phone browser and direct you to the associated website.

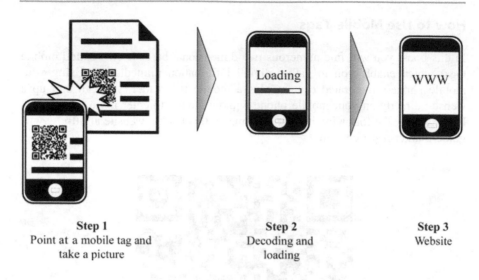

Step 1	**Step 2**	**Step 3**
Point at a mobile tag and	Decoding and	Website
take a picture	loading	

For Instructors

Besides those benefits described above, this book is also designed to make teaching using this book as easy as possible. Each chapter comes with a set of detailed and professionally designed instructors' Microsoft PowerPoint slides for educators, tailored for this book, which can be easily adjusted to fit a specific course's needs. These are available on the website's instructor resources page at http://www.guide-market-research.com. You can gain access to the instructor's page by requesting login information under Service ▸ Instructor Support.

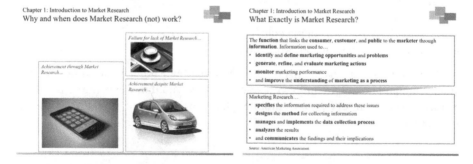

The book's web appendices are freely available on the accompanying website and provide supplementary information on analysis techniques, datasets, video files, and additional discussions of further methods not (entirely) covered in the book. Moreover, at the end of each chapter, there is a set of questions that can be used for in-class discussions.

If you have any remarks, suggestions, or ideas about this book, please drop us a line at marko.sarstedt@ovgu.de (Marko Sarstedt) or at erik.mooi@unimelb.edu.au (Erik Mooi). We appreciate any feedback on the book's concept and contents!

What's New in the Second Edition?

We've revised the second edition thoroughly. Some of the major changes in the second edition are:

- The second edition extends the **market research framework**. The market research process presented in the second chapter is fully integrated throughout the book, offering a clear and comprehensive guideline for readers.
- We increased the number of **pedagogical elements** throughout the book. Every chapter begins with a concise list of learning objectives, keywords, a short case study, and a chapter preview, highlighting the chapter contents. Chapters are organized in a more reader-friendly way, with more sections to facilitate navigation. Boxed features highlight additional contents on selected subjects.
- Learning market research vocabulary is essential for understanding the topic **Keywords** are therefore emphasized, are in italics, and are defined when they first appear. An extended glossary at the end of the book is a handy reference of the key terms.
- We have put considerable effort into **simplifying** and **streamlining** our explanations of the techniques. More figures and graphs, and less emphasis on formulas simplify the introduction of concepts. Furthermore, we have improved the click-through sequences, which guide the reader through SPSS and the real-world examples at the end of each chapter.
- The second edition contains substantial **new material** on all subjects. Most importantly, we extended the coverage of **secondary data** significantly, for example, in terms of the assessment of validity. We provide an extensive discussion of how secondary data can be made ready for analysis Internet and social networking data are emphasized even more, reflecting current market research trends. Likewise, we have extended the description of the data workflow (Chap. 5), which now includes detailed descriptions of outlier detection and missing value analysis. There is additional content in the context of regression analysis (e.g., moderation), factor analysis (e.g., choosing between principal components analysis and principal axis factoring), cluster analysis (e.g., validating and interpreting the cluster solution), and many more.
- **New Cases**, taken from real-life situations, illustrate the market research concepts discussed in each chapter. Almost all the cases draw on real-world data from companies or organizations around the globe, which gives the readers an opportunity to participate actively in the decision-making process.
- All the examples have been updated and now use **SPSS 22**. All the material reflects this new version of the program.

Acknowledgments

Thanks to all the students who have inspired us with their feedback and constantly reinforce our choice to stay in academia. Special thanks to our colleagues and good friends Joe F. Hair, Christian M. Ringle, Tobias Schütz, and Manfred Schwaiger for their continued support and help.

We have many people to thank for making this book possible. First, we would like to thank Springer, and particularly Barbara Fess and Marion Kreisel, for all of their help and for their willingness to publish this book. Second, Ilse Evertse has done a wonderful job (again!) proofreading major parts of our revisions. She is a great proofreader and we cannot recommend her enough! Drop her a line at stpubus@gmail.com if you need proofreading help. Third, we would like to thank Sebastian Lehmann, Janina Lettow, Doreen Neubert, Victor Schliwa, and Kati Zeller for their support with finalizing the manuscript and the PowerPoint slides. Finally, without the constant support and enduring patience of our families, friends, and colleagues, this book would not have been possible—thank you so much!

Finally, a large number of people have contributed to this book by reading chapters, providing examples, or datasets. For their insightful comments on the second or the previous edition of *A Concise Guide to Market Research*, we would like to thank those included in the "List of Contributors."

Contents

List of Contributors

Feray Adıgüzel Erasmus Universiteit Rotterdam, Rotterdam, The Netherlands

Ralf Aigner Wishbird, Mexico City, Mexico

Carolin Bock Technische Universität München, München, Germany

Cees J. P. M. de Bont Hong Kong Polytechnic, Hung Hom, Hong Kong

Bernd Erichson Otto von Guericke Universität Magdeburg, Magdeburg, Germany

Andrew M. Farrell Aston University, Birmingham, UK

Sebastian Fuchs thaltegos GmbH, München, Germany

David I. Gilliland Colorado State University, Fort Collins, CO, USA

Joe F. Hair Jr. Kennesaw State University, Kennesaw, GA, USA

Jörg Henseler University of Twente, Enschede, The Netherlands

Hester van Herk Vrije Universiteit Amsterdam, Amsterdam, The Netherlands

Emile F. J. Lancée Vrije Universiteit Amsterdam, Amsterdam, The Netherlands

Arjen van Lin Vrije Universiteit Amsterdam, Amsterdam, The Netherlands

Kobe Millet Vrije Universiteit Amsterdam, Amsterdam, The Netherlands

Irma Mooi-Reçi The University of Melbourne, Parkville, VIC, Australia

Leonard J. Paas Vrije Universiteit Amsterdam, Amsterdam, The Netherlands

Marcelo Gattermann Perin Pontifícia Universidade Católica do Rio Grande do Sul, Porto Alegre, Brazil

Wybe T. Popma University of Brighton, Brighton, UK

Sascha Raithel Ludwig-Maximilians-Universität München, München, Germany

Edward E. Rigdon Georgia State University, Atlanta, GA, USA

Christian M. Ringle Technische Universität Hamburg-Harburg, Hamburg, Germany

John Rudd Aston University, Birmingham, UK

Sebastian Scharf Campus M21, München, Germany

Tobias Schütz ESB Business School Reutlingen, Reutlingen, Germany

Philip Sugai International University of Japan, Minami-Uonuma, Niigata, Japan

Charles R. Taylor Villanova University, Philadelphia, PA, USA

Stefan Wagner ESMT European School of Management and Technology, Berlin, Germany

Eelke Wiersma Vrije Universiteit Amsterdam, Amsterdam, The Netherlands

Caroline Wiertz Cass Business School, London, UK

Learning Objectives

After reading this chapter, you should understand:
- What market and marketing research are and how they differ.
- How practitioner and academic market(ing) research differ and where they are similar.
- When market research should be conducted.
- Who provides market research and the importance of the market research industry.

Keywords

Full service and limited service providers • Market and marketing research • Syndicated data

1.1 Introduction

When Toyota developed the Prius – a highly fuel-efficient car using a hybrid petrol/electric engine – it took a gamble on a grand scale. Honda and General Motors' previous attempts to develop frugal (electric) cars had not worked well. Just like Honda and General Motors, Toyota had also been working on developing a frugal car but focused on a system integrating a petrol and electric engine. These development efforts led Toyota to start a project called Global Twenty-first Century aimed at developing a car with a fuel economy that was at least 50% better than similar-sized cars. This project nearly came to a halt in 1995 when Toyota encountered substantial technological problems. The company solved these problems, using nearly a thousand engineers, and launched the car, called the Prius, in Japan in 1997. Internal Toyota predictions suggested that the car was either going to be an instant hit, or that the take-up of the product would be slow, as it takes time

M. Sarstedt and E. Mooi, *A Concise Guide to Market Research*,
Springer Texts in Business and Economics, DOI 10.1007/978-3-642-53965-7_1,
© Springer-Verlag Berlin Heidelberg 2014

to teach dealers and consumers about the technology. In 1999, Toyota made the decision to start working on launching the Prius in the US. Initial market research showed that it was going to be a difficult task. Some consumers thought it was too small for the US and some thought the positioning of the controls was poor for US drivers. There were other issues too, such as the design, which many thought was too strongly geared toward Japanese drivers.

While preparing for the launch, Toyota conducted further market research, which could, however, not reveal who the potential buyers of the car would be. Initially, Toyota thought the car might be tempting for people concerned with the environment but market research dispelled this belief. Environmentalists dislike technology in general and money is a big issue for this group. A technologically complex and expensive car such as the Prius was therefore unlikely to appeal to them. Further market research did little to identify any other good market segment. Despite the lack of conclusive findings, Toyota decided to sell the car anyway and to await public reactions. Before the launch, Toyota put a market research system in place to track the initial sales and identify where customers bought the car. After the formal launch in 2000, this system quickly found that the car was being bought by celebrities to demonstrate their concern for the environment. Somewhat later, Toyota noticed substantially increased sales figures when ordinary consumers became aware of the car's appeal to celebrities. It appeared that consumers were willing to purchase cars endorsed by celebrities.

CNW Market Research, a market research company specialized in the automotive industry, attributed part of the Prius's success to its unique design, which clearly demonstrated that Prius owners were driving a different car. After substantial increases in the petrol price, and changes to the car (based on extensive market research) to increase its appeal, Toyota reached total sales of over three million and is now the market leader in hybrid petrol/electric cars.

This example shows that while market research occasionally helps, sometimes it contributes little or even fails. There are many reasons why the success of market research varies. These reasons include the budget available for research, support for market research in the organization, implementation, and the research skills of the market researchers. In this book, we will guide you through the practicalities of the basic market research process step by step. These discussions, explanations, facts, and methods will help you carry out market research successfully.

1.2   What Is Market and Marketing Research?

Market research can mean several things. It can be the process by which we gain insight into how markets work, a function in an organization, or it can refer to the outcomes of research, such as a database of customer purchases or a report including recommendations. In this book, we focus on the market research process, starting by identifying and formulating the problem, continuing by determining the research design, determining the sample and method of data collection, collecting the data, analyzing the data, interpreting, discussing, and presenting the findings, and ending with the follow-up.

Some people consider *marketing research* and *market research* to be synonymous, whereas others regard these as different concepts. The American Marketing Association, the largest marketing association in North America, defines marketing research as follows:

> The function that links the consumer, customer, and public to the marketer through information – information used to identify and define marketing opportunities and problems; generate, refine, and evaluate marketing actions; monitor marketing performance; and improve understanding of marketing as a process. Marketing research specifies the information required to address these issues, designs the method for collecting information, manages and implements the data collection process, analyzes the results, and communicates the findings and their implications (American Marketing Association 2004).

On the other hand, ESOMAR, the world organization for market, consumer and societal research, defines market research as:

> The systematic gathering and interpretation of information about individuals or organizations using the statistical and analytical methods and techniques of the applied social sciences to gain insight or support decision making. The identity of respondents will not be revealed to the user of the information without explicit consent and no sales approach will be made to them as a direct result of their having provided information (ICC/ESOMAR international code on market and social research 2007).

Both definitions overlap substantially but the definition of the AMA focuses on marketing research as a *function* (e.g., a department in an organization), whereas the ESOMAR definition focuses on the *process*. In this book, we focus on the process and, thus, on market research.

1.3   Market Research by Practitioners and Academics

Both practitioners and academics are involved in marketing and market research. Academic and practitioner views of market(ing) research differ in many ways, but also have many communalities.

A key difference is the target group. Academics almost exclusively conduct research with the goal of publishing in esteemed journals. Highly esteemed journals include: the *Journal of Marketing*, *Journal of Marketing Research*, *Journal of the Academy of Marketing Science*, and the *International Journal of Research in Marketing*. Practitioners' target group is the client, whose needs and standards include: relevance, practicality, generalizability, and timeliness. Journals, on the other hand, frequently emphasize methodological rigor and consistency. Academic journals are often difficult to read and understand, while practitioner reports should be easy to read.

Academics and practitioners differ substantially in their use of and focus on methods. Practitioners have adapted some of the methods, such as cluster analysis and factor analysis that academics have developed or refined.[1] Developing methods is often a goal in itself for academics. Practitioners are more concerned about the value of applying specific methods. Standards also differ. Practitioners' data collection methods are mostly guided by clear principles and professional conduct as advocated by ESOMAR and the AMSRS (see https://www.esomar.org/ knowledge-and-standards/codes-and-guidelines.php and http://www.amsrs.com.au/ documents/item/194, for examples). Universities or schools sometimes impose data collection and analysis standards on academics, but these tend to be general. Interestingly, many practitioners claim that their methods meet academic standards, but academics never claim that their methods are based on practitioner standards.

Besides these differences, there are also many similarities. For example, good measurement is paramount for academics as well as practitioners. Furthermore, academics and practitioners should be interested in each others' work; academics can learn much from the practical issues faced by practitioners while practitioners can gain much from understanding tools, techniques, and concepts that academics develop. The need to learn from each other was underlined by Reibstein et al. (2009) who issued an urgent call for the academic marketing community to focus on relevant business problems.[2]

1.4   When Should Market Research (Not) Be Conducted?

Market research serves a number of useful roles in organizations. Most importantly, market research can help organizations by providing answers to questions firms may have about their customers and competitors; answers that could help such firms increase their performance. Specific questions related to this include identifying market opportunities, measuring customer satisfaction, and assessing market shares. Some of these questions arise ad hoc, perhaps due to issues that the top management, or one of the departments or divisions have perceived. Much of the research is, however, programmatic; it arises because firms systematically evaluate elements of the market. An example of this type of research is conducted by Subway, the restaurant chain, which systematically measures customer satisfaction. This type of research does not usually have a distinct beginning and end (contrary to ad hoc research) but is executed continuously over time and leads to daily, weekly, or monthly reports.

The decision to conduct market research may be taken when managers face an uncertain situation and when the costs of undertaking good research are (much) lower than the expected benefits of making good decisions. Researching trivial issues or issues that cannot be changed is not helpful.

Other issues to consider are the politics within the organization; if the decision to go ahead has already been made (as in the Prius example in the introduction), market research is unnecessary. If it is conducted and supports the decision, it is of

---

[1] Roberts et al. (2014) explore the impact of marketing science tools on the practice of marketing.
[2] See Lee and Greenley (2010) for a further discussion.

little value (and those undertaking the research may be biased towards supporting the decision), while market research is ignored if it rejects the decision.

Moreover, organizations often need to make very quick decisions, for example when responding to competitive price changes, unexpected changes in regulation or the economic climate. In such situations, however, market research may only be included after decisions have already been made. Therefore, when urgent decisions have to be made, research should mostly not be undertaken.

1.5   Who Provides Market Research?

Many organizations have people, departments, or other companies working for them to provide market research. In Fig. 1.1, we show who these providers of market research are.

Most market research is provided internally through specialized market research departments or people tasked with this function. It appears that about 75% of organizations have at least one person tasked with carrying out market research. This percentage is similar across most industries, although it is much less in government sectors and, particularly, in health care (Churchill and Iacobucci 2009).

In larger organizations, internally provided market research is usually undertaken by a sub department of the marketing department. Sometimes this sub department is not connected to a marketing department but is connected to other organizational functions, such as corporate planning or sales (Rouziès and Hulland 2014). Many large organizations even have a separate market research department. This system of having a separate market research department or merging it with other departments seems to become more widespread with the marketing function increasingly devolving into other functions within organizations (Sheth and Sisodia 2006).

The external providers of market research are a powerful economic force. In 2012, external providers had a turnover of about $18.70 billion collectively (Honomichl 2013). The market research industry has also become a global field with companies such as The Nielsen Company (USA), Kantar (UK), GfK

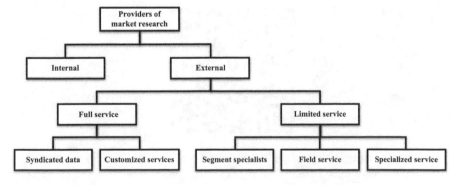

Fig. 1.1 The providers of market research

(Germany), and Ipsos (France) playing major roles outside their home markets. External providers of market research are either full or limited service providers.

Full service providers are large market research companies such as The Nielsen Company (http://www.nielsen.com), Kantar (http://www.kantar.com), and GfK (http://www.gfk.com). These large companies provide syndicated data as well as customized services. *Syndicated data* are data collected in a standard format and not specifically collected for a single client. These data, or analyses based on the data, are then sold to multiple clients. Syndicated data are mostly collected by large marketing research firms, as they have the resources to collect large amounts of data and can spread the costs of doing so over a number of clients. For example, The Nielsen Company collects syndicated data in several forms: Nielsen's Netratings, containing information on digital media; Nielsen Ratings, which details the type of consumer who listens to the radio, watches TV, or reads print media; and Nielsen Homescan, which consists of panel information on the purchases consumers make. These large firms also offer *customized services* by conducting studies for a specific client. These customized services can be very specific, such as helping a client with carrying out specific analyses.

The Nielsen People Meter
Measuring TV audiences is critical for advertisers. Yet, measuring the number of viewers per program has become more difficult as households nowadays have multiple TVs and may have different viewing platforms. In addition, "time shift" technologies such as Video-on-demand and the TIVO have further complicated the tracking of viewer behavior. Nielsen has measured TV, and other media use for over 25 years using a device called the People Meter. This device measures usage of each TV viewing platform and instantly transmits the results back to Nielsen, allowing for instant measurement. These devices are installed in over 20,000 households in the US.

In the following video, leaders and experts from The Nielsen Company discuss how the People Meter works.

https://www.youtube.com/watch?v=jYrVijea0UM

Compared to full service providers, which undertake nearly all market research activities, *limited service providers* specialize in one or more services and tend to be smaller companies. In fact, many of the specialized market research companies are one-man businesses with the owner, after (or besides) a practitioner or academic career, offering his or her specialized services. Although there are many different types of limited service firms, we only discuss three of them: those focused on segmentation, field service, and specialized services.

Segment specialists concentrate on specific market segments. An example of such specialists is Skytrax which focuses on market research in the airline and airport sector. Other segment specialists do not focus on a particular industry but on a type of customer. Ethnic Focus (http://www.ethnicfocus.com/), a UK-based market research firm, for example, focuses on understanding ethnic minorities.

Field service firms, such as Survey Sampling International (http://www. surveysampling.com/), focus on executing surveys, for example, determining samples, sample sizes, and collecting data. Some of these firms also deal with translating surveys, providing addresses and contact details.

Specialized Service firms are a catch-all term for firms that have specific technical skills, only focusing on specific products, or aspects of products such as market research on taste and smell. Specialized firms may also concentrate on a few highly specific market research techniques, or may focus on one or more highly specialized analysis techniques, such as time series analysis, panel data analysis, or quantitative text analysis. A prominent example of a specialized service firm is Envirosell (http://www.envirosell.com), a research and consultancy firm that analyzes consumer behavior in commercial environments.

The choice between these full service and limited service market research firms boils down to a tradeoff between what they can provide (if it is highly specialized, you may not have much choice) and the price of doing so. In addition, if you have to combine several studies to gain further insight, full service firms may be better than multiple limited service firms. Obviously, the fit and feel *with* the provider are highly important too!

Review Questions

1. What is market research? Try to explain what market research is in your own words.
2. Imagine you are the head of a division of Procter & Gamble. You are just about ready to launch a new shampoo but are uncertain about who might buy it. Is it useful to conduct a market research study? Should you delay the launch of the product?
3. Try to find the websites of a few market research firms. Look, for example, at the services provided by GfK and the Nielsen Company and compare the extent of

their offerings to those of specialized firms such as those listed on, for example, http://www.greenbook.org
4. If you have a specialized research question, such as what market opportunities there are for selling music to ethnic minorities, would you use a full service or limited service firm (or both)? Please discuss the benefits and drawbacks.

Further Readings

American Marketing Association at http://www.marketingpower.com
Website of the American Marketing Association. Provides information on their activities and also links to two of the premier marketing journals, the Journal of Marketing and the Journal of Marketing Research.
Marketing Research Association at http://www.mra-net.org
The Marketing Research Association is based in the US and focuses on providing knowledge, advice, and standards to those working in the market research profession.
The British Market Research Society at http://www.mrs.org.uk
The website of the British Market Research society contains a searchable directory of market research providers and useful information on market research careers and jobs.
Associação Brasileira de Empresas de Pesquisa (Brazilian Association of Research Companies) at http://www.abep.org/novo/default.aspx
The website of the Brazilian Association of Research Companies. It documents research ethics, standards, etc.
ESOMAR at http://www.esomar.org
The website of ESOMAR, the world organization for market, consumer and societal research. Amongst other activities, ESOMAR sets ethical and technical standards for market research and publishes books and reports on market research.
GreenBook: The guide for buyers of marketing research services at http://www.greenbook.org
This website provides an overview of many different types of limited service firms.

References

AMA Definition of Marketing. (2004). http://www.Marketingpower.com/AboutAMA/pages/definitionofmarketing.aspx
Churchill, G. A., & Iaccobucci, D. (2009). *Marketing research: Methodological foundation* (10th ed.). Mason, OH: Thomson.
Honomichl, J. (2013). 2013 Honomichl Top 50. *Marketing News 47*(August), 20–58.
ICC/ESOMAR international code on market and social research (2007) http://www.netcasearbitration.com/uploadedFiles/ICC/policy/marketing/Statements/ICCESOMAR_Code_English.pdf

Lee, N., & Greenley, G. (2010). The theory-practice divide: Thoughts from the editors and senior advisory board of EJM. *European Journal of Marketing, 44*(1/2), 5–20.

Reibstein, D. J., Day, G., & Wind, J. (2009). Guest editorial: Is marketing academia losing its way? *Journal of Marketing, 73*(4), 1–3.

Rouziès, D., & Hulland, J. (2014). Does marketing and sales integration always pay off? Evidence from a social capital perspective. *Journal of the Academy of Marketing Science* (in press).

Sheth J. N., & Sisodia, R. S. (Eds.) (2006). Does marketing need reform? In Does marketing need reform? Fresh perspective on the future. Armonk, NY: M.E. Sharpe.

The Market Research Process

2

Learning Objectives

After reading this chapter, you should understand:
- How to determine a research design.
- The differences between, and examples of, exploratory research, descriptive research, and causal research.
- What causality is.
- The market research process.

Keywords

Causal research • Descriptive research • Ethnographies • Exploratory research • Focus groups • Hypotheses • Interviews • Lab and field experiments • Observational studies • Scanner data

Planning a successful market research process is complex as Best Western, a worldwide association of hotels headquartered in Phoenix, Arizona, discovered. When they tried to expand the Best Western brand, they planned a substantial research process to find answers to seven major marketing questions. Answering these questions required involving several research firms, such as PriceWaterhouseCoopers. These firms then collected data to gain insights into customers, non-customers, and influencers in nine different countries.

How do organizations plan for market research processes? In this chapter, we explore the market research process and various types of research.

M. Sarstedt and E. Mooi, *A Concise Guide to Market Research*,
Springer Texts in Business and Economics, DOI 10.1007/978-3-642-53965-7_2,
© Springer-Verlag Berlin Heidelberg 2014

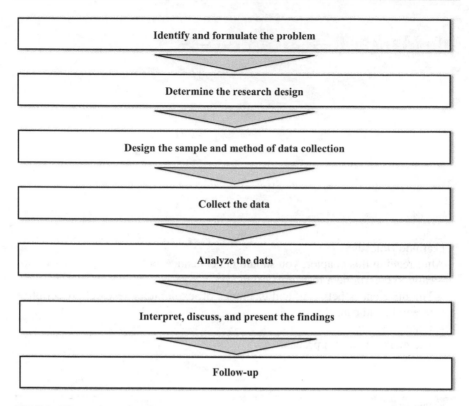

Fig. 2.1 The market research process

2.1   Introduction

Executing professional market research requires good planning. In this chapter, we introduce the planning of market research projects, starting with identifying and formulating the problem and ending with presenting the findings and the follow-up (see Fig. 2.1). This chapter is also an outline for the chapters to come.

2.2   Identify and Formulate the Problem

The first step in setting up a market research process involves identifying and formulating the research problem. Identifying the research problem is valuable, but also difficult. To identify the "right" research problem, we have to first identify the marketing symptoms or marketing opportunities. The *marketing symptom* is a problem that an organization faces. Examples of a marketing symptom include declining market shares, increasing numbers of complaints, or new products that consumers do not adopt. In some cases, there is no real existing problem but rather a *marketing opportunity*, such as potential benefits offered by new channels and products, or emerging market opportunities that need to be explored.

Organizations should identify the *marketing problem* or *marketing opportunity*, if they want to undertake market research. The marketing problem or marketing opportunity explores what underlies the marketing symptom by asking questions such as:

– *Why* is our market share declining?
– *Why* does the number of complaints increase?
– *Why* are our new products not successful?
– *How* can we enter the market for 3D printers?

Marketing problems can be divided into three categories:
– Ambiguous problems
– Somewhat defined problems, and
– Clearly defined problems.

Ambiguous problems occur when we know very little about the issues important to solve them. For example, the introduction of radically new technologies or products is often surrounded by ambiguity. When Amazon started selling products online, critical but little understood issues arose, such as how to deal with the (return) logistics and encouraging customers to purchase.

When we face *somewhat defined problems*, we know the issues (and variables) that are important for solving the problem, but not how they are related. For example, when an organization wants to export products, it is relatively easy to obtain all sorts of information, for example, on market sizes, economic development, and the political and legal system. However, how these variables impact exporting success may be very uncertain.

When we face *clearly defined problems*, both the issues and variables that are important, and their relationships are clear. However, we do not know how to make the best possible choice. Thus, we face a problem of how to optimize the situation. A clearly defined problem may arise when organizations want to change their prices. While organizations know that increasing (or decreasing) prices generally results in decreased (increased) demand, the precise relationship (i.e., how many units do we sell less when the price is increased by $1?) is unknown.

2.3   Determine the Research Design

The research design is related to the identification and formulation of the problem. Research problems and research designs are highly related. If we start working on an issue that has never been researched before, we seem to enter a funnel where we initially ask exploratory questions because we as yet know little about the issues we face. These exploratory questions are best answered using an exploratory research design. Once we have a clearer picture of the research issue after exploratory research, we move further into the funnel. Typically, we want to learn more by describing the research problem in terms of

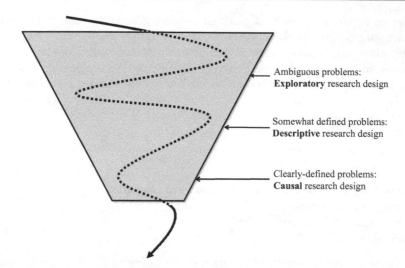

Fig. 2.2 The relationship between the marketing problem and the research design

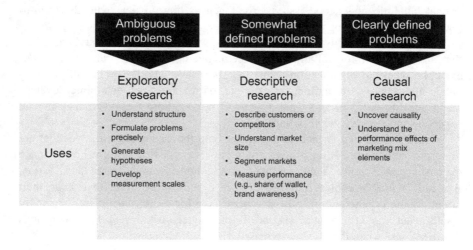

Fig. 2.3 Uses of exploratory, descriptive, and causal research

descriptive research. Once we have a reasonably complete picture of all the issues, it may be time to determine exactly how key variables are linked. Thus, we move to the narrowest part of the funnel. We do this through causal (not *casual*!) research (Fig. 2.2).

Each research design has different uses and requires the application of different analysis techniques. For example, whereas exploratory research can help to formulate problems exactly or structure them, causal research provides exact insights into how variables relate. In Fig. 2.3, we provide several examples of different types of research, which we will discuss in the following.

2.3.1   Exploratory Research

As its name suggests, the objective of exploratory research is to explore a problem or situation. As such, exploratory research has several key uses in solving ambiguous problems. It can help organizations formulate their problems exactly. Through initial research, such as interviewing potential customers, opportunities and pitfalls may be identified that help to determine or refine the research problem. It is crucial to discuss this information with the client to ensure that your findings are helpful. Such initial research also helps establish priorities (what is *nice* to know and what is *important* to know?) and to eliminate impractical ideas. For example, market research helped Toyota dispel the belief that people concerned with the environment would buy the Prius, as this target group has an aversion to high technology and lacks spending power.

2.3.2   Uses of Exploratory Research

Exploratory research may be used to formulate problems precisely. For example, depth interviews, focus groups, projective techniques, observational studies, and ethnographies are often used to achieve this. In the following, we briefly introduce each technique but provide more detailed descriptions in Chap. 4.

Depth interviews consist of interviewer asking an interviewee a number of questions. Depth interviews are unique in that they allow for probing on a one-to-one basis, fostering interaction between the interviewer and the respondent.

Focus groups usually have between 4 and 6 participants who, led by a moderator, discuss a particular subject. The key difference between an interview and focus group is that focus group participants can interact with one another (e.g., "What do you mean by…?", "How does this differ from….."), thereby providing insight into group dynamics.

Projective techniques present people with pictures, words, or other stimuli to which they respond. For example, a researcher could ask what people think of BMW owners ("A BMW owner is someone who….") or could show them a picture of a BMW and ask them what they associate the picture with. Moreover, when designing new products, market researchers can use different pictures and words to create analogies to existing products and product categories, thus making the adoption of new products more attractive (Feiereisen et al. 2008).

Observational studies are frequently used to refine research questions and clarify issues. Observational studies require an observer to monitor and interpret participants' behavior. For example, someone could monitor how consumers spend their time in shops or how they walk through the aisles of a supermarket. These studies require the presence of a person, camera or other tracking devices, such as radio frequency identification (RFID) chips, to monitor behavior. Other observational studies may consist of click stream data that tracks information on the web pages people have visited. Observational studies can also be useful to understand how people consume and/or use products. Such studies found, for example, that 5% or more of baby food in Japan is eaten by the elderly. Clearly such insights help in a country where birth rates are dropping and manufacturers have responded by labelling their produce as "food for ages 0–100" (Businessweek, January 26th, 2003).

In their paper entitled "An Exploratory Look at Supermarket Shopping Paths," Larson et al. (2005) analyze the paths taken by individual shoppers in a grocery store, as provided by RFID tags located on their shopping carts. The results provide new perspectives on many long-standing perceptions of shopper travel behavior within a supermarket, including ideas related to aisle traffic, special promotional displays, and perimeter shopping patterns.

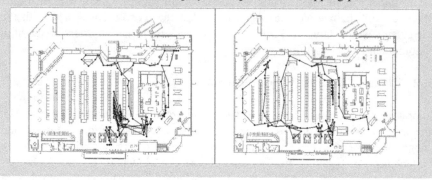

Ethnographies (or ethnographic studies) originate from anthropology. In ethnographic research a researcher interacts with consumers over a period to observe and ask questions. Such studies can consist of, for example, a researcher living with a family to observe how people buy, consume, and dispose products. For example, the market research company BBDO used ethnographies to understand consumers' rituals. The company found that many consumer rituals are ingrained in consumers in certain countries, but not in others. For example, women in Colombia, Brazil, and Japan are more than twice as likely to apply make-up when in their cars than women in other countries. These findings can help marketers in many ways.

Exploratory research can also help establish research priorities. What is important to know and what is less important? For example, a *literature search* may reveal that there are useful previous studies and that new market research is not necessary. Eliminating impractical ideas may also be achieved through exploratory research. Again, literature searches, just like interviews, may be useful to eliminate impractical ideas.

Another helpful aspect of exploratory research is the generation of *hypotheses*. A hypothesis is a claim made about a population, which can be tested by using sample results. For example, one could hypothesize that at least 10% of people in France are aware of a certain product. Marketers frequently put forward such hypotheses because they help structure decision making processes. In Chap. 6, we discuss the nature of hypotheses and how they can be tested in further detail.

Another use of exploratory research is to develop *measurement scales*. For example, what questions can we use to measure customer satisfaction? What questions work best in our context? Do potential respondents understand the wording, or do we need to make changes? Exploratory research can help us answer such questions. For example, an exploratory literature search may contain measurement scales that tell us how to measure important variables such as corporate reputation and service quality.

2.3.3 Descriptive Research

As its name implies, descriptive research is all about describing certain phenomena, characteristics or functions. It can focus on one variable (e.g., profitability) or on two or more variables at the same time ("What is the relationship between market share and profitability?" and "How does temperature relate to sales of ice cream?"). Such descriptive research often builds upon previous exploratory research. After all, to describe something, we must have a good idea of what we need to measure and how we should measure it. Key ways in which descriptive research can help us include describing customers, competitors, market segments, and measuring performance.

2.3.4 Uses of Descriptive Research

Market researchers conduct descriptive research for many purposes. These include, for example, describing customers or competitors. For instance, how large is the UK market for pre-packed cookies? How large is the worldwide market for cruises priced $10,000 and more? How many new products did our competitors launch last year? Descriptive research helps us answer such questions. For example, the Nielsen Company has vast amounts of data available in the form of *scanner data*. Scanner data are mostly collected at the checkout of a supermarket where details about each product sold are entered into a vast database. By using scanner data, it is, for example, possible to describe the market for pre-packed cookies in the UK.

Descriptive research is frequently used to segment markets. As companies often cannot connect with all (potential) customers individually, they divide markets into groups of (potential) customers with similar needs and wants. These are called *segments*. Firms can then target each of these segments by positioning themselves in a unique segment (such as Ferrari in the high-end sports car market). There are many market research companies specializing in market segmentation, such as Claritas, which developed a segmentation scheme for the US market called PRIZM (Potential Ratings Index by Zip Markets). PRIZM segments consumers along a multitude of attitudinal, behavioral, and demographic characteristics and companies can use this to better target their customers. Segments have names, such as Up-and-Comers (young professionals with a college degree and a mid-level income) and Backcountry Folk (older, often retired people with a high school degree and low income).

Another important function of descriptive market research is to measure performance. Nearly all companies regularly track their sales across specific product categories to evaluate the firm, managers, or specific employees' performance. Such descriptive work overlaps the finance or accounting departments' responsibilities. However, market researchers also frequently measure performance using measures that are quite specific to marketing, such as *share of wallet* (i.e., how much do people spend on a certain brand or company in a product category?) and *brand awareness* (i.e., do you know brand/company X?), or the *Net Promotor Score*, a customer loyalty metric for brands or firms.

2.3.5 Causal Research

Market researchers undertake causal research less frequently than exploratory or descriptive research. Nevertheless, it is important to understand the delicate relationships between important marketing variables. Causal research is used to understand the effects of one variable (e.g., the wording in advertising) on another variable (e.g., understanding as a result of advertising). It provides exact insights into how variables relate and may be useful as a test run for trying out changes in the marketing mix. The key usage of causal research is to uncover *causality*. Causality is the relationship between an event (the cause) and a second event (the effect), when the second event is a consequence of the first. To claim causality, we need to meet the following four requirements:
- Relationship between cause and effect,
- Time order,
- Control for other factors, and
- Availability of theory.

First, the cause needs to be *related* to the effect. For example, if we want to determine whether price increases cause sales to drop, there should be a negative relationship or correlation between price increases and sales decreases (see Chap. 5). Note that people often confuse correlation and causality. Just because there is some type of relationship between two variables does not mean that the one caused the other (see Box 2.1).

Second, the cause needs to come before the effect. This is the requirement of *time order*. Obviously, a price increase can only have a causal effect on sales if it occured before sales decrease.

Third, we need to *control for other factors*. If we increase the price, sales may go up because competitors increase their prices even more. Controlling for other factors is difficult, but not impossible. In experiments, we design studies so that external factors' effect is nil, or as close to nil as possible. This is achieved by, for example, conducting experiments in labs where, environmental factors such as conditions are constant (controlled for). To control for other factors, we can also use statistical tools that account for external influences. These statistical tools include analysis of variance (see Chap. 6), regression analysis (see Chap. 7), and structural equation modeling (see end of Chap. 8).

Fourth, an important criterion is that there needs to be a good *explanatory theory*. Without theory our effects may be due to chance and no "real" effect may be present. For example, we may observe that when we advertise, sales decrease. Without any good explanation for this (such as that people dislike the advertisement), we cannot claim that there is a causal relationship.

Box 2.1 Correlation does not imply causation

Correlation between two variables does not automatically imply causality. For example, in Fig. 2.4 US fatal motor vehicle crashes (per 100,000 people) are plotted against the harvested area of melons (in 1,000 acres) between 1996 and 2005.

Clearly, the picture shows a trend. If the harvested area of melons increases, the number of US fatal motor vehicle crashes increases. This is a correlation and the first requirement to determine causality. Where the story falls short in determining causality is explanatory theory. What possible mechanism could explain the findings? Other examples of *spurious correlations* not implying causality include the following:

– As ice cream sales increase, the rate of drowning deaths increases sharply. Therefore, ice cream causes drowning.
– As the number of pirates decreased, so did global temperatures increase. Therefore, global warming is caused by a lack of pirates.

If the above facts were to be presented, most people would be highly skeptical and would not interpret these facts as describing a causal mechanism. For other mechanisms, the situation is much less clear-cut. Think of claims that are part of everyday market research, such as "The new advertisement campaign caused a sharp increase in sales," "Our company's sponsorship activities helped improve our company's reputation," or "Declining sales figures are caused by competitors' aggressive price policies." Even if there is a correlation, the other requirements to determine causality may not be met. Causal research may help us to determine if causality really exists in these situations.

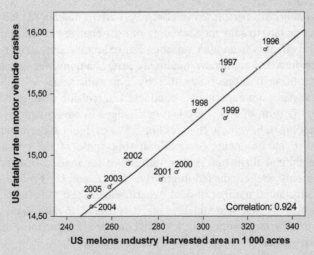

Fig. 2.4 Correlation and causation. The data were taken from the NHTSA Traffic Safety Facts, DOT HS 810 780, and the United States Department of Agriculture, National Agricultural Statistics Service

(continued)

Box 2.1 (continued)

Some of the above and additional examples can be found in Huff (1993) or on Wikipedia. Furthermore, check http://www.tylervigen.com/ for some entertaining examples of spurious correlations.

http://en.wikipedia.org/wiki/Correlation_does_not_imply_causation

2.3.6 Uses of Causal Research

Experiments are a key type of causal research and come in the form of either lab or field experiments.

Lab experiments are performed in controlled environments (usually in a company or academic lab) to gain understanding of how changes in one variable (called *stimulus*) cause changes in another variable. For example, substantial experimental research is conducted to gain understanding of how changing websites helps people navigate better through online stores, thereby increasing sales.

Field experiments are experiments conducted in real-life settings where a stimulus (often in the form of a new product or changes in advertising) is provided to gain understanding of how these changes impact sales. Field experiments are not set up in controlled environments (thus eliminating some of the causality claim's strength), but their realism makes them attractive for market research purposes. Field experiments are conducted regularly. For example, Procter & Gamble conducted a substantial number of field experiments to test the effects of different pricing strategies to help ease challenges and brand loyalty issues related to promotional pricing (see mobile tag and URL in Box 2.2 for more information). We discuss experimental set-ups in more detail in Chap. 4.

Test markets are a particular form of field experiments in which organizations in a geographically defined area introduce new products and services, or change the marketing mix to gauge consumer reactions. For example, Acxiom and GFK's Behaviorscan provide test market services. Picking a controlled and geographically

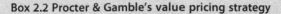

Box 2.2 Procter & Gamble's value pricing strategy

http://www.zibs.com/neslin.shtml

defined test market is difficult. Test markets help marketers learn about consumer response, thus reducing the risks associated with a nationwide rollout of new products/services or changes in the marketing mix. In Chap. 4, we discuss test markets in more depth.

2.4   Design the Sample and Method of Data Collection

After having determined the research design, we need to design a sampling plan and choose a data-collecting method. This involves deciding whether to use existing (secondary) data or to conduct primary research. We discuss this in further detail in Chap. 3.

2.5   Collect the Data

Collecting data is a practical but sometimes difficult part of the market research process. How do we design a survey? How do we measure attitudes toward a product, brand, or company if we cannot observe these attitudes directly? How do we get CEOs to respond? Dealing with such issues requires careful planning and knowledge of the marketing process. We discuss related key issues in Chap. 4.

2.6   Analyze the Data

Analyzing data requires technical skills. We discuss how to enter, clean, and describe data in Chap. 5. After this, we introduce key techniques, such as hypothesis testing and analysis of variance (ANOVA), regression analysis, factor analysis, and cluster analysis in Chaps. 6–9. In each of these chapters, we discuss the key theoretical choices and issues market researchers face when using these techniques. We also illustrate how researchers can deal practically with these theoretical choices and issues, using the market-leading software package IBM SPSS Statistics.

2.7   Interpret, Discuss, and Present the Findings

When executing the market research process, one's immediate goals are interpreting, discussing, and presenting the findings. Consequently, researchers should provide detailed answers and actionable suggestions based on data and analysis techniques. The last step is to clearly communicate the findings and recommendations to help decision making and implementation. This is further discussed in Chap. 10.

2.8   Follow-Up

Market researchers often stop when the results have been interpreted, discussed, and presented. However, following up on the research findings is important too. Implementing market research findings sometimes requires further research because suggestions or recommendations may not be feasible or practical and market conditions may have changed. From a market research firm's perspective, follow-up research on previously conducted research can be a good way of entering new deals to conduct further research.

Some market research never ends. For example, many firms track customer satisfaction over time. Even such research can have follow-ups, for example management may wish to know about drops in customer satisfaction.

Review Questions

1. What is market research? Try to explain what market research is in your own words.
2. Why do we follow a structured process when conducting market research? Are there any shortcuts you can take? Compare, for example, Qualtrix's market research process (http://www.qualtrics.com/blog/marketing-research-process/) with the process discussed above. What are the similarities and differences?
3. Describe what exploratory, descriptive, and causal research are and how these are related to one another. Provide an example of each type of research.
4. What are the four requirements for claiming causality? Do we meet these requirements in the following situations?

- Good design caused the Apple iPad to outsell its direct competitors.
- Using Aspirin makes headaches disappear.
- More advertising causes greater sales.

Further Readings

Levitt, S. D., & Dubner, S. J. (2005). *Freakonomics. A rogue economist explores the hidden side of everything.* New York, NY: HarperCollins.

An entertaining book that discusses statistical (mis)conceptions and introduces cases where people confuse correlation and causation.

Levitt, S. D., & Dubner, S. J. (2009). *Superfreakonomics.* New York, NY: HarperCollins.

The follow-up book on Freakonomics. Also worth a read.

Nielsen Retail Measurement at http://www.nielsen.com/us/en/nielsen-solutions/nielsen-measurement/nielsen-retail-measurement.html

Pearl, J. (2009). *Causality, Models, reasoning, and inference.* New York, NY: Cambridge University Press.

This book provides a comprehensive exposition of modern analysis of causation. Strongly recommended for readers with a sound background in statistics.

This website details some of the data the Nielsen company has available.

PRIZM by Claritas at http://www.claritas.com/MyBestSegments/Default.jsp?ID=20

This website allows looking up lifestyle segments at the zip level in the US.

References

Feiereisen, S., Wong, V., & Broderick, A. J. (2008). Analogies and mental simulations in learning for really new products: The role of visual attention. *Journal of Product Innovation Management, 25*(6), 593–607.

Huff, D. (1993). *How to lie with statistics.* New York, NY: W. W. Norton & Company.

Larson, J. S., Bradlow, E. T., & Fader, P. S. (2005). An exploratory look at supermarket shopping paths. *International Journal of Research in Marketing, 22*(4), 395–414. http://papers.ssrn.com/sol3/papers.cfm?abstract_id=723821.

Data

3

Learning Objectives

After reading this chapter you should understand:
- How to explain what kind of data you use.
- The differences between primary and secondary data
- The differences between quantitative and qualitative data.
- What the unit of analysis is.
- When observations are independent and when they are dependent.
- The difference between dependent and independent variables.
- Different measurement scales and equidistance.
- Validity and reliability from a conceptual viewpoint.
- How to set up different sampling designs.
- How to determine acceptable sample sizes.

Keywords

Case • Construct • Data • Equidistance • Item • Measurement scaling • Observation • Operationalization • Primary and secondary data • Qualitative and quantitative data • Reliability • Sample sizes • Sampling • Scale development • Validity • Variable

3.1 Introduction

Data lie at the heart of conducting market research. By *data* we mean a collection of facts that can be used as a basis for analysis, reasoning, or discussions. Think, for example, of the answers people give to surveys, existing company records, or observations of shoppers' behaviors.

In practice, "good" data are very important because they form the basis for useful market research. In this chapter, we will discuss some of the different types of data. This will help you describe what data you use and why. Subsequently, we discuss strategies to collect data in Chap. 4.

M. Sarstedt and E. Mooi, *A Concise Guide to Market Research*,
Springer Texts in Business and Economics, DOI 10.1007/978-3-642-53965-7_3,
© Springer-Verlag Berlin Heidelberg 2014

3.2   Types of Data

Before we start discussing data, it is a good idea to introduce some terminology. In the next sections, we will discuss the following four concepts:
– Variables,
– Constants,
– Cases, and
– Constructs.

A *variable* is an attribute whose value can change. For example, the price of a product is an attribute of that product and typically varies over time. If the price does not change, it is a *constant*. Although marketers often talk about variables, they also use the word item, which usually refers to a survey question put to a respondent. A *case* (or *observation*) consists of all the observed variables that belong to an object such as a customer, a company or a country.

The relationship between variables and cases is that within one case we usually find multiple variables. Table 3.1 includes six variables; *type of car bought*, *age* and *gender*, as well as *brand_1*, *brand_2*, and *brand_3* which capture statements related to brand trust. In the lower rows, you can see four observations.

Table 3.1 Quantitative data

Variable name	Type of car bought	Age	Gender	Brand_1	Brand_2	Brand_3
Description	Name of car bought	Age in years	Gender	This brand's product claims are believable	This brand delivers what it promises	This brand has a name that you can trust
Customer 1	BMW 328i	29	1	6	5	7
Customer 2	Mercedes C180K	45	0	6	6	6
Customer 3	VW Passat 2.0 TFSI	35	0	7	5	5
Customer 4	BMW 525ix	61	1	5	4	5

Coding for *gender*: 0=male, 1=female
Coding for *brand_1*, *brand_2*, and *brand_3*: 1=fully disagree, 7=fully agree

Another important term that is frequently used in market research is *construct*, which refers to a variable that is not directly observable (i.e., a *latent variable*). More precisely, a construct is a latent concept that researchers can define in conceptual terms but cannot measure directly (i.e., the respondent cannot articulate a single response that will totally and perfectly provide a measure of that concept). For example, constructs such as satisfaction, loyalty, or brand trust cannot be measured directly. However, we can measure indicators or manifestations of what we have agreed to call satisfaction, loyalty, or brand trust using several variables (or *items*). This requires combining these items to form a so called multi-item scale which can be used to measure a construct. Through multiple items, which all imperfectly capture a construct, we can create a measure, which better captures a construct. On the contrary, *type of car bought* from Table 3.1 is not a construct as this trait is directly observable. For example, we can directly see if a car is a BMW 328i or a Mercedes C180K.

Similar to creating constructs, we can create an *index* of sets of variables. For example, we can create an index of information search activities, which is the sum of the information that customers require from dealers, promotional materials, the Internet, and other sources. This measure of information search activities is also referred to as a *composite measure* but, unlike a construct, the items in an index define the trait to be measured. For example, the *Retail Price Index* consists of a "shopping" bag of common retail products multiplied by their price. Unlike a construct, each item in a scale perfectly captures a part of the index.

The procedure of combining several items is called *scale development, operatio-nalization*, or, in the case of an index, *index construction*. These procedures involve a combination of theory and statistical analysis, such as factor analysis (discussed in Chap. 8) aimed at developing an appropriate measure of a construct. For example, in Table 3.1, *brand_1*, *brand_2*, and *brand_3* are items that belong to a construct called *brand trust* (as defined by Erdem and Swait 2004). The construct is not an individual item that you see in the list, but it is captured by calculating the average of a number of related items. Thus, for brand trust, the score for customer 1 is $(6 + 5 + 7)/3 = 6$.

But how do we decide which and how many items to use when measuring specific constructs? To answer these questions, market researchers make use of scale development procedures which follow an iterative process with several steps and feedback loops. For example, DeVellis (2011) provides a thorough introduction to scale development. Unfortunately, scale development requires much (technical) expertise. Describing each step goes beyond the scope of this book. However, for many scales you do not need to use this procedure, as existing scales can be found in scale handbooks, such as the *Handbook of Marketing Scales* by Bearden et al. (2011). Furthermore, marketing and management journals frequently publish research articles that introduce new scales, such as for the reputation of non-profit organizations (for example Sarstedt and Schloderer 2010) or refine existing scales (for example Kuppelwieser and Sarstedt 2014). We introduce two distinctions that are often used to discuss constructs in Box 3.1.

Box 3.1 Types of constructs

Reflective vs. *formative constructs*: for reflective constructs, there is a causal relationship from the construct to the items, indicating that the items reflect the construct. Our example on brand trust suggests a reflective construct as the items reflect trust. Thus, if a respondent changes his assessment of brand trust (e.g., because of a negative brand experience), this reflects in the answers to the three items. Reflective constructs typically use multiple items (3 or more) to increase measurement stability and accuracy. If we have multiple items, we can use analysis techniques to inform us about the quality of measurement such as factor or reliability analysis (discussed in Chap. 8).

(continued)

Box 3.1 (continued)

Formative constructs consist of a number of items that define a construct. A typical example is socioeconomic status, which is formed by a combination of education, income, occupation, and residence. If any of these measures increases, socioeconomic status would increase (even if the other items did not change). Conversely, if a person's socioeconomic status increases, this would not go hand in hand with an increase in all four measures. This distinction is important when operationalizing constructs, as it requires different approaches to decide on the type and number of items. Specifically, reliability analyses (discussed in Chap. 8) cannot be used for formative measures. For an overview of this distinction, see Diamantopoulos and Winklhofer (2001) or Diamantopoulos et al. (2008).

Multi-item constructs vs. *single-item constructs*: Rather than using a large number of items to measure constructs, practitioners often use a single item. For example, we may use only "This brand has a name that you can trust" to measure brand trust instead of all three items. While this is a good way to make the questionnaire shorter, it also reduces the quality of your measures. Generally, you should avoid using single items as they have a pronounced negative impact on your findings. Only in very specific situations is the use of single items justifiable from an empirical perspective. See Diamantopoulos et al. (2012) for a discussion.

3.2.1 Primary and Secondary Data

Generally, we can distinguish between two types of data: *primary* and *secondary data*. While *primary data* are data that a researcher has collected for a specific purpose, *secondary data* are collected by another researcher for another purpose.

An example of secondary data is the US Consumer Expenditure Survey (http://www.bls.gov/cex/), which makes data available on what people in the US buy, such as insurances, personal care items, or food. It also includes the prices people pay for these products and services. Since these data have already been collected, they are secondary data. If a researcher sends out a survey with various questions to find an answer to a specific issue, the collected data are primary data. If primary data are re-used to answer another research question, it becomes secondary data.

Secondary data can either be *internal* or *external* (or a mix of both). Internal secondary data are data that an organization or individual already has collected, but wants to use for (other) research purposes. For example, we can use sales data to investigate the success of new products, or we can use the warranty claims people make to investigate why certain products are defective. External secondary data are data that other companies, organizations, or individuals have available, sometimes at a cost.

Table 3.2 The advantages and disadvantages of secondary and primary data

	Secondary data	Primary data
Advantages	– Tends to be cheaper – Sample sizes tend to be greater – Tend to have more authority – Are usually quick to access – Are easier to compare to other research that uses the same data – Are sometimes more accurate (e.g., data on competitors)	– Are recent – Are specific for the purpose – Are proprietary
Disadvantages	– May be outdated – May not completely fit the problem – There may be errors hidden in the data – difficult to assess data quality – Usually contains only factual data – No control over data collection – May not be reported in the required form (e.g., different units of measurement, definitions, aggregation levels of the data)	– Are usually more expensive – Take longer to collect

Secondary and primary data have their own specific advantages and disadvantages, which we illustrate in Table 3.2. Generally, the most important reasons for using secondary data are that they tend to be cheaper and quick to obtain access to (although there can be lengthy processes involved). For example, if you want to have access to the US Consumer Expenditure Survey, all you have to do is point your web browser to http://www.bls.gov/cex/pumdhome.htm and download the required files. Furthermore, the authority and competence of some of these research organizations might be a factor. For example, the claim that Europeans spend 9% of their annual income on health may be more believable if it comes from Eurostat (the statistical office of the European Community) than if it came from a single survey conducted through primary research.

However, important drawbacks of secondary data are that they may not answer your research question. If you are, for example, interested in the sales of a specific product (and not in a product or service category), the US Expenditure Survey may not help much. In addition, if you are interested in reasons why people buy products, this type of data may not help answer your question. Lastly, as you did not control the data collection, there may be errors in the data. Box 3.2 shows an example of inconsistent results in two well-known surveys on Internet usage.

In contrast, primary data tend to be highly specific because the researcher (you!) can influence what the research comprises. In addition, primary research can be carried out when and where it is required and cannot be accessed by competitors. However, gathering primary data often requires much time and effort and, therefore, is usually expensive compared to secondary data.

As a rule, start looking for secondary data first. If they are available, and of acceptable quality, use them! We will discuss ways to gather primary and secondary data in Chap. 4.

Box 3.2 Contradictory results in secondary data

IAB Europe (http://www.iabeurope.eu) is a trade organization for media companies such as CNN Interactive and Yahoo! Europe focused on interactive business. The Mediascope study issued yearly by the IAB provides insight into the European population's media consumption habits. For example, according to their 2008 study, 47% of all Germans were online every single day. However, this contradicts the results from the well-known German General Survey (ALLBUS) issued by the Leibniz Institute for Social Sciences (http://www.gesis.org), according to which merely 26% of Germans used the Internet on a daily basis in 2008.

3.2.2   Quantitative and Qualitative Data

Data can be *quantitative* or *qualitative*. Quantitative data are presented in values, whereas qualitative data are not. Qualitative data can take many forms such as words, stories, observations, pictures, or audio. The distinction between qualitative and quantitative data is not as black-and-white as it seems, because quantitative data are based on qualitative judgments. For example, the questions on brand trust in Table 3.1 take the values of 1–7. There is no reason why we could not have used other values to code these answers, but it is common practice to code answers of a construct's items on a range of 1–5 or 1–7.

In addition, when data are "raw," we often label them qualitative data, although researchers can code attributes of the data, thereby turning it into quantitative data. Think, for example, of how people respond to a new product in an interview. We can code this by setting neutral responses to 0, somewhat positive responses to 1, positive responses to 2, and very positive responses to 3. We have thus turned qualitative data into quantitative data. This is also qualitative data's strength and weakness; qualitative data are very rich but can be interpreted in many different ways. Thus, the process of interpreting qualitative data is subjective. To reduce some of these problems, qualitative data should be coded by (multiple) trained researchers. The distinction between quantitative and qualitative data is closely related to that between quantitative and qualitative research, which we discuss in Box 3.3. Most people think of quantitative data as being more factual and precise than qualitative data, but this is not necessarily true. Rather, what is important is how well qualitative data have been collected and/or coded into quantitative data.

3.3   Unit of Analysis

The unit of analysis is the level at which a variable is measured. Researchers often ignore this aspect, but it is crucial because it determines what we can learn from the data. Typical measurement levels include respondents, customers, stores, companies, or countries. It is best to use data at the lowest possible level, because

> **Box 3.3 Quantitative and qualitative research**
> Market researchers often label themselves as either *quantitative* or *qualitative researchers*. The two types of researchers use different methodologies, different types of data, and focus on different research questions. Most people regard the difference between qualitative and quantitative as one between numbers and words, with quantitative researchers focusing on numbers and qualitative researchers on words. This distinction is not accurate, as many qualitative researchers use numbers in their analyses. Rather, the distinction should be made according to when the information is *quantified*. If we know which possible values occur in the data before the research starts, we conduct quantitative research. If we only know this after the data have been collected, we conduct qualitative research. Think of it in this way: if we ask survey questions and use a few closed questions such as "Is this product of good quality?" and the respondents can choose between "Completely disagree," "Somewhat disagree," "Neutral," "Somewhat agree," and "Completely agree," we know that the data we will obtain from this will – at most – contain five different values. Because we know all possible values before hand, the data is *quantified* beforehand. If, on the other hand, we ask someone, "Is this product of good quality?," he or she could give many different answers, such as "Yes," "No," "Perhaps," "Last time yes, but lately...". This means we have no idea what the possible answer values are. Therefore, this data is qualitative. We can, however, recode these qualitative data and assign values to each response. Thus, we quantify the data, allowing further statistical analysis.
>
> Qualitative and quantitative research are equally important in the market research industry in terms of money spent on services.[1] Practically, market research is often hard to categorize in qualitative or quantitative as it may include elements of both. Research that includes both elements is sometimes called hybrid or fused market research, or mixed methodology.

this provides more detail and if we need these data at another level, we can *aggregate the data*. Aggregating data means that we sum up a variable at a lower level to create a variable at a higher level. For example, if we know how many cars all car dealers in a country sell, we can take the sum of all dealer sales, to create a variable measuring countrywide car sales. Aggregation is not possible if we have incomplete or missing data at lower levels.

---

[1] See http://www.e-focusgroups.com/press/online_article.html

3.4   Dependence of Observations

A key issue for any data is the degree to which observations are related. If we have exactly one observation from each individual, store, company, or country, we label the observations *independent*. That is, the observations are completely unrelated. If we have multiple observations of each individual, store, company, or country, we label them *dependent*. For example, we could ask respondents to rate a type of Cola, then show them an advertisement, and again ask them to rate the same type of Cola. Although the advertisement may influence the respondents, it is likely that the first response and second response will be related. That is, if the respondents first rated the Cola negatively, the chance is higher that they will continue to rate the Cola negative rather than positive after the advertisement. If the data are dependent, this often impacts what type of analysis we should use. For example, in Chap. 6 we discuss the difference between the independent samples t-test (for independent observations) and the paired samples t-test (for dependent observations).

3.5   Dependent and Independent Variables

Dependent variables represent the outcome that market researchers study while *independent variables* are those used to explain the dependent variable(s). For example, if we use the amount of advertising to explain sales, then advertising is the independent variable and sales the dependent.

This distinction is artificial, as all variables depend on other variables. For example, the amount of advertising depends on how important the product is for a company, the company's strategy, and other factors. However, the distinction is frequently used in the application of statistical methods. While researching relationships among variables, we need to distinguish between dependent and independent variables beforehand, based on theory and practical considerations.

3.6   Measurement Scaling

Not all data are equal! For example, we can calculate the average age of the respondents of Table 3.1 but it would not make much sense to calculate the average gender. Why is this? The values that we have assigned male (0) or female (1) respondents are arbitrary; we could just as well have given males the value of 1 and female the value of 0, or we could have used the values of 1 and 2. Therefore, choosing a different coding would result in different results. *Measurement scaling* refers to two things: the variables we use for measuring a certain construct (see discussion above) and the level at which a variable is measured which we discuss in this section. This can be highly confusing!

There are four levels of measurement:

- Nominal scale,
- Ordinal scale,
- Interval scale, and
- Ratio scale.

These scales relate to how we quantify what we measure. It is vital to know the scale on which something is measured because, as the gender example above illustrates, the measurement scale determines what analysis techniques we can, or cannot, use. For example, as indicated above, it makes no sense to calculate the average gender of respondents. We will come back to this issue in Chap. 5 and beyond.

The *nominal scale* is the most basic level at which we can measure something. Essentially, if we use a nominal scale, we substitute a word for a numerical value. For example, we could code what types of soft drinks are bought as follows: Coca Cola = 1, Pepsi Cola = 2, Seven-Up = 3. In this example, the numerical values represent nothing more than a label.

The *ordinal scale* provides more information. If a variable is measured on an ordinal scale, in- or decreases of values give meaningful information. For example, if we code customers' usage of a product as non-user = 0, light user = 1, and heavy user = 2, we know that if the value of the usage variable increases, the usage also increases. Therefore, something measured with an ordinal scale provides information about the *order* of our observations. However, we do not know if the differences in the order are equally spaced. That is, we do not know if the difference between "non-user" and "light user" is the same as between "light user" and "heavy user," even though the difference in values (0–1 and 1–2) is equal.

If something is measured on an *interval scale*, we have precise information on the rank order at which something is measured and we can interpret the magnitude of the differences in values directly. For example, if the temperature is 25°C, we know that if it drops to 20°C, the *difference* is exactly 5°C. This difference of 5°C is the same as the increase from 25°C to 30°C. This exact "spacing" is called *equidistance*. Equidistant scales are necessary for some analysis techniques, such as factor analysis (discussed in Chap. 8). What the interval scale does not give us, is an absolute zero point. If the temperature is 0°C it may feel cold, but the temperature can drop further. The value of 0 therefore does not mean that there is no temperature at all.

The *ratio scale* provides the most information. If something is measured on a ratio scale, we know that a value of 0 means that that particular variable is not present. For example, if a customer buys no products (value = 0) then he or she really buys no products. Or, if we spend no money on advertising a new product (value = 0), we really spend no money. Therefore, the *zero point* or origin of the variable is equal to 0.

While it is relatively easy to distinguish the nominal and interval scales, it is sometimes hard to see the difference between the interval and ratio scales. For most statistical methods, the difference between the interval and ratio scales can be ignored. In SPSS, both scales are combined into one scale called the *quantitative scale* or *metric scale*. Table 3.3 shows the differences between these four scales.

Table 3.3 Measurement Scaling

	Label	Order	Differences	Origin is 0
Nominal scale	✓			
Ordinal scale	✓	✓		
Interval scale	✓	✓	✓	
Ratio scale	✓	✓	✓	✓

3.7   Validity and Reliability

In any market research process, it is paramount to use "good" measures. Good measures are those that measure what they are supposed to measure and do so consistently. For example, if we are interested in knowing if customers like a new TV commercial, we could show a commercial and ask the following two questions afterwards:

1. "Did you enjoy watching the commercial?," and
2. "Did the commercial provide the essential information necessary for a purchase decision?"

How do we know if these questions really measure whether or not the viewers liked the commercial? We can think of this as a measurement problem through which we relate what we want to measure – whether existing customers like a new TV commercial – with what we actually measure in terms of the questions we ask. If these relate perfectly, our actual measurement is equal to what we intend to measure and we have no measurement error. If these do not relate perfectly, we have *measurement error*.

This measurement error can be divided into a *systematic* and a *random* error. We can express this as follows, where X_O stands for the observed score (i.e., what the customers indicated), X_T for the true score (i.e., what the customers' true liking of the commercial is), E_S for the systematic error, and E_R for the random error.

$$X_O = X_T + E_S + E_R$$

Systematic error is a measurement error through which we consistently measure higher, or lower, than we actually want to measure. If we were to ask, for example, customers to evaluate a TV commercial and offer them remuneration in return, they may provide more favorable information than they would otherwise have. This may cause us to think that the TV commercial is systematically more enjoyable than it is in reality. There may also be random errors. Some customers may be having a good day and indicate that they like a commercial whereas others, who are having a bad day, may do the opposite.

Fig. 3.1 Validity and
reliability

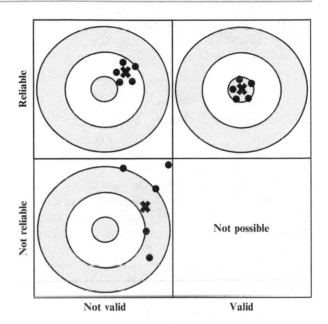

Systematic errors cause the actual measurement to be consistently higher, or lower, than what it should be. On the other hand random error causes (random) variation between what we actually measure and what we want to measure.

The systematic and random error concepts are important because they relate to a measure's validity and reliability. *Validity* refers to whether we are measuring what we want to measure and, therefore, to a situation where the systematic error E_S is zero. *Reliability* is the degree to which what we measure is free from random error and, therefore, relates to a situation where the E_R is zero. In Fig. 3.1, we illustrate the difference between reliability and validity by means of a target comparison. In this analogy, repeated measurements (e.g., of a customer's satisfaction with a specific service) are compared to arrows that are shot at a target. To measure each score, we have five measurements (indicated by the black circles) whose average is indicated by a cross. Validity describes the cross's proximity to the bull's eye at the target center. The closer the average to the true score, the higher the validity. If several arrows are fired, reliability is the degree to which the arrows are apart. When all arrows are close together, the measure is reliable, even though it is not necessarily near the bull's eye. This corresponds to the upper left box where we have a scenario in which the measure is reliable but not valid. In the upper right box, both reliability and validity are given. In the lower left box, though, we have a situation in which the measure is neither reliable, nor valid. Obviously, this is because the repeated measurements are scattered around and the average does not match the true score. However, even if the latter were the case (i.e., if the cross were in the bull's eye), we would still not consider the measure valid. An unreliable measure can never be valid because we cannot distinguish the systematic error from the random error. If we repeated the measurement, say, five more times, the random error would likely shift the cross in a different position. Thus, reliability is a necessary condition for validity. This is also why the scenario not reliable/valid (lower right box) is not included as it is not possible for a measure to be valid, but not reliable.

3.7.1 Types of Validity

For some variables, such as length or income, we can objectively verify what the true score is. For constructs such as satisfaction, loyalty or brand trust, this is impossible. From a philosophical point of view, one could even argue that there is no "true" score for a construct. So how do we know if a measure is valid? Because there is no direct way to know what it is that we are measuring, there are several forms of validity, including construct, face, content, predictive, and criterion validity. These types of validity help us understand the association between what we should measure and what we actually measure.

Construct validity relates to the correspondence between a measure at the conceptual level and a purported measure. Construct validity includes the different types of validity discussed next.

Face validity is an absolute minimum requirement for a variable to be valid and refers to whether a variable reflects what you want to measure. Essentially, face validity exists if a measure seems to make sense. For example, if you want to measure trust, using items such as "this company is honest and truthful" makes quite a lot of sense, whereas "this company is not well known" makes much less sense. Researchers should agree on face validity before starting the actual measurement (i.e., handing out the questions to respondents). Face validity is often determined by using a sample of experts who discuss and agree on the degree of face validity (this is also referred to as *expert validity*).

Content validity is strongly related to face validity but is more formalized. To assess content validity, researchers need to first define what they want to measure and discuss what is included in the definition and what not. For example, trust between businesses is often defined as the extent to which a firm believes that its exchange partner is honest and/or benevolent (Geyskens et al. 1998). This definition clearly indicates what should be mentioned in the questions used to measure trust (honesty and benevolence). After researchers have defined what they want to measure, questions have to be developed that relate closely to the definition. Consequently, content validity is mostly achieved before the actual measurement.

Predictive validity can be tested if we know that a measure should relate to an outcome. For example, loyalty should lead to people purchasing a product, or a measure of satisfaction should be predictive of people not complaining about a product or service. Assessing predictive validity requires collecting data at two points in time and therefore requires a greater effort.

Criterion validity is closely related to predictive validity, with the one difference that we examine the relationship between two constructs measured at the same time.[2]

3.7.2 Types of Reliability

How do we know if a measure is reliable? Reliability can be assessed by three key factors: stability of the measurement, internal consistency reliability, and inter-rater reliability.

Stability of the measurement means that if we measure something twice (also called *test–retest reliability*) we expect similar outcomes. Stability of measurement requires a market researcher to have collected two data samples and is therefore costly and could prolong the research process. Operationally, researchers administer the same test to the same sample on two different occasions and evaluate how strongly the measurements are related (more precisely, they compute correlations between the measurements; see Chap. 5 for an introduction to correlations). For a measure to be reliable, that is, stable over time, we would expect the two measurements to correlate highly. This approach is not without problems. For example, it is often hard, if not impossible, to survey the same people twice. Furthermore, the respondents may learn from past surveys, leading to "practice effects." For example, it may be easier to recall events the second time a survey is administered. Moreover, test–retest approaches do not work when the survey is about specific time points. If we ask respondents to provide information on their last restaurant experience, the second test might relate to a different restaurant experience. Thus, test–retest reliability can only be assessed for variables that are relatively stable over time.

Internal consistency reliability is by far the most common way of assessing reliability. Internal consistency reliability requires researchers to simultaneously use multiple items to measure the same concept. Think, for example, of the set of questions commonly used to measure brand trust (i.e., "This brand's product claims are believable," "This brand delivers what it promises," and "This brand has a name that you can trust"). If these items relate strongly, there is a considerable degree of internal consistency. There are several ways to calculate indices of internal consistency, including split-half reliability and Cronbach's α (pronounced as alpha), which we discuss in Chap. 8.

Inter-rater reliability is a particular type of reliability that is often used to assess the reliability of secondary data or qualitative data. If you want to measure, for example, which are the most ethical organizations in an industry, you could ask several experts to provide a rating and then calculate the degree to which their answers relate.

---

[2] There are other types of validity, such as discriminant validity (see Chap. 8) and nomological validity. See Netemeyer et al. (2003) for an overview.

3.8   Population and Sampling

A *population* is the group of units about which we want to make judgments. These units can be groups of individuals, customers, companies, products, or just about any subject in which you are interested. Populations can be defined very broadly, such as the people living in Canada, or very narrowly, such as the directors of large hospitals in Belgium. What defines a population depends on the research conducted and the goal of the research.

Sampling is the process through which we select cases from a population. The most important aspect of sampling is that the sample selected is *representative* of the population. With representative we mean that the characteristics of the sample closely match those of the population. In Box 3.4, we discuss how to determine whether a sample is representative of the population.

Box 3.4 Is my sample representative of the population?
Market researchers consider it important that their sample is representative of the population. How can we see if this is so?
– The best way to test whether the sample relates to the population is to use a dataset with information on the population. For example, the Amadeus and Orbis databases provide information at the population level. We can (statistically) compare the information from these databases to the sample selected. The Amadeus database is available at http://www.bvdinfo.com.
– You can use (industry) experts to judge the quality of your sample. They may look at issues such as the type and proportion of organizations in your sample and population.
– To check whether the responses of people included in your research do not differ significantly from non-respondents (which would lead to your sample nor being representative), you can use the *Armstrong and Overton procedure*. This procedure calls for comparing the first 50% of respondents to the last 50% with regard to key demographic variables. The idea behind this procedure is that later respondents more closely match the characteristics of non-respondents. If these differences are not significant (e.g., through hypothesis tests, discussed in Chap. 6), we find some support that there is little, or no, response bias (see Armstrong and Overton 1977). This procedure is sometimes implemented by comparing the last wave of respondents in a survey design against earlier waves. There is some evidence this procedure is better than the original procedure of Armstrong and Overton (Lindner et al. 2001).
– Using follow-up procedures, a small sample of randomly chosen non-respondents can be contacted again to ask for cooperation. This small sample can be compared against the responses that were obtained earlier to test for any differences.

(continued)

Box 3.4 (continued)

http://www.bvdinfo.com

When we develop a sampling strategy, we have three key choices:
- Census,
- Probability sampling, and
- Non-probability sampling.

If we get lucky and somehow manage to include every unit of the population in our study, we have conducted a *census* study (so, strictly speaking, this is not sampling). Census studies are rare because they are very costly and because missing just a small part of the population can have dramatic consequences. For example, if we were to conduct a census study among directors of banks in Luxemburg, we may miss out on a few because they were too busy to participate. If these busy directors happen to be those of the very largest companies, any information we collect would underestimate the effects of variables that are more important in large banks. Census studies work best if the population is small, well-defined, and accessible. Sometimes census studies are also conducted for specific reasons. For example, the US Census Bureau is required to hold a census of all persons resident in the US every 10 years. Check out the US Census Bureau's YouTube channel using the mobile tag or URL in Box 3.5 to find out more about the US Census Bureau.

Box 3.5 The US census

http://www.youtube.com/uscensusbureau#p/

If we select part of the population, we can distinguish two types of approaches: probability sampling and non-probability sampling. Figure 3.2 provides an overview of the different sampling procedures, which we will discuss in the following sections.

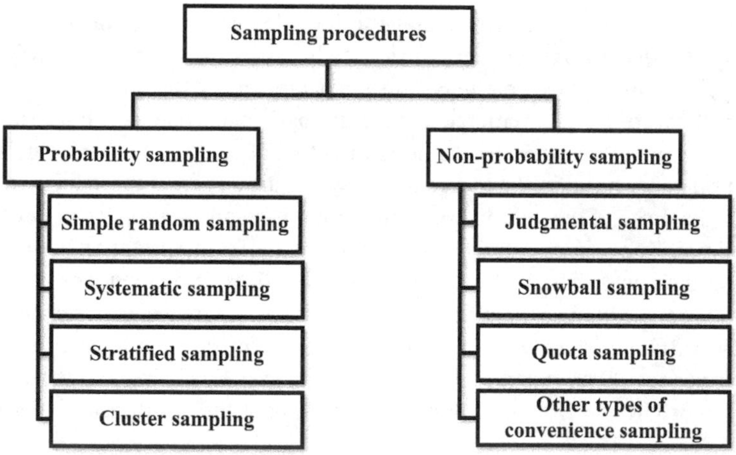

Fig. 3.2 Sampling procedures

3.8.1 Probability Sampling

Probability sampling approaches provide every individual in the population a chance (not equal to zero) of being included in the sample. This is often achieved by using an accurate *sampling frame*. A sampling frame is a list of individuals in the population. There are various sampling frames, such as Dun & Bradstreet's Selectory database (includes executives and companies), the Mint databases (includes companies in North and South Americas, Italy, Korea, the Netherlands, and the UK), or telephone directories. These sampling frames rarely completely cover the population of interest and often include some outdated information, but due to their ease of use and availability they are frequently used. If the sampling frame and population are very similar, we have little *sampling frame error*, which is the degree to which sample frames represent the population. Starting from a good-quality sampling frame, we can use several methods to select units from the sampling frame.

The easiest way is to use *simple random sampling*, which is achieved by randomly selecting the number of cases required. This can be achieved by using specialized software, or using Microsoft Excel or SPSS.[3] Specifically, Microsoft Excel can create random numbers between 0 and 1 (using the RAND() function). Next you choose those individuals from the sampling frame where the random value falls in a certain range. The range depends on the percentage of respondents needed. For example, if you wish to approach 5% of the sampling frame, you could set the range from 0.00 to 0.05.

Systematic sampling uses a different procedure. We first randomize the order of all observations, number them and, finally, select every nth observation. For example, if our sampling frame consists of 1,000 firms and we wish to select just 100 firms, we could select the 1st observation, the 11th, the 21st, etc. until we reach the end of the sampling frame and have our 100 observations.

Stratified sampling and cluster sampling are more elaborate techniques of probability sampling, which require dividing the sampling frame into different groups. When we use *stratified sampling*, we divide the population into several different homogenous groups called *strata*. These strata are based on key sample characteristics, such as different departments in organizations or the area in which consumers live. Subsequently we draw a random number of observations from each strata. While stratified sampling is more complex and requires accurate knowledge of the sampling frame and population, it also helps to assure that the sampling frame's characteristics are similar to those of the sample.

Cluster sampling requires dividing the population into different heterogeneous groups with each group's characteristics similar to those of the population. For example, we can divide the consumers of one particular country into different provinces, counties, or councils. Several of these groups can perhaps be created on the basis of key characteristics (e.g., income, political preference, household composition) that are very similar (representative) to those of the population. We can select one or more of these representative groups and use random sampling to select our observations from this group. This technique requires knowledge of the

---

[3] By going to *Data* in the SPSS menu options, then *Select Cases*, followed by *Random sample of cases*, you can indicate what percentage or exact number of cases you want to be randomly selected from the sampling frame. The use of SPSS will be discussed in detail in Chap. 5 and beyond.

sampling frame and population, but is convenient because gathering data from one group is cheaper and less time consuming.

Generally, all probability sampling methods allow for drawing representative samples from the target population. However, simple random sampling and, in particular, stratified sampling are considered superior in terms of drawing representative samples.

3.8.2   Non-probability Sampling

Non-probability sampling procedures do not give every individual in the population an equal chance of being included in the sample. This is a drawback, because the resulting sample is most certainly not representative of the population, which may bias results of subsequent analyses. Nevertheless, non-probability sampling procedures are frequently used as they are easily executed, and are typically less costly than probability sampling methods.

Judgmental sampling is based on researchers taking an informed guess regarding which individuals should be included. For example, research companies often have panels of respondents who are continuously used in research. Asking these people to participate in a new study may provide useful information if we know, from experience, that the panel has little sampling frame error.

Snowball sampling is predominantly used if access to individuals is difficult. People such as directors, doctors, or high-level managers often have little time and are, consequently, difficult to involve. If we can ask just a few of these people to provide names and details of others in a similar position, we can expand our sample quickly and access them. Similarly, if you post a link to an online questionnaire on your Facebook page (or send out a link via email) and ask your friends to share it with others, this is snowball sampling through referrals to people who would be difficult to access otherwise.

In *quota sampling*, we select observations according to some fixed quota. That is, observations are selected into the sample on the basis of pre-specified characteristics so that the total sample has the same distribution of characteristics assumed to exist in the population being studied. In other words, the researcher aims to represent the major characteristics of the population by sampling a proportional amount of each (which makes the approach similar to stratified sampling). Let's say, for example, that you want to obtain a quota sample of 100 people based on gender. First you would need to find out the proportion of the population that is men and the proportion that is women. If you found out the larger population is 40% women and 60% men, you would need a sample of 40 women and 60 men for a total of 100 respondents. You would start sampling and continue until you got those proportions and then you would stop. So, if you've already got 40 women for the sample, but not 60 men, you would continue to sample men and discard any female respondents that came along.

What makes *quota sampling* a non-probability technique is that the selection of the observations does not occur randomly. That is, once the quota has been fulfilled for a certain characteristic (e.g., females), you do not allow any more observations with this specific characteristic in the sample. This systematic component of the sampling approach can introduce a sampling error. Nevertheless, quota sampling is very effective for little cost, making it the most prominent sampling procedure in practitioner market research.

Finally, *convenience sampling* is a catch-all term for methods (including the three non-probability sampling techniques just described) in which the researcher makes a subjective judgment. For example, we can use *mall intercepts* to ask people in a shopping mall if they want to fill out a survey. The researcher's control over who ends up in the sample is limited and influenced by situational factors.

3.9 Sample Sizes

After determining the sampling procedure, we have to determine the sample size. Larger sample sizes increase the precision of the research, but are also much more expensive to collect. The gains in precision decrease as the sample size increases (in Box 6.3 we discuss the question whether a sample size can be too large in the context of significance testing). It may seem surprising that relatively small sample sizes are precise, but the strength of samples comes from accurately selecting samples, rather than through sample size. Furthermore, the required sample size has very little relation to the population size. That is, a sample of 100 employees from a company with 100,000 employees can be nearly as accurate as selecting 100 employees from a company with 1,000 employees.

There are some problems in selecting sample sizes. The first is that market research companies often push their clients towards accepting large sample sizes. Since the fee for market research services is often directly dependent on the sample size, increasing the sample size increases the market research company's profit. Second, if we want to compare different groups, we need to multiply the required sample by the number of groups included. That is, if 150 observations are sufficient to measure how much people spend on organic food, 2 times 150 observations are necessary to compare singles and couples' expenditure on organic food.

The figures mentioned above are net sample sizes; that is, these are the actual (usable) number of observations we should have. Owing to *non-response* (discussed in Chaps. 4 and 5), a multiple of the initial sample size is normally necessary to obtain the desired sample size. Before collecting data, we should have an idea of the percentage of respondents we are likely to reach (often fairly high), a percentage estimate of the respondents willing to help (often low), as well as a percentage estimate of the respondents likely to fill out the survey correctly (often high). For example, if we expect to reach 80% of the identifiable respondents, and if 25% are likely to help, and 75% of those who help are likely to fully fill out the questionnaire, only 15% (0.80·0.25·0.75) of identifiable respondents are in this case likely to provide a usable response. Thus, if we wish to obtain a net sample size of 100, we need to send out $\left(\dfrac{\text{desired sample size}}{\text{likely usable responses}} \right) = 100/0.15 = 667$ surveys. In Chap. 4, we will discuss how we can increase response rates (the percentage of people willing to help).

Review Questions

1. Please explain the difference between items and constructs.
2. What is the difference between reflective and formative constructs?
3. Explain the difference between quantitative and qualitative data and give examples of each type.
4. What is the scale on which the following variables are measured?
   - The amount of money spent by a customer on shoes.
   - The country-of-origin of a product.
   - The number of times an individual makes a complaint.
   - The grades of a test.
   - The color of a mobile phone.
5. Try to find two websites that contain secondary data and also discuss what kind of data are described. Are these qualitative or quantitative data? What is the unit of analysis and how are the data measured?
6. What is "good data"?
7. Discuss the concepts of reliability and validity. How do they relate to each other?
8. Please comment on the following statement: "Face and content validity are essentially the same."
9. What is the difference between predictive and criterion validity?
10. Imagine you have just been asked to execute a market research study to estimate the market for notebooks priced $300 or less. What sampling approach would you propose to the client?
11. Imagine that a university decides to evaluate their students' satisfaction. To do so, employees issue a questionnaire to every 10th student coming to the student cafeteria on one weekday. Which type of sampling is conducted in this situation? Can the resulting sample be representative of the population?

Further Readings

Carmines, E. G., & Zeller, R. A. (1979). *Reliability and validity assessment.* Beverly Hills, CA: Sage.
Carmines and Zeller provide an in-depth discussion of different types of reliability and validity, including how to assess them.
Churchill, G. A. (1979). A paradigm for developing better measures for marketing constructs. *Journal of Marketing Research, 16*(1), 64–73.
Probably the most widely cited marketing research article to this day. This paper marked the start of a rethinking process on how to adequately measure constructs.
Diamantopoulos A, Winklhofer HM (2001) Index construction with formative indicators: an alternative to scale development. J Mark Res 38(2):269–277.
In this seminal article the authors provide guidelines how to operationalize formative constructs.
Cochran, W. G. (1977). *Sampling techniques. Wiley series in probability and mathematical statistics* (3rd ed.). New York, NY: Wiley.

This is a seminal text on sampling techniques which provides a thorough introduction into this topic. However, please note that most descriptions are rather technical and require a sound understanding of statistics.

DeVellis, R. F. (2011). *Scale development: theory and applications* (3rd ed.). Thousand Oaks, CA: Sage.

This is a very accessible book which guides the reader through the classic way of developing multi-item scales. The text does not discuss how to operationalize formative constructs, though.

Marketing Scales Database at http://www.marketingscales.com/search/search.php

This website offers an easy-to-search database of marketing-related scales. For every scale a description is given, the scale origin and reliability and validity are discussed and the items are given.

Netemeyer, R. G., Bearden, W. O., & Sharma, S. (2003). *Scaling procedures: Issues and applications.* Thousand Oaks, CA: Sage.

Like DeVellis (2011), this book presents an excellent introduction into the principles of scale development of measurement in general.

References

Armstrong, J. S., & Overton, T. S. (1977). Estimating nonresponse bias in mail surveys. *Journal of Marketing Research, 14*(3), 396–403.

Bearden, W. O., Netemeyer, R. G., & Haws, K. L. (2011). *Handbook of marketing scales. Multi-item measures for marketing and consumer behavior research* (3rd ed.). Thousand Oaks, CA: Sage.

DeVellis, R. F. (2011). *Scale development: Theory and applications* (3rd ed.). Thousand Oaks, CA: Sage.

Diamantopoulos, A., Riefler, P., & Roth, K. P. (2008). Advancing formative measurement models. *Journal of Business Research, 61*(12), 1203–1218.

Diamantopoulos, A., Sarstedt, M., Fuchs, C., Wilczynski, P., & Kaiser, S. (2012). Guidelines for choosing between multi-item and single-item scales for construct measurement: A predictive validity perspective. *Journal of the Academy of Marketing Science, 40*(3), 434–449.

Diamantopoulos, A., & Winklhofer, H. M. (2001). Index construction with formative indicators: An alternative to scale development. *Journal of Marketing Research, 38*(2), 269–277.

Erdem, T., & Swait, J. (2004). Brand credibility, brand consideration, and choice. *Journal of Consumer Research, 31*(1), 191–198.

Geyskens, I., Steenkamp, J.-B. E. M., & Kumar, N. (1998). Generalizations about trust in marketing channel relationships using meta-analysis. *International Journal of Research in Marketing, 15*(3), 223–248.

Kuppelwieser, V., & Sarstedt, M. (2014). Confusion about the dimensionality and measurement specification of the future time perspective scale. *International Journal of Advertising, 33*(1), 113–136.

Lindner, J. R., Murphy, T. H., & Briers, G. E. (2001). Handling nonresponse in social science research. *Journal of Agricultural Education, 42*(4), 43–53.

Netemeyer, R. G., Bearden, W. O., & Sharma, S. (2003). *Scaling procedures: Issues and applications.* Thousand Oaks, CA: Sage.

Sarstedt, M., & Schloderer, M. P. (2010). Developing a measurement approach for reputation of nonprofit organizations. *International Journal of Nonprofit and Voluntary Sector Marketing, 15*(3), 276–299.

Getting Data

4

Learning Objectives

After reading this chapter, you should understand:
- How to find secondary data and decide on its suitability.
- How to collect primary data.
- How to design a basic questionnaire.
- How to set up basic experiments.
- How to set up basic qualitative research.

Keywords

Constant sum scale • CRM • Depth interviews • Directly and indirectly observed qualitative data • Ethnographies • Experiments • Face-to-face interviewing • Focus groups • Internal and external secondary data • Likert scale • Mall surveys • Mixed mode • Observational studies • Projective techniques • Semantic differential scale • Surveys • Telephone interviews • Test markets • Web surveys

4.1 Introduction

In the previous chapter, we discussed some of the key theoretical concepts and choices associated with collecting data. These concepts and choices included validity, reliability, sampling, and sample sizes. We also discussed different types of data. Building on Chap. 3, this chapter discusses the practicalities of collecting data. First, we discuss how to work with secondary data. Market researchers should always consider secondary data before collecting primary data, as secondary data usually takes less time to collect and does not depend on the respondents' willingness to participate. Although secondary data are already collected data, you usually need to spend considerable effort preparing it for analysis. If you find that secondary data are unavailable or outdated, primary data may have to be collected. In the

M. Sarstedt and E. Mooi, *A Concise Guide to Market Research*,
Springer Texts in Business and Economics, DOI 10.1007/978-3-642-53965-7_4,
© Springer-Verlag Berlin Heidelberg 2014

sections that follow, we discuss how to collect primary data through observations and surveys. Thereafter, we discuss experiments.

We introduce the practicalities of secondary data prior to those of primary data. In Figure 4.1, we provide an overview of some types of secondary and primary, data. These and some other types will be discussed in this chapter.

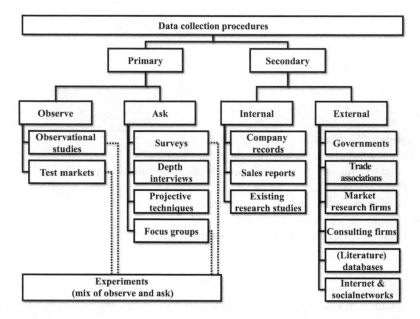

Fig. 4.1 Types of primary and secondary data sources

4.2   Secondary Data

Secondary data are data that have already been gathered, often for a different research purpose and some time ago. Secondary data comprises internal secondary data, external secondary data, or a mix of both.

4.2.1   Internal Secondary Data

Internal secondary data are data that companies compiled for various reporting and analysis purposes. Much of this data are collected and stored with the idea that "you can't manage what you don't measure."[1] Large companies have systems in place, such as accounting and *Enterprise Resource Planning* (ERP) systems, in which vast

---

[1] This quote has been attributed to Peter Drucker.

amounts of data on customers, transactions, and performance are stored. In general terms, internal secondary data comprise the following:

- Company records,
- Sales reports, and
- Existing research studies.

Company records are a firm's repository of information. They may contain data from different business functions, such as finance, or *Customer Relationship Management* (CRM). Finance may provide internal reviews of organizations' financial well-being and may provide strategic advice as they have access to a firm's financial and operational data. CRM is a term that refers to a system of databases and analysis software to track and predict customer behavior. Firms such as IBM, Microsoft, and Oracle market the database systems on which the analysis software runs. These database management systems often include information on, for example, purchasing behavior, (geo-) demographic customer data, and the after-sales service provided. This information is compiled to allow marketers to track individual customers over different sales channels and types of products in order to tailor their offerings to their customers. A number of information technology companies, such as SAP, Oracle, and Salesforce.com sell the analysis software that runs on top of these databases. Companies often use CRM systems to, for example, identify customer trends, calculate the profitability per customer, or identify opportunities for selling new or different products. The CRM market is substantial, generating over \$20 billion in 2013.[2]

Sales reports are created when products and services are sold to business-to-business clients. Many of these reports detail discussions held with clients and the products and services sold. Consequently, they can provide insights into customers' needs. Sales reports are also a means of retaining customers' suggestions regarding products and services and can therefore be a productive source of information. For example, DeMonaco et al. (2005) discovered that 59% of existing drugs had uses other than those that the producing company described. Because it is important to be aware of a drug's uses, sales discussions with doctors, hospitals, and research institutes can help the company market these drugs. When sales reports are available, they are often part of a CRM system.

Existing research studies are a good source of secondary data. You should carefully consider whether existing research studies are still useful and what you can learn from them. Even if you believe the findings of such studies to be outdated, the measures that they contain may be very useful. In order to use existing research studies, it is important that enough of their details should be available.

4.2.2 External Secondary Data

External secondary data has been compiled outside the company for many purposes. The important sources of secondary data, which we discuss next, include:

---

[2] See http://www.forbes.com/sites/louiscolumbus/2013/06/18/gartner-predictscrm-will-be-a-36b-market-by-2017/

- Governments,
- Trade associations,
- Market research firms,
- Consulting firms,
- (Literature) databases, and
- Internet & social networks.

Governments often provide data that can be used for market research purposes. For example, The *CIA World Fact Book* provides information on the economy, politics, and other issues of nearly every country in the world. Eurostat (the statistics office of the European Union) provides detailed information on the economy and different market sectors of the European Union. Much of this information is free of charge and is an easy starting point for market research studies.

CIA World Fact Book	Eurostat
https://www.cia.gov/library/publications/ the world-factbook/	http://epp.eurostat.ec.europa.eu/portal/page/ portal/eurostat/home/
Wolfram Alpha	JD Power's Initial Quality Study
http://www.wolframalpha.com/ (e.g. type in air purifiers to see the market variety in air purifiers).	http://autos.jdpower.com/ratings/quality.

Trade associations are organizations representing different companies whose purpose is to promote their common interests. For example, the Auto Alliance – which consists of US automakers – provides information on the sector and lists the key issues it faces. The European Federation of Pharmaceutical Industries and Associations represents 1,900 pharmaceutical companies operating in Europe. The federation provides a detailed list of key figures and facts, and regularly offers statistics on the industry. Most other trade associations also provide lists that include the members' names and addresses. These can be used, for example, as a sampling frame (see Chap. 3). Most trade associations consider identifying their members' opinions a key task and therefore regularly collect data. These data are often included in reports that may be downloaded from the organization's website. Such reports can be a short-cut to identifying key issues and challenges in specific industries. Sometimes, these reports are free of charge, but non-members usually need to pay a (mostly substantial) fee.

Market research firms are another source of secondary data. Particularly large market research firms provide syndicated data that different clients can use (see Chap. 1). *Syndicated data* are standardized, processed information made available to multiple (potential) clients, usually for a substantial fee. Syndicated data often allows the client's key measures (such as satisfaction or market share) to be compared against the rest of the market. Some examples of syndicated data include the J.D. Power Initial Quality Study, which provides insights into the initial quality of cars in the US, while the J.D. Power Vehicle Ownership Satisfaction Study contains similar data on other markets, such as New Zealand and Germany. Another prominent example of syndicated data is GfK Etilize, which we introduce in Box 4.1.

Box 4.1 GfK's Etilize

GfK Etilize provides resellers, distributors, manufacturers, and website portals with product data. It offers aggregated data on more than 7 million products from 20,000 manufacturers in 30 countries, and in 20 languages. The database provides details on IT, consumer electronics, household appliances, and other products. GfK Etilize also provides insight into new products being launched by providing 70,000 new information sheets that describe new products or product changes every month. The data can also be used to map product categories. Such information helps its clients understand the market structure, or identify cross-selling or up-selling possibilities. See http://www.etilize.com for more details, including a demo of its products.

Consulting firms are a rich source of secondary data. Most firms publish full reports or summaries of reports on their website. For example, McKinsey & Company publish the *McKinsey Quarterly*, a business journal that includes articles on current business trends, issues, problems, and solutions. Oliver Wyman publishes regular reports on trends and issues across many different industries. Other consulting firms, such as Gartner and Forrester provide panel data on various topics. This data can be purchased and used for secondary analysis. For example, Forrester maintains databases on market segmentation, the allocation of budgets across firms, and the degree to which consumers adopt various innovations. Consulting firms provide general advice, information, and knowledge, while market research firms only focus on marketing-related applications. In practice, there is some overlap in the activities that consulting and market research firms undertake.

(Literature) databases comprise professional and academic journals, newspapers, and books. Some of the prominent literature databases are ProQuest (http://www.proquest.co.uk) and JSTOR (http://www.jstor.org). ProQuest contains over 9,000 trade journals, business publications, and leading academic journals, including highly regarded publications such as the *Journal of Marketing* and the *Journal of Marketing Research*. A subscription is needed to gain access. Academic institutions often provide their students, and sometimes their alumni, with access to these journals. JSTOR is similar to ProQuest but is mostly aimed at academics. Consequently, it provides access to nearly all leading academic journals. A helpful feature of JSTOR is that the first page of academic articles (which usually contains the abstract) can be read free of charge. In addition, JSTOR's information is searchable via Google Scholar (discussed in Box 4.2). Certain database firms make firm-level data, such as names and addresses, available. For example, Bureau van Dijk (http://www.bvdep.com/), as well as Dun and Bradstreet (http://www.dnb.com) publish extensive lists that contain the names of firms, the industry in which they operate, their profitability, key activities, and address information. This information is often used as a sampling frame for surveys.

Internet data are a catchall term that refers to data stored to track peoples' behavior on the Internet. Such data consists of *page requests* and *sessions*. A page request refers to people clicking on a link or entering a specific Internet address. A session is a series of these requests and is often identified by the IP number, a specific address that uniquely identifies the receiver for a period of time, or through a *tracking cookie*. With this information, researchers can calculate when and why people move from one page to another. A specific type of information that often interests researchers is the *conversion rate*, which is the ratio of the number of purchases relative to the number of unique visitors (often identified by their IP address or login details).

Social networking data, such as that provided by LinkedIn, Twitter, or Facebook, provides valuable information in the form of social networking profiles, which include personal details and information. This information reflects how people would like others to perceive them and, thus, indicates consumers' intentions. Product or company-related user groups are of specific interest to market researchers. Take, for example, comments posted on a Facebook group site, such as that of BMW or Heineken. An analysis of the postings helps provide an understanding of how people perceive these brands. Interpretations of such postings usually include analyzing five elements: the agent (who is posting?), the act (what happened, i.e., what aspect does the posting refer to?), the agency (what media is used to perform the action), the scene (what is the background situation?), and the purpose (why do the agents act?). By analyzing this qualitative information, market researchers can gain insight into consumers' motives and actions. For example, Casteleyn et al. (2009) show that the Facebook posts on Heineken reveal that the brand has a negative image in Belgium. Several companies, such as Attensity (http://www.attensity.com) have software tools to analyze text information

Fig. 4.2 Snapshot of http://www.socialmention.com

and provide statistics, such as the number of mentions or complaints. A good example is www.socialmention.com, which aggregates data from different websites (including blogs) and provides a snapshot of how people and objects are rated on various dimensions. These dimensions include the strength, measured by the frequency of mentions, and the sentiment, which is the ratio of positive mentions to negative mentions. It also includes the probability of people mentioning the specific term more than once and the average number of mentions per user (reach). More detailed information on the sources of these four characteristics is also included. The snapshot in Fig. 4.2 shows part of the information when searching for "Toyota Prius."

Social websites also provide quantitative information. For example, Facebook's Ad Manager, provides information on the effectiveness of advertising on Facebook, including measures, such as the click-through-rate, and demographics, such as gender or location.

A popular term in the context of Internet and social networking data is *big data*. Big data describes very large datasets that typically include a mix of quantitative and qualitative data in very large volumes that are automatically analyzed, often with the task of making predictions. There is not one commonly accepted definition but it is clear that big data is quickly emerging. Big data is not unique to market research but spans boundaries, often including IT, strategy, marketing, and other parts of organizations.

Netflix, a provider of videos and movies, is a company that relies on big data. One challenge for Netflix is that it pays upfront for videos and movies and needs to understand which customers might buy afterwards. Netflix analyzes 2 billion hours of video each month to understand their customers and to determine which videos and movies will become hits.

Walmart, the largest retailer in the world, also uses big data. One of Walmart's challenges is to proactively suggest products and services to its customers. Using big data, Walmart connects information from many sources, including their location, and uses a product database to find related products. This helps Walmart make online recommendations.

4.3   Conducting Secondary Data Research

In Chap. 2, we discussed the market research process, starting with identifying and formulating the research question, followed by determining the research design. Once these two have been set, your attention should turn to designing the sample and method of data collection. For secondary data, this task involves the steps shown in Fig. 4.3.

4.3.1   Assess Availability of Secondary Data

Much of the secondary data we have just discussed is easily accessed through *search engines*. Search engines (such as Google, Yahoo, or Bing) provide access to many sources of secondary information. Furthermore, a large number of (specialist) databases (see the ⃝ Web Appendix → Chap. 4) also provide access to secondary data.

Search engines work by regularly crawling through the Internet to update their contents. Algorithms that include how websites are linked and other peoples' searches evaluate this content and present a set of results. Undertaking searches by means of search engines requires careful thought. For example, the word order is important (put keywords first) and operators (such as +, −, and ~) may have to be added to restrict searches. In Box 4.2, we discuss the basics of searching the Internet using Google.

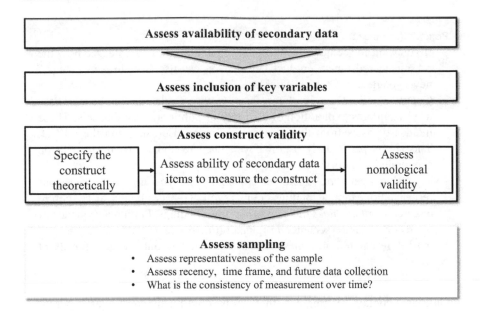

Fig. 4.3 Assessing secondary data

Box 4.2 Searching for secondary data using Google

Most people use Google daily, so why not use it for market research purposes too? Google has an easy interface but if you use the standard search box, you may not find the data you are looking for. How do you then find useful data?

- You could use Google Scholar (http://scholar.google.com) if you are looking for scholarly information such as that found in academic journals. While you can *search* for information from anywhere, specific search items can usually only be accessed if you have an organizational, university, or library password.
- By using Google Books (http://books.google.com/books), you can enter several keywords to easily search within a very large catalogue of books. Google clearly indicates the books in which the search results are found and also the pages on which the keywords occur. A cool tool of Google books is the Ngram tool (http://books.google.com/ngrams/), which shows the relative frequency with which words are used.
- Under *advanced search* on the Google homepage, you can command Google to only return searches from, for example, Excel documents by selecting *Microsoft Excel* under *file type*. Since data are often stored in spreadsheets, this is a good way to search for data. Under advanced search, you can also command Google to only provide searches of university sites by typing in *.edu* in *Search Within Site or Domain*.

(continued)

Box 4.2 (continued)

– If you want to see news from some time ago to, for example, see how the press received a new product launch, you can use Google News (http:// news.google.com/archivesearch).
– Google Public Data Explorer (http://www.google.com/publicdata/direc tory) facilitates exploration of a variety of public-interest datasets. These include datasets from the US Census Bureau, Eurostat, and the OECD. This site is particularly useful if you want to obtain visualized data on economic indicators.
– Try using operators. Operators are signs that you use to restrict your research. For example, putting a minus symbol (−) (without a space) before a search word *excludes* this word from your findings. Putting a sequence of words or an entire sentence in quotation marks (e.g., "a concise guide to market research") indicates that Google should only search for exact matches.

Databases contain existing data that can be used for market research purposes, which we discussed in the section "External Secondary Data." Additionally, Lightspeed Research (http://www.lightspeedresearch.com/), for example, maintains several databases, such as the Travel & Leisure Specialty Panel, which provides details on the vacations and holidays of selected market segments. GfK provides several databases that track retail sales. Nielsen maintains a large consumer panel of some 250,000 households in 27 countries. Clearly, it is not possible to provide an exhaustive list of what is available, but an online search, a market research agency, or expert should help you quickly identify the options.

Once a potential secondary data source has been located, the next task is to evaluate the available data. It is important to critically assess the fit of the (potential) data against your needs. Figure 4.3 provides a set of criteria to help evaluate this fit.

4.3.2 Assess Inclusion of Key Variables

Measurement is a first element to assess. It consists of a set of criteria. First, one should check if the desired variables are included in the source. Clearly, the key variables you are interested in, or could use, should be part of the data. Also check if these measures are included at the required level of analysis, which is called the aggregation level (see Chap. 3). For example, the American Customer Satisfaction Index (ACSI) satisfaction dataset reports on satisfaction at the company level.[3] If researchers need measurement of satisfaction at a product, service, or store level, these data are inappropriate.

---

[3] See http://www.theacsi.org/about-acsi/frequently-asked-questions#how_are_company for a detailed description of how ACSI data are collected.

4.3.3 Assess Construct Validity

After checking that the desired variables are included in the source, the construct validity should be assessed (see Chap. 3 for a discussion of validity). Validity relates to whether variables measure what they should measure. Construct validity is a general term relating to how a variable is defined conceptually and its suggested (empirical) measure. Houston (2002) has establishes a three-step method to assess the construct validity of secondary data measures.

- First, specify the theoretical definition of the construct you are interested in. Satisfaction is, for example, often defined as the degree to which an experience conforms to expectations and the ideal.
- Second, compare your intended measure against this theoretical definition (or another acceptable definition of satisfaction). Conceptually, the items should fit closely.
- Third, assess if these items have nomological validity. For example, satisfaction has been argued to be driven by customer expectations, perceived quality, and value, as well as to correlate with customer loyalty (Ringle et al. 2010). As such, you would expect the measure of satisfaction that you are evaluating to correlate with these measures (if included in the database).

Taking these three steps is important as construct validity is often poor when secondary data are used.[4] See Raithel et al. (2012) for an application of this three step process.

If there are multiple sources of secondary data, identical measures can be correlated to assess construct validity. For example, the Thomson Reuter SDC Platinum and the Bioscan database of the American Health Consultants both include key descriptors of firms and financial information; they therefore have a considerable overlap regarding the measures included. This may raise questions as to which databases are most suitable, particularly if the measures do not correlate highly. Fortunately, some comparisons of databases have been made. For example, Schilling (2009) compares several databases, including SDC Platinum.

4.3.4 Assess Sampling

Next, the sampling process of the collected secondary data should be assessed. First, assess the population and the representativeness of the sample drawn from it. Take, for example, the Nielsen Homescan data. The sampling process of this data collection effort is based on probability sampling, which can lead to representative samples.[5] Sellers of secondary data often emphasize the size of the data collected, but good sampling is more important than sample size! When sampling issues arise, these can be difficult to detect in secondary data, because the documents explaining

---

[4] Issues related to construct validity in business marketing are discussed by, for example, Rindfleisch and Heide (1997). A more general discussion follows in Houston (2002).

[5] See http://ageconsearch.umn.edu/bitstream/19344/1/sp05ha07.pdf

the methodology behind secondary data (bases) rarely discuss the data collection's weaknesses. For example, in many commercial mailing lists 25% (or more) of the firms included routinely have outdated contact information, are bankrupt, or otherwise not accurately recorded. This means that the number of contactable firms is structurally lower than the number of actual firms. Whether this is problematic depends on the purpose of the research. For example, descriptive statistics may be inaccurate if data are missing.

The recency of the data, the time period over which the data was collected, and the future intentions to collect data have to be assessed next. The data should be recent enough to allow decisions to be based on it. The timespan of the data collection and the intervals at which it was collected (in years, months, weeks, or in even more detail) should match the research question. For example, when introducing new products, market penetration is an important variable. Data on market penetration should be recent enough so that it is still useful. Also consider whether the data will be updated in the future and the frequency of such updates. Spending considerable time on getting to know data that will not be refreshed can be frustrating! Other measurement issues include definitions that change over time. For example, many firms changed their definitions of loyalty from behavioral (actual purchases) to attitudinal (commitment or intentions). This makes comparisons over time difficult, as measures can only be compared if the definitions are consistent.

4.4   Conducting Primary Data Research

Primary data are gathered for a specific research project or task. There are two ways to gather primary data. You can *observe* consumers' behavior, for example, through observational studies, or test markets. Alternatively, you can ask consumers directly through surveys, depth interviews, predictive techniques, or focus groups. Experiments are a special type of research, which is typically a combination of observing and asking. We provide an overview of various types of primary data collection methods in Fig. 4.1.

Next, we briefly introduce observing as a method of collecting primary data. We proceed by discussing how to set up surveys. Since surveys are the main means of collecting primary data by asking, we discuss the process of undertaking survey research in enough detail to allow you to set up your own survey-based research project. We then discuss depth interviews, including a special type of test used in these interviews (projective techniques). Lastly, we discuss combinations of observing and asking – the basics of conducting experimental research.

4.4.1   Collecting Primary Data Through Observations

Observational studies can provide important insights that are not available through other market research techniques. Observational techniques shed light on consumers' and employees' behavior and can help answer questions, such as how consumers walk through supermarkets, how they consume and dispose of products,

Fig. 4.4 The EyeSee mannequin

and how employees spend their working day. Observational techniques are normally used to understand what people are doing, rather than understand *why* people are doing something. They work well when people find it difficult to put what they are doing into words, such as when people from different ethnic backgrounds shop.

Most observational studies use video recording equipment, or trained researchers, who observe what people do unobtrusively (e.g., through one-way mirrors or by using recording equipment). Recently, researchers started using computer chips (called RFIDs) as observational equipment to trace consumers' shopping paths within a supermarket. Almax, an Italian company, has developed a special type of observational equipment. Their EyeSee product is an in-store mannequin equipped with a camera and audio recording equipment. The product also comes with software to analyze the camera recordings and provides statistical and contextual information, such as the demographics of the shoppers. Such information is useful to develop targeted marketing strategies. For example, it was found that Chinese visitors prefer to shop in Spanish stores after 4 PM, prompting these stores to increase their Chinese-speaking staff at these hours. Figure 4.4 shows what the EyeSee mannequin looks like.

A specific type of observational studies is *mystery shopping,* in which a trained researcher is asked to visit a store or restaurant and consume their products/services. For example, McDonalds and Selfridges, a UK retail chain, use mystery shoppers (see Box 4.3 for an MSNBC video on mystery shopping).

Sometimes observational studies are conducted in households; researchers participate in a household to see how people buy, consume, and dispose of products/services. The type of study in which the researcher is a participant is called an *ethnography*. An example of an ethnography is Volkswagen's Moonraker project, in which a number of Volkswagen employees followed American drivers to gain an understanding of how their usage of and preferences for automobiles differ from those of European drivers.[6]

Test markets are a useful, but costly, type of market research in which a company introduces a new product or service in a specific geographic market. Sometimes, test markets are also used to understand how consumers react to different marketing mix instruments, such as changes in pricing, distribution, or advertising and communication. Thus, test marketing is about changing the product or service offering in a real market and gauging consumers' reactions. While the results from such studies provide important insights into consumer behavior in a real-world setting, they are expensive and difficult to conduct. Some frequently used test markets include Hassloch in Germany, as well as Indianapolis and Nashville in the US.

Box 4.3 Using mystery shopping to improve customer service

https://www.youtube.com/watch?v=JK2p6GMhs0I

4.4.2   Collecting Quantitative Data: Designing Questionnaires

There is little doubt that questionnaires are the mainstay of primary market research. While it may seem easy to create a questionnaire (just ask what you want to know, right?), there are many issues that could turn good intentions into bad results. In this section, we discuss the key design choices to produce good surveys. A good survey requires at least six steps. First, determine the goal of the survey. Next, determine the type of questionnaire and method of administration. Thereafter, decide on the questions and the scale, the design of the questionnaire, and conclude by pretesting and administering the questionnaire. We show these steps in Fig. 4.5.

---

[6] See http://www.businessweek.com/autos/autobeat/archives/2006/01/there_have_been.html

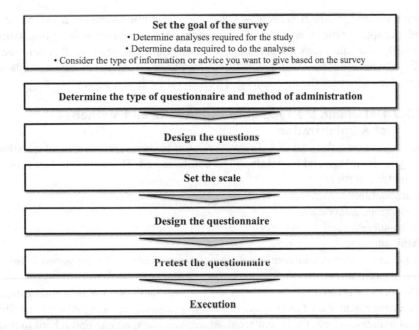

Fig. 4.5 Steps in designing questionnaires

4.4.2.1 Set the Goal of the Survey

Before you start designing the questionnaire, it is vital to consider the goal of the survey. Is it to collect quantitative data on the background of customers, to assess customer satisfaction, or do you want to understand why and how customers complain? These different goals influence the type of questions asked (such as open-ended or closed-ended questions), the method of administration (e.g., by mail or on the Web), and other design issues are discussed below. We discuss three sub-aspects that are important to consider when designing surveys.

First, it is important to consider the *analyses required for the study* early in the design process. For example, if a study's goal is to determine market segments, you should most probably use cluster analysis (cluster analysis is discussed in Chap. 9). Similarly, if the study's goal is to develop a way to systematically measure customer satisfaction, you are likely to use factor analysis (see Chap. 8).

A second step is to consider what *types of data* these analyses require. Cluster analysis, for example, often requires equidistant data (see Chap. 3), meaning that researchers need to use a type of questionnaire that can produce this data. On the other hand, factor analysis usually requires data that includes different, but related, questions. If researchers use factor analysis to distinguish between the different aspects of consumer satisfaction, they need to design a survey that allows them to conduct factor analysis.

A third point to consider is the information or *advice you want to give based on the study.* Say you are asked to help understand check-in waiting times at an airport. If the specific question is to understand how many minutes travelers are willing to wait before becoming dissatisfied, you should be able to provide answers to how much travelers' satisfaction decreases as the waiting time increases. If, on the other hand, the specific question is to understand how people perceive waiting time (short or long), your questions should focus on how travelers perceive this time and, perhaps, what influences their perception. Thus, the information or advice you want to provide influences the questions that you should ask in a survey.

4.4.2.2 Determine the Type of Questionnaire and Method of Administration

After determining the goal of a survey, you need to decide on the type of questionnaire you should use and how it should be administered. There are four key ways to administer a survey:
– Personal interviews,
– Telephone interviews,
– Web surveys, and
– Mail surveys.
In some cases, researchers combine different ways of administering surveys. This is called a *mixed mode*.

Personal interviews (or *face-to-face interviews*) can obtain high response rates, since engagement with the respondents are maximized, allowing rich information (visual expressions, etc.) to be collected. Moreover, since people find it hard to walk away from interviews, it is possible to collect answers to a reasonably lengthy set of questions. Consequently, personal interviews can support long surveys. It is also the best type of data collection for open-ended responses. In situations where the respondent is initially unknown, this may be the only feasible data collection type. Consequently, depth interviews may be highly preferable, but they are also the most costly per respondent. This is less of a concern if only small samples are required (where personal interviewing could be the most efficient). Other issues with personal interviews include the possibility of interviewer bias (i.e., a bias resulting from the interviewer's behavior, for example, in terms of his/her reactions or presentation of the questions), respondent bias to sensitive items, and that the data collection usually takes more time. Researchers normally use personal interviewing when they require an in-depth exploration of opinions. Such interviewing may also help if drop out is a key concern. For example, if they collect data from executives around the globe, using methods other than face-to-face interviewing may lead to excessive non-response in countries such as Russia or China where face-to-face interviews are seen as a sign of respect and appreciation for time used. A frequently used term in the context of depth interviewing is *CAPI*, which is an abbreviation of *Computer-Assisted Personal Interviews*. CAPI involves using computers during the interviewing process to, for example, route the interviewer through a series of questions, or to enter responses directly. Similarly, in *CASI* (*Computer-Assisted Self Interviews*) the respondent uses a computer to complete the survey questionnaire without an interviewer administering it.

Telephone interviewing allows researchers to collect data quickly. It also supports open-ended responses, though not as well as personal interviews do. Moreover, there is only a moderate control of interviewer bias, since interviewers follow predetermined protocols, and the respondent's interactions with others during the interview is strongly controlled. Telephone interviewing can be a good compromise between the low cost of mail and the richness of depth interviews. Similar to CAPI, *CATI* refers to *Computer-Assisted Telephone Interviews*. Telephone surveys are an important method of administering surveys. In the 1990s telephone interviews were typically conducted over fixed lines but mobile phone usage has soared since. In many countries mobile phone adoption rates are higher than landline adoption was (especially in African countries and India). This has caused market researchers to be increasingly interested in using mobile phones for survey purposes. The cost of calling mobile phones is still higher than calling landlines, but is decreasing.

Can market researchers simply switch to calling mobile phones? Research suggests not. In many countries, users of mobile phones differ from the country's general population in that they are younger, more educated, and represent a smaller household size. Moreover, the process of surveying by calling mobile phones differs from using landlines. For example, the likelihood of full completion of surveys is higher for mobile calling, although completion takes around 10% longer (Vincente et al. 2008). Researchers should be aware that calling mobile phones differs from calling landlines and that those who use mobile phones are unlikely to represent the general population of a country.

Web surveys (sometimes referred to as *CAWI*, or *Computer-Assisted Web Interviews*) are often the least expensive to administer and can be fast in terms of data collection, particularly since they can be set up very quickly. Researchers can administer Web surveys to very large populations, even internationally, because, besides the fixed costs of setting up a survey, the marginal costs of administering additional Web surveys is relatively low.

Many firms specializing in carrying out Web surveys will ask $0.30 (or more) to process every additional respondent, which is substantially lower than the costs of telephone interviews, depth interviews or mail surveys. It is easy to obtain precise quotes quickly. For example, Qualtrix Panels (http://qualtrics.com/panel-management/) allows a specific type of respondent and a desired sample size to be chosen. For example, using Qualtrix's sample to survey 500 current owners of cars to measure their satisfaction costs $2,500 for a 10-minute survey. This cost increases sharply if samples are hard to access and/or need to be compensated for their time. For example, surveying 500 purchasing managers by means of a 10-minute survey costs approximately $19,500.

Web surveys also support complex survey designs with elaborate branching and skip patterns that depend on the response. For example, Web surveys allow different surveys to be created for different types of products. Also, as web surveys reveal questions progressively to the respondents, the option exists to channel respondents to the next question based on their earlier responses. This procedure is called *adaptive questioning*. In addition, Web surveys can be created that allow respondents to automatically skip questions if they do not apply. For example, if a respondent has no experience using Apple's iPad, researchers can create surveys that do not ask questions about this product. The central drawback of Web surveys is the difficulty of drawing random samples, since Web access is known to be biased regarding income, race, gender, and age. Some firms, like Toluna (http://www.toluna.com) or Qualtrix (http://qualtrics.com), provide representative panels to address this concern. Another issue with Web surveys is that they impose similar burdens on the respondents as mail surveys do (see below). This makes administering long Web surveys difficult. Moreover, open-ended questions tend to be problematic because few respondents are likely to provide answers, leading to low item response. There is evidence that properly conducted Web surveys lead to data as good as that obtained from mail surveys, and that they can provide better results than personal interviews due to the lack of an interviewer and subsequent interviewer bias (Bronner and Ton 2007; Deutskens et al. 2006). In addition, in Web surveys, the respondents are less exposed to evaluation apprehension and are less inclined to respond with socially desirable behavior.[7] Web surveys are also used when a quick "straw poll" is needed on a subject.

It is important to distinguish between true web-based surveys used for collecting information on which marketing decisions will be based and polls, or very short surveys on websites that are used to increase interactivity. These polls/short surveys are used to attract and keep people interested in websites and are thus not part of market research. For example, the USA Today (http://www. usatoday.com/), an American newspaper, regularly publishes short polls on their main website.

Mail surveys are paper-based surveys sent out to respondents. They are a more expensive type of survey research and are best used for sensitive items. As no interviewer is present, there is no interviewer bias. However, mail surveys are a poor choice for complex survey designs, such as when respondents need to skip a large number of questions depending on previously asked questions, as this means that the respondent needs to correctly interpret the survey structure. Open-ended items are also problematic because few people are likely to provide answers to such questions if the survey is administered on paper. Other problems include a lack of control over the environment in which the respondent fills out the survey and that mail surveys take longer than telephone or Web surveys. However, in some situations, mail surveys are the only way to gather data. For example, while executives rarely respond to Web-based surveys, they are more likely to respond to paper-based surveys. More-over, if the participants cannot easily access the Web (such as employees working in supermarkets, cashiers, etc.), handing out paper surveys is likely more successful.

---

[7] For a comparison between CASI, CAPI and CATI with respect to differences in response behavior, see Bronner and Ton (2007).

Mixed mode approaches are increasingly used by market researchers. An example of a mixed mode survey is when potential respondents are first approached telephonically and asked to participate and confirm their email addresses, after which they are given access to a Web survey. Mixed mode approaches could also be used in cases where people are first sent a paper survey and are then called if they fail to respond to the survey.

Mixed mode approaches may help because they signal that the survey is important. They may also help response rates, as people who are more visually oriented prefer mail and Web surveys, whereas those who are aurally oriented prefer telephone surveys. By providing different modes, people can use the mode they prefer most. A downside of mixed mode surveys is that they are expensive and require a detailed address list (including a telephone number and matching email address). However, the most serious issue with mixed mode surveys is are systematic (non) response issues. For example, when filling out mail surveys, the respondents have more time than when providing answers by telephone. If respondents need this time to think about their answers, the responses obtained through mail surveys may differ systematically from those obtained by means of telephone surveying.

4.4.2.3 Design the Questions

Designing questions (items) for a survey, whether it is for a personal interview, Web survey, or mail survey, requires a great deal of thought. Take, for example, the survey item in Fig. 4.6:

Fig. 4.6 Example of a bad survey item

It is unlikely that people are able to give meaningful answers to such a question. First, using negation ("not") in sentences makes questions hard to understand. Second, the reader may not have an iPhone, or may not even know what it is. Third, the answer categories are unequally spaced. That is, the difference from neutral to disagree is unequal to the distance from neutral to completely agree. These issues are likely to create difficulties in understanding and answering questions which may, in turn, cause validity and reliability issues.

When designing survey questions, there are at least three essential rules you should keep in mind.

As a *first rule*, ask yourself whether everyone will be able to answer each question. If the question is, for example, about the quality of train transport and the respondent always travels by car, his or her answers will be meaningless. However, the framing of questions is important since, for example, questions about why that particular respondent does not use the train can be meaningful answers.

As a *second rule*, you should check whether respondents are able to construct or recall an answer. If you require details that possibly occurred a long time ago (e.g., what information did the real estate agent provide when you bought/rented your current house?), the respondents may have to "make up" an answer, which could also lead to validity and reliability issues.

As a *third rule*, assess whether the respondents will be willing to answer the questions. If questions are considered sensitive (e.g., referring to sexuality, money, etc.), respondents may adjust their answers (e.g., by reporting higher or lower incomes than are actually true). They may also not answer such questions at all. You have to determine whether these questions are necessary to attain the research objective. If they are not, omit them from the survey. What comprises a sensitive question is subjective and differs across cultures, age categories, and other variables. Use your common sense and, if necessary, expert judgment to decide whether the questions are appropriate. In addition, make sure you pretest the survey and ask those participants whether they were reluctant to provide certain answers. In some cases, a reformulation of the question can avoid this issue. For example, instead of directly asking about respondents' disposable income, you can provide various answering categories, which might increase their willingness to answer this question.

A survey's length is another issue that may make respondents reluctant to answer questions. Many people are willing to provide answers to a short questionnaire but are reluctant to even start with a lengthy survey. As the length of the survey increases, respondents' willingness and ability to complete it decrease.

Providing specifics on what is "too long" in the world of surveys is hard. The mode of surveying and the importance of the survey to the respondent help determine a maximum. Vesta Research (http://www.verstaresearch.com/blog/rules-of-thumb-for-survey-length/) suggests about 20 minutes for a telephone and a web-based (5 minutes when mobile phones are contacted) survey. 10 minutes appears to be the practical maximum for social media-based surveys. Personal interviews and mail surveys can be much longer, depending on the context. For example, surveys comprising personal interviews on topics that respondents find important, could take up to 2 hours. However, when topics are less important, mail surveys and personal interviews need to be considerably shorter.

A final issue that has a significant bearing on respondents' willingness to answer specific questions is the question type in terms of using *open-ended* or *closed-ended* questions. Open-ended questions provide little or no structure for respondents' answers. Generally, the researcher asks a question and the respondent writes down his or her answer in a box. Open-ended questions (also called *verbatim items* in the market research world) are flexible and allow explanation, but the drawback is that respondents may feel reluctant to provide such detailed information. In addition, their interpretation requires substantial coding. This coding issue arises when respondents provide many different answers (such as "sometimes," "maybe," "occasionally," or "once in a while") and the researcher has to divide these into categories (such as very infrequently, infrequently, frequently, and very frequently) for further statistical analysis. This coding is very time-consuming, subjective, and difficult. On the other hand, closed-ended questions provide a few categories from which the respondent can choose by ticking an appropriate answer. When open-ended and closed-ended questions are compared, open-ended questions usually have much lower response rates.

4.4.2.4 Set the Scale

When deciding on scales two separate decisions need to be made. First you need to decide on the type of scale. Second, you need to set the properties of the scale you chose.

Type of Scale

Marketing research and practice have provided a variety of scale types. In the following, we will discuss the most important (and useful) ones:
- Likert scales,
- Semantic differential scales, and
- Rank order scales.

The type of scaling where all categories are named and respondents indicate the degree to which they (dis)agree is called a *Likert scale*. Likert scales are used to establish the degree of agreement with a specific statement. Such a statement could be "I am satisfied with my mortgage provider." The degree of agreement is usually set by scale endings ranging from completely disagree to completely agree. Likert scales are used very frequently and are relatively easy to administer. A caveat with Likert scales is that the statement should be phrased in such a way that complete agreement, or disagreement, is possible. For example, "completely agreeing" with the statement "I have never received a spam email" is almost impossible. If the statement is too positive or negative, it is unlikely that the endings of the scale will be used, thereby reducing the number of answer categories actually used.

The *semantic differential scale* uses an opposing pair of words (young/old, masculine/feminine) and respondents then indicate to what extent they agree with that word. These scales are widely used in market research. As with Likert scales, 5 or 7 answer categories are commonly used (see the next section regarding the number of answer categories you should use). We provide an example of the semantic differential scale in Fig. 4.7, in which respondents can mark their perception of how important online evaluations are for those having to decide on a hotel. The advantages of semantic differential scales include their ability to profile respondents or objects (such as products or companies) in a simple way.

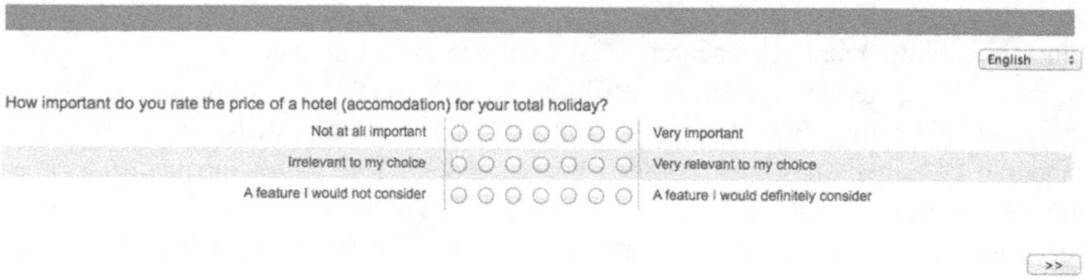

How important do you rate the price of a hotel (accomodation) for your total holiday?

Not at all important	○	○	○	○	○	○	○	Very important
Irrelevant to my choice	○	○	○	○	○	○	○	Very relevant to my choice
A feature I would not consider	○	○	○	○	○	○	○	A feature I would definitely consider

Fig. 4.7 Example of a 7-point semantic differential scale

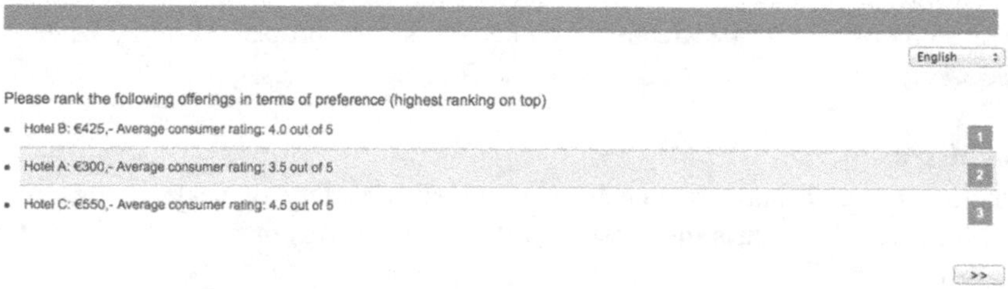

Please rank the following offerings in terms of preference (highest ranking on top)

- Hotel B: €425,- Average consumer rating: 4.0 out of 5 — **1**
- Hotel A: €300,- Average consumer rating: 3.5 out of 5 — **2**
- Hotel C: €550,- Average consumer rating: 4.5 out of 5 — **3**

Fig. 4.8 Example of a rank order scale

Rank order scales are a unique type of scale, as they force respondents to compare alternatives. In its basic form, a rank order scale (see Fig. 4.8 for an example) asks the respondent to indicate which alternative they rank highest, which alternative they rank second-highest, etc. The respondents therefore need to balance their answers instead of merely stating that everything is important. In a more complicated form, rank order scales ask the respondent to allocate a certain total number of points (often 100) to a number of alternatives. This is called the *constant sum scale*. Constant sum scales work well when a small number of answer categories is used (typically up to 5). Generally, respondents find constant scales that have 6 or 7 answer categories somewhat challenging, while constant scales that have 8 or more categories are very difficult to answer. The latter are thus best avoided.

In addition to these types of scaling, there are other types, such as graphic rating scales, which use pictures to indicate categories, and the *MaxDiff scale* in which respondents indicate the most and least applicable items. We introduce the MaxDiff scale in the ✍ Web Appendix (→ Chap. 4).

Properties of the Scale

After deciding on the type of scale, it is time to set the properties of the scale. The properties that need to be set include the following:

– The number of answer categories,
– Whether or not to use an undecided option, and
– Whether or not to use a balanced scale.

Number of answer categories: When using closed-ended questions, the number of answer categories needs to be determined. In its simplest form, a survey could use just two answer categories (yes/no). Multiple categories (such as, "completely disagree," "disagree," "neutral," "agree," "completely agree") are used more frequently to allow for more nuances. In determining how many scale categories to use, one has to balance having more variation in responses versus asking too much of the respondents. There is some evidence that 7-point scales are better than 5-point scales in terms of obtaining more variation in responses. A study analyzing 259 academic marketing studies suggests that 5-point (24.2%) and 7-point (43.9%) scales are the most common by far (Peterson 1997). Ten-point scales are most commonly used for practical market research. However, scales with a large number of answer categories often confuse respondents because the wording differences between the scale points become trivial. For example, differences between "tend to agree" and "somewhat agree" are subtle and respondents may not pick them up. Moreover, scales with many answer categories increase a survey's length. You could, of course, also use 4-point or 6-point scales (by deleting the neutral choice). If you wish to force the respondents to be positive or negative, you should use a *forced-choice* (Likert) *scale*. This could bias the answers, thereby leading to validity issues. By providing a "neutral" category choice, namely the *free-choice* (Likert) *scale*, the respondents are not forced to give a positive or negative answer. Many respondents feel more comfortable about participating in a survey when offered free-choice scales. Whatever you decide, provide descriptions of all the answer categories (such as "agree" or "neutral") to help the respondents answer

When designing answer categories, use scale categories that are exclusive, so that answers do not overlap (e.g., age categories 0–4, 5–10 etc.). A question is how to choose the spacing of categories. For example, should we divide US household income in categories 0–$9,999, $10.000–$19.999, $20,000 higher or use some other way of setting categories? One suggestion is to use narrower categories if the variable is easy to recall by the respondent. A second suggestion is to space the categories such that as researchers, we expect approximately equal number of observations in categories. In the example above we may find that most households have an income of $20.000 or higher and that categories 0–$9,999 and $10.000–$19.999 are used infrequently. It is best to choose categories where equal percentages are expected such as 0–$24,999, $25.000–$44.999, $45.000–$69.999, $70.000–$109.999, $110.000 and higher. Although the range in each category differs, we can reasonably expect that each category should hold about 20% of responses if we randomly sample US households (see http://en.wikipedia.org/wiki/House hold_income_in_the_United_States#Household_income_over_time).

Sometimes a scaling with an infinite number of answer categories is used (without providing answer categories). This seems very precise because the respondent can tick any answer on the scale. However, in practice, these are imprecise because respondents do not, for example, know where along the line "untrustworthy" falls. Another drawback of an infinite number of answer categories is that entering and analyzing the responses are time-consuming because this involves measuring the distance from one side of the scale to the answer that the respondent ticked. We provide two examples of such a semantic differential scale in the Web appendix (⌨ Web Appendix → Chap. 4).

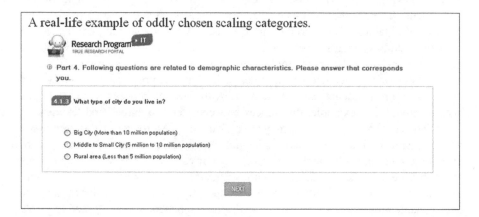

Undecided option: A related choice is to include an "undecided" category in the scaling. Using an undecided category allows the researcher to distinguish between those respondents who have a clear opinion and those who do not. Moreover, it may make answering the survey slightly easier for the respondents. While these are good reasons for including this category, the drawback is that there will then be missing observations. If a large number of respondents choose not to answer, this will substantially reduce the number of surveys that can be used for analysis. Generally, when designing surveys, you should include an "undecided" or "don't know" category as answers to questions that the respondent might genuinely not know, for example, when factual questions are asked. For other types of questions (such as on attitudes or preferences) the "undecided" or "don't know" category should not be included, as researchers are interested in respondents' perceptions regardless of their knowledge of the subject matter.

Balanced scale: A balanced scale has an equal number of positive and negative scale categories. For example, in a 5-point Likert scale, we may have two negative categories (completely disagree and disagree), a neutral option, and two positive categories (agree and completely agree). Besides this, the wording in a balanced scale should reflect equal distances between the scale items. If this is the case, we can claim that the scale is equidistant which is a requirement for its use in many analysis techniques. Therefore, we strongly recommend using a balanced scale. A caveat of balanced scales is that many constructs cannot have negative values. For example, one can have some trust in a company or very little trust, but negative trust is highly unlikely. If a scale item cannot be negative, you will have to resort to an unbalanced scale in which the endpoints of the scales are unlikely to be exact opposites. Table 4.1 summarizes the key choices we have to make when designing surveys.

Table 4.1 A summary of some of the key choices when designing surveys

Choice	Actions
Can all the respondents answer the question asked?	Ensure that all potential respondents can answer all items. If they cannot, ask screener questions to direct them. If the respondents cannot answer questions, they should be able to skip them.
Can the respondents construct/recall answers?	If the answer is no, you should use other methods to obtain information (e.g., secondary data or observations). Moreover, you should ask the respondents about major aspects before zooming in on details to help them recall answers.
Do the respondents want to answer each question?	If the questions concern "sensitive" subjects, check whether they can be omitted. If not, stress the confidentiality of the answers and mention why these answers are useful for the researcher, the respondent, or society before introducing them.
Should you use open-ended or closed-ended questions?	Keep the subsequent coding in mind. If easy coding is possible beforehand, design a set of exhaustive answer categories. Further, remember that open-ended scale items have a much lower response rate than closed-ended items.
What scaling categories should you use (closed-ended questions only)	Use Likert scales, semantic differential scales, or rank order scales.
Should you use a forced-choice or open-choice scale?	Respondents feel most comfortable with the open-choice scale. However, if an even number of scale categories is used, the forced-choice scale is most common, since the scaling can become uneven if it isn't.
Should you include an "undecided"/ "don't know" category?	Only for questions that the respondent might genuinely not know, should a "don't know" category be included. If included, place this at the end of the scale.
Should you use a balanced scale?	Always use a balanced scale. There should be an exact number of positive and negative wordings in the scale items. The words at the ends of the scale should be exact opposites.

Do's and Don'ts in Designing Survey Questions

When designing survey questions, there are a number of do's and don'ts, which we discuss in the following. Always use simple words and avoid using jargon or slang if not all the respondents are likely to understand it. There is good evidence that short sentences work better than longer sentences because they are easier to understand (Holbrook et al. 2006). Thus, try to keep survey questions short and simple. Moreover, avoid using the word *not* or *no* where possible. This is particularly important when other words in the same sentence are negative, such as "unable," or "unhelpful" because sentences with two negatives (called a double negative) are hard to understand. For example, a question such as "I do not use the email function in my iPhone because it is unintuitive" is quite hard to follow.

Also avoid the use of *vague quantifiers* such as "frequent" or "occasionally" (Dillman 2007). Vague quantifiers make it difficult for respondents to answer questions (what exactly is meant by "occasionally"?). They also make comparing responses difficult. After all, what one person considers "occasionally," may be "frequent" for another. Instead, it is better to use frames that are precise ("once a week").

Never suggest an answer, for example, by asking "Company X has done very well, how do you rate it?" In addition, avoid *double-barreled questions* at all costs; these are questions in which a respondent can agree with one part of the question but not the other, or cannot answer without accepting a particular assumption. Examples of double-barreled questions include: "Is the sales personnel polite and responsive?" and "In general, are you satisfied with the products and services of company X?"

Lastly, when you run simultaneous surveys in different countries, make use of professional translators as translation is a complex process. Functionally translating one language into another is quite easy and many websites, such as Google translate (http://translate.google.com/) can do this. However, translating surveys requires preserving conceptual equivalence of whole sentences and paragraphs; current software applications and websites cannot ensure this. In addition, cultural differences may require changes to the entire instrument format or procedure. A technique to establish conceptual equivalence across languages is back-translation. *Back-translation* requires translating a survey instrument into another language after which the translated survey instrument is translated into the original language by another translator. After the back-translation, the original and back-translated instruments are compared and points of divergence are noted. The translation is then corrected to more accurately reflect the intent of the wording in the original language.

In Fig. 4.9, we provide a few examples of poorly designed survey questions followed by better-worded equivalents. These questions relate to how satisfied iPhone users are with performance, reliability, and after-service.

4.4.2.5 Design the Questionnaire

After determining the individual questions, you have to integrate these, together with other elements, to create the questionnaire. This involves the following elements:
- Designing the starting pages of the questionnaire,
- Choosing the order of the questions, and
- Designing the layout and format.

Starting pages of the questionnaire: At the beginning of each questionnaire, the importance and goal are usually described to stress that the results will be treated confidentially, and to mention what they will be used for. This is usually followed by an example question (and answer), to demonstrate how the survey should be filled out.

Poor: The question is double-barreled: it asks about performance and reliability

	Strongly disagree	Somewhat disagree	Neutral	Somewhat agree	Completely agree
I am satisfied with the performance and reliability of my Apple iPhone	0	0	0	0	0

Better: Separate the question into two questions

	Strongly disagree	Somewhat disagree	Neutral	Somewhat agree	Completely agree
I am satisfied with the performance of my Apple iPhone	0	0	0	0	0
I am satisfied with the reliability of my Apple iPhone	0	0	0	0	0

Poor: The question cannot be answered by those who have not experienced after-sales service.

	Strongly disagree	Somewhat disagree	Neutral	Somewhat agree	Completely agree
I am satisfied with the after-sales service of my Apple iPhone	0	0	0	0	0

Better: The question uses branching

	No	Yes
1.1: Have you used Apple's after-sales service for your iPhone?	0	0
If you answered yes, please proceed to question 1.2.; otherwise, skip question 1.2 and proceed to question 1.3		

	Strongly disagree	Somewhat disagree	Neutral	Somewhat agree	Completely agree
1.2: I am satisfied with the after-sales service that Apple provided for my iPhone	0	0	0	0	0

Fig. 4.9 (continued)

Poor: Question design will likely cause inflated expectations ("everything is very important")

	Not at all important	Not important	Neutral	Important	Very important
Which of the following iPhone features do you find most important?					
Camera	0	0	0	0	0
Music player	0	0	0	0	0
App store	0	0	0	0	0
Web browser	0	0	0	0	0
Mail client	0	0	0	0	0

Better: Use rank order scale

	Rank
Rank the following iPhone features from most to least important. Begin by picking out the feature you think is most important and assign it the number 1. Then find the second most important and assign it the number 2, etc.	
Camera	___
Music player	___
App store	___
Web browser	___
Mail client	___

Fig. 4.9 Examples of good and bad practice in designing survey questions

If questions relate to a specific issue, moment, or transaction, you should indicate this clearly at the very beginning. For example, "Please provide answers to the following questions, keeping the purchase of product X in mind." If applicable, you should also point out that your survey is conducted in collaboration with a university, a recognized research institute, or a known charity, as this generally increases respondents' willingness to participate. Moreover, do not forget to provide a name and contact details for those participants who have questions, or in case technical problems arise. Consider including a picture of the research team as this increases response rates. Lastly, you should thank the respondents for their time and describe how the questionnaire should be returned (for mail surveys).

Order of the questions: Choosing the appropriate order of questions is crucial because it determines the logical flow of the questionnaire and therefore contributes to high response rates. The order of questions is usually as follows:

1. Screeners or classification questions come first. These questions determine what parts of the survey a respondent should fill out.
2. Next, insert the key variables of the study. This includes the dependent variables, followed by the independent variables.
3. Use a funnel approach. That is, ask questions that are more general first and then move on to details. This makes answering the questions easier as the order helps the respondents recall. Make sure that sensitive questions are put at the very end of this section.
4. Demographics are placed last if they are not part of the screening questions. If you ask demographic questions, always check whether they are relevant with regard to the research goal. In addition, check if these demographics are likely to lead to non-response. Asking about demographics, like income, educational attainment, or health, may result in a substantial number of respondents refusing to answer. If such sensitive demographics are not necessary, omit them from the survey. Note that in certain countries asking about a respondent's demographic characteristics means you have to abide by specific laws, such as the Data Protection Act 1998 in the UK.

If your questionnaire contains several sections (e.g., in the first section you ask about the respondents' buying attitudes and in the following section about their satisfaction with the company's services), you should make the changing context clear to the respondents.

Layout and format of the survey: The layout of both mail and web-based surveys should be concise and should conserve space where possible. In Box 4.4, we discuss further design issues that should be considered when planning surveys.

Box 4.4 Design issues when planning surveys
Avoid using small and colored fonts, which reduce readability. For mail-based surveys, booklets work well, since postage is cheaper if surveys fit in standard envelopes. If this is not possible, single-sided stapled paper can also work. For web-based surveys, it is good to have a counter letting the respondents know what percentage of the questions they have already filled out. This gives them some indication of how much time they still have to spend on completing the survey. Make sure the layout is simple and follows older and accepted Web standards. This step allows respondents with older and/or non-standard browsers or computers to fill out the survey. In addition, take into consideration that many people access Web surveys through mobile phones and tablet computers. Using older and accepted Web standards will cause these respondents a minimum number of technical problems.

4.4.2.6 Pretest the Questionnaire

We have already mentioned the importance of pretesting the survey several times. Before any survey is sent out, you should pretest the questionnaire to enhance its clarity and to ensure the client's acceptance of the survey. Once the questionnaire is in the field, there is no way back! You can pretest questionnaires in two ways. In its simplest form, you can use a few experts (say 3–6) to read the survey, fill it out, and comment on it. Many web-based survey tools allow researchers to create a pretested version of their survey, in which there is a text box for comments behind every question. Experienced market researchers are able to spot most issues right away and should be employed to pretest surveys. If you aim for a very high quality survey, you should also send out a set of preliminary (but proofread) questionnaires to a small sample consisting of 50–100 respondents. The responses (or lack thereof) usually indicate possible problems and the preliminary data may be analyzed to determine the potential results. Never skip pretesting due to time issues, since you are likely to run into problems later!

Box 4.5 Dillman's (2007) recommendations on how to increase response rates
It is becoming increasingly difficult to get people to fill out surveys. This may be due to over-surveying, dishonest firms that disguise sales as research, and a lack of time. In his book, *Mail and Internet Surveys*, Dillman (2007) discusses four steps to increase response rates:

1. Send out a pre-notice letter indicating the importance of the study and announcing that a survey will be sent out shortly.
2. Send out the survey with a sponsor letter, again indicating the importance of the study.
3. Follow up after 3–4 weeks with both a thank you note (for those who responded) and a new survey plus a reminder (for those who did not respond).
4. Call or email those who have not responded still and send out a thank you note to those who replied in the second round.

Further, Dillman (2007) points out that names and addresses should be error free. Furthermore, he recommends using a respondent-friendly questionnaire in the form of a booklet, providing return envelopes, and personalizing correspondence.

An increasingly important aspect of survey research is to induce potential respondents to participate. In addition to Dillman's (2007) recommendations on how to increase response rates (Box 4.5), incentives are increasingly used. A simple example of such an incentive is to provide potential respondents with a cash reward. In the US, one-Dollar bills are often used for this purpose. Respondents who participate in (online) research panels often receive points that can be exchanged for products and services. For example, Research Now, a market research company, provides its Canadian panel members AirMiles that can be exchanged for free flights, amongst others. A special type of incentive is to indicate that, for every returned survey, money will be donated to a charity. ESOMAR, the world organization for market and social research (see Chap. 10), suggests that incentives for interviews or surveys should "be kept to a minimum level proportionate to the amount of their time involved, and should not be more than the normal hourly fee charged by that person for their professional consultancy or advice."

Another incentive is to give the participants a chance to win a product or service. For example, you could randomly give away iPods or holidays to a number of participants. By providing them with a chance to win, the participants need to disclose their name and address so that they can be reached. While this is not part of the research itself, some respondents may feel uncomfortable to provide contact details, which could potentially reduce response rates.

Finally, a type of incentive that may help participation (particularly in professional settings) is reporting the findings to the participants. This can be done by providing a general report of the study and its findings, or by providing a customized report detailing the participant's responses and comparing them with all the other responses (e.g., www.selfsurvey.com). Obviously, anonymity needs to be assured so that the participants cannot compare their answers with those of other individual responses.

4.5 Basic Qualitative Research

Qualitative research is mostly used to gain an understanding of *why* certain things happen. It can be used in an exploratory context by defining problems in more detail, or by developing hypotheses to be tested in subsequent research. Qualitative research also allows researchers to learn about consumers' perspectives and vocabulary, especially when the context (e.g., the industry) is unknown to them. As such, qualitative research offers importance guidance when little is known about consumers' attitudes and perceptions or the market.

Qualitative research leads to the collection of qualitative data as discussed in Chap. 3. One can collect qualitative data by explicitly informing the participants that you are doing research (*directly observed qualitative data*), or you can simple observe the participants' behavior without the them being explicitly aware of the research goals (*indirectly observed qualitative data*). There are ethical issues associated with conducting research when the participants are not aware of the research purpose. Always check regulations regarding what is allowed in your context and what not. It is always advisable to brief the participants on their role and the goal of the research after the data has been collected.

The two key forms of directly observed qualitative data are depth interviews and focus groups. Together, they comprise most of the conducted qualitative market research. First, we will discuss depth interviews which are – as the terms suggests – interviews conducted with one participant at a time, allowing for high levels of personal interaction between the interviewer and respondent. Next, we will discuss projective techniques, a frequently used type of testing procedure in depth interviews. Lastly, we will introduce focus group discussions, which are conducted with multiple participants.

4.5.1 Depth Interviews

Depth interviews are qualitative conversations with participants about a specific topic. These participants are often consumers, but they may also be the decision-makers in a market research study, who are interviewed to gain an understanding of their clients' needs. They may also be government or company representatives. Interviews vary in their level of structure. In their simplest form, interviews are unstructured and the participants talk about a topic in general. This works well if you want to obtain insight into a topic, or as an initial step in a research process. Interviews can also be fully structured, meaning all questions and possible answer categories are decided in advance. This leads to the collecting of quantitative data. However, most depth interviews for gathering qualitative data are semi-structured and contain a series of questions that need to be addressed, but that have no specific format regarding what the answers should look like. The person interviewed can make additional remarks, or discuss somewhat related issues, but is not allowed to wander off too far. In these types of interviews, the interviewer often asks questions like "that's interesting, could you explain?," or "how come...?" to probe further into the issue. In highly structured interviews, the interviewer has a fixed set of questions and often a fixed amount of time for each person's response. The goal of structured interviews is to maximize the comparability of the answers. Consequently, the set-up of the questions and the structure of the answers need to be similar.

Depth interviews are unique in that they allow for probing on a one-to-one basis, fostering interaction between the interviewer and interviewee. Depth interviews also work well when those being interviewed have very little time and when they do not want the information to be shared with the other study participants. This is, for example, likely to be the case when you discuss marketing strategy decisions with CEOs. The drawbacks of depth interviews include the amount of time the researcher needs to spend on the interview itself and on traveling (if the interview is conducted face-to-face and not via the telephone), as well as transcribing the interview.

When conducting depth interviews, a set format is usually followed. First, the interview details are discussed, such as confidentiality issues, the topic of the interview, the structure, and the duration. Moreover, the interviewer should disclose whether the interview is being recorded and inform the interviewee that there is no right or wrong answer, just opinions on the subject. The interviewer should also try to be open and keep eye contact with the interviewee. Interviewers can end an interview by informing their respondents that they have reached the last question and thanking them for their time.

Interviews are often used to investigate *means-end* issues in which researchers try to understand what ends consumers aim to satisfy and which means (consumption) they use to do so. A means-end approach involves determining the *attributes* of a product first. These are the functional product features, such as the speed a car can reach or its acceleration. Subsequently, researchers look at the *functional consequences* that follow from the product benefits. This could be driving fast. The *psychosocial consequences*, or personal benefits, are derived from the functional benefits and, in this example, could include an enhanced status, or being regarded as successful. Finally, the psychosocial benefits are linked to people's personal *values* or life goals, such as a desire for success or acceptance. Analyzing and identifying the relationships between these steps is called *laddering*.

4.5.2 Projective Techniques

Projective techniques describe a special type of testing procedure, usually used in depth interviews. They work by providing participants with a stimulus and gauging their responses. Although participants in projective techniques know that they are participating in a market research study, they may not be aware of the research's specific purpose. The stimuli provided in projective techniques are ambiguous and require a response from the participants. A key form of projective techniques is *sentence completion*, for example:

> An iPhone user is someone who: ....
> The Apple brand makes me think of: ....
> iPhones are most liked by: ....

In this example, the respondents are asked to express their feelings, ideas, and opinions in a free format.

Projective techniques' advantage is that they allow for responses when people are unlikely to respond if they were to know the exact purpose of the study. Thus, projective techniques can overcome self-censoring and allow expression and fantasy. In addition, they can change a participant's perspective. Think of the previous example. If the participants are users of the Apple iPhone, the sentence completion example asks how they think other people regard them, not what they think of the Apple iPhone. A drawback is that projective techniques require the interpretation and coding of responses, which can be difficult.

4.5.3 Focus Groups

Focus groups are interviews conducted among a number of respondents at the same time and led by a *moderator*. This moderator leads the interview, structures it, and often plays a central role in transcribing the interview later. Focus groups are usually semi or highly structured. The group usually comprises between 4 and 6 people to allow for interaction between the participants and to ensure that all the participants have a say. The duration of a focus group interview varies, but is often between 30 and 90 minutes for focus groups of company employees and between 60 to 120 minutes for consumers. When focus groups are held with company employees, moderators usually travel to the company and conducts their focus group in a room. When consumers are involved, moderators often travel to a market research company, or hotel, where a conference room is used for the focus group. Market research companies often have special conference rooms with equipment like one-way mirrors, built-in microphones, and video recording devices.

How are focus groups structured? They usually start with the moderator introducing the topic and discussing the background. Everyone is introduced to establish rapport. Subsequently, the moderator tries to get the members of the focus group to speak to one another, instead of asking the moderator for confirmation. Once the focus group members start discussing topics with one another, the moderator tries to stay in the background, merely ensuring that the discussions stay on-topic. Afterwards, the participants are briefed and the discussions are transcribed for further analysis.

Table 4.2 Comparing focus groups and depth interviews

	Focus groups	Depth interviews
Group interactions	Group interaction is present. This may stimulate new thoughts from respondents.	There is no group interaction. Therefore, stimulation for new ideas from the respondents comes from the interviewer.
Group/peer pressure	Group pressure and stimulation may clarify and challenge thinking. Peer pressure and role playing.	In the absence of group pressure, the respondents' thinking is not challenged. With one respondent, role playing is minimized and there is no peer pressure.
Respondent competition	Respondents compete with one another for time to talk. There is less time to obtain in-depth details from each participant.	Individuals are alone with the interviewer and can express their thoughts in a non-competitive environment. There is more time to obtain detailed information.
Peer influence	Responses in a group may be biased by other group members' opinions.	With one respondent, there is no potential of other respondents influencing this person.
Subject sensitivity	If the subject is sensitive, respondents may be hesitant to talk freely in the presence of other people.	If the subject is sensitive, respondents may be more likely to talk.
Stimuli	The volume of stimulus materials that can be used is somewhat limited.	A fairly large amount of stimulus material can be used.
Interviewer schedule	It may be difficult to assemble 8 or 10 respondents if they are a difficult type to recruit (such as busy executives).	Individual interviews are easier to schedule.

Focus groups have distinct advantages: they are relatively cheap compared to depth interviews, they work well with issues that are important socially or which require spontaneity. They are also useful for developing new ideas. On the downside, focus groups do not offer the same ability as interviews to probe, and also run a greater risk of going off-topic. Moreover, a few focus group members may dominate the discussion and, especially in larger focus groups, "voting" behavior may occur, hindering real discussions and the development of new ideas. Table 4.2 summarizes the key differences between focus groups and depth interviews.

4.6 Collecting Primary Data Through Experimental Research

In Chap. 2, we discussed causal research and briefly introduced experiments as a means of conducting research. The goal of designing experiments is to control for as many influencing factors as possible in an effort to avoid unintended influences. Experiments are typically conducted by manipulating one variable, or a few, at a time. For example, we can change the price of a product, the type of product, or the package size to determine whether these changes affect important outcomes such as attitudes, satisfaction, or intentions. Often, simple field observations cannot establish these relationships as inferring causality can be problematic. Imagine a company that wants to introduce a new type of soft drink aimed at health-conscious consumers. If the product were to fail, the managers would probably conclude that the consumers did not like the product. However, many (often unobserved) variables, such as price cuts by competitors, changing health concerns, and a lack of availability, can also influence new products' success.

4.6.1 Principles of Experimental Research

An *experiment* deliberately imposes a *treatment* on a group of subjects in the interest of observing the response. This way, experiments attempt to isolate how one particular change affects an outcome. The outcome(s) is (are) the *dependent variable(s)* and the *independent variable(s)* (also referred to as *factors*) are used to explain the outcomes. To examine the influence of the independent variable(s) on the dependent variable(s), *treatments* or *stimuli* are administered to the participants. These are supposed to manipulate participants in that they put them into different situations. A simple form of treatment could be an advertisement with and without humor. In this case, the humor is the independent variable, which can take two *levels* (i.e., with or without humor). If we manipulate, for example, the price between low, medium, and high, we have three levels. When selecting independent variables, we typically include those marketers care about and which are related to the marketing and design of the products and services.

Care should be taken not to include too many of these variables in order to keep the experiment manageable. An experiment that includes four independent variables, each of which has three levels, and which includes every possible combination (called a *full factorial design*) requires $4^3 = 64$ experiments. Large numbers of levels (5 or more) will increase the complexity and cost of the research dramatically. Finally, *extraneous variables,* such as the age or income of the participant in the experiment, are not changed as part of the experiment. However, it might be important to control for their influence when setting up the experimental design.

4.6.2 Experimental Designs

Experimental design refers to an experiment's structure. There are various types of experimental designs. To clearly separate the different experimental designs, researchers have developed the following notation:

O:	A formal observation or measurement of the dependent variable. Subscripts below an observation O such as $_1$ or $_2$, indicate measurements at different points in time.
X:	The test participants' exposure to an experimental treatment.
R:	The random assignment of participants. Randomization ensures control over extraneous variables and increases the experiment's reliability and validity.

In the following, we will discuss the most prominent experimental designs:
- One-shot case study,
- Before-after design,
- Before-after design with a control group, and
- Solomon four-group design.

The simplest form of experiment is the *one-shot case study*. This type of experiment is structured as follows:[8]

X	O_1

This means we have one treatment (indicated by X), such as a new advertising campaign. After the treatment, we await reactions and then measure the outcome of the manipulation (indicated by O_1), such as the participants' willingness to purchase the advertised product. This type of experimental set-up is common but does not tell us if the effect is causal. One reason for this is that we did not measure anything before the treatment and therefore cannot assess what the relationship between the treatment and outcome is. The participants' willingness to purchase the product was perhaps higher before they were shown the advertisement. As we did not measure their willingness to purchase before the treatment, such an issue cannot be ruled out. Thus, causality cannot be established with this design.

---

[8] If one symbol follows after another, it means that the first symbol precedes the next one in time.

The simplest type of experiment that allows us to make causal inferences – within certain limits – is the *before-after design* for one group. The notation for this design is:

O_1	X	O_2

We have one measurement before (O_1) and one after a treatment (O_2). Thus, this type of design can be used to determine whether an advertisement has a positive, negative, or no effect on the participants' willingness to purchase the product.

A problem with this type of design is that we do not have a standard of comparison with which to contrast the change between O_1 and O_2. While the advertisement may have increased the participants' willingness to purchase, this might have been even higher if no advertisement had been launched at all. The reason for this is that the before-after-design does not control for influences occurring between the two measurements. For example, negative publicity after the initial measurement could influence the subsequent measurement. These issues make the "real" effect of the advertisement hard to assess.

If we want to have a much better chance of identifying the "real" effect of a treatment, we need a more complex setup, called the *before-after experiment with a control group*. In this design, a control group is added which is not subjected to the treatment X. The notation of this type of experiment is:

Experimental group (R)	O_1	X	O_2
Control group (R)	O_3		O_4

The effect attributed to the experiment is the difference between O_1 and O_2 minus that of O_3 and O_4. For example, if the participants' willingness to purchase increases much stronger in the experimental group (i.e., O_2 is much higher than O_1) than in the control group (i.e., O_4 is slightly higher than or equal to O_3), the advertisement has had an impact on the participants.

An important element of this experimental design is the random assignment of participants to the experimental and control groups (indicated by R). This means that, for any given treatment, every participant has an equal probability of being chosen for one of the two groups. This ensures that participants with different characteristics are spread randomly (and, it is hoped, equally) among the treatment(s), which will neutralize *self-selection*. Self-selection occurs when participants can select themselves into the experimental or control group. For example, if participants who like sweets participate in a cookie tasting test, they will certainly make an effort to give the treatment (cookie) a try! See Mooi and Gilliland (2013) for an example of self-selection and an analysis method.

However, the before-after experiment with a control group still has limitations. The initial measurement O_1 may alert the participants that they are being studied, which may bias the post measurement O_2. This effect is also referred to as *before measurement effect*. Likewise, because of the initial measurement O_1, the participants may drop out of the experiment, leading to no recorded response for O_2. In case there is a systematic reason for participant drop out, the experiment's validity is threatened.

The *Solomon four-group design* is an experimental design accounting for before measurement effects and is structured as follows:

Experimental group 1 (R)	O_1	X	O_2
Control group 1 (R)	O_3		O_4
Experimental group 2 (R)		X	O_5
Control group 2 (R)			O_6

The design is much more complex, as we need to measure the effects six times and administer two stimuli. This method provides the power to control for the before measurement effect of O_1 on O_2. The design also provides several measures of the effect of the treatment (i.e., (O_2-O_4), $(O_2-O_1)-(O_4-O_3)$, and (O_6-O_5)). If there is agreement among these measures, the inferences about the effect of the treatment are much stronger.

In Chap. 6, we discuss how to analyze experimental data using ANOVA and various other tests.

Review Questions

1. What is the difference between primary and secondary data? Can primary data become secondary data?
2. Please search and download two examples of secondary data sources that you found through the Internet. Discuss two potential market research questions that each dataset can answer.
3. Please download one of Ipsos's reports on satisfaction at http://ec.europa.eu/consumers/cons_int/serv_gen/cons_satisf/consumer_service_finrep_en.pdf. Examine how they measured satisfaction. Can you establish construct validity of this satisfaction measure, using the three-step method by Houston (2002)?
4. Imagine you are asked to understand what consumer characteristics make them likely to buy a Honda Insight Hybrid car (see http://automobiles.honda.com/insight-hybrid/). How would you collect the data? Would you start with secondary data, or would you start collecting primary data directly? Do you think it is appropriate to collect qualitative data? If so, at what stage of the process?
5. What are the different reasons for choosing interviews rather than focus groups? What choice would you make if you want to understand CEOs' perceptions of the economy, and what would seem appropriate when you want to understand how consumers feel about a newly introduced TV program?
6. Describe the Solomon four-group design and explain, which problems of simpler experimental design it controls for.
7. If you were to set up an experiment to ascertain what type of product package (new or existing) customers prefer, what type of experiment would you choose? Please discuss.

Further Readings

Campbell, D. T., & Stanley, J. C. (1966). *Experimental and quasi-experimental designs for research*. Chicago: Wadsworth Publishing.
Cook, T. D., & Campbell, D. T. (1979). *Quasi-experimentation: Design and analysis issues for field settings*. Chicago, IL: Wadsworth Publishing.
   These are the two great books on experimental research.
Dillman, D. A., Smyth, J. D., & Christian, L. M. (2009). *Internet, mail, and mixed-mode surveys: The tailored design method*. Hoboken, NJ: Wiley.
   This book gives an excellent overview of how to create questionnaires and how to execute them. Mixed-mode surveys and web surveys are paid significant attention.
FocusGroupTips.com (http://www.focusgrouptips.com).
   This website provides a thorough explanation of how to set-up focus groups from planning to reporting the results.
Lietz, P. (2010). Current state of the art in questionnaire design: a review of the literature. *International Journal of Market Research, 52*(2), 249–272.
   Reviews survey design choices from an academic perspective.
Mystery Shopping Providers Association (http://www.mysteryshop.org/).
   This website discusses the mystery shopping industry in Asia, Europe, North America, and South America.
Veludo-de-Oliveira, T. M, Ikeda, A. A., & Campomar, M. C. (2006). Laddering in the practice of marketing research: Barriers and solutions. *Qualitative Market Research: An International Journal, 9*(3), 297–306.
   This article provides an overview of laddering, the various forms of laddering, and biases that may result and how these should be overcome.

References

Bronner, F., & Ton, K. (2007). The live or digital interviewer. A comparison between CASI, CAPI and CATI with respect to differences in response behaviour. *International Journal of Market Research, 49*(2), 167–190.
Casteleyn, J., André, M., & Kris, R. (2009). How to use facebook in your market research. *International Journal of Market Research, 51*(4), 439–447.
DeMonaco, H. J., Ayfer, A., & Hippel, E. V. (2005). The major role of clinicians in the discovery of off-label drug therapies. *Pharmacotherapy, 26*(3), 323–332.
Deutskens, E., de Jong, A., de Ruyter, K., & Martin, W. (2006). Comparing the generalizability of online and mail surveys in cross-national service quality research. *Marketing Letters, 17*(2), 119–136.
Dillman, D. A. (2007). *Mail and internet surveys*. New Jersey: Wiley.
Holbrook, A., Cho, Y. I. K., & Johnson, T. (2006). The impact of question and respondent characteristics on comprehension and mapping difficulties. *Public Opinion Quarterly, 70*(4), 565–595.
Houston, M. B. (2002). Assessing the validity of secondary data proxies for marketing constructs. *Journal of Business Research, 57*(2), 154–161.
Mooi, E., & Gilliland, D. I. (2013). How contracts and enforcement explain transaction outcomes. *International Journal of Research in Marketing, 30*(4), 395–405.

Peterson, R. A. (1997). A quantitative analysis of rating-scale response variability. *Marketing Letters, 8*(1), 9–21.

Raithel, S., Sarstedt, M., Scharf, S., & Schwaiger, M. (2012). On the value relevance of customer satisfaction. Multiple drivers in multiple markets. *Journal of the Academy of Marketing Science, 40*(4), 509–525.

Rindfleisch, A., & Heide, J. B. (1997). Transaction cost analysis: Past, present, and future applications. *Journal of Marketing, 61*(4), 30–54.

Ringle, C. M., Sarstedt, M., & Mooi, E. A. (2010). Response-based segmentation using FIMIX-PLS. Theoretical foundations and an application to American customer satisfaction index data. *Annals of Information Systems, 8*(1), 19–49.

Schilling, M. A. (2009). Understanding the alliance data. *Strategic Management Journal, 30*(3), 233–260.

Vincente, P., Reis, E., & Santos, M. (2008). Using mobile phones for survey research. *International Journal of Market Research, 51*(5), 613–633.

Descriptive Statistics

5

Learning Objectives

After reading this chapter, you should understand:
- The workflow involved in a market research study.
- Univariate and bivariate descriptive graphs and statistics.
- How to deal with missing values.
- How to transform data (z-transformation, log transformation, creating dummies, aggregating variables).
- How to identify and deal with outliers.
- What a codebook is.
- The basics of using IBM SPSS Statistics.

Keywords

Bar chart • Box plot • Codebook • Correlation • Covariance • Crosstabs • Dummies • Frequency table • Histogram • Interquartile range • Interviewer fraud • Line chart • Log transformation • Mean • Median • Mode • Outliers • Pie chart • Range • Scatter plots • SPSS • Standard deviation • Suspicious response patterns • Variance • Workflow • z-transformation

This chapter has two purposes: first, we discuss how to keep track of the entering, cleaning, describing, and transforming of data. We call these steps the *workflow* of data. Second, we discuss how we can describe data using a software package called IBM SPSS Statistics (abbreviated as SPSS).

5.1   The Workflow of Data

Market research projects involving data become more efficient and effective if a proper *workflow* is in place. A workflow is a strategy to keep track of the entering, cleaning, describing, and transforming of data. These data may have been collected

M. Sarstedt and E. Mooi, *A Concise Guide to Market Research*,
Springer Texts in Business and Economics, DOI 10.1007/978-3-642-53965-7_5,
© Springer-Verlag Berlin Heidelberg 2014

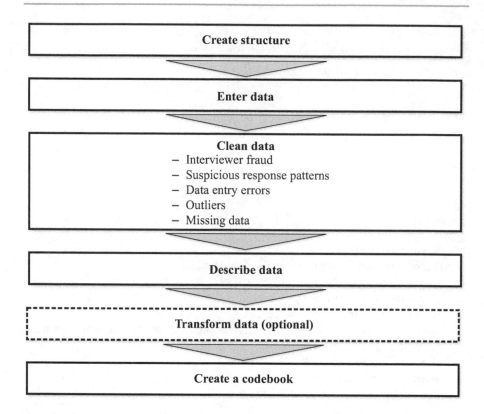

Fig. 5.1 The workflow of data

through surveys or may be secondary data. Haphazardly entering, cleaning, and analyzing bits of data is not a good strategy, since it increases one's likelihood of making mistakes and makes it hard to replicate results. Moreover, without a good workflow of data, it becomes hard to document the research process and cooperate on projects. For example, how can you outsource the data analysis, if you cannot indicate what the data are about or what specific values mean? Finally, a lack of a good workflow increases one's risk of having to duplicate work or even of losing all of your data due to accidents. In Fig. 5.1, we show the steps necessary to create and describe a dataset after the data have been collected.

5.2   Create Structure

The basic idea of setting up a good workflow is that good planning allows the researcher to save time and allows other researchers to do their share of the analysis and/or replicate the research. After the data collection phase, the first step is to save the available data. We recommend keeping track of the dataset by providing data and data-related files in separate directories. We can do this with Windows Explorer or the Apple Mac's Finder. This directory should have subdirectories for at least the data

Table 5.1 Example of a directory structure for saving market research related files

Directory name	Subdirectory name	Example file names
2014_TV market project	Data files	TV_market.sav
		TV_market.zip
		TV_market rev1.sav
		TV_market rev2.sav
	Output files	Missing data analysis rev2.spv
		Descriptives rev2.spv
		Factor analysis rev2.spv
		Regression analysis rev2.spv
	Syntax files	Missing data analysis.sps
		Descriptives.sps
		Factor analysis.sp
		Regression analysis.sps
	Temporary	Missing data analysis rev1.spv
		Descriptives rev1.spv
		Factor analysis rev1.spv
		Regression analysis rev1.spv
	Related files	Codebook.docx
		Survey.pdf
		Initial findings–presentation to client.pptx
		Findings–presentation to client.pptx
		Recommendations rev1.docx
		Recommendations rev2.docx

files, the output, syntax, a temporary directory, and a directory with files that are directly related, such as the survey used to collect the data. In Table 5.1, we show an example of a directory structure. Within the main directory, there are five subdirectories, each with distinct files. Notice that in the *Data files* directory, we have the original dataset, two modified datasets (one without missing data and one which includes several transformations of the data) as well as a *.zip* file that contains the original dataset. If the data file is contained in a *.zip* file, it is unlikely to be modified and can be easily opened if the working file is accidentally overwritten or deleted. In the *Output files*, *Syntax files*, and *Temporary* directories, we provided each file with the suffix *rev1* or *rev2*. We use *rev* (abbreviation of *revision*), however, you could choose to use another file name, as long as it clearly indicates the revision on which you are working. Finally, in the *Related Files* directory, we have a codebook (more on this later), the survey, two presentations, and two documents containing recommendations.

Another aspect to creating structure is to properly set up the variables for your study. This involves making decisions on the following elements:

– Variable names,
– Variable labels,
– Data type, and
– Coding of variables.

The *variable names* should be clear and short so that they can be read in the dialog boxes. For example, if you have three questions on product satisfaction, three on loyalty, and several descriptors (age and gender), you could code these as *satisfaction1-satisfaction3*, *loyalty1-loyalty3*, *age*, and *gender*.

In SPSS, and most other statistical software programs, you can include *variable labels*, which describe what each variable stands for. The description typically includes the original question if the data were collected using surveys.

Before running any analyses, we have to indicate what *data types* have been entered. For example, you can collect data based on values (*Numeric* in SPSS) or on text (*String* in SPSS). In SPSS, you can indicate the measurement level; nominal data, ordinal data, or scale data (for ratio and interval scaled data).

Another point to consider is the *coding of variables*. Coding means assigning values to specific questions. When quantitative data are collected, the task is relatively easy; for Likert and semantic differential scales, we use values that correspond with the answers. For example, for a 7-point Likert scale, responses can be coded as 1–7 or as 0–6 (with 0 being the most negative and 6 being the most positive response). Open-ended questions (qualitative data) require more effort; typically, a three step process is involved. First, we collect all responses. In the second step, we group all responses. Determining the number of groups and to which group a response belongs is the major challenge in this step. To prevent the process from becoming too subjective, usually two or three market researchers code the responses and discuss any arising differences. The third step is providing a value for each group.

Once a system is set up to keep track of your progress, you need to consider safeguarding your files. Large companies usually have systems for creating *backups* (extra copies of files as a safeguard). If you are working alone or for a small company, you will most probably have to take care of this yourself. You could save your most recent and second most recent version of your file on a separate drive. Always keep at least two and never keep both backups in the same place as theft, fire, or an accident could still mean you'll lose all of your work! To prevent such issues, you should make use of cloud storage services such as Dropbox or Google Drive.

5.3   Enter Data

Capturing the data is the next step for primary data. How do we enter survey or experimental data into a dataset? For large datasets, or datasets created by professional firms, specialized software is often used. For example Epidata (http://www.epidata.dk) is frequently used to enter data from paper-based surveys, Entryware's mobile survey (http://www.techneos.com) is commonly deployed to enter data from personal intercepts or face-to-face interviewing, while, Voxco's Interviewer CATI is often used for telephone interviewing. The SPSS Data Collection Family (http://www.spss.com/software/data-collection) is a suite of different software packages specifically designed to collect and (automatically) enter data collected from online, telephone, and paper-based surveys.

Small firms or individual firms may not have access to such software and may need to enter data manually. You can enter data directly into SPSS. However, a drawback of directly entering data is the risk of making typing errors. Professional software such as Epidata can directly check if values are admissible. For example, if a survey question has only two answer categories such as gender (coded 0/1), Epidata and other packages can directly check if the value entered is 0 or 1, and not any other value. Moreover, if you are collecting very large amounts of data that require multiple typists, specialized software needs to be used. When entering data, check whether a substantial number of surveys or survey questions were left blank and note this.

5.4 Clean Data

Cleaning data is the next step in the workflow. It requires checking for the following:
- Interviewer fraud,
- Suspicious response patterns,
- Data entry errors,
- Outliers, and
- Missing data.

These issues require researchers to make decisions very carefully. In the following, we discuss each issue in greater detail.

5.4.1 Interviewer Fraud

Interviewer fraud is a difficult and serious issue. It ranges from interviewers "helping" respondents provide answers to entire surveys being falsified. Interviewer fraud often leads to incorrect results. Fortunately, we can avoid and detect interviewer fraud in various ways. First, never base interviewers' compensation on the number of completed responses they submit. Once data have been collected, and if multiple interviewers were used, each of whom collected a reasonably large number of responses (> 100), the way they selected respondents should be similar. We would therefore expect the average responses obtained to also be similar. Using the techniques discussed in Chap. 6, we can test this. Furthermore, the persons interviewed can be contacted afterwards for their feedback on the survey. If a substantial number of people do not claim to have been interviewed, interviewer fraud is likely. Furthermore, if people were previously interviewed on a similar subject, the factual variables (education, address, etc.) should not have changed much. Using descriptive statistics, we can check this. If substantial interviewer fraud is suspected, the data should be discarded. Since the costs of discarding data are substantial; firms should therefore also check for interviewer fraud during the data collection process.

5.4.2 Suspicious Response Patterns

Before analyzing data, we need to identify *suspicious response patterns*. There are two types of response patterns we need to look for:
- Straight lining, and
- Inconsistencies in answers.

Straight lining occurs when a respondent marks the same response in almost all the questions. For example, if a 7-point scale is used to obtain answers and the response pattern is 4 (the middle response) in almost all the items in the question-naire, then that respondent should mostly (see below) be removed from the dataset. Similarly, if the respondent selects only 1s, or only 7s in all the items, this respondent should mostly be removed.

However, it is important to note that such *middle response styles* and *extreme response styles* (i.e., respondents' tendency to select the mid or end points of a response scale) are culture-specific. Similarly, respondents from different cultures have different tendencies regarding agreeing with questions, regardless of the question content; this tendency is also referred to as *acquiescence*. For example, respondents from Spanish-speaking countries tend to show higher extreme response styles and high acquiescence, while East Asian (Japanese and Chinese) respondents show a relatively high level of middle response style. Within Europe, the Greeks stand out as having the highest level of acquiescence and an extreme response style. Harzing (2005) and Johnson et al. (2005) provide a review of culture effects on response behavior.

Inconsistencies in answers also need to be addressed before analyzing your data. Many surveys start with one or more screening questions. The purpose of a screening question is to ensure that only individuals who meet the prescribed criteria complete the survey. For example, a survey of mobile phone users may screen for individuals who own an Apple iPhone. If, later in the survey, an individual indicates that he/she is an Android user, this respondent should be removed from the dataset.

Surveys often ask the same question with slight variations, especially when reflective measures (see Box 3.1) are used. If a respondent gives a different answer to very similar questions, this may raise a red flag and could suggest that the respondent did not read the questions closely, or simply marked answers randomly to complete the survey as quickly as possible.

5.4.3 Data Entry Errors

When data are entered manually, *data entry errors* occur routinely. Fortunately, such errors are easy to spot if they occur outside the variable's range. That is, if an item is measured using a 7-point scale, the lowest value should be 1 (or 0) and the highest 7 (or 6). Using descriptive statistics (minimum, maximum, and range; see next section), we can check if this is true. Data entry errors should always be corrected by going back to the original survey. If we cannot go back (e.g., because the data were collected using face-to-face interviews), we need to delete this specific observation for this specific variable.

More subtle errors – for example, incorrectly entering a score of 4 as 3 – are difficult to detect using statistics. One way to check for these data entry errors is to randomly select observations and compare the entered responses with the original survey. We do, of course, expect a small number of errors (below 1%). If many typing errors occurred, the dataset should be entered again.

5.4.4 Outliers

Data often contain *outliers*. Outliers are values that differ totally from all the other observations and they can influence results substantially. For example, if we compare the average income of 20 households, we may find that the incomes range between $20,000 and $100,000, with the average being $45,000. If we considered an additional household with an income of, say $1 million, this would substantially increase the average. If the outlier is a valid case, should we retain this, for example, to compute the average?

5.4.4.1 Types of Outliers

Outliers must be interpreted in the context of the study and this interpretation should be based on the types of information they provide. Depending on the source of their uniqueness, outliers can be classified into three categories:

– The first type of outlier is produced by data collection or entry errors. For example, if we ask people to indicate their household income in thousands of US dollars, some respondents may just indicate theirs in US dollars (not thousands). Obviously, there is a substantial difference between $30 and $30,000! Moreover, (as discussed before) clear data entry errors occur quite often. Outliers produced by data collection or entry errors should be deleted, or we need to determine the correct values, for example, by going back to the respondents (see discussion above).

– A second type of outlier occurs because exceptionally high or low values are a part of reality. While such observations can influence results significantly, they are sometimes highly important for researchers, because the characteristics of outliers can be insightful. Think, for example, of companies that are extremely successful, or users with specific needs long before most of the relevant marketplace also need them (i.e., lead users). Deleting such outliers is not appropriate, but it is necessary to discuss the impact of outliers on the results.

Malcolm Gladwell's (2008) book "Outliers: The Story of Success" is an entertaining study of how some people became exceptionally successful (outliers).

– A third type of outlier occurs when combinations of variables are exceptionally rare. For example, if we look at income and expenditure on holidays, we may find someone who earns $100,000 and spends $90,000 of his/her income on holidays. Such combinations are unique and have a very strong impact on the results, particularly on correlations. In such situations, the outlier should be retained unless specific evidence suggests that the outlier is not a valid member of the population under study. It would also be very useful to flag such outliers and discuss their impact on the results.

5.4.4.2 Detecting Outliers

In a simple form, outliers can be detected using univariate or bivariate graphs and statistics.[1] When searching for outliers, we should use multiple approaches to ensure that we detect all the observations that can be classified as outliers. In the following, we discuss both routes to outlier detection:

Univariate Detection

The univariate detection of outliers examines the distribution of observations of each variable with the aim of identifying those cases falling outside the range of the 'usual' values. In other words, finding outliers means finding observations with very low or very high variable values. This can be achieved by calculating the minimum and maximum value of each variable, as well as the range. Another useful option for detecting outliers is by means of box plots, which we introduce in greater detail in the *Describe Data* section. Box plots are a means of visualizing the distribution of a variable, pinpointing those observations that fall outside the range of the 'usual' values.

It is important to recognize that there will always be observations with extreme values in one or more variables. However, we should strive to identify those outliers that are truly distinctive.

Bivariate Detection

Complementing the univariate perspective, we can also examine pairs of variables to identify observations whose combinations of variables are exceptionally rare. This is done by means of a scatter plot, which plots all observations in a graph where the x-axis represents the first variable and the y-axis the second (usually *dependent*) variable (see the *Describe Data* section). Observations that fall markedly outside the range of the other observations will show as isolated points in the scatter plot.

A drawback of this approach is the potentially large number of scatter plots that we need to draw. For example, with 10 variables, we need to draw 45 scatter plots to map all possible combinations of variables! Consequently, we should limit the

---

[1] There are multivariate techniques which consider three, or more, variables simultaneously to detect outliers. See Hair et al. (2010) for an introduction, and Agarwal (2013) for a more detailed methodological discussion.

analysis to specific relationships between variables, such as the relationship between a dependent and independent variable in a regression. Scatterplots with large numbers of observations are often problematic when we wish to detect outliers, as there is usually not just one dot, or a few isolated dots, just a decreasing density of observations where it is difficult to determine a cutoff point.

5.4.4.3 Dealing with Outliers

In a final step, we need to decide whether to delete or retain outliers. This decision requires determining whether we have an explanation for these high or low values. If there is an explanation (e.g., because some exceptionally wealthy people were included in the sample), outliers are typically retained, because they are a representative element of the population. However, their impact on the analysis results should be carefully evaluated. That is, one should run two analyses, one with and another without the outliers to ensure that a very few (extreme) observations do not influence the results substantially. If the explanation is that these outliners are most probably due to a typing or data entry error, we always delete them. If there is no clear explanation, outliers should be retained.

5.4.5 Missing Data

Market researchers often have to deal with the issue of *missing data*. There are two levels at which missing data occur:

– Entire surveys are missing (survey non-response)
– Respondents have not answered all the items (item non-response)

Survey non-response occurs when entire surveys are missing. Survey non-response is very common because only 5–25% of respondents fill out surveys. Although higher percentages are possible, they are not the norm in one-shot surveys. Issues such as inaccurate address lists, a lack of interest and time, people confusing market research with selling, and privacy issues have led response rates to drop over the last decade. Moreover, the amount of market research has increased, leading to respondent fatigue and a further decline in the response rates. The issue of survey response is best dealt with by designing surveys and the survey procedure properly (see Box 4.4 in Chap. 4 for suggestions).

Item non-response occurs when respondents do not provide answers to certain questions. Item non-response is common and 2–10% of questions usually remain unanswered. However, this number is greatly dependent on several factors, such as the subject matter, the length of the questionnaire, and the method of administration. The non-response can be much higher with respect to questions that many people considered sensitive (such as income).

The key issue with item non-response is the type of pattern that the missing data follow. Do the missing values occur randomly, or is there some type of underlying system? Once we have identified the type of missing data, we need to decide how to treat them. Figure 5.2 illustrates the process of missing data treatment, which we will discuss in the following.

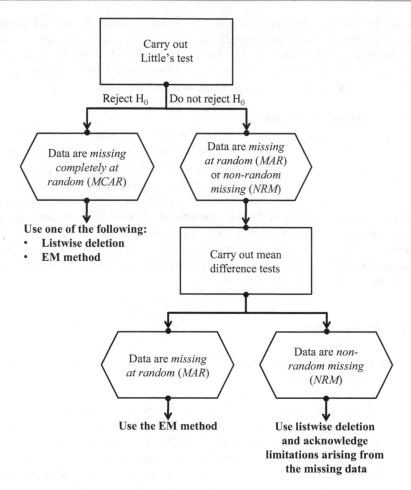

Fig. 5.2 Treating missing data

5.4.5.1 The Three Types of Missing Data: Paradise, Purgatory, and Hell

We generally distinguish between three types of missing data:

– Missing completely at random ("paradise"),
– Missing at random ("purgatory"), and
– Non-random missing ("hell").

Data are *missing completely at random (MCAR)*, when the probability that an data point(e.g., Y_i) is missing is unrelated to the value of Y_i, or to the value of any other variables. MCAR data occur when there is no systematic reason for certain data points being missing. For example, this happens when paper-based surveys are lost in the mail, when the Internet server hosting the web survey broke down temporarily, or the data were entered incorrectly. Why is MCAR paradise? When data are MCAR, observations with missing data are indistinguishable from those with complete data. Therefore, most missing data techniques will work well and any analysis based on MCAR data will be unbiased. Unfortunately, however, data are rarely MCAR.

It is another issue occurs if a missing data point (e.g., Y_i) is unrelated to the value of Y_i, but depends on another variable. In this case, we consider the data *missing at random (MAR)*. The term MAR is unfortunate because many people confuse it with MCAR; however, the label has stuck. For example, women are less likely to reveal their income. That is, the probability of missing data depends on the gender and on not on the income. Why is MAR purgatory? When data are MAR, the missing value pattern is not random, but this can be handled by more sophisticated missing data techniques.

Lastly, data are *non-random missing (NRM)* when the probability that a data point (e.g., Y_i) is missing depends on the variable Y. For example, very affluent and poor people are less likely to indicate their income. Thus, missing values in income depend on the income variable. This is the most severe type of missing data ("hell"), as even sophisticated missing data techniques do not provide satisfactory solutions. Thus, any result based on NRM data should be considered with extreme caution. NRM data can best be prevented by extensive pretesting and consultations with experts in order to avoid designing surveys that are likely to cause problematic response behavior. For example, we could use income categories instead of directly querying the respondents' income, or we could simply omit the income variable.

5.4.5.2 Testing for the Type of Missing Data

When dealing with missing data, we must ascertain the type of missing data. If the dataset is small, it should be easy to spot patterns by using univariate or bivariate graphs, tables or statistics (see next section). For example, using a scatter plot, we can analyze whether a certain value in one variable is related to a missing value in another variable. However, as the sample size and the number of variables increase, missing data patterns become more difficult to identify. Similarly, when we have only few observations, patterns are difficult to spot. In these cases, we should use one (or both) of the following diagnostic tests to identify missing data patterns:
– Little's MCAR test, and
– Mean difference tests.

Little's (1998) MCAR test analyzes the pattern of the missing data in all the variables and compares it with the pattern expected if the data were randomly missing. The MCAR test can be conducted using the *SPSS Missing Value Analysis* module. If the test indicates no significant differences between the two patterns, the missing data can be classified as MCAR. Put differently in statistical terms (see Chap. 6):
– If we reject the null hypothesis, we assume that the data are MCAR.
– If we do not reject the null hypothesis, the data are either MAR or NRM.

If the data cannot be assumed to be MCAR, we need to test whether the missing pattern is caused by another variable in the data set by using the procedures discussed in Chap. 6. For example, we can run a two-independent samples *t*-test to explore whether there is a significant difference in the mean of a continuous) variable (e.g., income) between the group with missing values and the group without missing values. In respect of nominal or ordinal variables, we could tabulate the occurrence of non-responses against different groups' responses. If we put the (categorical)

Table 5.2 Example of
response issues

	Low income	Medium income	High income
Response	65	95	70
Non-response	35	5	30
N = 300			

variable about which we have concerns in one column of a table, and the number of (non-)response in another, a table similar to Table 5.2 is produced.

Using the χ^2-test (pronounced as *chi-square* (which we discuss under nonparametric tests in the ⏻ Web Appendix → Chap. 6), we can test if there is a significant relationship between the respondents' (non-)response in a certain variable and their income. In the present example, this test would clearly indicate that there is a significant relationship between the respondents' income and the (non-)response behavior in another variable, supporting the assumption that the data are MAR.

5.4.5.3 Dealing with Missing Data

Research has suggested a broad range of approaches for dealing with missing data. We present the following three popular approaches, which are also integrated into SPSS' *Missing Value Analysis* module:
– Listwise deletion,
– Pairwise deletion, and
– Expectation maximization (EM) method.

Listwise deletion (also referred to as *casewise deletion*) uses only those observations with complete responses in respect of all the variables considered in the analysis. If any of the variables used have missing values, the observation is omitted from the computation. If many observations have some missing responses, this approach can substantially decrease the usable sample size.

Instead of discarding all observations with missing values, *pairwise deletion* uses all observations with complete responses in the calculation of the statistics. For example, assume we want to calculate the mean of three variables (Y_1, Y_2, and Y_3). To estimate the mean, all valid values in Y_1, Y_2, and Y_3 are used in the computation. That is, if a respondent has a missing value in Y_3, the valid values in Y_1 and Y_2 are still used to calculate the mean. Consequently, different calculations in the analysis may be based on different sample sizes, which can severely bias the results and even lead to inadmissible solutions. Some researchers therefore call this approach "unwise deletion" and we also advise against its use.

The expectation maximization method, commonly referred to as the *EM method* is a more complex approach to missing data treatment. It is an iterative, two-step procedure in which each iteration consists of an E (expectation) step and an M (maximization) step. Given the observed values and current estimates of the parameters (e.g., the means, standard deviations, or correlations), the E step finds the expected value of the missing data. In the M step, these parameters are re-estimated by assuming that the missing values have been replaced with the expected values. This way, the EM method finds a suitable value, which is then used to *impute* (i.e., substitute) the missing value.

Now that we have learnt about the different approaches for handling missing data, there is still one unanswered question: Which one should you use? As can be seen in Fig. 5.2, if the data are MCAR, you should use listwise deletion, unless this step decreases the usable sample size substantially (e.g., below a minimum sample size required for running a certain analysis procedure). Alternatively, the EM method should be used. When the data are not MCAR, listwise deletion (just like pairwise deletion) yields biased results. Therefore, when the data are MAR, you should to use the EM method. However, when the data are NRM, the EM method provides inaccurate results. Consequently, you should choose listwise deletion and acknowledge the limitations arising from the missing data.

Table 5.3 summarizes the data cleaning issues discussed in this section.

Table 5.3 Data cleaning issues and how to deal with them

Problem	Action
Interviewer fraud	– Check respondents if they were interviewed and correlate with previous data if available.
Suspicious response patterns	– Check for straight lining. – Consider cultural differences in response behavior (middle and extreme response styles, acquiescence). – Check for inconsistencies in response behavior.
Data entry errors	– Use descriptive statistics (minimum, maximum, range) to check for obvious typing errors. – Compare a subset of surveys to the dataset to check for inconsistencies.

Outliers	– Identify outliers by means of univariate descriptive statistics (minimum, maximum, range), box plots, and scatter plots.
	– Outliers are usually retained unless they...
	    – ... are a result of data entry errors,
	    – ... do not fit the objective of the research, or
	    – ... influence the results severely (but report results with and without outliers for transparancy).

Missing data	– Check the type of missing data by running Little's MCAR test and, if necessary, mean differences tests. – When the data are MCAR, use listwise deletion or the EM method. – When the data are MAR, use the EM method. – When the data are NRM, use listwise deletion and acknowledge the limitations arising from the missing data.

5.5   Describe Data

Once we have performed the previous steps, we can turn to the task of describing the data. Data can be described one variable at a time (*univariate descriptives*) or in terms of the relationship between two variables (*bivariate descriptives*). We further

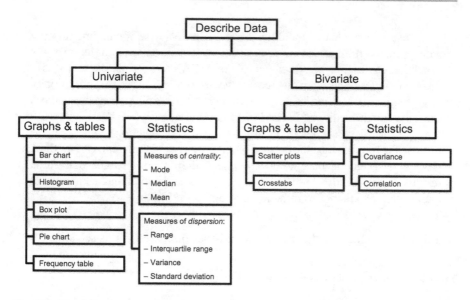

Fig. 5.3 The different types of descriptive statistics

divide univariate and bivariate descriptives into graphs and tables as well as statistics.

The choice between the two depends on what information we want to convey. Often graphs and tables can tell a reader with a limited background in statistics a great deal. However, graphs and tables can also mislead readers, as we will discuss later in Chap. 10 (Box 10.1). On the other hand, statistics require some background knowledge but have the advantage that they take up little space and are exact. We summarize the different types of descriptive statistics in Fig. 5.3.

5.5.1   Univariate Graphs and Tables

In this section, we discuss the most prominent types of *univariate graphs* and *tables*:
– Bar chart,
– Histogram,
– Box plot,
– Pie chart, and
– Frequency table.

In Fig. 5.4, these different types of charts are used to show technical information, prices and ratings of TVs, sold in Germany.

A *bar chart* is a graphical representation of a single categorical variable representing frequencies of occurences of each value. Each variable value is represented by a separate bar with the height of each bar indicating the number of

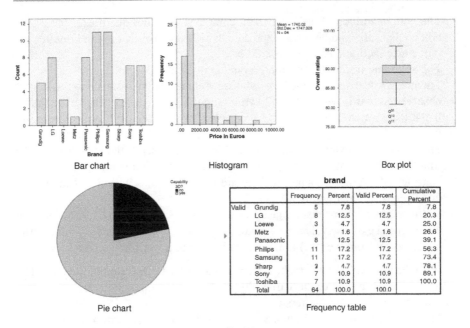

Fig. 5.4 Several univariate graphs, charts, and tables

times this value is observed. However, each bar's height can also represent other indices such as measures of centrality or dispersion for different groups of data (see next section). Bar charts are primarily useful for describing nominal or ordinal variables. For interval or ratio-scaled variables, histograms should be used.

The *histogram* is a graph that shows how frequently categories made from a continuous variable occur. Different from the bar chart, however, the variable values on the x-axis are divided into (non-overlapping) classes of equal width. For example, if you create a histogram for the variable *age*, you can use classes of 0–10, 11–20, etc. A histogram is commonly used to examine the distribution of a variable. For this purpose a curve following a specific distribution (e.g., normal) is superimposed on the bars to assess the correspondence of the actual distribution to the desired (e.g., normal) distribution.

Histograms plot continuous variables with ranges of the variables grouped into intervals (bins) while bar charts plot nominal and ordinal variables.

Another way of displaying the distribution of a (continuous) variable is by means of a *box plot* (also referred to as *box-and-whisker plot*). The *box plot* is a pictorial representation of a variable's distribution which builds on several statistical indices (see next section). The following elements constitute a box plot:

- The bottom and top of the box describe the first and third quartiles. That is, the box contains the middle 50% of the data, which is equivalent to the interquartile range (see section *Univariate Statistics*).
- The solid line inside the box represents the median.
- The upper line extending the box (whisker) represents the distance to the largest observation that is within the following range: 3rd quartile + interquartile range. If there are no obervations within this range, the line is equal to the maximum value.
- The lower line extending the box (*whisker*) represents the distance to the smallest observation that is within the following range: 1st quartile − interquartile range. If there are no obervations within this range, the line is equal to the minimum value.
- Outliers (observations that range between 1.0 and 3.0 quartile ranges away from the box) and extreme values (observations that range more than 3.0 interquartile ranges away from the box) are depicted by symbols outside the whiskers.

With the box plot, we can make statements about the dispersion of the data. The larger the box, the greater the variability of the observations. Furthermore, a box plot helps us identifying outliers in the data.

The *pie chart* visualizes how a variable's different values are distributed. Pie charts are easy to understand and work well if the number of values a variable takes on is small (less than 10), which makes them more useful for nominal and ordinal variables. Pie charts are particularly useful for displaying percentages of variables, because people interpret the entire pie as being 100%, and can easily see how often a variable's value occurs.

A *frequency table* is a table that includes all possible values of a variable and how often they occur. It is similar to both the histogram and pie chart in that it shows the distribution of a variable's possible values. However, in a frequency table, all values are indicated exactly. As with pie charts, frequency tables are primarily useful for variables measured on a nominal or ordinal scale.

5.5.2 Univariate Statistics

Univariate statistics fall into two groups: those describing centrality and those describing the dispersion of variables. We will discuss these two types of measures separately. Box 5.1 at the end of this section provides a sample calculation of the statistics used on a small set of values.

5.5.2.1 Measures of Centrality
Measures of centrality (or the central tendency) are statistical indices of a "typical" or "average" score. There are three main types of measures of centrality:
- Mode,
- Median, and
- Mean.

The simplest measure of centrality is the *mode*. It is the most frequently occurring value in a dataset. Since the mode is simply identified by counting the number of occurrences of each value, it can be used on all scales, including the nominal scale.

The *median* is the value that occurs in the middle of the set of scores if they are ranked from smallest to the largest, and therefore separates the lowest 50% of cases from the highest 50% of cases. For example, if 50% of the products in a market cost less than $1,000, then this is the median price. Identifying the median requires at least ordinal data (i.e., it cannot be used with nominal data).

The most commonly used measure of centrality is the *mean* (also called the arithmetic mean or, simply, the average). The mean (abbreviated as $\bar{x}$) is the sum of each observation's value divided by the number of observations:

$$\bar{x} = \frac{Sum(x)}{n} = \frac{1}{n}\sum_{i=1}^{n} x_i$$

In the formula above, x_i refers to observation i of variable x and n to the total number of observations. The mean is only useful for interval or ratio-scaled variables.

Several variations of the mean exist. For example, the *geometric mean* is an average that is useful for sets of positive values that are interpreted according to their product and not their sum (which the arithmetic mean does), such as rates of growth. The *harmonic mean* is an average used for values defined in relation to a unit, for example, speed (the distance per unit of time).

Each measure of centrality has its own use. The mean is most frequently used, but is sensitive to very small or large values. Conversely, neither the mode nor the median is sensitive to outliers. As a consequence, the relationship between the mean, median, and mode provides us with valuable information about the distribution of a variable. If the mean, median, and mode are about the same, the variable is likely to be symmetrically distributed. If the mean differs from the median and mode, this suggests that the variable is asymmetrically distributed and/or contains outliers. This is the case when we examine the prices of a set of products valued $500, $530, $530, and $10,000; both the median and the mode are $530, while the mean is $2,890. This example illustrates why only focusing on measures of centrality can be quite misleading when characterizing a variable. To gain a more complete picture, we also need to consider the variable's dispersion.

A lighthearted description of the mode, median, and mean

http://tinyurl.com/mode-median-mean

5.5.2.2 Measures of Dispersion

Measures of dispersion provide researchers with information about the variability of the data; that is, how far the values are spread out. We differentiate between three types of measures of dispersion:

– Range,
– Interquartile range,
– Variance, and
– Standard deviation.

The *range* is the simplest measure of dispersion. It is the difference between the highest value and the lowest value in a dataset and can be used on data measured at least on an ordinal scale. The range is of limited use as a measure of dispersion, because it provides information on extreme values and not necessarily on "typical" values. However, the range is valuable when screening data, as it allows for identifying data entry errors. For example, a range of more than 6 on a 7-point Likert scale would indicate an incorrect data entry.

The *interquartile range* is the difference between the 3rd and 1st quartile. The 1st quartile corresponds to the value separating the 25% lowest values from the 75% largest values if the values are ordered sequentially. Correspondingly, the 3rd quartile separates the 75% lowest from the 25% highest values. The interquartile range is particularly important for drawing box plots.

A common measures of dispersion is the *variance* (abbreviated as s^2). The variance is the sum of the squared differences between all of a variable's values and its mean, divided by the sample size minus 1. As such, it is only useful if the data are interval or ratio-scaled.

$$s^2 = \frac{\sum_{i=1}^{n} (x_i - \bar{x})^2}{n - 1}$$

The variance tells us how strongly observations vary around the mean. A low variance indicates that the observations tend to be very close to the mean; a high variance indicates that the observations are spread out over a large range of values. If squared differences are used between the observations and the mean, positive and negative differences cannot cancel each other. Likewise, values that lie far from the mean increase the variance more strongly than those that are close to the mean.

The most commonly used measure of dispersion is the *standard deviation* (abbreviated as s). It is the square root of – and, therefore, a special case of – the variance:

$$s = \sqrt{s^2} = \sqrt{\frac{\sum_{i=1}^{n}(x_i - \bar{x})^2}{n-1}}$$

Essentially, the variance and standard deviation provide the same information, but – unlike the variance – the standard deviation is expressed in the same units as the mean. Because of this characteristic, the following holds for normally distributed variables (this will be discussed in later chapters):
- 66% of all observations are between plus and minus one standard deviation unit from the mean,
- 95% of all observations are between plus and minus two standard deviation units from the mean, and
- 99% of all observations are between plus and minus three standard deviation units from the mean.

Thus, if the mean price is $1,000 and the standard deviation is $150, 66% of all the prices fall between $850 and $1,150, 95% fall between $700 and $1,300, and 99% of all the observations fall between $550 and $1,450.

5.5.3 Bivariate Graphs and Tables

There are a number of *bivariate graphs* and *tables*, of which the scatter plot and the crosstab are the most important. Furthermore, several of the graphs, charts, and tables discussed in the context of univariate analysis can be used for bivariate analysis. For example, box plots can be used to display the distribution of a variable in each group (category) of nominal variables.

A *scatter plot* uses both the y and x-axis to show how two variables relate to one another. If the observations almost form a straight line in a scatter plot, the two variables are strongly related (i.e., they have a high correlation). If the observations are equally distributed in a scatter plot, the relationship is low, or even zero.[2] Sometimes, a third variable, corresponding to the color or size (e.g., a *bubble plot*) of the data points, is included in a scatter plot, thus adding another dimension to the plot.

Crosstabs (also referred to as *contingency tables*) are tables in a matrix format that show the frequency distribution of nominal or ordinal variables. They are the

---

[2] A similar type of chart is the *line chart*. In a line chart, measurement points are ordered (typically by their x-axis value) and joined with straight line segments.

equivalent of a scatter plot used to analyze the relationship between two variables. While crosstabs are usually used for showing the relationship between two variables, they can also be used for three or more variables, which, however, makes them difficult to grasp. Crosstabs are of particular importance in the context of the χ^2-test (pronounced as *chi-square*), which we discuss under nonparametric tests in the ⁀Web Appendix → Chap. 6.

5.5.4   Bivariate Statistics

Bivariate statistics involve the analysis of two variables in order to determine the empirical relationship between them. There are two key measures that indicate (linear) associations between two variables, whose computation we illustrate in Box 5.1:
– Covariance, and
– Correlation.

The *covariance* is the degree to which two variables vary. The covariance is the sum of the multiplication of the differences between each value of the x and y variables and their means, divided by the sample size minus 1:

$$Cov(x, y) = \frac{1}{n-1} \sum\nolimits_{i=1}^{n} (x_i - \bar{x}) \cdot (y_i - \bar{y})$$

The *correlation* (abbreviated as r) is a more important measure of how strongly two variables relate to each other. A *(Pearson) correlation* coefficient is calculated as follows:

$$r^2 = \frac{Cov(x_i, y_i)}{s_x \cdot s_y} = \frac{\sum_{i=1}^{n} (x_i - \bar{x}) \cdot (y_i - \bar{y})}{\sqrt{\sum_{i=1}^{n} (x_i - \bar{x})^2} \cdot \sqrt{\sum_{i=1}^{n} (y_i - \bar{y})^2}}$$

The numerator contains the covariance of x and y $(Cov(x,y))$, while the denominator contains the product of the standard deviations of x and y.[3] Thus, the correlation is the covariance divided by the product of the standard deviations. Therefore, the correlation is *standardized* and, unlike the covariance, is no longer dependent on the variables' original measurement. More precisely, the correlation coefficient ranges from -1 to 1, where -1 indicates a perfect negative relationship and 1 indicates a perfect positive relationship. A correlation coefficient of 0 indicates that there is no relationship. As a rule of thumb (Cohen 1988), an absolute correlation. . .
– . . . below 0.30 indicates a weak relationship,
– . . . between 0.30 and 0.49 indicates a moderate relationship, and
– . . . above 0.49 indicates a strong relationship.

---

[3] Note that the terms *n-1* in the numerator and denominator cancel each other and are therefore not displayed here.

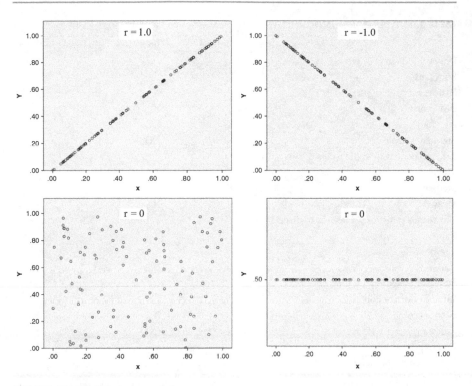

Fig. 5.5 Scatter plots and correlations

The scatter plots in Fig. 5.5 illustrate several correlations. If the observations almost form a straight line in the scatter plot (upper left and right in Fig. 5.5), the two variables have a high (absolute) correlation. If the observations are equally distributed in the scatter plot (lower left in Fig. 5.5), or one variable is a constant (lower right in Fig. 5.5), the correlation is (close to) zero.

There are several types of correlations that can be calculated, but only two are very important. Pearson's correlation coefficient is the most common and is often simply referred to as the correlation. Pearson's correlation is appropriate for calculating correlations between two interval or ratio-scaled variables. It can also be used when one variable is interval or ratio-scale whereas the other is, for example, binary. There are other correlation coefficients for variables measured on lower scale levels. Some examples are:

– *Spearman's correlation coefficient* and *Kendall's tau* for variables measured on an ordinal scale.
– *Contingency coefficient*, *Cramer's V*, and *Phi* for variables measured on a nominal scale. These statistical measures are used with crosstabs; we discuss these in the context of nonparametric tests in the ⁻⊕ Web Appendix of Chap. 6.

In Table 5.4, we indicate which descriptive statistics are useful for differently scaled variables. The brackets (X) indicate that the use of a graph, table or statistic is possible but not necessarily useful, usually because it would require collapsing the data into categories, resulting in a loss of information.

Table 5.4 Types of descriptive statistics for differently scaled variables

	Nominal	Ordinal	Interval & ratio (Scale in SPSS)
Univariate graphs & tables			
Bar chart	X	X	
Histogram			X
Box plot			X
Pie chart	X	X	(X)
Frequency table	X	X	(X)
Univariate statistics: Measures of centrality			
Mode	X	X	X
Median		X	X
Mean			X
Univariate statistics: Measures of dispersion			
Range		(X)	X
Interquartile range		(X)	X
Variance			X
Standard deviation			X
Bivariate graphs/tables			
Scatter plot			X
Crosstab	X	X	(X)
Bivariate statistics			
Contingency coefficient	X		
Cramer's V	X		
Phi	X		
Spearman's correlation		X	
Kendall's tau		X	
Pearson's correlation			X

Box 5.1 Sample calculation of univariate and bivariate statistics

Consider the following list of values for variables x and y, which we treat as ratio-scaled:

x	6	6	7	8	8	8	12	14	14
y	7	6	6	9	8	5	10	9	9

Measures of centrality for x:

Mode $= 8$

Median $= 8$

Mean $(\bar{x}) = \frac{1}{9}(6 + 6 + \ldots + 14 + 14) = \frac{83}{9} = 9.22$

Measures of dispersion for x:

Minimum $= 6$

Maximum $= 14$

Range $= 14\text{--}6 = 8$

(continued)

> **Box 5.1** continued
>
> Interquartile range $= 6.5$
>
> Variance $(s^2) = \frac{[(6-9.22)^2 + \ldots + (14-9.22)^2]}{9-1} = \frac{83.56}{8} = 10.44$
>
> Standard deviation $(s) = \sqrt{s^2} = \sqrt{10.44} = 3.23$
>
> *Measures of association between x and y:*
>
> Covariance $(\text{cov}(x,y)) = \frac{1}{9-1}[(6-9.22) \cdot (7-7.67) + \ldots + (14-9.22) \cdot$
>
> $(9-7.67)] = \frac{31.67}{8} = 3.96$
>
> Correlation $(r) = \frac{3.96}{3.23 \cdot 1.73} = 0.71$

5.6 Transform Data

Transforming data is an optional step in the workflow. Researchers transform data as it is necessary for certain analysis techniques, because it might help interpretation, or because it might help meet the assumptions of techniques that will be discussed in subsequent chapters. We distinguish two types of data transformation:
- Variable respecification, and
- Scale transformation.

5.6.1 Variable Respecification

Variable respecification involves transforming data to create new variables or to modify existing variables. The purpose of respecification is to create variables that are consistent with the objective of the study.

An example of a simple respecification is *recoding* a continuous variable into a categorical variable. For example, if we have a variable measuring a respondent's income, we could code incomes below $15,000 as low, those between $15,000 and $30,000 as medium, and everything above $30,000 as high. Thus, we use a simple rule to recode our original variable as a new variable.

A special way of recoding data is to create a dummy variable. *Dummy variables* (or simply *dummies*) are binary variables that indicate if a certain trait is present or not. For example, we can use a dummy variable to indicate that advertising was used during a particular period (value of the dummy is 1) or not (value of the dummy is 0). We can also use multiple dummies to capture categorical variables' effects. For example, three levels of advertising intensity (low, medium, and high) can be represented by means of two dummy variables: The first takes a value of 1 if the intensity is high (0 else), the second also takes a value 1 if the intensity is medium (0 else). If both dummies take the value 0, this indicates low advertising intensity. We always construct one dummy less than the number of categories. We explain dummies in further detail in the Web Appendix (⌨ Web Appendix → Chapter 5).

Creating *constructs* is a frequently used type of variable respecification. As described in Chap. 3, a construct is a concept which cannot be observed yet can be measured using multiple items, none of which relate perfectly with the construct. To compute a construct measure, we need to calculate the average (or the sum) of a number of related items. For example, the construct brand trust can be measured using the following three items:
- "This brand's product claims are believable"
- "This brand delivers what it promises" and
- "This brand has a name you can trust"

By calculating the average of these three items, we can form a *composite* of brand trust. If one respondent indicated 4, 3, and 6 on the three items' scale, we can calculate a construct score (also referred to as composite score) for this respondent as follows: $(4 + 3 + 6)/3 = 4.33$.

Similar to creating constructs, we can create an *index* of sets of variables. For example, we can create an index of information search activities, which is the sum of the information that customers require from dealers, promotional materials, the Internet, and other sources. This measure of information search activities is also referred to as a composite measure but, unlike a construct, the items in an index define the trait to be measured.

5.6.2   Scale Transformation

Scale transformation involves changing the variable values to ensure comparability with other variables or to make the data suitable for analysis. Different scales are often used to measure different variables. For example, we may use a 5-point Likert scale for one set of variables and a 7-point Likert scale for a different set of variables in our survey. Owing to the differences in scaling, it would not be meaningful to make comparisons across the measurement scales of any respondent. These differences can be corrected by *standardizing variables*.

A popular way of standardizing data is by rescaling the data so that the mean of the variable is 0 and the standard deviation is 1. This type of standardization is called the *z-transformation*. Mathematically, standardized scores z_i (also called *z-scores*) can be obtained by subtracting the mean $\bar{x}$ of every observation x_i and dividing it by the standard deviation s. That is:

$$z_i = \frac{(x_i - \bar{x})}{s}$$

A *log transformation* – another type of transformation – is commonly used if we have skewed data. Skewed data occur if we have a variable that is asymmetrically distributed. For example, family income is often a highly skewed variable. The majority of people will have incomes around the median, and only a few will have very high incomes. However, no one will have a negative income leading to a "tail" to the right of the distribution. A histogram will quickly show whether data are skewed. Skewed data can be problematic in analyses, and using a log transformation it therefore common practice. A log transformation applies a base 10 logarithm to every observation.[4]

Finally, *aggregation* is a special type of transformation. Aggregation means that we take variables measured at a lower level to a higher level. For example, if we know the average of customers' satisfaction and from which stores they buy, we can calculate the average satisfaction at the store level. Aggregation only works one way (from lower to higher levels) and is useful if we want to compare groups.

While transforming data is often necessary to ensure comparability among variables, or to make the data suitable for analysis, there are also drawbacks to this procedure. Most notably, we may lose information through most transformations. For example, recoding income in US dollars (measured at the ratio scale) into a "low" and "high" income category will result in an ordinal variable. Thus, in the transformation process, we have lost information by going from a ratio to an ordinal scale. A simple rule of thumb is that information is lost if we cannot move back from the transformed to the original variable. Another drawback is that transformed data are often more difficult to interpret. For example, log($) is much more difficult to interpret and less intuitive than simply using US dollars.

5.7 Create a Codebook

After all the variables have been organized and cleaned and some initial descriptives have been calculated, a *codebook* is often created. A codebook contains essential details of the data file to allow the data to be shared. In large projects, multiple people usually work on data analysis and entry. Therefore, we need to keep track of the data to minimize errors. Even if just a single researcher is involved, it is still a good idea to create a codebook, as this helps the client use the data and helps if the same data are used later on. On the website accompanying this book (✐ Web Appendix → Chap. 5), we briefly discuss how to create a codebook using SPSS. Codebooks usually have the following structure:

Introduction: The introduction discusses the goal of the data collection, why the data are useful, who participated, and how the data collection effort was conducted (mail, Internet, etc.).

Questionnaire(s): It is common practice to include copies of all types of questionnaires used. Thus, if different questionnaires were used for different respondents (e.g., for French and Italian respondents), a copy of each original

---

[4] The logarithm is calculated as follows: If $x = y^b$, then $y = log_b(x)$ where x is the original variable, b the logarithm's base, and y the exponent. For example, log 10 of 100 is 2. Logarithms cannot be calculated for negative values (such as household debt) and for the value of zero.

questionnaire should be included. Differences in wording may explain the results of the study afterwards, particularly in cross-national studies, even if a back-translation was used (see Chap. 4). These are not the questionnaires received from the respondents themselves but blank copies of each type of questionnaire used. Most codebooks include details of the name of each variable behind the items used. If a dataset was compiled using secondary measures (or a combination of primary and secondary data), the secondary datasets are often briefly discussed (what version was used, when it was accessed, etc.).

Description of the variables: This section includes a verbal description of each variable used. It is useful to provide the variable name as used in the data file, a description of what the variable is supposed to measure, and whether the measure has been used previously. You should also describe the measurement level (see Chap. 3).

Summary statistics: This section includes descriptive statistics of each variable. The average (only for interval and ratio-scaled data), minimum, and maximum are often shown. In addition, the number of observations and usable observations (excluding observations with missing values) are included, just like a histogram (if applicable).

Datasets: This last section includes the names of the datasets and sometimes the names of all the revisions of the used datasets. Sometimes, codebooks include the file date to assure that the right files are used.

5.8   Introduction to SPSS

SPSS is a computer package specializing in quantitative data analysis. It is widely used by market researchers. It is powerful, able to deal with large datasets, and relatively easy to use.

In this book, we use version 22 of IBM SPSS Statistics for Mac (which we simply refer to as SPSS). Prior versions (16 or higher) for Microsoft Windows, Mac, or Linux can also be used for all examples throughout the book. The differences between the versions are small enough so that all examples in the book work with all versions.

The regular SPSS package is available at a substantial fee for commercial use. However, large discounts are available for educational use. To obtain these discounts, it is best to go to your university's IT department and enquire if you can purchase a special student license. You can also download a trial version from www.spss.com.

In the next sections, we will use the ▶ sign to indicate that you have to click on something with your mouse. Options, menu items or drop-down lists that you have to look up in dialog boxes are printed in **bold**, just like elements of SPSS output. Variable names, data files or data formats are printed in *italics* to differentiate them from the rest of the text.

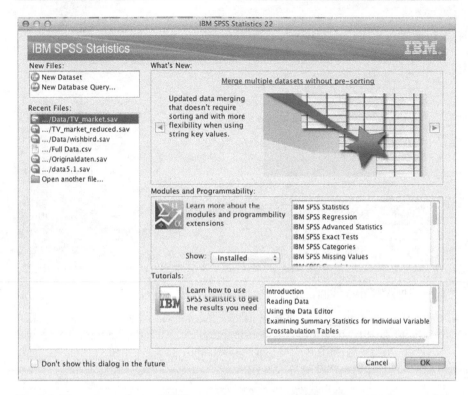

Fig. 5.6 The start-up screen of SPSS

5.8.1   Finding Your Way in SPSS

If you start up SPSS for the first time, it presents a screen similar to Fig. 5.6, unless a previous user has ticked the **Don't show this dialog in the future** box. In that case, you will see a screen similar to Fig. 5.7, but without an active dataset.

In the startup screen, SPSS indicates several options to create or open datasets. The options that you should use are either **Recent Files**, under which you can find a list with recently opened data files, or **New Files**. To open an unlisted file, simply choose **Open another file**... and click **OK** (alternatively, you can click **Cancel**, and then go to ▶ File ▶ Open ▶ Data). Then search for the directory in which the files are kept, click on the file and then on ▶ Open. For the subsequent examples and illustrations, we use a dataset called *TV_market.sav* (✋ Web Appendix → Chap. 5). This dataset contains technical information, prices and ratings of TVs, provided by CHIP Online (www.chip.de), the web portal of one of Germany's largest computer and communications magazine. More precisely, the dataset contains information on the following aspects:

– Brand
– Model type

Fig. 5.7 The SPSS data editor

	brand	model	price	overall_rating	price_rating	quality_picture_rating	quality_3d_rating	quality_sound_rating	quality_equipment_rating	quality_ergonomics_rating
1	Samsung	UE32ES6300	594.99	94.60	77	91	90	98	99	100
2	Panasonic	TX-L32ETW5	554.99	93.10	75	95	100	98	100	83
3	Samsung	UE32ES5700	590.00	91.70	73	95	-99	94	95	92
4	LG	32LM620S	500.00	91.50	82	92	99	95	95	89
5	LG	32LA6608	394.00	90.50	81	91	92	93	95	87
6	LG	32LS575S	500.00	89.90	79	91	-99	95	95	95
7	Toshiba	32TL933G	495.37	88.60	79	97	69	84	92	71
8	Toshiba	32L2333DG	278.99	84.90	100	100	-99	100	74	60
9	Grundig	32VLE7130BF	444.89	83.00	72	93	-99	92	83	66
10	Grundig	32VLC6110C	447.99	77.60	62	92	-99	94	72	57
11	Toshiba	32EL933G	289.97	76.20	70	89	-99	77	64	65
12	Philips	40PFL8008S	1199.00	95.50	61	100	100	95	92	95
13	Samsung	UE40F8090	1029.00	95.00	66	94	93	87	99	100
14	Samsung	UE40F7090SL	920.00	92.20	70	91	93	90	95	96
15	Sony	KDL-40HX855	1178.99	91.70	59	93	86	93	91	91
16	Philips	40PFL8007K	999.00	91.40	60	89	90	91	96	97
17	Samsung	UE40F6470	519.00	91.00	100	90	95	92	93	90
18	Samsung	UE40ES6300	670.00	90.60	84	91	84	79	92	100
19	Panasonic	TX-L42ETW60	745.00	90.60	80	86	98	94	92	98
20	Philips	42PFL6008K	739.00	90.50	77	89	93	90	88	97
21	Philips	40PFL5507K	679.00	89.40	85	89	79	88	92	89
22	Philips	40PFL7007K	699.00	88.30	69	88	93	100	84	97

- Overall product rating, which is an index of various product feature ratings such as picture quality, sound, energy consumption etc. All ratings are measured on a scale from 1 (very bad) to 100 (very good), and
- Technical features such as screen size.

SPSS uses multiple file formats. The .sav file format contains data only. SPSS also allows you to open other file formats such as Excel (.xls and .xlsx) and text files (such as .txt and .dat). Once these files are open, they can be conveniently saved into SPSS's own .sav file format. If you are on SPSS's main screen (see Fig. 5.7) simply go to File ▶ Open ▶ Files of type (select the file format) and double click on the file you wish to open.

SPSS uses two windows. The **SPSS Statistics Data Editor** contains the data and information on the variables in the dataset and the **SPSS Statistics Viewer,** which contains the output produced by the analyses. In the following, we will discuss these two windows separately.

Tip: The notation you will see in this book follows the US style. That is, commas are used to separate thousands (1,000) while decimal points are used to separate whole values from fractions. If you want to change the notation to US style, go to SPSS, then ▶ File ▶ New ▶ Syntax and type in *SET LOCALE = 'English'*. You also need to type in the last point. Now press enter and type in *EXECUTE*. (again, including the point) in the next line. Now run the syntax by choosing Run ▶ All in the syntax window. SPSS will then permanently apply the US style notation the next time you use SPSS.

5.8.2 SPSS Statistics Data Editor

In the **SPSS Statistics Data Editor** (Fig. 5.7), you will find the dataset *TV_market. sav*. This dataset's variables are included in the columns and their names are indicated at the top of each column. The cases are in the rows, which are numbered from 1 onwards. If you click on the **Variable View** tab at the bottom of the screen, SPSS will show you a screen similar to Fig. 5.8. In the **Variable View**, SPSS provides information on the variables included in your dataset:

- **Name**: Here you can indicate the name of the variable. It is best to provide very short names. Variable names must begin with letters (A to Z) or one of the following special characters (@, # or $). Subsequent characters can include letters (A to Z), numbers (0-9), a dot (.), and _, @, #, or $. Note that neither spaces nor other special characters (e.g., %, &,/) are allowed.
- **Type**: Here you can specify what your variable represents. **Numeric** refers to values and **String** refers to words. String is useful if you want to include open-ended answers, email addresses or any other type of information that cannot be adequately captured by numbers. For example, in the dataset *TV_market.sav*, *model* is a string variable, capturing the model type of each TV. With **Dollar** or **Custom Currency**, you can indicate that your variable represents money.

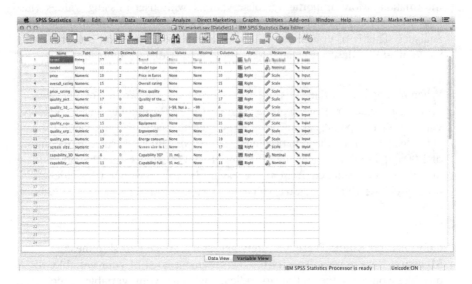

Fig. 5.8 The variable view

- **Width** and **Decimals**: These elements indicate the amount of space available for your variables values.
- **Labels**: Here you can provide a longer description of your variables (called variable labels). This can either be the definition of the variables or the original survey question.
- **Values**: Here you can indicate what a certain value represents (called value labels). For example, for the variable *capability_3D*, which is measured on a nominal scale, 0 represents "no" and 1 "yes."

– **Missing**: Here you can indicate one or more missing value(s). Generally, SPSS
deals with missing values in two ways. If you have blanks in your variables (i.e.,
you haven't entered any data for a specific observation), SPSS treats these as
system-missing values. These are indicated in SPSS by means of a dot (•).
Alternatively, you can define user-missing values that are meant to signify a
missing observation. By defining user-missing values, we can indicate why
specific scores are missing (e.g., the question didn't apply to the respondent or
the respondent refused to answer). In SPSS, you should preferably define user-
missing values as this at least allows the true missing values to be separated from
data that were not recorded (no value was entered). The options under **Missing**
provide three options to indicate user-defined missing values. The first option is
No missing values, which is the default setting and indicates that no values are
user-defined missing. The other two options, **Discrete missing values** and
Range plus one optional discrete missing value, provide a means to express
user-defined missing values. To do so, simply enter values that record that an
observation is missing. Each separate value should indicate separate reasons for
missing values. For example −99 may record that a respondent could not
answer, and −98 that the respondent was unwilling to answer, and −97 might
record "other" reasons.[5] Thus, missing values can provide us with valuable
information. More importantly, observations with user-missing values (just
like with system-missing values) are excluded from data manipulation and
analyses. This is of course essential as, for example, including a user-missing
value of −99 in descriptive analyses would greatly distort the results.

> When picking user-defined missing values, take those that would not otherwise
> occur in the data. For example, for a variable *age*, 1,000 might be an acceptable
> value, as that response cannot occur. However, the same missing value for a
> variable *income* might lead to problems, as a respondent might have an income
> of 1,000. If 1,000 is indicated as a (user-defined) missing value, this observa-
> tion would be excluded from further analysis. By convention, researchers
> usually choose (high) negative values to designate missing such as −99 or
> −999.

– **Columns** and **Align**: These are rarely necessary, so we will skip these.
– **Measure**: Here you can specify the measurement level of your variable. SPSS
provides you with the option to indicate whether your variable is nominal,
ordinal, or whether it is interval or ratio-scaled. The combination of the last
two categories is called **Scale** in SPSS. Note that several procedures such as
creating graphs require that all measurement levels are specified correctly.
– The last **Role** option is not necessary for basic analysis.

---

[5] In the dataset *TV_market.sav*, the variable *quality_3D_rating* has −99 defined as missing value,
indicating that the rating is not applicable as the corresponding TV does not have 3D functionality.

5.8.3   SPSS Statistics Viewer

The **SPSS Statistics Viewer** is a separate window, which opens after you carry out an action in SPSS. The viewer contains the output that you may have produced. If you are used to working with software such as Microsoft Excel, where the data and output are included in a single screen, this may be a little confusing at first. Another aspect of the viewer screen is that it does not change your output once made. Unlike, for example, Microsoft Excel, changing the data after an analysis does not dynamically update the results.

The output produced in SPSS can be saved using the *.spv* file format that is particular to SPSS. To partially remedy this, SPSS provides the option to export the output to Microsoft Word, Excel, or PowerPoint, PDF, HTML, or text. It is also possible to export output as a picture. You can find these export options in the Statistics Viewer under File ▶ Export.

SPSS Menu Functions

In SPSS, you find a number of commands in the menu bar. These include File, ▶ Edit, ▶ View, ▶ Data, ▶ Transform, ▶ Analyze, and ▶ Graphs. In this section, we will briefly discuss these commands. The commands ▶ Analyze and ▶ Graphs will be discussed in greater detail in the example, later in this chapter. The last four commands are ▶ Utilities, ▶ Add-ons, ▶ Windows, and ▶ Help. You are unlikely to need the first three functions but the help function may come in handy if you need further guidance. Under help, you also find a set of tutorials that can show you how to use most of the commands included in SPSS.

In addition to the menu functionalities, we can run SPSS by using its command language, called **SPSS syntax**. You can think of it as a programming language that SPSS uses to "translate" those elements on which you have clicked in the menus into commands that SPSS can understand. Discussing the syntax in great detail is beyond the scope of this book but, as the syntax offers a convenient way to execute analysis, we offer an introduction in the Web appendix (⚘ Web Appendix → Chap. 5). Also, Collier (2010) provides a thorough introduction into this subject. Syntax can be saved (as a *.sps* file) for later use. This is particularly useful if you conduct the same analyses over different datasets. Think, for example, of standardized marketing reports on daily, weekly, or monthly sales.

Under ▶ File, you find all the commands that deal with the opening and closing of files. Under this command, you will find subcommands that you can use to open different types of files, save files, and create files. If you open a dataset, you will notice that SPSS also opens a new screen. Note that SPSS can open several datasets simultaneously. You can easily switch from dataset to dataset by just clicking on the one which you would like to activate. Active datasets are marked with a green plus sign at the top left of the **Data View** and **Variable View** screen.

Under ▶ Edit, you will find subcommands to copy and paste data. Moreover, you will find two options to insert cases or variables. If you have constructed a dataset but need to enter additional data, you can use this to add an additional variable and subsequently add data. **Edit** also contains the **Find** subcommand with which you can look for specific cases or observations. Finally, under ▶ Edit ▶ Options, you find a large number of options, including how SPSS formats tables, and where the default file directories are located.

Under ▶ View, you find several options, of which the **Value Labels** option is the most useful. Value labels are words or short sentences used to indicate what each value represents. For example for *capability_3D, yes* would be the value label used to indicate that the corresponding TV has 3D functionality. SPSS shows value labels in the SPSS Data Editor window if you click on ▶ View, and then on **Value Labels**.

Under the ▶ Data command, you will find many subcommands to change or restructure your dataset. The most prominent option is the ▶ Sort Cases subcommand with which you can sort your data based on the values of a variable. You could, for example, sort the data based on the prices of the TVs. The ▶ Split File subcommand is useful if you want to compare output across different groups, for example, if you want to compare different brands. Moreover, we can carry out separate analyses over different groups using the **Split File** command. Another very useful command is ▶ Data ▶ Select Cases, which allows you to select the observations that you want to analyze. Under ▶ Transform, we find several options to create new variables from existing variables. For example, the first subcommand is **Compute Variable**. This command allows you to create a new variable from one (or more) existing variables. Also included under the ▶ Transform command are two subcommands to recode variables (▶ Recode into Same Variables and ▶ Recode into Different Variables). These commands allow you to recode variable values or to summarize sets of values into one value. For example, using the **Recode into Different Variables** command, you could generate a new variable that takes the value 1 if *overall_rating* is higher than 70, and 0 else.

Under ▶ Analyze, you find numerous analysis procedures, several of which we will discuss in the remainder of the book. For example, under **Descriptive Statistics**, you can request univariate and bivariate statistics. Under **Regression**, SPSS provides numerous types of regression techniques.

Lastly, under ▶ Graphs, there are two subcommand, the **Chart Builder** and **Legacy Dialogs**. The Chart Builder is an interactive tool that allows you to design basic and more complex charts. In order to use the **Chart Builder**, all variables' measurement levels must be correctly specified. The Legacy Dialogs command allows for a menu-driven selection of different chart types.

Some of the previous commands are also accessible by means of shortcut symbols in **Data View** screen's menu bar. As these are very convenient, we present the most frequently used shortcuts in Table 5.5.

Table 5.5 Shortcut symbols	Symbol	Action
		Open dataset
		Save the active dataset
		Recall recently used dialogs
		Undo a user action
		Find
		Split file
		Select cases
		Show value labels

5.9   Data Management in SPSS

In this section, we will illustrate the use of some of the most commonly used commands for managing data in SPSS using the *TV_market.sav* dataset. These include the following:

– Split file,
– Select cases,
– Compute variables, and
– Recode into same/different variables.

5.9.1   Split File

The *split file* command allows you to split the dataset on the basis of grouping variables. If the split file function is activated, all subsequent analyses will be done separately for each group of data, as defined by the grouping variable.

By clicking on ▶ Data ▶ Split File, a dialog box similar to Fig. 5.9 will open. All you need to do is to enter the variable that indicates the grouping (select **Compare groups**) and move the grouping variable (e.g., *brand*) into the **Groups Based on** box. SPSS will automatically carry out all subsequent analyses of each subgroup separately. If you want to revert to analyzing the whole dataset, you need to go to ▶ Data ▶ Split File, then click on **Analyze all cases, do not create groups**.

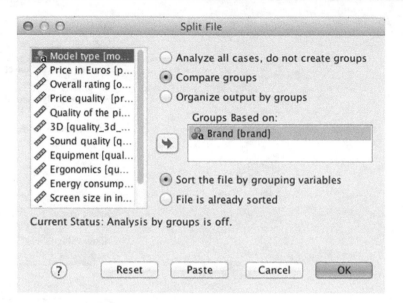

Fig. 5.9 Split file command

> It is a common mistake to forget to turn off the split file command. Failing to do so results in all subsequent analyses being carried out for each group separately!

5.9.2   Select Cases

Using the *select cases* command (▶ Data ▶ Select Cases), you can select certain observations for all subsequent analyses. After clicking on this command, SPSS shows a dialog box where you can select the cases that you want to analyze. If you select **If condition is satisfied** and click on **If. . .**, you will see a new screen similar to Fig. 5.10 where you can select a subset of the data. For example, you can tell SPSS to consider only those cases where the overall rating is higher than 90 by entering *overall_rating* $> = 90$. SPSS will only use the selected observations in subsequent analyses, and will omit the others (these are crossed out in the **Data View** screen). Remember to turn the selection off if you do not need it by going back to ▶ Data ▶ Select Cases and then click on **All cases**.

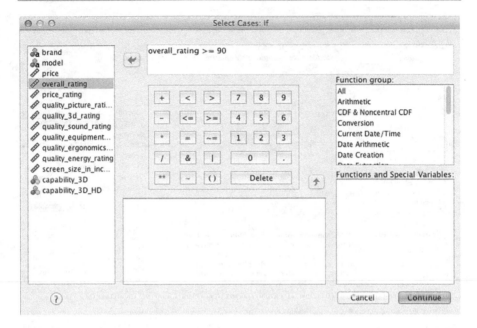

Fig. 5.10 Select cases

5.9.3   Compute Variables

The *compute variable* command allows you to create a new variable from one
(or more) existing variables. For example, if you want to create a composite score of
some type (see Chap. 3), you need to calculate the average of several variables. In
the following, we will use the command to compute a new index from the mean of
the following three rating variables: *price_rating*, *quality_picture_rating*, and
quality_sound_rating. After clicking on ▶ Transform ▶ Compute Variable,
SPSS shows a dialog box similar to Fig. 5.11.

In this dialog box, you can enter the name of the variable you want to create
under **Target Variable.** Under **Numeric Expression** you have to indicate how the
new variable will be created. In the example, we create a new index variable called
rating_index, which is the average of variables *price_rating*, *quality_pic-
ture_rating*, and *quality_sound_rating*. You can use the buttons in the dialog box
to build the formulas that create the new variable (such as the + and − button), or
you can use any of the built-in functions that are found under **Function group**.
SPSS provides a short explanation of each function (in this example, we selected
the **Mean** function).

5.9.4   Recode Into Same/Different Variables

Also included under the ▶ Transform command are two subcommands to *recode
variables*; ▶ Recode into Same Variables and ▶ Recode into Different Variables.

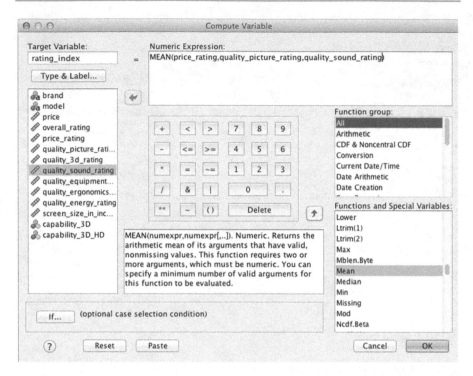

Fig. 5.11 Compute new variables

We always recommend using the recode into different variables option. If you were to use recode into the same variables, any changes you make to the variable will result in the deletion of the original variable. Thus, if you ever want to go back to the original data, you either need to have saved a previous version, or have to enter all the data again as SPSS cannot undo these actions! The recode subcommands allow you to change the scaling of a variable. This is useful if you want to create dummies or create categories of existing variables.

For example, if you want to create a dummy variable to compare cheap and expensive TVs, you could divide the variable *price* into cheap (say, €1,000 or less) and expensive (say, more than €1,000). Figure 5.12 shows the dialog box used for recoding into different variables.

In Fig. 5.12, we see several boxes. The first box at the far left shows all variables included in the dataset. This is the input for the recode process. To recode a variable, move it to the middle box by using the arrow located between the left and middle boxes. On the far right, you see an **Output Variable** box in which you should enter the name of the variable and an explanatory label you want to create. In the **Label** box below, you can specify a variable label. Our newly generated variable is *price_dummy* and has the label *Dummy variable price*. After entering the name and label, click on **Change**. You will then see that, in the middle box, an arrow is drawn between the original and new variables (see the circle in Fig. 5.12). The next step is to tell SPSS what values need to be recoded. Do this by clicking on

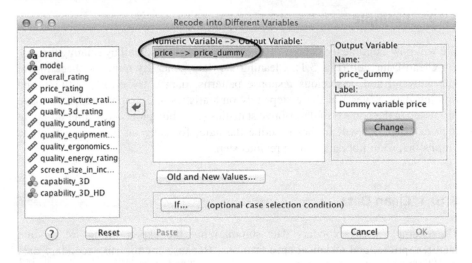

Fig. 5.12 Recode into different variables

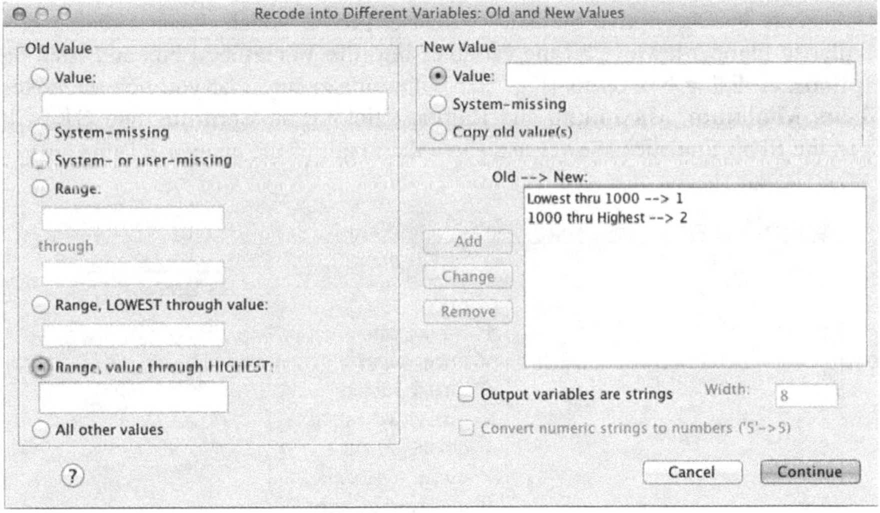

Fig. 5.13 Recode options

Old and New Values. After this, SPSS will present a dialog box similar to Fig. 5.13.

On the left of this dialog box, you should indicate the values of the original variable that you want to recode. In our example, we used the option **Range, LOWEST through value:** to indicate that we want to recode all values of 1,000 or less, and **Range, value through HIGHEST:** to indicate that we want to recode all values of more than 1,000. On the right, you need to indicate the new values for the new variable (in our example, 1 and 2). Finally, confirm your changes by clicking on **Continue** and **OK**.

5.10 Example

We will now examine the dataset *TV_market.sav* in closer detail by running through the Clean Data step (Fig. 5.1). Cleaning the data generally requires checking for interviewer fraud, suspicious response patterns, data entry errors, outliers, and missing data. Several of these steps rely on statistics and graphs, which we have discussed in the context of descriptive statistics (e.g., box plots and scatter plots). In the next step, we will further describe the data, focusing on those statistics and graphs that were not part of the previous step.

5.10.1 Clean Data

The example uses secondary data summarizing the expert ratings of product features, prices, and technical specifications. Because it concerns secondary data used before, we do not check for interviewer fraud or suspicious response patterns.

To examine whether any data entry errors occurred, we first examine the minimum and maximum values, as well each variable's range. To do so, click on ▶ Analyze ▶ Descriptive Statistics ▶ Descriptives, which opens a dialog box similar to Fig. 5.14. Move all the variables into the **Variable(s)** box and click on **Options**. A dialog box opens (Fig. 5.15), now make sure that you tick the boxes **Mean**, **Minimum**, **Maximum**, and **Range**. Clicking on **Continue** and **OK** will open the SPSS Statistics Viewer and show the result of the analysis (Table 5.6).

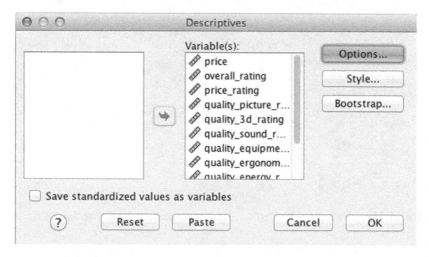

Fig. 5.14 Descriptives menu

As we can see, all of the rating variables' values fall into the regular range between 1 and 100. For example, *price_rating* has a minimum value of 14 and a maximum value of 100, yielding a range of 86. Similarly, and as expected, the two

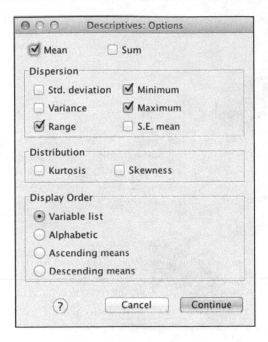

Fig. 5.15 Descriptives options

Table 5.6 Descriptive statistics

Descriptive Statistics

	N	Range	Minimum	Maximum	Mean
price	66	34721.01	278.99	35000.00	2440.3220
overall_rating	66	19.70	76.20	95.90	88.4061
price_rating	66	86	14	100	69.08
quality_picture_rating	66	16	84	100	92.12
quality_3d_rating	52	40	60	100	89.10
quality_sound_rating	66	35	65	100	89.12
quality_equipment_rating	66	36	64	100	89.02
quality_ergonomics_rating	66	43	57	100	83.38
quality_energy_rating	66	62	38	100	74.21
screen_size_in_inches	66	53	32	85	46.76
capability_3D	66	1	0	1	.79
capability_3D_HD	66	1	0	1	.53
Valid N (listwise)	52				

binary variables *capability_3D* and *capability_3D_HD* have minimum values of 0 and maximum values of 1. However, the variable *price* gives rise to concern. Here, the maximum value is 35,000, which is much higher than the minimum value (278.99) and the mean (2,440.32). While this finding could be the result of a data

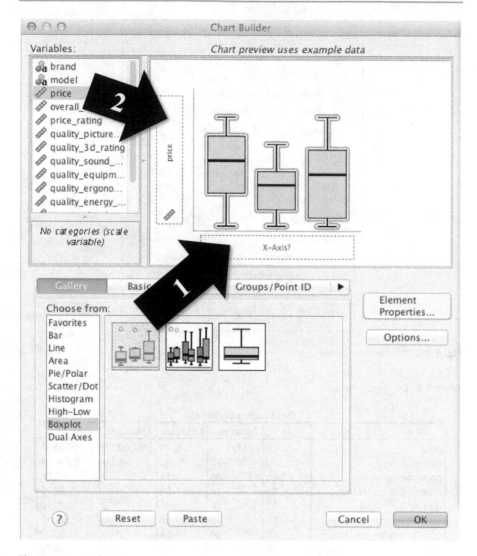

Fig. 5.16 Chart builder

entry error, it could also indicate that there are extremely expensive TVs listed in the dataset. We will examine this issue further in the next step, the outlier detection.

The examination of the maximum values indicated that there is potentially at least one outlier in the dataset. We will examine the distribution of the variable price by means of a box plot (i.e., univariate outlier detection). To do so, go to ▶ Graphs ▶ Chart Builder, which will open an interactive dialog box similar to Fig. 5.16.

In a first step, you need to select the correct graph from the **Gallery**. Go to **Boxplot** in the **Choose from** box and drag and drop the first box plot element into

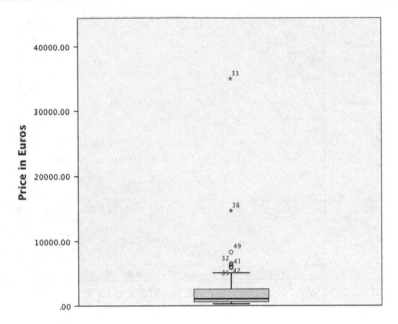

Fig. 5.17 Box plot

the preview field (see arrow 1 in Fig. 5.16). Next, select *price* from the **Variables** box and drag and drop it onto the **Y-Axis?** field in the preview (see arrow 2 in Fig. 5.16). When clicking on **OK**, a box plot similar to Fig. 5.17 shows.

The box plot shows the median distribution of TV prices with a thick horizontal bar. It also shows TV prices are highly skewed (i.e., there are a few observations in the upper part that are very far removed from the median). Note that SPSS differentiates between outliers (indicated by the circles; i.e., observations between 1.5 and 3.0 interquartile ranges from the box) and extreme values (indicated by asterisks; i.e., observations more than 3.0 interquartile ranges from the box). Particularly the latter should give rise to concern.

As we can see, there are two extreme values in the dataset. The numbers next to the asterisks indicate the case number in our dataset (i.e., cases 33 and 38). An Internet search for these two TVs (Samsung UE85S9 and LG 84LM960V) shows that these are in fact exceptionally expensive. Thus, our findings are not a result of data entry errors.

We can further examine these two cases by creating a scatter plot of *price* and *overall_rating*. To do so, open the interactive chart builder (▶ Graphs ▶ Chart Builder) and select **Scatter/Dot** from the **Gallery**. Next, drag and drop the first scatter plot element into the preview field, and move the *price* onto the **Y-Axis?** field and *overall_rating* onto the **X-Axis?** field. After clicking on **OK**, SPSS will show a scatter plot similar to Fig. 5.18. If you double-click on the figure and select the target symbol, you can select individual datapoints to see their case number. In this example, we highlighted the two datapoints, which are isolated from the rest.

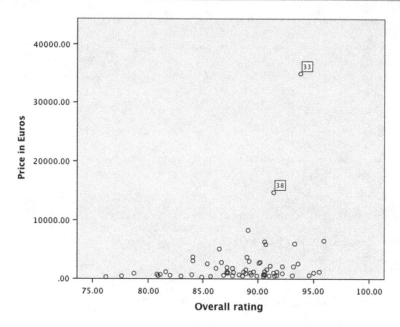

Fig 5.18 Scatter plot of *price* and *overall_rating*

As we can see, these two points correspond to the two cases we identified previously in the univariate outlier detection.

Given the results of the univariate and bivariate outlier detection, how should we deal with these two extreme cases? If we aim to provide an overview of the standard TV market (rather than the exclusive high end market), we should delete these two cases from the analysis. To do so, go back to the SPSS Statistics Data Editor, and delete cases 33 and 38 from the dataset. Next, go to ▶ File ▶ Save as and save the dataset as *TV_market_reduced.sav*.[6] While one could also ague that the other cases, designated as outliers (e.g., cases 49 and 32) should be considered candidates for removal, we decide to retain these cases for now as these TV models are much closer to the rest of the market in terms of price.

In a final step, we run a missing value analysis (▶ Analyze ▶ Missing Value Analysis). In the dialog box that opens (Fig. 5.19), we need to include all the rating variables, as well as the price in the **Quantitative Variables** box and the two binary variables (*capability_3D* and *capability_3D_HD*) in the **Categorical Variables** box. As *brand* and *model* are string variables, we cannot conduct a missing value analysis with these two variables.

Because of the nature of the dataset, there is no need to run Little's MCAR test on the data (see the following discussion). To do this, select **EM** from the **Estimation** box at the right of Fig. 5.19. The test results will then show just below the output tables.

---

[6] Note that all following analyses will be based on the reduced dataset *TV_market_reduced.sav*.

Fig. 5.19 Missing value analysis

Table 5.7 Missing value analysis results

Univariate Statistics

	N	Mean	Std. Deviation	Missing		No. of Extremes[a]	
				Count	Percent	Low	High
price	64	1740.0195	1747.32835	0	.0	0	6
overall_rating	64	88.2750	4.30710	0	.0	3	0
price_rating	64	70.62	17.712	0	.0	0	0
quality_picture_rating	64	91.98	3.756	0	.0	1	5
quality_3d_rating	50	88.78	8.774	14	21.9	3	0
quality_sound_rating	64	89.00	6.958	0	.0	1	0
quality_equipment_rating	64	88.83	7.234	0	.0	2	0
quality_ergonomics_rating	64	83.08	11.567	0	.0	0	0
quality_energy_rating	64	75.23	14.560	0	.0	0	0
screen_size_in_inches	64	45.58	10.583	0	.0	0	9
capability_3D	64			0	.0		
capability_3D_HD	64			0	.0		

a. Number of cases outside the range (Q1 - 1.5*IQR, Q3 + 1.5*IQR).

By clicking on **OK**, a results table similar to Table 5.7 will appear. The analysis shows that the vast majority of variables have no missing values. The only exception is *quality_3d_rating*, which has 14 missing values (21.9%). Given that not all TVs in the dataset have 3D functionalities, this result should not come as a surprise.

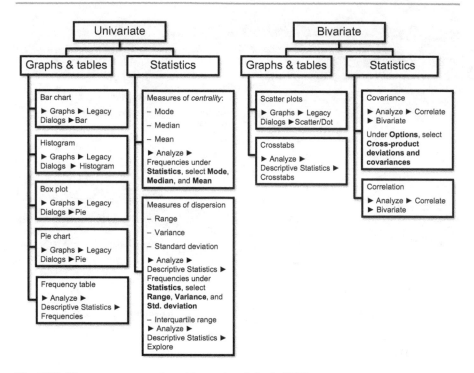

Fig. 5.20 How to request graphs, tables, and statistics in SPSS

Therefore, there is no need for any type of missing data treatment, because the corresponding rating category does not apply to these 14 cases.

This final analysis step concludes the cleaning of the dataset. We can now continue with the description of the data.

5.10.2 Describe Data

In the next step, we describe the data in more detail, focusing on those statistics and graphs that were not part of the previous step. To do so, we make use of descriptive statistics (▶ Analyze ▶ Descriptive Statistics) and graphs (▶ Graphs). As discussed earlier, the ▶ Graphs command is divided into two subcommands, the **Chart Builder** and **Legacy Dialogs**. As we have illustrated the use of the Chart Builder in the previous section, we refer to the legacy dialogs in the following sections.[7] In Fig. 5.20, we show how each previously discussed graph, table, and statistic can be requested in SPSS.

---

[7] As we had already introduced box plots in the sections on univariate outlier detection, we do not repeat the discussion here.

5.10.2.1 Univariate Graphs and Tables
Bar Charts

Bar charts are made by clicking on ▶ Graphs ▶ Legacy Dialogs ▶ Bar. Next, SPSS will ask you to choose a type of bar chart (**Simple, Clustered,** or **Stacked**) and what the data in the bar chart represents (**Summaries for groups of cases, Summaries of separate variables,** or **Values of individual cases**). For a simple bar chart, click on **Define** and then move the variable for which you want to create a bar chart in the **Category Axis** box. Under **Bars Represent**, you can indicate what the bars stand for. Choosing **N of cases** or **% of Cases** provides a graph that looks like a histogram, while choosing **Other statistic (e.g., mean)** can be helpful to summarize a variable's average values across different groups. The groups then need to be identified in the **Category Axis.** Next, enter the variable that should be summarized in the **Variable** box. For example, go to ▶ Graphs ▶ Legacy Dialogs ▶ Bar, then click on **Simple** and **Define**. Subsequently, enter *brand* under **Category axis**. SPSS will then show a graph similar to Fig. 5.21.

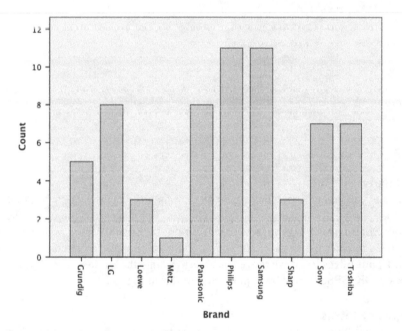

Fig. 5.21 A bar chart

Histograms

Histograms are created by clicking on ▶ Graphs ▶ Legacy Dialogs and then on ▶ Histogram. SPSS will then produce a dialog box in which you have to enter the variable for which you want to produce a histogram under **Variable**. If you want to create multiple histograms on top of or next to each other, you can add a variable for which multiple histograms need to be made under **Rows** or **Columns**. For example, if you move *price* into the **Variable** box, SPSS will produce a histogram as in Fig. 5.22.

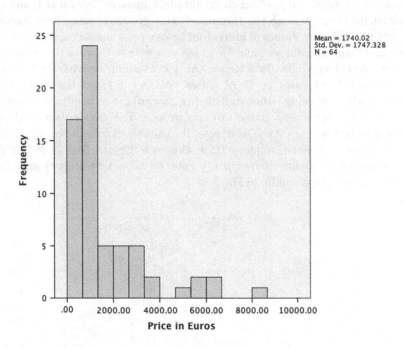

Fig. 5.22 A histogram

Pie Charts
Pie charts can be made by clicking on ▶ Graphs ▶ Legacy Dialogs ▶ Pie. SPSS will then ask you to make one of three choices. For a standard pie chart, the first option (**Summaries for groups of cases**) is best. In the subsequent dialog box, you only need to enter the variable for which you want to make a pie chart in the box titled **Define Slices by**. If we move *capability_3d* into the **Define Slices by** box, and click on **OK**, SPSS will show a pie chart similar to Fig. 5.23.

Frequency Tables
A frequency table can be made by clicking on ▶ Analyze ▶ Descriptive Statistics ▶ Frequencies. You can enter as many variables as you want, as SPSS will make separate frequency tables for each variable. Then click on **OK**. If we use *brand*, SPSS will produce tables similar to Table 5.8. The first table only includes the number of observations, while the second includes the actual frequency table.

5.10.2.2 Univariate Statistics
The mean, mode, and median are easily calculated in SPSS by going to ▶ Analyze ▶ Descriptive Statistics ▶ Frequencies. If you just need these three descriptives,

Fig. 5.23 Pie chart

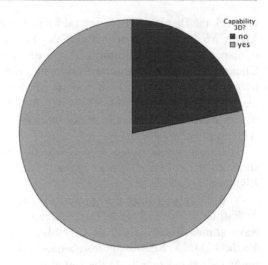

Capability
3D?
■ no
☐ yes

Table 5.8 Example of a crosstab

Statistics

brand

N	Valid	64
	Missing	0

brand

		Frequency	Percent	Valid Percent	Cumulative Percent
Valid	Grundig	5	7.8	7.8	7.8
	LG	8	12.5	12.5	20.3
	Loewe	3	4.7	4.7	25.0
	Metz	1	1.6	1.6	26.6
	Panasonic	8	12.5	12.5	39.1
	Philips	11	17.2	17.2	56.3
	Samsung	11	17.2	17.2	73.4
	Sharp	3	4.7	4.7	78.1
	Sony	7	10.9	10.9	89.1
	Toshiba	7	10.9	10.9	100.0
	Total	64	100.0	100.0	

uncheck the **Display Frequency tables** box. Under **Statistics**, you can then check **Mean**, **Median**, and **Mode**. In this dialog box, you can also select various measures of dispersion such as **Minimum**, **Maximum**, **Range**, **Variance** and **Std. deviation**. Clicking on **Continue** and then **OK** will show you the requested statistics in the output window. Notice that if you ask SPSS to calculate descriptives, it will also display **Valid N (listwise)**. The value indicated behind this, is the number of observations for which we have full information available (i.e., those observations without missing values).

The interquartile range is available by going to ▶ Analyze ▶ Descriptive statistics ▶ Explore. You need to put the variable(s) of interest in the **Dependent List** box.

You can also conduct a z-transformation using descriptive statistics dialog option. Go to ▶ Analyze ▶ Descriptive statistics ▶ Descriptives. Then click on **Save standardized values as variables**. For every variable you enter into the **Variable(s)** box, SPSS will create a new variable (adding the prefix z), standardize the variable, and save it. In the **Label** column under **Variable View** it will even show the original value label preceded by *Zscore:* to indicate that you have transformed that particular variable.

5.10.2.3 Bivariate Graphs and Tables
Scatter Plots
We already requested a simple scatter plot in the context of (bivariate) outlier detection, but SPSS can produce more complex plots. Scatter plots can be made easily by going to ▶ Graphs ▶ Legacy Dialogs ▶ Scatter/Dot. Subsequently, SPSS shows five different options:

1. **Simple Scatter**: this plots two variables against each other.
2. **Matrix Scatter**: this plot creates scatter plots for multiple variables simultaneously. To create an example of a matrix scatter plot, go to ▶ Graphs ▶ Legacy Dialogs ▶ Scatter/Dot. Then click on **Matrix Scatter** and **Define**. Enter, for example, *price*, *overall_rating*, and *price_rating* under **Matrix Variables**. The resulting graph shows separate scatter plots for all combinations of the three matrix variables (Fig. 5.24).
3. **Simple Dot** graph: Plots individual observations as the values of a numeric variable, for example by stacking dots on the x-axis.
4. **Overlay Scatter**: This plot shows different groups within one scatter plot.
5. **3-D Scatter**: Plots the relationships between 3 variables.

Crosstabs
Crosstabs are useful to describe data, particularly if your variables are nominally or ordinally scaled. Crosstabs are made by going to ▶ Analyze ▶ Descriptive Statistics ▶ Crosstabs. You can enter multiple variables under **Row(s)** and **Column(s)**, but crosstabs are easiest to interpret if you enter just one variable under **Row(s)** and one under **Column(s)**. Try making a crosstab by going to ▶ Analyze ▶ Descriptive Statistics ▶ Crosstabs. Under **Row(s)** you can enter *brand*

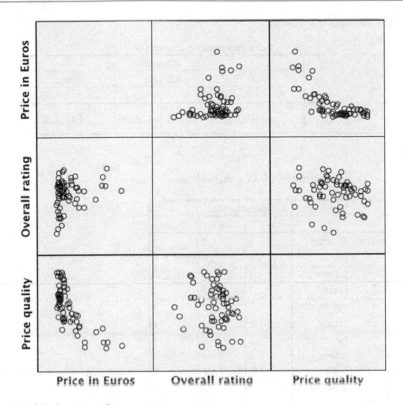

Fig. 5.24 Matrix scatter plot

and *capability_3D* under **Column(s)**. If you then click on **OK**, SPSS produces a table (see Table 5.9).

5.10.2.4 Bivariate Statistics: Correlations

In SPSS, we can calculate bivariate correlations by going to ▶ Analyze ▶ Correlate ▶ Bivariate. In the dialog box that pops up, we can select the type of correlation coefficient and the variables to be considered in the analysis. For example, enter *price*, *overall_rating*, and *price_rating* in the **Variables** box and choose **Pearson** under **Correlation Coefficients**.[8] When you click on **OK**, SPSS will produce a correlation matrix similar to Table 5.10.

The correlation matrix in Table 5.10 shows the correlation between each pairwise combination of three variables. For example, the correlation between *price* and *overall_rating* is 0.244, which is rather weak. Conversely, with a value of -0.738, the correlation between *price* and *price_rating* is very high. Under N, SPSS indicates the number of observations used to calculate each correlation

---

[8] You can also ask for the covariances to be shown by selecting **Cross-product deviations and covariances** under **Options**.

Table 5.9 Example of a crosstab

Case Processing Summary

	Cases					
	Valid		Missing		Total	
	N	Percent	N	Percent	N	Percent
brand * capability_3D	64	100.0%	0	0.0%	64	100.0%

brand * capability_3D Crosstabulation

Count

		capability_3D		Total
		no	yes	
brand	Grundig	4	1	5
	LG	1	7	8
	Loewe	1	2	3
	Metz	1	0	1
	Panasonic	0	8	8
	Philips	1	10	11
	Samsung	2	9	11
	Sharp	1	2	3
	Sony	0	7	7
	Toshiba	3	4	7
Total		14	50	64

Table 5.10 Correlation matrix produced in SPSS

Correlations

		price	overall_rating	price_rating
price	Pearson Correlation	1	.244	-.738[**]
	Sig. (2-tailed)		.052	.000
	N	64	64	64
overall_rating	Pearson Correlation	.244	1	-.144
	Sig. (2-tailed)	.052		.256
	N	64	64	64
price_rating	Pearson Correlation	-.738[**]	-.144	1
	Sig. (2-tailed)	.000	.256	
	N	64	64	64

[**]. Correlation is significant at the 0.01 level (2-tailed).

(64 observations) and gives the significance, which *Sig. (2-tailed)* indicates. We discuss what this means in Chap. 6.

5.11   Cadbury and the UK Chocolate Market (Case Study)

The UK chocolate market achieved annual sales of £7.68 billion in 2012. Six subcategories of chocolates are used to identify the different chocolate segments: boxed chocolate, molded bars, seasonal chocolate, countlines, straightlines, and "other."

Chocolate confectionery industry insights

http://www.globalbusinessinsights.com/content/rbcg0125m.pdf

To understand the UK chocolate market for molded chocolate bars, we have a dataset *(chocolate.sav)* that includes a large supermarket's weekly sales of 100g molded chocolate bars from January 2012 onwards. This data file can be downloaded on the book's website (☝ Web Appendix → Chap. 5). This file contains a set of variables. Once you have opened the dataset and clicked on **Variable View**, you will see the set of variables we discuss next.

The first variable is *week*, indicating the week of the year and starts with Week 1 of January 2012. The last observation for 2012 ends with observation 52, but the variable continues to count onwards for 16 weeks in 2013. The next variable is *sales*, which indicates the weekly sales of 100g Cadbury bars in £. Next, four price variables are included, *price1-price4*, which indicate the price of Cadbury, Nestlé, Guylian, and Milka in £. Next, *advertising1-advertising4* indicate the amount of £ the supermarket spent on advertising each product during that week. A subsequent block of variables, *pop1-pop4*, indicate whether the products were promoted in the supermarket using a point of purchase advertising. This variable is measured as yes/no. Variables *promo1-promo4* indicate whether the product was put at the end of the supermarket aisle - where it is more noticeable. Lastly, *temperature* indicates the weekly average temperature in degrees Celsius.

You have been tasked to provide descriptive statistics for a client, using this available dataset. To help you with this task, the client has prepared a number of questions:

1. Do Cadbury's chocolate sales vary substantially across different weeks? When are Cadbury's sales at their highest? Please create an appropriate graph to illustrate any patterns.
2. Please tabulate point-of-purchase advertising for Cadbury against point-of-purchase advertising for Nestlé. Also create a few further crosstabs. What are the implications of these crosstabs?
3. How do Cadbury's sales relate to the price of Cadbury? What is the strength of the relationship?
4. Which descriptive statistics are appropriate to describe the usage of advertising? Which are appropriate to describe point-of-purchase advertising?

Review Questions

1. Imagine you are given a dataset on car sales in different regions and are asked to calculate descriptive statistics. How would you set up the analysis procedure?
2. What summary statistics could best be used to describe the change in profits over the last five years? What types of descriptives work best to determine the market shares of five different types of insurance providers? Should we use just one or multiple descriptives?
3. What information do we need to determine if a case is an outlier? What are the benefits and drawbacks of deleting outliers?
4. Download the US 2007–2011 5-Year American/Puerto Rican Community Survey Codebook at https://usa.ipums.org/usa/resources/codebooks/Data Dict0711. pdf. Is this codebook clear? What do you think of its structure?

Further Readings

Cohen, J., Cohen, P., West, S. G., & Aiken, L. S. (2003). *Applied multiple regression/correlation analysis for the behavioral sciences* (3rd ed.). Mahwah, NJ: Lawrence Erlbaum Associates.

This is the seminal book on correlation (and regression) analysis which provides a detailed overview into this field. It is aimed at experienced researchers.

Field, A. (2013). *Discovering statistics using SPSS* (4th ed.). London: Sage.

In Chap. 7 of his book, Andy Field provides a very thorough introduction into the principles of correlation analysis from an application-oriented point of view.

Hair, J. F., Jr., Black, W. C., Babin, B. J., & Anderson, R. E. (2010). *Multivariate data analysis. A global perspective* (7th ed.). Upper Saddle River, NJ: Prentice-Hall.

A widely used book on multivariate data analysis. Chapter 2 of this book discusses missing data issues.

Levesque, R., *Programming and data management for IBM SPSS Statistics 20*. Chicago, SPSS, Inc.

An advanced book demonstrating how to manage data in SPSS. Can be downloaded for free at http://tinyurl.com/programming-SPSS

SPSS Learning Modules at http://www.ats.ucla.edu/stat/spss/modules/.

On this website further data organization issues are discussed. This is useful if you already have a dataset, but cannot use it because of the way the data are organized.

SticiGui at http://www.stat.berkeley.edu/~stark/SticiGui/Text/correlation.htm.

This websites interactively demonstrates how strong correlations are for different datasets.

References

Agarwal, C. C. (2013). *Outlier analysis*. New York, NY: Springer.

Cohen, J. (1988). *Statistical power analysis for the behavioral sciences* (2nd ed.). Hillsdale, NJ: Lawrence Erlbaum Associates.

Collier, J. (2010). *Using SPSS syntax: A beginner's guide*. Thousand Oaks, CA: Sage.

Gladwell, M. (2008). *Outliers: the story of success*. New York, NY: Little, Brown, and Company.

Hair, J. F., Jr., Black, W. C., Babin, B. J., & Anderson, R. E. (2010). *Multivariate data analysis. A global perspective* (7th ed.). Upper Saddle River, NJ: Pearson.

Harzing, A. W. (2005). Response styles in cross-national survey research: A 26-country study. *International Journal of Cross Cultural Management, 6*(2), 243–266.

Johnson, T., Kulesa, P., Lic, I., Cho, Y. I., & Shavitt, S. (2005). The relation between culture and response styles. Evidence from 19 countries. *Journal of Cross-Cultural Psychology, 36*(2), 264–277.

Little, R. J. A. (1998). A test of missing completely at random for multivariate data with missing values. *Journal of the American Statistical Association, 83*(404), 1198–1202.

Hypothesis Testing & ANOVA

Learning Objectives

After reading this chapter you should understand:
- The logic of hypothesis testing.
- The steps involved in hypothesis testing.
- What test statistics are.
- Types of error in hypothesis testing.
- Common types of t-tests, one-way and two-way ANOVA.
- How to interpret SPSS outputs.

Keywords:

α-Inflation • Degrees of freedom • F-test • Familywise error rate • Independent and paired samples t-test • Kolmogorov–Smirnov-test • Levene's test • Null and alternative hypothesis • One-sample and two-samples t-tests • One-tailed and two-tailed tests • One way and two way ANOVA • p value • Parametric and nonparametric tests • Post hoc tests • Power of a test • Shapiro–Wilk test • Significance • Statistical significance • t-test • Type I and type II error • z-test

Founded in 2012, wishbird (http://wishbird.net) has become Mexico's leading online marketplace for adventure tours and leisure experiences. Activities range from cooking courses, gourmet dinners, wellness treatments to scuba diving, driving rally cars, skydiving, and everything in between. In an effort to expand to other Latin American markets, wishbird's management decides to analyze their customer base by exploring customers' buying behavior and their perception of the website wishbird.net. Results from hypothesis tests reveal significant differences between male and female customers. Furthermore, the results of an ANOVA analysis show that customers' perceived ease-of-use of the website significantly influences sales.

M. Sarstedt and E. Mooi, *A Concise Guide to Market Research*,
Springer Texts in Business and Economics, DOI 10.1007/978-3-642-53965-7_6,
© Springer-Verlag Berlin Heidelberg 2014

6.1   Introduction

In the previous chapter, we learned about descriptive statistics, such as means and standard deviations, and the insights that can be gained from such measures. Often, we use descriptive statistics to compare groups. For example, we might be interested in investigating whether men or women spend more money on the Internet. Assume that the mean amount that a sample of men spends online is $200 per year against the mean of $250 for the women sample. Two means drawn from different samples are almost always different (in a mathematical sense), but are these differences also statistically significant?

To determine statistical significance, we need to ascertain whether this finding is attributable to chance or if these findings are likely due to significant differences. If the difference is so large that it is unlikely to have occurred by chance, we call this *statistical significance*. Whether results are statistically significant depends on several factors, including variation in the sample data and the number of observations.

In this chapter, we will introduce hypothesis testing which allows for the determination of statistical significance. As statistical significance is a precursor to establishing practical significance, hypothesis testing is of fundamental importance for market research.

6.2   Understanding Hypothesis Testing

Hypothesis testing is a claim about a statistic characterizing a population (such as a mean or correlation) that can be subjected to statistical testing. Such a claim refers to a situation that we might find support for or reject. A hypothesis may comprise a claim about the difference between two sample statistics (e.g., is there a difference in mean spending between males and females). It can also be a judgment of a population value of a certain statistic (e.g., the average amount of time that teenagers spend on the Internet per day is four hours).

Subject to the type of claim made in the hypothesis, we have to choose an appropriate statistical test, of which there are many, with different tests suitable for different research situations. In this chapter, we will focus on *parametric tests* used to examine hypotheses that relate to differences in means. Parametric tests assume that the variable of interest follows a specific statistical distribution (usually a normal distribution). On the contrary, *nonparametric tests* do not require any distributional assumptions.

The most popular parametric test for examining means is the *t-test*. The t-test can be used to compare one mean with a given value (e.g., do males spend more than $150 a year online?). We call this type a *one-sample t-test*. Alternatively, we can test the difference between two samples (e.g., do males spend more than females?). In this latter case, we talk about a *two-samples t-tests* but then we need to differentiate whether we are analyzing two *independent samples* or two *paired samples*.

Independent samples t-tests consider two distinct groups, such as males vs. females or users vs. non-users. Conversely, paired samples t-tests relate to the same set of respondents and thus, occur when respondents are surveyed multiple times. This situation occurs in pre-test/post-test studies designed to measure a variable before and after a treatment. An example is the before-after experimental design discussed in Chap. 4.

Often, we are interested in examining the differences between means found in more than two groups of respondents. For example, we might be interested in evaluating differences in satisfaction between low, medium, and high income customer segments. Instead of carrying out several paired comparisons through separate t-tests, we should use *Analysis of Variance (ANOVA)*. ANOVA is useful for complex research questions, such as when three or more means need to be compared, as ANOVA can analyze multiple differences in one analysis. While there are many types of ANOVA, we focus on the most common types, the one-way and two-way ANOVA.

Figure 6.1 provides a guideline for choosing the appropriate parametric test for comparing means, including the associated SPSS menu options. We will discuss all of these as well as the decisions involved in the choice of test in the remainder of the chapter.

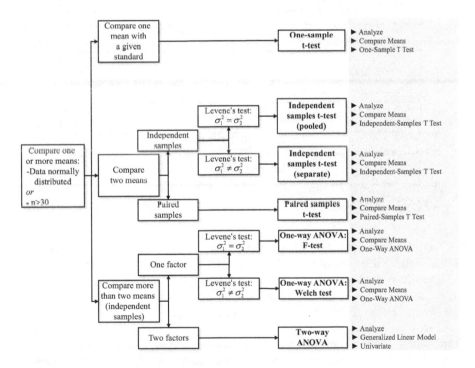

Fig. 6.1 Parametric tests for comparing means

No type of hypothesis testing can validate hypotheses with absolute certainty. The problem is that we have to rely on sample data to make inferences and, as we have not included the whole population in our analysis, there is some probability that we have reached the wrong conclusion. However, we can set an acceptable probability (called the *significance level*) that we will accept a wrong hypothesis. Once we have chosen the significance level, information is obtained from the sample and used to calculate a *test statistic*. Based on the test statistic, we can now decide how likely it is that the claim stated in the hypothesis is supported. On the basis of our final decision to either reject or support the hypothesis, we can then draw market research conclusions. Figure 6.2 illustrates the steps involved in hypothesis testing.

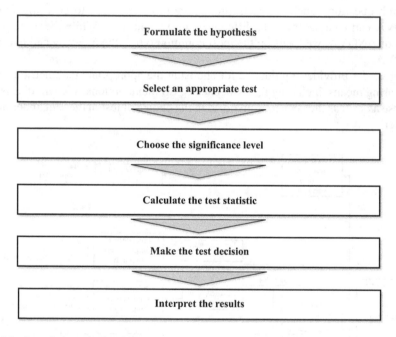

Fig. 6.2 Steps in hypothesis testing

To illustrate the process of hypothesis testing, consider the following example. Suppose that a department store chain wants to evaluate the effectiveness of three different in-store promotion campaigns (1) point of sale display, (2) free tasting stand, and (3) in-store announcements. The management decides to conduct a one-week field experiment. The management chooses 30 stores randomly and randomly assigns ten stores to each campaign type. This random assignment is important to obtain results that may be generalized, because randomization should equalize the effect of factors that have not been accounted for in the experimental design (see Chap. 4).

Table 6.1 shows the number of products sold in each store/campaign in one week. These sales data are normally distributed, which is a necessary condition for

Table 6.1 Sales data

Service type	Sales (units)		
	Point of sale display (stores 1–10)	Free tasting stand (stores 11–20)	In-store announcements (stores 21–30)
Personal	50	55	45
Personal	52	55	50
Personal	43	49	45
Personal	48	57	46
Personal	47	55	42
Self service	45	49	43
Self service	44	48	42
Self service	49	54	45
Self service	51	54	47
Self service	44	44	42

correctly applying the parametric tests discussed in this chapter. We will discuss what this means and how we can evaluate whether the data are normally distributed later in this chapter. The table also contains information on the service type (personal or self service). We will need this information to illustrate the concept of a two-way ANOVA later in this chapter, so let us ignore this column for now.

In what follows, we use these data to carry out different mean comparisons using parametric tests. We illustrate these tests by means of basic formulas. Although we will use SPSS to execute the tests, a basic knowledge of the test formulas will help you understand how the tests work. Hopefully, you will find out that the formulas are not at all as complicated as you might have thought! Most of these formulas contain Greek characters with which you might not be familiar. That's why we have included a table with a description of these characters in the ⌐ Web Appendix (→Additional Material).

6.3 Testing Hypotheses about One Mean

6.3.1 Formulate the Hypothesis

Hypothesis testing starts with the formulation of a null and alternative hypothesis. A *null hypothesis* (indicated as H_0) is a statement expecting no difference or no effect. Conversely, an *alternative hypothesis* (represented as H_1) is one in which some difference is expected – it supplements the null hypothesis. Examples of potential null and alternative hypotheses on the campaign types are:

- H_0: There's no difference in the mean sales between stores that installed a point of sale display and those that installed a free tasting stand (statistically, the average sales of the point of sale display = average sales of the free tasting stand)

H_1: There's a difference in the mean sales between stores that installed a point of sale display and those that installed a free tasting stand (statistically, the average sales of the point of sale display $\neq$ average sales of the free tasting stand).

– H_0: The mean sales in stores that installed a point of sale display are at least 45 units.

H_1: The mean sales in stores that installed a point of sale display are more than 45 units.

When carrying out a statistical test, we always test the null hypothesis. This test can have two outcomes:

1. We reject the null hypothesis, thus finding support for the alternative hypothesis. This outcome is, of course, desirable in most analyses, as we generally want to show that something (such as a promotion campaign) has an effect on a certain outcome (e.g., sales). This is why we frame the effect that we want to show in the alternative hypothesis.

> Researchers always refer to the alternative hypothesis as the hypothesis that is tested!

2. We do not reject the null hypothesis. However, it would be incorrect to conclude then that the null hypothesis is true, as it is not possible to "prove" the non-existence of a certain effect or condition. For example, one can examine any number of crows and find that they are all black, yet that would not make the statement "There are no white crows" true. Only sighting one white crow will prove its existence.

> Each hypothesis test inevitably has a certain degree of uncertainty so that even if we reject a null hypothesis, we can never be fully certain that this was the correct decision. Therefore, knowledgeable market researchers use terms such as "reject the null hypothesis," or "find support for the alternative hypothesis" when they discuss the findings. Terms like "prove the hypothesis" should never be part of any discussion on statistically tested hypotheses.

Returning to our example, the department store managers might be interested in evaluating whether the point of sale display has a positive effect on product sales. The management may consider the campaign a success if sales are higher than the 45 units normally sold (you can likewise choose any other value – the idea is to test the sample mean against a given standard). But what does "generally higher" mean?

Just looking at the data clearly suggests that sales are higher than 45. However, we are not interested in the sample result as much as to assess whether this result is likely due to sample variation.

An appropriate way to formulate the hypotheses is:

$$H_0 : \mu \leq 45$$

$$H_1 : \mu > 45$$

In words, H_0 states that the population mean – indicated by μ – is equal to or smaller than 45, whereas H_1 states that the population mean is larger than 45.

It is important to note that the hypothesis always refers to a population parameter, in this case the population mean, represented by μ (pronounced as *mu*). It is convention that Greek characters represent population parameters and not a sample statistic (e.g., the sample mean indicated by $\bar{x}$). In the end, we want to make inferences regarding the population, not the sample, given the basic assumption that the sample is representative!

If the null hypothesis H_0 is rejected, then the alternative hypothesis H_1 will be accepted and the promotion campaign can be considered a success. On the other hand, if H_0 is not rejected, we conclude that the campaign did not have a positive impact on product sales in the population. Of course, with *conclude*, we still mean that this is what the test indicates and not that this is an absolute certainty.

In this example, we consider a *directional hypothesis* as the two hypotheses are expressed in one direction relative to the standard of 45 units: We presume that the campaign has a positive effect on product sales, which is expressed in hypothesis H_1. More precisely, we consider a right-tailed hypothesis because H_1 presumes that the population mean is actually higher than a given standard. Alternatively, suppose that we were interested in determining whether the product sales differ from the 45 units, either being higher or lower. In this case, a *non-directional hypothesis* would be required, which can be written as follows:

$$H_0 : \mu = 45$$

$$H_1 : \mu \neq 45$$

The difference between the two general types of hypothesis is that a directional hypothesis looks for an increase or a decrease in a parameter (such as a population mean) relative to a specific standard. On the contrary, non-directional hypotheses look for any difference in the parameter from the selected standard.

6.3.2   Select an Appropriate Test

To choose an appropriate statistical test, we have to consider the purpose of the hypothesis test as well as the conditions under which the test is applied. Depending on the distribution of the test variable, this decision involves the choice between a parametric and nonparametric test. Furthermore, we have to decide whether to use a one-tailed or two-tailed test.

6.3.2.1 Parametric vs. Nonparametric Tests

The *parametric tests* we discuss in this chapter assume that the test variable – which needs to be measured on at least an interval scale – is normally distributed. In our numerical example of the promotion campaign, we already assumed that the sales are normally distributed. In practice, we usually lack this information.

To test whether the data are normally distributed, we can use two tests, the *Kolmogorov–Smirnov test (with Lilliefors correction)*, and the *Shapiro–Wilk test*. We describe these in more detail in Box 6.1 and provide an example, executed in SPSS, toward the end of this chapter. If the Kolmogorov–Smirnov or Shapiro–Wilk test suggests that the test variable is not normally distributed, you should use nonparametric tests, which do not make distributional assumptions (Web Appendix → Chap. 6).

The good news is that parametric tests we discuss in this chapter are generally quite robust against violations of the normality assumption. That is, if the test statistic obtained is much below the critical value, deviations from normality matter little. If the test statistic is close to the critical value, for example the obtained p-value (introduced later) is 0.04, and n is smaller than 30, deviations from normality could matter. Still, such deviations are usually no more than a p-value of 0.01 units apart, even if severe deviations from normality are present (Boneau 1960). Thus, even if the Kolmogorov–Smirnov or Shapiro–Wilk test suggests that the data are not normally distributed, we don't have to be concerned that the parametric test results are grossly wrong. Specifically, where we compare means, we can simply apply one of the parametric tests with a low risk of error, provided we have sample sizes greater than 30.

However, if this is not the case, we have to revert to *nonparametric tests*. Nonparametric tests are also the method of choice when the test variable is not measured on an interval or ratio scale. For example, the *Mann-Whitney U test* is used to compare differences between two independent groups when the test variable is ordinal. On the contrary, the χ^2 test is used when nominal variables are involved. In the Web Appendix (→ Chap. 6), we provide an introduction to popular nonparametric tests. There, we specifically discuss the χ^2-tests (pronounced as *chi-square*).

Box 6.1 Normality tests

An important (nonparametric) test for normality is the *one-sample Kolmogorov–Smirnov test*. We can use it to test whether or not a variable is normally distributed. Somewhat surprisingly, the test's null hypothesis is that the variable follows a specific distribution (e.g., the normal distribution). This means that only if the test result is insignificant, that is the null hypothesis is not rejected, can we assume that the data are drawn from the specific distribution against which it is tested. Technically, when assuming a normal distribution, the Kolmogorov–Smirnov test compares the sample scores with an artificial set of normally distributed scores that has the same mean and standard deviation as the sample data. However, this approach is known to yield biased results which are corrected for through the Lilliefors correction (1967). The Lilliefors correction considers the fact that we do not know the true mean and standard deviation of the population. An issue with the Kolmogorov–Smirnov test is that it is very sensitive when used on very large samples and often rejects the null hypothesis if very small deviations are present.

The *Shapiro–Wilk* test also tests the null hypothesis that the test variable under consideration is normally distributed. Thus, rejecting the Shapiro–Wilk test provides evidence that the variable is not normally distributed. It is best used for sample sizes of less than 50. A drawback of the Shapiro–Wilk test is that it works poorly if the variable you are testing has many identical values, in which case you should use the Kolmogorov–Smirnov test with Lilliefors correction.

To conduct the Kolmogorov–Smirnov test with Lilliefors correction and the Shapiro–Wilk test in SPSS, we have to go to ▶ Analyze ▶ Descriptive Statistics ▶ Explore ▶ Plots and choose the **Normality plots with tests** option (note that the menu option ▶ Analyze ▶ Nonparametric Tests ▶ Legacy Dialogs ▶ 1-Sample K-S will yield the standard Kolmogorov–Smirnov test whose results oftentimes diverge heavily from its counterpart with Lilliefors correction). We will discuss these tests using SPSS in this chapter's case study.

6.3.2.2 One-tailed vs. Two-tailed Tests

In statistical significance testing, a *one-tailed test* and *two-tailed test* are alternative ways of computing the statistical significance of a test statistic, depending on whether the hypothesis is expressed directionally or not (alternative names are one-sided and two-sided tests). The terminology "tail" is because the extremes of distributions are often small, as in the normal distribution or "bell curve," pictured in Fig. 6.4 later in this chapter.

Researchers usually employ two-tailed tests as these are stricter (and therefore generally considered more appropriate) when it comes to revealing significant effects. However, the universal use of two-tailed tests is not without problems. Because two-tailed tests, by their very nature, do not reflect any directionality in a hypothesis, the logical connection between the statistical test and the hypothesis is lost when the latter is directional. So, from a conceptual perspective, it is more appropriate to engage in one-tailed testing when the hypothesis is directional.

For example, when a research hypothesis presumes a positive relationship between two variables, right-tailed testing is appropriate; when the presumed relationship is negative, then left-tailed testing is appropriate. The use of two-tailed testing for directional hypothesis is also valuable as it identifies significant effects that occur in the opposite direction from the one anticipated. Imagine that you developed and advertising campaign that you believe is an improvement over an existing campaign. You wish to maximize your ability to detect the improvement, so you opt for a one-tailed test. In doing so, you fail to test for the possibility that the new campaign is less effective than the old one. This is an extreme example but it illustrates a danger of inappropriate use of a one-tailed test.

Cho and Abe (2012) analyzed 2,307 research hypotheses in major marketing journals and found that over 90.9% were directional. However, to test these directional hypotheses, 74.8% of the articles used two-tailed testing, while only 10.6% used one-tailed testing and the remaining 14.6% were unclassifiable.

6.3.3 Choose the Significance Level

Each statistical test is associated with some degree of uncertainty. In statistical testing, two types of errors can occur (Fig. 6.3):
1. A true null hypothesis can be incorrectly rejected (type I or α error), and
2. A false null hypothesis is not rejected (type II or β error).

In our example, a type I error would occur if we found that the point of sale display increased sales, when in fact it did not increase, or may even have decreased sales. Accordingly, a type II error would occur if we did not reject the null hypothesis, which would suggest that the campaign was not successful, even though, in reality, it did significantly increase sales.

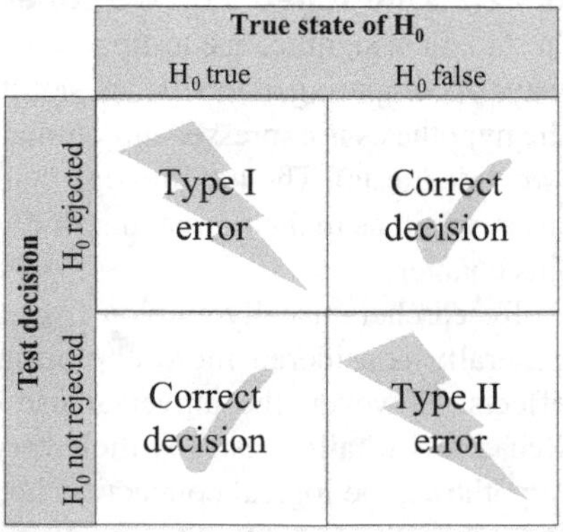

Fig. 6.3 Type I and type II errors

		True state of H_0	
		H_0 true	H_0 false
Test decision	H_0 rejected	Type I error	Correct decision
	H_0 not rejected	Correct decision	Type II error

A problem with hypothesis testing is that we don't know the true state of H_0. Fortunately, we can establish a level of confidence that a true null hypothesis will not be erroneously rejected.

Thus, before carrying out a test, we should decide on the maximum probability of a type I error that we want to allow for. This probability is represented by the Greek character α (pronounced as *alpha*) and is called the *significance level*. In market research reports, this is indicated by phrases such as, "this test result is significant at a 5% level." This means that the researcher allowed for a maximum chance of 5% of mistakenly rejecting a true null hypothesis and that the actual chance, based on the data, turned out to be lower than this.

> Practitioners, usually refer to "significant" in a different, non-statistical context. What they call significant refers to differences that are large enough to influence the decision making process. Perhaps the analysis discloses a significant market segment (i.e., large enough to matter), or the sample reveals such a significant change in consumer behavior that the company needs to change its behavior. Whether results are practically significant (i.e., relevant for decision making), depends on management's perception of whether the difference is large enough to require specific action. It is important to separate statistical significance from practical significance. Statistical significance might imply practical significance but does not need to.

The selection of a particular α value depends on the research setting and the costs associated with a type I error. Usually, α is set to 0.01, 0.05, or 0.10, which corresponds to 1%, 5%, or 10%. Most often, an α-level of 0.05 is used, but when researchers want to be very conservative or strict in their testing, α is set to 0.01. Especially in experiments, α is often set to lower levels. In studies that are exploratory, an α of 0.10 is commonly used.

> Rules of thumb for setting the significance level:
> – $\alpha = 0.10$ in exploratory studies,
> – $\alpha = 0.01$ in experimental studies, and
> – $\alpha = 0.05$ for all other studies.

An α-level of 0.10 means that if you carry out ten tests and reject the null hypothesis every time, your decision in favor of the alternative hypothesis was, on average, wrong once. This might not sound too high a probability, but when much is at stake (e.g., withdrawing a product because of low satisfaction ratings as indicated by hypothesis testing) then 10% is a high α-level. But why don't we simply set α to 0.0001% to really minimize the probability of a type I error? Obviously, setting α to such a low level would make the erroneous rejection of H_0 very unlikely.

Unfortunately, this approach introduces another problem; the probability of a type I error is inversely related to that of a type II error, so that the smaller the risk of one type of error, the higher the risk of the other! However, since a type I error is considered more severe than a type II error, we directly control the former by setting α to a desired level.

Another important concept related to this is the *power of a statistical test* (defined by $1 - \beta$, where β is the probability of a type II error), which represents the probability of rejecting a null hypothesis when it is in fact false (i.e., not making a type II error). Obviously, you would want the power of a test to be as high as possible. However, as indicated before, when α is small, the occurrence of a type I error is much reduced, but then β, the probability of a type II error, is large.[1] This is why α is usually set to the levels described above, which ensures that the test has an acceptable level of statistical power. As a rule of thumb, a statistical power of 0.80 is considered satisfactory. The good news is that both α and β, the probability of incorrect findings, can be controlled for by increasing the sample size: For a given level of α, increasing the sample size will decrease β. See Box 6.2 for further information on statistical power.

Box 6.2 Statistical power

A common problem that market researchers encounter is calculating the sample size required to yield a certain test power, given a predetermined level of α. Unfortunately, computing the required sample size (*power analyses*) can become complicated, depending on the test or procedure we use. However, SPSS provides an add-on module called "Sample Power," which can be used to carry out such analyses. In addition, the Internet offers a wide selection of downloadable applications and interactive Web programs for this purpose. One particular sophisticated and easy-to-use program is G*Power 3.0 which is available at no charge from http://www.psycho.uni-duesseldorf.de/abteilungen/aap/gpower3/.

As an alternative, Cohen (1992) provides a convenient presentation of required sample sizes for different types of tests. For example, detecting the presence of differences between two independent sample means for α = 0.05 and a power of β = 0.80, requires n = 26 for large differences, n = 64 for medium differences, and n = 393 for small differences. This demonstrates sample size requirements go up disproportionally when the effect that needs to be detected becomes smaller.

---

[1] Note that the power of a statistical test may depend on a number of factors which may be particular to a specific testing situation. However, power nearly always depends on (1) the chosen significance level, and (2) the magnitude of the effect of interest in the population.

6.3.4 Calculate the Test Statistic

After having decided on the appropriate test as well as the significance level, we can proceed by calculating the test statistic using the sample data at hand. In our example we make use of a *one-sample t-test*, whose test statistic is computed as follows:

$$t = \frac{\bar{x} - \mu}{s_{\bar{x}}}$$

Here $\bar{x}$ is the sample mean and μ is the hypothesized population mean, and $s_{\bar{x}}$ the standard error. Let's first take a look at the formula's numerator, which describes the difference between the sample mean $\bar{x}$ and the hypothesized population mean μ. If the point of sale display was highly successful, we would expect $\bar{x}$ to be much higher than μ, leading to a positive difference between the two in the formula's numerator.

Using the data from Table 6.1, we can compute the sample mean as follows:

$$\bar{x} = \frac{1}{n}\sum_{i=1}^{n} x_i = (50 + 52 + \dots + 51 + 44) = 47.30$$

When comparing the calculated sample mean (47.30) with the hypothesized mean (45), we find a difference of 2.30.

$$\bar{x} - \mu = 47.30 - 45 = 2.30$$

At first sight, therefore, it appears as if the campaign was successful; sales during the time of the campaign were higher than those that the store normally encounters. However, we have not yet considered the variation in the dataset, which is accounted for by s_x. The problem is that if we had taken another sample from the population, for example, by using data from a different period, the new sample mean would most likely have been different from that which we first encountered. To account for this problem, we have to divide the mean difference $\bar{x} - \mu$ by the *standard error* of $\bar{x}$ (indicated as $s_{\bar{x}}$), which represents the uncertainty of the sample estimate.

This sounds very abstract, so what does this mean? The sample mean is usually used as an estimator of the population mean; that is, we assume that the sample and population means are identical. However, when we draw different samples from the same population, we will most likely obtain different sample means. The standard error tells us how much variability we can expect is in the mean across different samples from the same population. Therefore, a large value for the standard error indicates that a specific sample mean may not adequately reflect the population mean.

Why do we have to divide the difference $\bar{x} - \mu$ by the standard error $s_{\bar{x}}$? Proceeding from the calculation of the test statistic above, we see that when the standard error is very low (i.e., there is a low level of variation or uncertainty in the data), the value in the test statistic's denominator is also small, which results in a higher value for the t-test statistic. Higher t-values favor the rejection of the null hypothesis, which implies that the alternative hypothesis is supported (see next section). In other words: The lower the standard error $s_{\bar{x}}$, the greater the probability that the population represented by the sample truly differs from the selected standard in terms of the average number of units sold. But how do we compute the standard error? It is computed by dividing the sample standard deviation (s), by the square root of the number of observations (n):

$$s_x = \frac{s}{\sqrt{n}} = \frac{\sqrt{\frac{1}{n-1}\sum_{i=1}^{n}(x_i - \bar{x})^2}}{\sqrt{n}}$$

As we can see, a low standard deviation s decreases the standard error (which means less ambiguity when making inferences from these data). That is, less variation in the data decreases the standard error and thus favors the rejection of the null hypothesis. Note that the standard error also depends on the sample size n. By increasing the number of observations, we have more information available, thus reducing the standard error. Consequently, for a certain standard deviation, a higher n goes hand in hand with lower $s_{\bar{x}}$ which is why we generally want to have high sample sizes (within certain limits, see Box 6.3).

Box 6.3 Can a sample size be too large?
In a certain sense, even posing this question is heresy! Market researchers are usually trained to think that large sample sizes are good because of their positive relationship with the goodness of inferences. However, it doesn't seem logical that the claim for high sample sizes should never be discussed. As long as our primary interest lies in the precise estimation of an effect (which will play a greater role when we discuss regression analysis), then the larger the sample, the better. If we want to come as close as possible to a true parameter, increasing the sample size will generally provide more precise results.

There are at least three issues with this argument. First, all else being equal, if you increase the sample size excessively, even marginal effects become statistically significant. However, statistically significant does not mean managerially relevant! In the end, we might run into problems when wanting to determine which effects really matter and how priorities should be assigned.

Second, academics especially are inclined to disregard the relationship between the (often considerable) costs associated with obtaining additional observations and the additional information provided by these observations. In fact, the incremental value provided by each additional observation

(continued)

Box 6.3 (continued)

decreases with increasing sample size. Consequently, there is little reason to work with an extremely high number of observations as, within reason, these do not provide much more information than fewer observations.

Third, not every study's purpose is the precise estimation of an effect. Instead, many studies are exploratory in nature, and we try to map out the main relationships in some area. These studies serve to guide us in directions that we might pursue in further, more refined studies. Specifically, we often want to find those statistical associations that are relatively strong and that hold promise of a considerable relationship that is worth researching in greater detail. We do not want to waste time and effort on negligible effects. For these exploratory purposes, we generally don't need very large sample sizes.

In summary, with a higher mean difference $\bar{x} - \mu$ and lower levels of uncertainty in the data (i.e., lower values in $s_{\bar{x}}$), there is a greater likelihood that we can assume that the promotion campaign has a positive effect on sales.[2]

In summary, the test statistic is nothing but the ratio of the variation, which is due to a real effect (expressed in the numerator), and the variation caused by different factors that are not accounted for in our analysis (expressed in the denominator). In this context, we also use the terms *systematic variation* and *unsystematic variation*. If you understood this basic principle, you will have no problems understanding most other parametric statistical tests.

Let's go back to the example and compute the standard error as follows

$$s_{\bar{x}} = \frac{\sqrt{\frac{1}{10-1}\left[(50 - 47.30)^2 + \cdots + (44 - 47.30)^2\right]}}{\sqrt{10}} = \frac{3.199}{\sqrt{10}} = 1.012$$

Thus, the result of the test statistic is

$$t = \frac{\bar{x} - \mu}{s_{\bar{x}}} = \frac{2.30}{1.012} = 2.274$$

This test statistic applies when we compute the standard deviaton from a sample. In some situations, however, we might know the population's standard deviation, which necessitates the use of a different test, the z-text. (see Box 6.4)

---

[2] Note that most tests follow the same scheme. First, we compare a sample statistic, such as the sample mean, with some standard or the mean value of a different sample. Second, we divide this difference by another measure (i.e., the standard deviation or standard error), which captures the degree of uncertainty in the sample data.

Box 6.4 The z-test

Note that in the previous example, we used sample data to calculate the standard error $s_{\bar{x}}$. If we know the population's standard deviation beforehand we would have to apply a different test, called the *z-test*. The z-test follows a different statistical distribution (in this case, a normal instead of a t-distribution), which we have to consider when determining the critical value associated with a test statistic (we do this in the following step of hypothesis testing). Likewise, the z-test is typically used in situations when the sample size exceeds 30, because the t-distribution and normal distribution are almost identical in higher sample sizes.

As the t-test is slightly more accurate, SPSS only considers the t-test in its menu options. To avoid causing any confusion, we do not present the formulas associated with the z-test here, but we have included these in the ⤻ Web Appendix ($\rightarrow$ Chap. 6).

6.3.5   Make the Test Decision

Once we have calculated the test statistic, we can decide how likely it is that the claim stated in the hypothesis is correct. This is done by comparing the test statistic with the critical value that it must exceed (*Option 1*). Alternatively, we can calculate the actual probability of making a mistake when rejecting the null hypothesis and compare this value with the significance level (*Option 2*). In the following, we will discuss both options.

6.3.5.1 Option 1: Compare the Test Statistic with the Critical Value

In order to make a test decision, we have to determine the critical value, which the test statistic must exceed in order for the null hypothesis to be rejected. In our case, the critical value comes from a *t-distribution* and depends on two parameters:
1. The significance level, and
2. The degrees of freedom.

We already discussed the first point, so let's focus on the second. The *degrees of freedom* (usually abbreviated as "df") represents the amount of information available to estimate the test statistic. In general terms, an estimate's degrees of freedom (such as a variable's variance) are equal to the amount of independent information used (i.e., the number of observations) minus the number of parameters estimated.

> **Box 6.5 Degrees of freedom**
> Suppose you have a soccer team and 11 slots in the playing field. When the
> first player arrives, you have the choice of 11 positions in which you can place
> a player. By allocating the player to a position (e.g., right defense) one
> position is occupied. When the next player arrives, you can chose from 10
> positions. With every additional player that arrives, you will have fewer
> choices where to position each player. For the very last player, you have no
> freedom to choose where to put that player – there is only one spot left. Thus,
> there are 10 degrees of freedom. For 10 players you have some degree of
> choice, but for 1 player you don't. The degrees of freedom are the number of
> players minus 1.

The concept of degrees of freedom is very abstract, so let's look at a simple
example: Suppose you have a single sample with n observations to estimate a
variable's variance. Then, the degrees of freedom are equal to the number of
observations (n) minus the number of parameters estimated as intermediate steps
(in this case, 1 as we need to compute the mean, $\bar{x}$) and are therefore equal to $n-1$.
Field (2013) provides a vivid explanation which we adapted and present in Box 6.5.

The degrees of freedom for the t-statistic to test a hypothesis on one mean are also
$n - 1$; that is, $10 - 1 = 9$ in our example. We can find critical values for combinations
of significance levels and degrees of freedom in the t-distribution table as shown in
Table A1 in the ⁀ Web Appendix ($\rightarrow$ Additional Material). For 9 degrees of freedom
and using a significance level of, for example, 5% (i.e., $\alpha = 0.05$), the critical value of
the t-statistic is 1.833 (just look at the "significance level = 0.05" column and at line
"df = 9" in Table A1 in the ⁀ Web Appendix ($\rightarrow$ Additional Material)). This means
that for the probability of a type I error (i.e., falsely rejecting H_0) to be less than or
equal to 0.05, the value of the test statistic must be 1.833 or greater. In our case (right-
tailed test), the test statistic (2.274) clearly exceeds the critical value (1.833), which
suggests that we should reject the null hypothesis.[3]

Table 6.2 shows the decision rules for rejecting the null hypothesis for different
types of t-tests, where t_{test} describes the test statistic and $t_{critical}$ the critical value of a
significance level α. We always consider absolute test values as these may well be
negative (depending on the test's formulation), while the tabulated critical values
are always positive.

---

[3] To obtain the critical value, you can also use the TINV function provided in Microsoft Excel,
whose general form is "TINV(α, df)." Here, α represents the desired Type I error rate and df the
degrees of freedom. To carry out this computation, open a new Excel spreadsheet and type in
"=TINV(2*0.05,9)." Note that we have to specify "2*0.05" (or, directly 0.1) under α as we are
applying a one-tailed instead of a two-tailed test.

Table 6.2   Decision rules for testing decisions

Type of test	Null hypothesis (H$_0$)	Alternative hypothesis (H$_1$)	Reject H$_0$ if
Right-tailed test	$\mu \le$ value	$\mu >$ value	$|t_{test}| > t_{critical}(\alpha)$
Left-tailed test	$\mu \ge$ value	$\mu <$ value	$|t_{test}| > t_{critical}(\alpha)$
Two-tailed test	$\mu =$ value	$\mu \ne$ value	$|t_{test}| > t_{critical}\left(\frac{\alpha}{2}\right)$

Figure 6.4 summarizes this concept graphically. In this figure, you can see that the critical value $t_{critical}$ for an α-level of 5% divides the area under the curve into two parts. One part comprises 95% of the area, whereas the remaining part (also called the acceptance region, meaning that we accept the alternative hypothesis) represents the significance level α, that is, the remaining 5%. The test value $|t_{test}|$ defines the actual probability of erroneously rejecting a true null hypothesis, which is indicated by the area right of the dotted line. As $|t_{test}|$ is larger than $t_{critical}$, we can reject the null hypothesis. Note that Fig. 6.4 also indicates the p-value which we will describe in the following section.

Fig. 6.4 Relationship between test value, critical value, and p-value

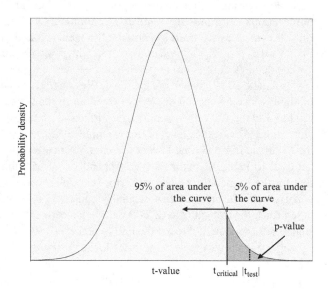

Important: Unlike one-sided tests, we have to divide α by 2 to obtain the critical value of a two-tailed test. This means that when using a significance level of 5%, we have to look under the 0.025 column in the t-distribution table. The reason is that a two-tailed test is somewhat "stricter" than a one-tailed test, because we test whether it is either lower *or* higher than a population value. Thus, we have to assume a tighter confidence level of $\alpha/2$ when looking up the critical value.

6.3.5.2 Option 2: Compare the p-value with the Significance Level

You might remember the above things in horror from your introductory statistics course and the good news is that we do not have to bother with statistical tables when working with SPSS. SPSS automatically calculates the probability of obtaining a test statistic at least as extreme as the one that is actually observed, conditional on the null hypothesis being supported. This probability is also referred to as the *p-value* or *probability value* (rather confusingly, it is usually denoted with **Sig.** – also in the SPSS outputs). In other words, the p-value is the probability of erroneously rejecting a true null hypothesis.

With regard to our example, the p-value is the answer to the following question: If the population mean is really lower than or equal to 45 (i.e., in reality, therefore, H_0 holds), what is the probability that random sampling would lead to a test statistic value of at least 2.274? This description shows that there is a relationship between the p-value and the test statistic. More precisely, these two measures are inversely related; the higher the test statistic, the lower the p-value and vice versa (see Fig. 6.4).

> The description of the p-value very similar to the significance level α, which describes the tolerable level of risk of rejecting a true null hypothesis. However, the difference is that the p-value is calculated using the sample, and that α is set by the researcher before the test outcome is observed.[4] Thus, we cannot simply transfer the interpretation that a long series of α-level tests will reject no more than $100 \cdot \alpha$ of true null hypotheses. Note that the p-value is not the probability of the null hypothesis being supported! Rather, we should interpret it as evidence against the null hypothesis. The α-level is an arbitrary and subjective value that the researcher assigns for the level of risk of making a type I error; the p-value is calculated from the available data.

The comparison of the p-value and the significance level allows the researcher to reject or not reject the null hypothesis. Specifically, if the p-value is smaller than or equal to the significance level, we reject the null hypothesis. Thus, when looking at test results in SPSS, we have to make use of the following decision rule – this should become second nature!

– p-value (**Sig.** in SPSS) $\leq \alpha \rightarrow$ reject H_0
– p-value (**Sig.** in SPSS) $> \alpha \rightarrow$ do not reject H_0

Note that this decision rule applies for two-tailed tests. In case you assume a directional hypothesis, you may want to apply a one-tailed test. In this case, you need to cut the p-value in half before comparing it to α, leading to the following decision rule:

– $0.5 \cdot$ p-value (**Sig.** in SPSS) $\leq \alpha \rightarrow$ reject H_0
– $0.5 \cdot$ p-value (**Sig.** in SPSS) $> \alpha \rightarrow$ do not reject H_0

---

[4] Unfortunately, there is quite some confusion about the difference between α and p-value. See Hubbard and Bayarri (2003) for a discussion.

No matter how small the p-value is in relation to α, it is only of interest whether p-value $\leq \alpha$ but not the specific value of p itself. Thus, a statement such as "this result is highly significant" is inappropriate, as the test results are binary in nature (i.e., they reject or don't reject, nothing more). Compare it with any binary condition from real life, such as pregnancies – it is not possible to be just a little bit pregnant!

In our example, the actual p-value is about 0.024, which is clearly below the significance level of 0.05. Thus, we can reject the null hypothesis and find support for the alternative hypothesis.[5]

6.3.6   Interpret the Results

The conclusion reached by hypothesis testing must be expressed in terms of the market research problem and the relevant managerial action that should be taken. In our example, we conclude that there is evidence that the point of sale display significantly increased sales during the week it was installed.

6.4   Comparing Two Means: Two-samples t-test

In the previous example, we examined a hypothesis relating to one sample and one mean. However, market researchers are often interested in comparing two sample means. As indicated in Fig. 6.1, two samples can either be *independent* or *paired*, depending on whether we compare two distinct groups (e.g., males vs. females) or the same group at different points in time (e.g., customers before and after being exposed to a treatment or campaign). Let's begin with two independent samples.

6.4.1   Two Independent Samples

Testing the relationship between two independent samples is very common in market research settings. Some common research questions are:
– Does heavy and light users' satisfaction with products differ?
– Do male customers spend more money online than female customers?
– Do US teenagers spend more time on Facebook than Australian teenagers?

---

[5] We don't have to conduct manual calculations and tables when working with SPSS. However, we can easily compute the p-value ourselves using the TDIST function in Microsoft Excel. The function has the general form "TDIST(t, df, tails)", where t describes the test value, df the degrees of freedom and *tails* specifies whether it's a one-tailed test (tails = 1) or two-tailed test (tails = 2). For our example, just open a new spreadsheet and type in "=TDIST(2.274,9,1)". Likewise, there are several webpages with Java-based modules (e.g., http://www.graphpad.com/quickcalcs/index.cfm) that calculate p-values and test statistic values.

Each of these hypotheses aims at evaluating whether two populations (e.g., heavy and light users), represented by samples, are significantly different in terms of certain key variables (e.g., satisfaction ratings).

To understand the principles of a two independent samples t-test, let's reconsider the previous example of a promotion campaign in a department store. Specifically, we want to test whether the population mean of the sales of the point of sale display (μ_1) differs from that of the free tasting stand (μ_2). Thus, the resulting null and alternative hypotheses are now:

$$H_0 : \mu_1 = \mu_2$$

$$H_1 : \mu_1 \neq \mu_2$$

In its general form, the test statistic of the two independent samples t-test – which is now distributed with $n_1 + n_2 - 2$ degrees of freedom – seems very similar to the one-sample t-test:

$$t = \frac{(\bar{x}_1 - \bar{x}_2) - (\mu_1 - \mu_2)}{s_{\bar{x}_1 - \bar{x}_2}}$$

Here, $\bar{x}_1$ is the mean of the first sample (with n_1 numbers of observations) and $\bar{x}_2$ is the mean of the second sample (with n_2 numbers of observations). The term $\mu_1 - \mu_2$ describes the hypothesized difference between the population means. In this case, $\mu_1 - \mu_2$ is zero as we assume that the means are equal, but we could likewise use another value in cases where we hypothesize a specific difference in population means. Lastly, $s_{\bar{x}_1 - \bar{x}_2}$ describes the estimated standard error, which comes in two forms:

1. If we assume that the two populations have the same variance (i.e., $\sigma_1^2 = \sigma_2^2$), we compute the standard error based on the so called *pooled* variance estimate:

$$s_{\bar{x}_1 - \bar{x}_2} = \sqrt{\frac{[(n_1 - 1) \cdot s_1^2 + (n_2 - 1) \cdot s_2^2]}{n_1 + n_2 - 2}} \cdot \sqrt{\frac{1}{n_1} + \frac{1}{n_2}}$$

2. Alternatively, if we assume that the population variances differ (i.e., $\sigma_1^2 \neq \sigma_2^2$), things become a little bit easier as we can use the *separate* variance estimate:

$$s_{\bar{x}_1 - \bar{x}_2} = \sqrt{\frac{s_1^2}{n_1} + \frac{s_2^2}{n_2}}$$

How do we determine whether the two populations have the same variance? This is done by means of an intermediate step that consists of another statistical test.

This test is known as the *F-test of sample variance* (also called *Levene's test*) and considers the following hypotheses:

$$H_0 : \sigma_1^2 = \sigma_2^2$$

$$H_1 : \sigma_1^2 \neq \sigma_2^2$$

The null hypothesis is that the two population variances are the same and the alternative hypothesis is that they differ. As the computation of this test statistic is rather complicated, we refrain from discussing it in detail. If you want to learn more about Levene's test and its application to the promotion campaign example, read up on it in the ✐ Web Appendix (→ Chap. 6).

In this example, the Levene's test provides support for the assumption that the variances in the population are equal, so that we have to make use of the pooled variance estimate. First, we estimate the variances of samples 1 and 2:

$$s_1^2 = \frac{1}{n_1 - 1} \sum_{i=1}^{10} (x_{1i} - \bar{x}_1)^2 = \frac{1}{10 - 1} [(50 - 47.30)^2 + \cdots + (44 - 47.30)^2]$$
$$= 10.233,$$

$$s_2^2 = \frac{1}{n_2 - 1} \sum_{i=1}^{10} (x_{2i} - \bar{x}_2)^2 = \frac{1}{10 - 1} [(55 - 52)^2 + \cdots + (44 - 52)^2] = 17.556,$$

and use these to obtain the estimated standard error:

$$s_{\bar{x}_1 - \bar{x}_2} = \sqrt{\frac{[(10 - 1) \cdot 10.233 + (10 - 1) \cdot 17.556]}{10 + 10 - 2}} \cdot \sqrt{\frac{1}{10} + \frac{1}{10}} = 1.667$$

Inserting the estimated standard error into the test statistic results in:

$$t = \frac{(\bar{x}_1 - \bar{x}_2) - (\mu_1 - \mu_1)}{s_{\bar{x}_1 - \bar{x}_2}} = \frac{(47.30 - 52) - 0}{1.667} = -2.819$$

As you can see, calculating these measures manually is not very difficult. Still, it is much easier to let SPSS do the calculations.

The test statistic follows a t-distribution with $n_1 + n_2 - 2$ degrees of freedom. In our case we have $10 + 10 - 2 = 18$ degrees of freedom. Looking at the statistical Table A1 in the ✐ Web Appendix (→ Additional Material), we can see that the critical value for a significance level of 5% is 2.101 (note that we are conducting a two-tailed test and, thus, have to look in the $\alpha = 0.025$ column). As the absolute value of -2.819 is greater than 2.101, we can reject the null hypothesis at a significance level of 5% and conclude that the means of the sales of the point of sale display (μ_1) and those of the free tasting stand (μ_2) differ in the population.

If we evaluated the results of the left-tailed test (i.e., $H_0 : \mu_1 \geq \mu_2$ and $H_1 : \mu_1 < \mu_2$) we find that sales of the point of sale display are significantly lower than those of the free tasting stand. Thus, the managerial recommendation would be to make use of free tasting stands when carrying out promotion campaigns, as this increases sales significantly over those of the point of sale display. Of course, in making the final decision, we would need to weigh the costs of the display and free tasting stand against the expected increase in sales.

6.4.2 Two Paired Samples

In the previous example, we compared the mean sales of two independent samples. Now, imagine that management wants to evaluate the effectiveness of the point of sale display in more detail. We have sales data for the week before point of sale display was installed, as well as the following week when this was not the case. Table 6.3 shows the sale figures of the 10 stores under consideration for the two experimental conditions (the point of sale display and no point of sale display). Again, you can assume that the data are normally distributed.

Table 6.3 Sales data (extended)

Store	Sales (units)	
	No point of sale display	Point of sale display
1	46	50
2	51	52
3	40	43
4	48	48
5	46	47
6	45	45
7	42	44
8	51	49
9	49	51
10	43	44

At first sight, it appears that the point of sale display yielded higher sales numbers: The mean of the sales in the week during which the point of sale display was installed (47.30) is slightly higher than in the week when it was not (46.10). However, the question is whether this difference is statistically significant.

Obviously, we cannot assume that we are comparing two independent samples, as each set of two samples originates from the same store, but at different points in time under different conditions. This means we have to examine the differences by means of a *paired samples t-test*. In this example, we want to test whether the sales of the point of sale display condition are significantly higher than when no display was installed. We can express this by means of the following hypotheses, where μ_d describes the population difference in sales:

$$H_0 : \mu_d \leq 0$$

$$H_1 : \mu_d > 0$$

We assume that the population difference is greater than zero since we suspect that the point of sale display ought to have significantly increased sales. This is expressed in the alternative hypothesis H_1, while the null hypothesis assumes that the point of sale display made no difference or even resulted in lower sales

To carry out this test, we have to define a new variable d_i, which captures the differences in sales between the two treatment conditions (point of sale display installed and not installed) for each of the stores. Thus:

$$d_1 = 50 - 46 = 4$$

$$d_2 = 52 - 51 = 1$$

$$\cdots$$

$$d_9 = 51 - 49 = 2$$

$$d_{10} = 44 - 43 = 1$$

Based on these results, we calculate the mean difference

$$\bar{d} = \frac{1}{n} \sum_{i=1}^{10} d_i = \frac{1}{10} (4 + 1 + \cdots + 2 + 1) = 1.2$$

as well as the standard error of this difference

$$s_{\bar{d}} = \frac{\sqrt{\frac{1}{n-1} \sum_{i=1}^{10} (d_i - \bar{d})^2}}{\sqrt{n}}$$

$$= \frac{\sqrt{\frac{1}{9}[(4 - 1.2)^2 + (1 - 1.2)^2 + \cdots + (2 - 1.2)^2 + (1 - 1.2)^2]}}{\sqrt{10}} = 0.533$$

As you might suspect, the test statistic is very similar to the ones discussed before. Specifically, we compare the mean difference $\bar{d}$ in our sample with the difference expected under the null hypothesis μ_d and divide this difference by the standard error $s_{\bar{d}}$. Thus, the test statistic is

$$t = \frac{\bar{d} - \mu_d}{s_{\bar{d}}} = \frac{1.2 - 0}{0.533} = 2.250,$$

which follows a t-distribution with $n - 1$ degrees of freedom, where n is the number of pairs that we compare. Assuming a significance level of 5%, we obtain the critical value by looking at Table A1 in the ⁀ Web Appendix (→Additional Material). In our example, with 9 degrees of freedom and using a significance level of 5% (i.e., $\alpha = 0.05$), the critical value of the t-statistic is 1.833. Since the test value is larger than the critical value, we can reject the null hypothesis and presume that the point of sale display really did increase sales.

6.5 Comparing More Than Two Means: Analysis of Variance (ANOVA)

Researchers are often interested in examining mean differences between more than two groups. For example:
- Do light, medium and heavy users differ with regard to their monthly disposable income?
- Do customers across four different types of demographic segments differ with regard to their attitude towards a certain brand?
- Is there a significant difference in hours spent on Facebook between US, UK and Australian teenagers?

Continuing with our previous example on promotion campaigns, we might be interested in whether there are significant sales differences between the stores in which the three different types of campaigns were launched. One way to tackle this research question would be to carry out multiple pairwise comparisons of all groups under consideration. In this example, doing so would require the following comparisons:
1. The point of sale display vs. the free tasting stand
2. The point of sale display vs. the in-store announcements and
3. The free tasting stand vs. the in-store announcements

While three comparisons seem to be easily manageable, you can imagine the difficulty that will arise when a greater number of groups are compared. For example, with 10 groups, we would have to carry out 45 group comparisons.[6]

Although such high numbers of comparisons become increasingly time consuming, there is a more severe problem associated with this approach, called *α-inflation*. This refers to the fact that the more tests you conduct at a certain significance level, the more likely you are to claim a significant result when this is not so (i.e., a type I error). Using a significance level of $\alpha = 0.05$ and making all possible pairwise comparisons of ten groups (i.e., 45 comparisons), the increase in the overall probability of a type I error (also referred to as the *familywise error rate*) is

---

[6] The number of pairwise comparisons is calculated as follows: $k \cdot (k - 1)/2$, with k the number of groups to compare.

$$\alpha^* = 1 - (1 - \alpha)^{45} = 1 - (1 - 0.05)^{45} = 0.901.$$

That is, there is a 90.1% probability of erroneously rejecting your null hypothesis in at least some of your 45 t-tests – far greater than the 5% for a single comparison! The problem is that you can never tell which of the comparisons provide results that are wrong and which are right.

Instead of carrying out many pairwise tests, market researchers use ANOVA, which allows a comparison of averages between three or more groups. In ANOVA, the variable that differentiates the groups is referred to as the *factor* (don't confuse this with the factors from factor analysis which we discuss in Chap. 8!). The values of a factor (i.e., as found for the different groups under consideration) are also referred to as *factor levels*.

In the example above on promotion campaigns, we considered only one factor with three levels, indicating the type of campaign. This is the simplest form of an ANOVA and is called *one-way ANOVA*. However, ANOVA allows us to consider more than one factor. For example, we might be interested in adding another grouping variable (e.g., the type of service offered), thus increasing the number of treatment conditions in our experiment. In this case, we would use a *two-way ANOVA* to analyze both factors' effect on the units sold (in isolation and jointly). ANOVA is in fact even more flexible in that you can also integrate metric independent variables and even several additional dependent variables. We first introduce the one-way ANOVA, followed by a brief discussion of the two-way ANOVA.[7] For a more detailed discussion of the latter, you can turn to the ⌁ Web Appendix ($\rightarrow$ Chap. 6).

6.5.1   Understanding One-Way ANOVA

As indicated above, ANOVA is used to examine mean differences between more than two groups.[8] In more formal terms, the objective of one-way ANOVA is to test the null hypothesis that the population means of the groups under consideration (defined by the factor and its levels) are equal. If we compare three groups, as in our example, the null hypothesis is:

$$H_0 : \mu_1 = \mu_2 = \mu_3$$

This hypothesis implies that the population means of all three promotion campaigns are identical (which is the same as saying that the campaigns have the same effect on mean sales). The alternative hypothesis is

---

[7] Field (2013) provides a detailed introduction to further ANOVA types such as multiple ANOVA (MANOVA) or an analysis of covariance (ANCOVA).

[8] Note that you can also apply ANOVA when comparing two groups, but as this will lead to the same results as the independent samples t-test, the latter is preferred.

$$H_1 : \text{At least two of } \mu_1, \mu_2, \text{ and } \mu_3 \text{ are different.}$$

Of course, before we even think of running an ANOVA in SPSS, we have to come up with a problem formulation, which requires us to identify the dependent variable and the factor, as well as its levels. Once this task is done, we can dig deeper into ANOVA by following the steps described in Fig. 6.5. We will discuss each step in more detail in the following sections.

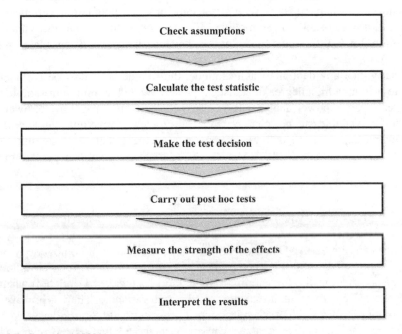

Fig. 6.5 Steps in ANOVA

6.5.1.1 Check Assumptions

ANOVA rests on the following series of assumptions, the first two of which are identical to the parametric tests discussed earlier:

– The dependent variable is measured on an interval or ratio scale,
– The dependent variable is normally distributed,
– The population variances in each group are identical, and
– The sample size is sufficiently high.

ANOVA is quite robust when these assumptions are violated, particularly in cases where the groups are sufficiently large and approximately equal in size. Consequently, we may also use ANOVA in situations when the dependent variable is ordinally scaled and not normally distributed, but then we should ensure that the group-specific sample sizes are equal.[9] Thus, if possible, it is useful to collect equal-sized samples of data across the groups.

When carrying out ANOVA the population variances in each group should be the same. Even though ANOVA is rather robust in this respect, violations of the assumption of homogeneous variances can significantly bias the results, especially when groups are of very unequal sample size.[10] Consequently, we should always test for homogeneity of variances, which is commonly done by using Levene's test. We already briefly touched upon this test and you can learn more about it in ↗ Web Appendix (→ Chap. 6). If Levene's test indicates that population variances are different, it is advisable to use modified F-tests such as the *Welch test*, which we discuss in Box 6.6 (the same holds for post hoc tests which we discuss later in this chapter).

Finally, like any data analysis technique, the sample size must be sufficiently high to warrant a high degree of statistical power. While the minimum sample size requires separate power analyses (e.g., using the software program G*Power 3.0 which is available at no charge from http://www.psycho.uni-duesseldorf.de/abteilungen/aap/gpower3/), there is general agreement that the bare minimum sample size per group is 20. However, 30 or more observations per group are desirable.

Box 6.6 Tests to use when variances are unequal and group-specific sample sizes different

When carrying out ANOVA, violations of the assumption of homogeneity of variances can have serious consequences, especially when group sizes are unequal. Specifically, the within-group variation is increased (inflated) when there are large groups in the data that exhibit high variances. There is however a solution to this problem when it occurs. Fortunately, SPSS provides us with two modified techniques that we can apply in these situations: Brown and Forsythe (1974) and Welch (1951) propose modified test statistics, which make adjustments if the variances are not homogeneous. While both techniques control the type I error well, past research has shown that the Welch test exhibits greater statistical power. Consequently, when population variances are different and groups are of very unequal sample sizes, it is best to use the Welch test.

---

[9] Nonparametric alternatives to ANOVA are, for example, the χ^2-test of independence (for nominal variables) and the Kruskal–Wallis test (for ordinal variables). See, for example, Field (2013).

[10] In fact, these two assumptions are interrelated, since unequal group sample sizes result in a greater probability that we will violate the homogeneity assumption.

6.5.1.2 Calculate the Test Statistic

The basic idea underlying the ANOVA is that it examines the dependent variable's variation across the samples and, based on this variation, determines whether there is reason to believe that the population means of the groups (or factor levels) differ significantly.

With regard to our example, each store's sales will likely deviate from the overall sales mean, as there will always be some variation. The question is whether the difference between each store's sales and the overall sales mean is likely to be caused by a specific promotion campaign or is due to a natural variation in sales. In order to disentangle the effect of the treatment (i.e., the promotion campaign type) and the natural variation ANOVA splits up the total variation in the data (indicated by SS_T) into two parts:

1) The between-group variation (SS_B), and
2) The within-group variation (SS_W).[11]

These three types of variation are estimates of the population variation. Conceptually, the relationship between the three types of variation is expressed as

$$SS_T = SS_B + SS_W$$

However, before we get into the maths, let's see what SS_B and SS_W are all about.

The Between-group Variation (SS_B)

SS_B refers to the variation in the dependent variable as expressed in the variation in the group means. In our example, it describes the variation in the sales mean values across the three treatment conditions (i.e., point of sale display, free tasting stand, and in-store announcements) in relation to the overall mean. However, what does SS_B tell us? Imagine a situation in which all mean values across the treatment conditions are the same. In other words, regardless of which campaign we choose, sales are always the same. Obviously, in such a case, we cannot claim that the different types of promotion campaigns had any influence on sales. On the other hand, if mean sales differ substantially across the three treatment conditions, we can assume that the campaigns influenced the sales to different degrees.

This is what is expressed by means of SS_B; it tells us how much variation can be explained by the fact that the differences in observations truly stem from different groups. Since SS_B can be considered "explained variation" (i.e., variation explained by the grouping of data and, thus, reflecting different effects), we would want SS_B to be as high as possible. However, there is no given standard of how high SS_B should be, as its magnitude depends on the scale level used (e.g., are we looking at 7-point Likert scales or an income variable?). Consequently, we can only interpret the explained variation expressed by SS_B in relation to the variation that is not explained by the grouping of data. This is where SS_W comes into play.

---

[11] SS is an abbreviation of "sum of squares" because the variation is calculated by means of squared differences between different types of values.

The Within-group Variation (SS$_W$)

As the name already suggests, SS$_W$ describes the variation in the dependent variable within each of the groups. In our example, SS$_W$ simply represents the variation in sales in each of the three treatment conditions. The smaller the variation within the groups, the greater the probability that all the observed variation can be explained by the grouping of data. It is obviously the ideal for this variation to be as small as possible. If there is much variation within some or all the groups, then this variation seems to be caused by some extraneous factor that was not accounted for in the experiment and not the grouping of data. For this reason, SS$_W$ is also referred to as "unexplained variation."

Unexplained variation can occur if we fail to account for important factors in our experimental design. For example, in some of the stores, the product might have been sold through self-service while in others personal service was available. This is a factor that we have not yet considered in our analysis, but which will be used when we look at two-way ANOVA later in the chapter. Nevertheless, some unexplained variation will always be present, regardless of how sophisticated our experimental design is and how many factors we consider. That is why unexplained variation is frequently called *(random) noise*.

Combining SS$_B$ and SS$_W$ into an Overall Picture

The comparison of SS$_B$ and SS$_W$ tells us whether the variation in the data is attributable to the grouping, which is desirable, or due to sources of variation not captured by the grouping. More precisely, ideally we want SS$_B$ to be as large as possible, whereas SS$_W$ should be as small as possible. This relationship is described in Fig. 6.6, which shows a scatter plot, visualizing sales across stores of our three different campaign types:

– Point of sale display (•),
– Free tasting stand (■), and
– In-store announcements (▲).

We indicate the group mean of each level by dashed lines. If the group means were all the same, the three dashed lines would be aligned and we would have to conclude that the campaigns have the same effect on sales. In such a situation, we could not expect the point of sale group to differ from the free tasting stand group or the in-store announcements group. Furthermore, we could not expect the free tasting stand group to differ from the in-store announcements group. On the other hand, if the dashed lines were on very different levels, we would probably conclude that the campaigns had significantly different effects on sales.

At the same time, we would like the variation within each of the groups to be as small as possible; that is, the vertical lines connecting the observations and the dashed lines should be short. In the most extreme case, all observations would lie on the dashed lines, implying that the grouping explains the variation in sales perfectly. This, however, hardly ever occurs.

It is easy to visualize from this diagram that if the vertical bars were all, say, twice as long, then it would be difficult or impossible to draw any meaningful

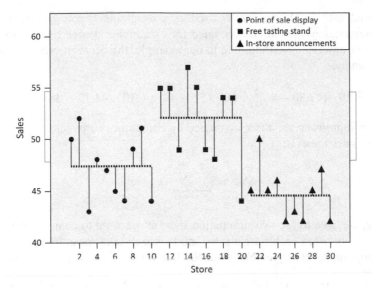

Fig. 6.6 Scatter plot of stores vs. sales

conclusions about the effects of the different campaigns. Too great a variation within the groups then swamps any variation across the groups. Based on the discussion above, we can calculate the three types of variation.

> Note that strictly speaking, the group-specific sample size in this example is too small to yield valid results as we would expect to have at least 20 observations per group. However, we restricted the sample size to 10 per group to show the manual calculation of the statistics.

1. The total variation, computed by comparing each store's sales with the overall mean $\bar{x}$, which is equal to 48 in our example:

$$SS_T = \sum_{i=1}^{n} (x_i - \bar{x})^2 = (50 - 48)^2 + (52 - 48)^2 + \cdots + (47 - 48)^2 + (42 - 48)^2 = 584$$

2. The between-group variation, computed by comparing each group's mean sales with the overall mean, is:

$$SS_B = \sum_{j=1}^{k} n_j(\bar{x}_j - \bar{x})^2$$

As you can see, besides index i, as previously discussed, we also have index j to represent the group sales means. Thus, $\bar{x}_j$ describes the mean in the j-th group and n_j the number of observations in that group. The overall number of groups is denoted with k. The term n_j is used as a weighting factor: groups that have many observations should be accounted for to a higher degree relative to groups with fewer observations. Returning to our example, the between-group variation is then given by:

$$SS_B = 10 \cdot (47.30 - 48)^2 + 10 \cdot (52 - 48)^2 + 10 \cdot (44.70 - 48)^2 = 273.80$$

3. The within-group variation, computed by comparing each store's sales with its group sales mean is:

$$SS_w = \sum_{j=1}^{k} \sum_{i=1}^{n_j} (x_{ij} - \bar{x}_j)$$

Here, we have to use two summation signs as we want to compute the squared differences between each store's sales and its group sales mean for all k groups in our set-up. In our example, this yields the following:

$$SS_W = [(50 - 47.30)^2 + \cdots + (44 - 47.30)^2] + [(55 - 52)^2 + \cdots$$
$$+ (44 - 52)^2] + [(45 - 44.70)^2 + \cdots + (42 - 44.70)^2]$$
$$= 310.20$$

In the previous steps, we discussed the comparison of the between-group and within-group variation. The higher the between-group variation is in relation to the within-group variation, the more likely it is that the grouping of the data are responsible for the different levels in the stores' sales and not the natural variation in all sales.

A suitable way to describe this relation is by forming an index with SS_B in the numerator and SS_W in the denominator. However, we do not use SS_B and SS_W directly, as these are based on summed values and, thus, are influenced by the number of scores summed. These results for SS_B and SS_W have to be normalized, which we do by dividing the values by their degrees of freedom to obtain the true "mean square" values MS_B (called between-group mean squares) and MS_W (called within-group mean squares). The resulting mean squares are:

$$MS_B = \frac{SS_B}{k - 1} \quad \text{and} \quad MS_W = \frac{SS_w}{n - k}$$

We use these mean squares to compute the following test statistic which we then compare with the critical value:

$$F = \frac{MS_B}{MS_W}$$

6.5.1.3 Make the Test Decision

Making the test decision in ANOVA is analogous to the t-tests discussed earlier with the only difference that the test statistic follows an F-distribution (as opposed to a t-distribution). Unlike the t-distribution, the F-distribution depends on two degrees of freedom: One corresponding to the between-group mean squares $(k - 1)$ and the other referring to the within-group mean squares $(n - k)$. Turning back to our example, we calculate the F-value as:

$$F = \frac{MS_B}{MS_W} = \frac{SS_B/_{k-1}}{SS_W/_{n-k}} = \frac{273.80/_{3-1}}{310.20/_{30-3}} = 11.916$$

For the promotion campaign example, the degrees of freedom are 2 and 27; therefore, looking at Table A2 in the ✋ Web Appendix ($\rightarrow$ Additional Material), we obtain a critical value of 3.354 for $\alpha = 0.05$. Note that we don't have to divide α by two when looking up the critical value! The reason is that we always test for equality of population means in ANOVA, rather than one being larger than the others. Thus, the distinction between one-tailed and two-tailed tests does not apply in this case. Because the calculated F-value is greater than the critical value, we reject the null hypothesis. Consequently, we can conclude that at least two of the population sales means for the three types of promotion campaigns differ significantly.

At first sight, it appears that the free tasting stand is most successful, as it exhibits the highest mean sales ($\bar{x}_2 = 52$) compared to the point of sale display ($\bar{x}_1 = 47.30$) and the in-store announcements ($\bar{x}_3 = 44.70$). However, note that rejecting the null hypothesis does not mean that all population means differ – it only means that at least two of the population means differ significantly! Market researchers often make this mistake, assuming that all means differ significantly when interpreting ANOVA results. Since we cannot, of course, conclude that all means differ from one another, this can present a problem. Consider the more complex example in which the factor under analysis does not only have three different levels, but ten. In an extreme case, nine of the population means could be the same while one is significantly different from the rest. It is clear that great care has to be taken when interpeting the result of the F-test.

How do we determine which of the mean values differs significantly from the others without stepping into the α-inflation trap discussed above? One way to deal with this problem is to use *post hoc tests* which we discuss in the next section.[12]

6.5.1.4 Carry Out Post Hoc Tests

The basic idea underlying post hoc tests is to perform tests on each pair of groups and to correct the level of significance for each test. This way, the overall type I error rate across all comparisons (i.e., the familywise error rate) remains constant at a certain

---

[12] Note that the application of post hoc tests only makes sense when the overall F-test finds a significant effect.

level such as $\alpha = 0.05$. The easiest way of maintaining the familywise error rate is to carry out each comparison at a statistical significance level of α divided by the number of comparisons made. This method is also known as the *Bonferroni correction*. In our example, we would use $0.05/3 = 0.017$ as our criterion for significance. Thus, in order to reject the null hypothesis that two population means are equal, the p-value would have to be smaller or equal to 0.017 (instead of 0.05!).

Thus, the Bonferroni adjustment is a very strict way of maintaining the familywise error rate. While this might at first sight not be problematic, there is a trade-off between controlling the familywise error rate and increasing the type II error, which would reduce the test's statistical power. By being very conservative in the type I error rate, such as when using the Bonferroni correction, a type II error may creep in and cause us to miss out on revealing some significant effect that actually exists in the population.

The good news is that there are alternatives to the Bonferroni correction. The bad news is that there are numerous types of post hoc tests – SPSS provides no less than 18! Generally, these tests detect pairs of groups whose mean values do not differ significantly (*homogeneous subsets*). However, all these tests are based on different assumptions and designed for different purposes, whose details are clearly beyond the scope of this book. Check out the SPSS help function for an overview and references.

The most widely used post hoc test in market research is Tukey's honestly significant difference test (usually simply called *Tukey's HSD*). Tukey's HSD is a very versatile test which controls for the type I error and is conservative in nature. A less conservative alternative is the *Ryan/Einot-Gabriel/Welsch Q procedure* (REGWQ), which also controls for the type I error rate but has a higher statistical power. These post hoc tests share two important properties:
1. they require an equal number of observations for each group (differences of a few observations are not problematic), and
2. they assume that the population variances are equal.

Fortunately, research has provided alternative post hoc tests for situations in which these properties are not met. When sample sizes differ clearly, it is advisable to use *Hochberg's GT2*, which has good power and can control the type I error. However, when population variances differ, this test becomes unreliable. Thus, in cases where our analysis suggests that population variances differ, it is best to use the *Games-Howell procedure* because it generally seems to offer the best performance. Figure 6.7 provides a guideline for choosing the appropriate post hoc test.

While post hoc tests provide a suitable way of carrying out pairwise comparisons among the groups while maintaining the familywise error rate, they do not allow making any statements regarding the strength of a factor's effects on the dependent variable. This is something we have to evaluate in a separate analysis step, which is discussed next.

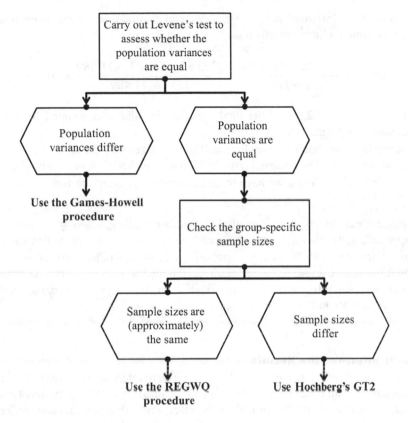

Fig. 6.7 Guideline for choosing the appropriate post hoc test

6.5.1.5 Measure the Strength of the Effects

To determine the strength of the effect (also *effect size*) that the factor exerts on the dependent variable, we can compute the η^2 (pronounced as *eta squared*) coefficient. It is the ratio of the between-group variation (SS_B) to the total variation (SS_T) and, as such, expresses the variance accounted for of the sample data. η^2 is often simply referred to as effect size and, can take on values between 0 and 1. If all groups have the same mean value, and we can thus assume that the factor has no influence on the dependent variable, η^2 is 0. Conversely, a high value implies that the factor exerts a strong influence on the dependent variable. In our example η^2 is:

$$\eta^2 = \frac{SS_B}{SS_T} = \frac{273.80}{584} = 0.469$$

The outcome indicates that 46.9% of the total variation in sales is explained by the promotion campaigns. Note that η^2 is often criticized as being inflated, for example, due to small sample sizes, which might in fact apply to our analysis.

To compensate for small sample sizes, we can compute ω (pronounced *omega squared*), which adjusts for this bias:

$$\omega^2 = \frac{SS_B - (k - 1) \cdot MS_W}{SS_T + MS_W} = \frac{273.80 - (3 - 1) \cdot 11.489}{584 + 11.489} = 0.421$$

In other words, 42.1% of the total variation in sales is accounted for by the promotion campaigns.

Generally, you should use ω^2 for small sample sizes (say 50 or less) and η^2 for larger sample sizes. Unfortunately, the SPSS one-way ANOVA procedure does not compute η^2 and ω^2. Thus, we have to do this manually, using the formulas above.

It is difficult to provide firm rules of thumb regarding when η^2 or ω^2 is appropriate, as this varies from research area to research area. However, since η^2 resembles the Pearson's correlation coefficient (Chap. 5) of linear relationships, we follow the suggestions provided in Chap. 5. Thus, we can consider values below 0.30 weak, values from 0.31 to 0.49 moderate and values of 0.50 and higher as strong.

6.5.1.6 Interpret the Results

Just as in any other type of analysis, the final step is to interpret the results. Based on our results, we can conclude that the promotion campaigns have a significant effect on sales. An analysis of the strength of the effects revealed that this association is moderate. Carrying out post hoc tests manually is difficult and, instead, we have to rely on SPSS to do the job. We will carry out several post hoc tests later in this chapter on an example.

6.5.2   Going Beyond One-way ANOVA: The Two-Way ANOVA

A logical extension of one-way ANOVA is to add a second factor to the analysis. For example, we could assume that, in addition to the different promotion campaigns, management also varied the type of service provided by offering either self-service or personal service (see column "Service type" in Table 6.1). In principle, a two-way ANOVA works the same way as a one-way ANOVA, except that the inclusion of a second factor necessitates the consideration of additional types of variation. Specifically, we now have to account for two types of between-group variations:

1. The between-group variation in factor 1 (i.e., promotion campaigns), and
2. The between-group variation in factor 2 (i.e., service type).

In its simplest usage, the two-way ANOVA assumes that these factors are mutually unrelated. However, in market research applications this is rarely the case, thereby requiring us to use the more complex case of related factors. When we take two related factors into account, we not only have to consider each factor's direct effect (also called *main effect*) on the dependent variable, but also the factors' *interaction effect*. Conceptually, an interaction effect is the additional effect due to combining two (or more) factors. Most importantly, this extra effect cannot be observed when considering each of the factors separately and thus reflects a concept known as *synergy*. There are many examples in everyday life where the whole is more than simply the sum of the parts as we know from cocktail drinks, music or paintings (for a very vivid example of interaction, see the link provided in Box 6.7).

Box 6.7 A different type of interaction

http://tinyurl.com/interact-coke

In our example, the free tasting stand might be the best promotion campaign when studied separately, but it could well be that when combined with personal service, the point of sale display is much more effective. A significant interaction effect indicates that the combination of the two factors is particularly effective or, on the other hand, ineffective, depending on the direction of the interaction effect. Conversely, an insignificant interaction effect suggests that we should choose the best level of the two factors and then use them in combination. The computation of these effects as well as discussion of further technical aspects go beyond the scope of this book but are discussed in the ⌀ Web Appendix (→ Chap. 6).

Table 6.4 provides an overview of steps involved when carrying out the following tests in SPSS: One-sample t-test, independent samples t-test, paired samples t-test, and the one-way ANOVA.

Table 6.4 Steps involved in carrying out t-tests and one-way ANOVA in SPSS

Theory	Action
One-sample t-test	
Compare mean value with a given standard	▶ Analyze ▶ Compare Means ▶ One-Sample T Test
Assumptions:	
Is the test variable measured on an interval or ratio scale?	Check Chap. 3 to determine the measurement level of the variables.
Are the observations independent?	Consult Chap. 3 to determine if the observations are independent.
Is the test variable normally distributed or is $n>30$?	If necessary, carry out normality tests: ▶ Analyze ▶ Descriptive Statistics ▶ Explore ▶ Plots. Check Normality plots with tests. For $n < 50$, interpret the Shapiro–Wilk test. If test variable exhibits many identical values or for higher sample sizes, use the Kolmogorov–Smirnov test (with Lilliefors correction).
Specification:	
Select the test variable	Enter the variable in the **Test Variable(s)** box
Specify the standard of comparison	Specify the test value in the **Test Value** box.
Results interpretation:	
Look at test results	Compare the p-value with the pre-defined significance level.
Independent samples t-test	
Compare the differences in the means of the independent samples	▶ Analyze ▶ Compare Means ▶ Independent-Samples T Test
Assumptions:	
Is the test variable measured on at least an interval scale?	Check Chap. 3 to determine the measurement level of your variables.
Are the observations independent?	Consult Chap. 3 to determine if the observations are independent.
Is the test variable normally distributed or is $n > 30$ in each of the groups?	If necessary, carry out normality tests: ▶ Analyze ▶ Descriptive Statistics ▶ Explore ▶ Plots. Enter the test variable in the **Dependent List** box and the grouping variable in the **Factor List** box. Check Normality plots with tests. For $n < 50$, interpret the Shapiro–Wilk test. If test variable exhibits many identical values or for higher sample sizes, use the Kolmogorov–Smirnov test (with Lilliefors correction).
Specification:	
Select the test variable and the grouping variable	Enter these in the **Test Variable(s)** and **Grouping Variable** boxes.
Results interpretation:	
Look at test results	If the Levene's test suggests equal population variances, interpret the t-value and its significance level based on the pooled variance estimate (upper row in SPSS output); if Levene's test suggests unequal population variances, interpret the t-value and its significance level based on the separate variance estimate (lower row in SPSS output).

(continued)

Table 6.4   (continued)

Theory	Action
Paired samples t-test	
Compare the differences in the means of the paired samples	▶ Analyze ▶ Compare Means ▶ Paired-Samples T Test
Assumptions:	
Are the test variables measured on an interval or ratio scale?	Check Chap. 3 to determine the measurement level of your variables.
Are the observations dependent?	Consult Chap. 3 to determine if the observations are dependent.
Are the test variable normally distributed or is $n > 30$ in each of the groups?	If necessary, carry out normality tests: ▶ Analyze ▶ Descriptive Statistics ▶ Explore ▶ Plots. Enter the test variable in the **Dependent List** box and the grouping variable in the **Factor List** box. Check Normality plots with tests. For $n < 50$, interpret the Shapiro–Wilk test. If test variable exhibits many identical values or for higher sample sizes, use the Kolmogorov Smirnov test (with Lilliefors correction).
Specification:	
Select the paired test variables	Enter these in the **Paired Variables** box.
Results interpretation:	
Look at test results	Compare the p-value with the pre-defined significance level.
One-way ANOVA	
Compare the means of three or more groups	▶ Analyze ▶ Compare Means ▶ One-Way ANOVA
Specification:	
Select the dependent variable and the factor (grouping variable)	Enter these in the **Dependent List** and **Factor** box.
Assumptions:	
Are there at least 20 observations per group?	Check Chap. 5 to determine the sample size in each group.
Is the dependent variable measured on an interval or ratio scale?	Check Chap. 3 to determine the measurement level of your variables.
Are the observations independent?	Consult Chap. 3 to determine if the observations are independent.
Is the dependent variable normally distributed in each of the groups?	Carry out normality tests: ▶ Analyze ▶ Descriptive Statistics ▶ Explore ▶ Plots. Enter the test variable in the **Dependent List** box and the grouping variable in the **Factor List** box. Check Normality plots with tests. For $n < 50$, interpret the Shapiro–Wilk test. If test variable exhibits many identical values or for higher sample sizes, use the Kolmogorov–Smirnov test (with Lilliefors correction).
Are the population variances equal?	Carry out Levene's test: ▶ Analyze ▶ Compare Means ▶ One-Way ANOVA ▶ Options ▶ Homogeneity of variance test

(continued)

Table 6.4 (continued)

Theory	Action
Results interpretation:	
Look at test results	Check the F-value and its significance level; if Levene's test suggests different population variances and the group sizes differ significantly, interpret using Welch test. ▶ Analyze ▶ Compare Means ▶ One-Way ANOVA ▶ Options ▶ Welch
Look at the strength of the effects	Use SPSS output to compute η^2 and ω^2 manually
Carry out pairwise comparisons	Carry out post hoc tests: ▶ Analyze ▶ Compare Means ▶ One-Way ANOVA ▶ Post Hoc Equal population variances assumed: - Use R-E-G-WQ if group sizes are equal - Use Hochberg's GT2 if group sizes differ.
	If unequal population variances assumed, use the Games–Howell procedure.

6.6   Example

Founded in 2012, Wishbird is Mexico's leading online marketplace for adventure tours and leisure experiences. Wishbird offers hundreds of experiences to choose from throughout Mexico. Activities range from cooking courses, gourmet dinners, wellness treatments to scuba diving, driving rally cars, skydiving, and everything in between. Wishbird is currently expanding to other Latin American markets.

After one year of operations, the company decided to consult a market research firm to explore the customers' buying behavior and their perception of the website. In a small-scale ad hoc study, the firm gathered data from a quota sample of 60 customers on the following variables (variable names in parentheses):

– Identification number (*id*)
– Respondent's gender (*gender*)
– Perceived image of wishbird.net (*image*)
– Perceived ease-of-use of wishbird.net (*ease*)
– Sales per respondent per year in USD (*sales*)

Using these dataset *wishbird.sav* (✇ Web Appendix → Chap. 6), the market research firm sought to identify potential areas of improvement for the website design and ideas on how to further explore relevant target groups in future advertising campaigns. Specifically, the firm wanted to answer the following two research questions:

1. Is there a significant difference in sales between male and female customers?
2. Does the website's perceived ease-of-use (measured in three categories: easy, neutral, and difficult) influence the customers' buying behavior?

Before conducting any testing procedure to answer the two research questions, we have to examine whether the variable of interest (i.e., sales in USD) is normally distributed within each of the groups (i.e., males/females and easy/neutral/difficult). The results of these analyses determine, whether we should consider parametric or nonparametric tests to test for group differences. This is done using normality test, which we can access by clicking ▶ Analyze ▶ Descriptive Statistics ▶ Explore. This will open a dialog box similar to Fig. 6.8.

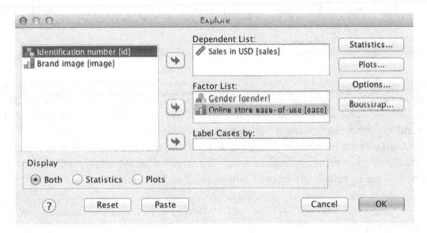

Fig. 6.8 One-sample Kolmogorov–Smirnov test dialog box

Enter the variable *sales* in the **Dependent List** box and the variables *gender* and *ease* in the **Factor List** box. By entering these two variables in the **Factor List** box, we request the following analyses to be done separately for each of the groups defined in *gender* and *ease*. Under **Plots**, we need to check **Normality plots with tests**. Next, click on **Continue** and then **OK** to run the analyses.

The outputs in Tables 6.5 and 6.6 show the results of the Kolmogorov–Smirnov as well as the Shapiro–Wilk test for both grouping variables (i.e., *gender* and *ease*). As we only have less than 50 observations in each of the groups being analyzed, we should interpret the Shapiro–Wilk test as it exhibits more statistical power in situations with small sample sizes. Remember that the p-value is the probability of obtaining a test statistic at least as extreme as the one actually observed,

Table 6.5 Normality test results for *gender*

Tests of Normality

gender		Kolmogorov-Smirnov[a]			Shapiro-Wilk		
		Statistic	df	Sig.	Statistic	df	Sig.
sales	female	.098	30	.200[*]	.962	30	.349
	male	.150	30	.082	.944	30	.120

*. This is a lower bound of the true significance.

a. Lilliefors Significance Correction

Table 6.6 Normality test results for *ease*

Tests of Normality

ease		Kolmogorov-Smirnov[a]			Shapiro-Wilk		
		Statistic	df	Sig.	Statistic	df	Sig.
sales	easy	.121	20	.200[*]	.936	20	.199
	neutral	.140	20	.200[*]	.950	20	.371
	difficult	.162	20	.179	.909	20	.062

*. This is a lower bound of the true significance.

a. Lilliefors Significance Correction

assuming that the null hypothesis is true. This means that if the p-value is smaller than or equal to our level of tolerance of the risk of rejecting a true null hypothesis (i.e., α), we should reject the null hypothesis. In these analyses, we follow the general convention by using a 5% significance level.

Because all the p-values are larger than 0.05, the null hypothesis that the data are normally distributed is not rejected at a 5% level. Consequently, we assume the sales data are normally distributed within each of the groups.

Research Question #1

The first question that we want to address is whether there is a difference in sales based on the respondents' gender. Using the previous test's results, we know that the sales variable is normally distributed for males and females and since it is also measured on an interval scale, we can use a parametric test. In this case, we examine two distinct groups of customers (i.e., males and females). Thus, looking at our guideline in Fig. 6.1, we have to use the independent samples t-test. To run this test, go to ▶ Analyze ▶ Compare Means ▶ Independent-Samples T Test to display a dialog box similar to Fig. 6.9.

Move *sales* to the **Test Variable(s)** box and move *gender* to the **Grouping Variable** box. Next, click **Define Groups** and a menu similar to that shown in Fig. 6.10 will appear in which you have to specify the grouping variable's values that identify the two groups you wish to compare. You can also specify a **Cut point**, which is particularly useful when you want to compare two groups based on an

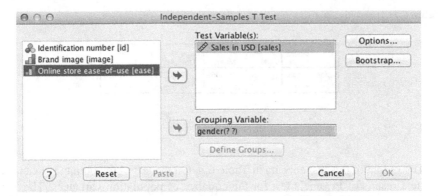

Fig. 6.9   Independent-samples t-test dialog box

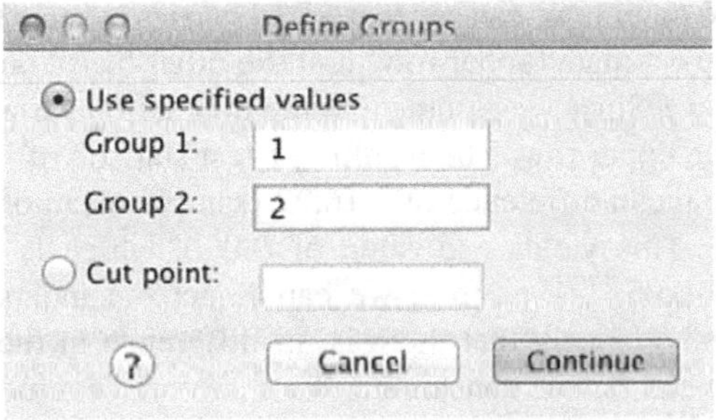

Fig. 6.10   Definition of groups

ordinal or continuous grouping variable. For example, if you want to compare younger vs. older members you could put all members below 30 years of age into one category and all who are 30 or above into the other category. When you indicate a cut point, observations with values less than the cut point form one group, while observations with values greater than or equal to the cut point form the other group. However, we will stick to the first option, using 1 for group 1 (females) and 2 for group 2 (males). Click on **Continue** and then on **OK** in the main menu. This will yield the outputs shown in Table 6.7.

Looking at the descriptive statistics in Table 6.7, we can see that female customers have a lower mean in sales (approx. 86.39 USD) than male customers (approx. 102.61 USD). At first sight, it appears that the sales are really different between these two groups, but, as we learned before, we have to take the variation in the data into account to test whether this difference is also present in the population.

Table 6.7 Descriptive statistics (group statistics)

Group Statistics

	gender	N	Mean	Std. Deviation	Std. Error Mean
sales	female	30	86.3869	14.80299	2.70264
	male	30	102.6061	16.95573	3.09568

The output of this test appears in Table 6.8. On the left of the output, we can see the test results of Levene's test for the equality of population variances. The low F-value of 0.247 already suggests that we cannot reject the null hypothesis that the population variances are equal. This is also mirrored in the large p-value of 0.621 (**Sig.** in Table 6.8), which lies far above our α-level of 0.05. Looking at the central and right part of the output, we can see that SPSS carries out two tests, one based on the pooled variance estimate (upper row) and the other based on separate variance estimates (lower row). Since we assume that the population variances are equal, we have to consider the upper row. The resulting t-test statistic of −3.947 is negative due to the negative mean difference of −16.22 (sample mean of group 1 – sample mean of group 2). This yields a p-value of 0.000, which is clearly below the threshold value of 0.05.[13] Therefore, we can reject the independent samples t-test's null hypothesis, namely that there is no difference in the population mean sales between male and female consumers. We therefore conclude that the sales for men and women differ significantly.

Table 6.8 Independent samples t-test result

Independent Samples Test

		Levene's Test for Equality of Variances		t-test for Equality of Means						
									95% Confidence Interval of the Difference	
		F	Sig.	t	df	Sig. (2-tailed)	Mean Difference	Std. Error Difference	Lower	Upper
sales	Equal variances assumed	.247	.621	-3.947	58	.000	-16.21918	4.10944	-24.44512	-7.99324
	Equal variances not assumed			-3.947	56.963	.000	-16.21918	4.10944	-24.44831	-7.99005

---

[13] Note that the p-value is not truly zero as SPSS just truncates the rightmost digits. If you double-click on the output and again on the p-value, you will see that the factual p-value is 0.000217.

Research Question #2

In the second analysis, we want to examine whether the customers' perceived ease-of-use of wishbird.net's online appearance has a significant effect on sales. Reconsidering the guideline in Fig. 6.1, we can see that a one-way ANOVA is the method of choice for answering this research question. Clicking on ▶ Analyze ▶ Compare Means ▶ One-Way ANOVA will open a dialog box similar to Fig. 6.11.

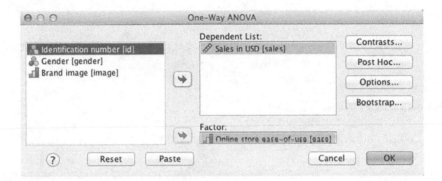

Fig. 6.11 One-way ANOVA dialog box

We start off by moving the *sales* variable to the **Dependent List** box and the ease-of-use variable (*ease*) to the **Factor** box (remember that in ANOVA, factor refers to the grouping variable). Under **Options**, we can request several statistics (Fig. 6.12). As discussed above, we have to determine whether the assumption of homogenous variances is met. For this purpose – just as in the independent samples t-test – we have to consider Levene's test, which we can request by choosing the **Homogeneity of variance test**. Because we do not yet know whether the population variances are equal or not, we should choose the statistic **Welch** (for the Welch test). Also, make sure you tick the boxes next to **Descriptive** as well as **Means plot** (Fig. 6.12). Click **Continue**.

Under **Post Hoc** (Fig. 6.13) we can specify a series of post hoc tests for multiple group comparisons. Since we do not yet know the result of Levene's test, we choose the Ryan/Einot-Gabriel/Welsch Q procedure (**R-E-G-W Q**) if we can assume equal variances. We choose the **Games-Howell** if we have to reject Levene's test's null hypothesis that population variances are equal. Since group sizes are equal, there is no need to select **Hochberg's GT2**. Next, click on **Continue** to get back to the main menu.

In the main menu, click on **OK** to run the analysis. Table 6.9 shows the descriptive results. Not unexpectedly, the higher the customers rate the perceived ease-of-use of the online store, the greater the sales. This is also illustrated in the means plot in Fig. 6.14.

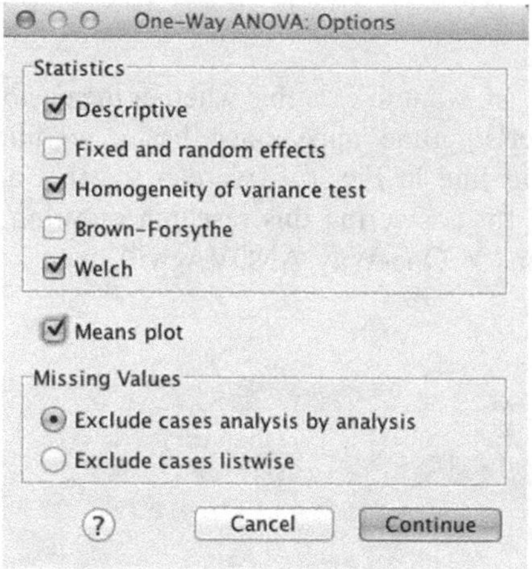

Fig. 6.12 Options for one-way ANOVA

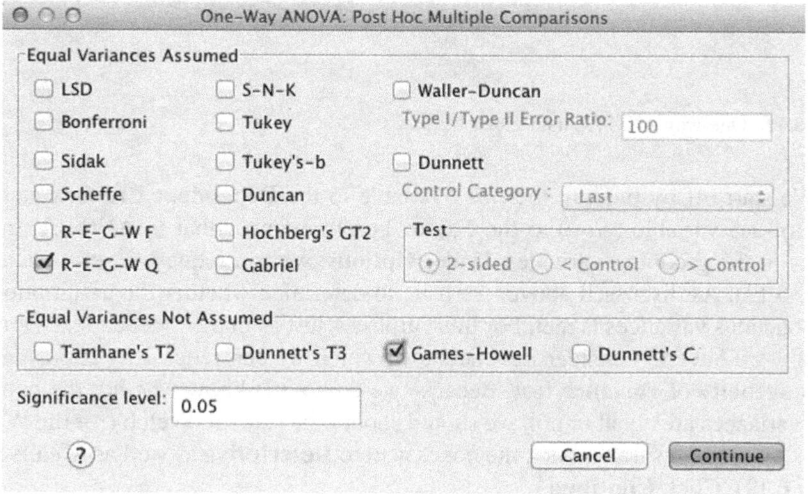

Fig. 6.13 Post hoc tests

Before we can evaluate the ANOVA's results, we have to take a closer look at the results of Levene's test as shown in Table 6.10. Levene's test clearly suggests that the population variances are equal, as the test's p-value (0.341) is well above 0.05. Thus, to decide whether at least one group mean differs from the others, we should consider using the regular F-test, rather than the Welch test.

Table 6.11 shows that we can reject the null hypothesis that the sales of the three groups of customers are equal (Sig. = 0.001 which is smaller than 0.05). More precisely, this result suggests that at least two group means differ significantly.

Table 6.9 Descriptive statistics

Descriptives

sales

	N	Mean	Std. Deviation	Std. Error	95% Confidence Interval for Mean		Minimum	Maximum
					Lower Bound	Upper Bound		
easy	20	103.5312	15.68420	3.50709	96.1907	110.8716	83.10	134.06
neutral	20	96.3088	14.18816	3.17257	89.6686	102.9491	74.66	122.05
difficult	20	83.6494	17.90034	4.00264	75.2718	92.0270	57.78	108.74
Total	60	94.4965	17.77356	2.29456	89.9051	99.0879	57.78	134.06

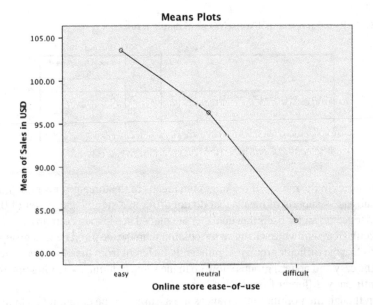

Fig. 6.14 Means plot

Table 6.10 Levene's test output (test of homogeneity of variances)

Test of Homogeneity of Variances

sales

Levene Statistic	df1	df2	Sig.
1.095	2	57	.341

To evaluate whether all groups are mutually different or only two, we take a look at the post hoc test results. As Levene's test showed that the population variances are equal (and since the group sizes are equal), we are primarily interested in the Ryan/Einot-Gabriel/Welsch Q-procedure's result (Table 6.12). This table is a summary of

Table 6.11 ANOVA results

ANOVA

sales

	Sum of Squares	df	Mean Square	F	Sig.
Between Groups	4051.378	2	2025.689	7.916	.001
Within Groups	14586.684	57	255.907		
Total	18638.062	59			

Table 6.12 Ryan/Einot-Gabriel/Welsch Q procedure's result

sales

	ease	N	Subset for alpha = 0.05	
			1	2
Ryan-Einot-Gabriel-Welsch Range	difficult	20	83.6494	
	neutral	20		96.3088
	easy	20		103.5312
	Sig.		1.000	.159

Means for groups in homogeneous subsets are displayed.

the differences in the means. It organizes the means of the three groups into "homogeneous subsets" – subsets of means that do not differ at a significance level of 0.05 are grouped together, and subsets that do differ are placed in separate columns. Notice how the difficult group shows up in a separate column than the easy and neutral groups. This indicates that the difficult group is significantly different from the other two in terms of sales. The easy and neutral groups show up in the same column, indicating that they are not significantly different from each other.

Even though the population variances are assumed to be equal, let us take a look at the results of the Games-Howell procedure (Table 6.13) for the sake of comprehensiveness. There are several comparisons listed in the table. In the first row, you can see the comparison between the easy group and neutral group. The difference between the means of these two groups is 7.22 units. Following this row across, we see that this difference is statistically insignificant ($p = 0.290$). On the contrary in the row below this, we can see that the difference between the easy and difficult group (19.88) is significant, as $p = 0.002$, which is below 0.05. Lastly, the comparison of the neutral and difficult group (two rows below) also renders a significant result.

Finally, we want to examine the strength of the effect by computing η^2 and ω^2 manually (remember that SPSS does not provide us with these measures when running the one-way ANOVA).[14] Using the information from Table 6.11, we can easily compute the measures as follows:

---

[14] Note. however, that you SPSS offers the option to compute η^2 by going to Analyze ▶ Compare Means ▶ Means. Under **Options**, you can request an ANOVA table including η^2.

$$\eta^2 = \frac{SS_B}{SS_T} = \frac{4,051.378}{18,638.062} = 0.217$$

$$\omega^2 = \frac{SS_B - (k-1) \cdot MS_W}{SS_T + MS_W} = \frac{4,051.378 - (3-1) \cdot 255.907}{18,638.062 + 255.907} = 0.187$$

Table 6.13   Games-Howell test result

Multiple Comparisons

Dependent Variable: sales

			Mean Difference (I-J)	Std. Error	Sig.	95% Confidence Interval	
	(I) ease	(J) ease				Lower Bound	Upper Bound
Games-Howell	easy	neutral	7.22235	4.72915	.290	-4.3159	18.7606
		difficult	19.88175*	5.32173	.002	6.8939	32.8696
	neutral	easy	-7.22235	4.72915	.290	-18.7606	4.3159
		difficult	12.65940*	5.10748	.046	.1769	25.1419
	difficult	easy	-19.88175*	5.32173	.002	-32.8696	-6.8939
		neutral	-12.65940*	5.10748	.046	-25.1419	-.1769

*. The mean difference is significant at the 0.05 level.

As we can see, the strength of the effect is weak as it is below 0.30. Taken jointly, these results suggest that the buying behavior of customers is little influenced by their perceived ease-of-use of wishbird.net's online store. Of course, improving the online store's navigation or layout might boost sales across all three groups jointly, but it will not necessarily introduce differences in sales between the groups.

So far, we have considered only one factor in the ANOVA but we could easily extend this example by simultaneously considering a second factor, say one which captures the customers' perceived image of the Wishbird brand. This would then require the application of a two-way ANOVA, which we discuss in the Web Appendix (⊖ Web Appendix → Chap. 6).

6.7   Customer Analysis at Crédit Samouel (Case Study)

In 2013, Crédit Samouel, a globally operating bank underwent a massive re-branding campaign. In the course of this campaign, the bank's product range was also restructured and service and customer orientation were improved. In addition, a comprehensive marketing campaign was launched, aimed at increasing the bank's customer base by one million new customers by 2020.

In an effort to control the campaign's success and to align the marketing actions, the management decided to conduct an analysis of newly acquired customers. Specifically, the management is interested in evaluating the segment customers aged 30 and below. To do so, the marketing department surveyed the following characteristics of 251 randomly drawn new customers (variable names in parentheses):

- Gender (*gender*)
- Bank deposit in Euro (*deposit*)
- Does the customer currently attend school/university? (*training*)
- Customer's age specified in three categories (*age_cat*)

Use the data provided in *bank.sav* (⌖ Web Appendix → Chap. 6) to answer the following research questions:

1. Which test do we have to apply to find out whether there is a significant difference in bank deposits between male and female customers? Do we meet the assumptions necessary to conduct this test? Also use an appropriate normality test and interpret the result. Does the result give rise to any cause for concern? Carry out an appropriate test to answer the initial research question.
2. Is there a significant difference in bank deposits between customers who are still studying and those that are not?
3. Which type of test or procedure would you use to evaluate whether bank deposits differ significantly between the three age categories? Carry out this procedure and interpret the results.
4. Reconsider the previous question and, using post hoc tests, evaluate whether there are significant differences between the three age groups.
5. Is there a significant interaction effect between the variables *training* and *age_cat* in terms of the customers' deposit?
6. On the basis of your analysis results, please provide recommendations on how to align future marketing actions for the management team.

Review Questions

1. Describe the steps involved in hypothesis testing in your own words.
2. Explain the concept of the p-value and explain how it relates to the significance level α.
3. What level of α would you choose for the following types of market research studies? Give reasons for your answers.
   (a) An initial study on the preferences for mobile phone colors.
   (b) The production quality of Rolex watches.
   (c) A repeat study on differences in preference for either Coca Cola or Pepsi.

4. Write two hypotheses for each of the example studies in question 3, including the null hypothesis and alternative hypothesis.
5. Describe the difference between independent and paired samples t-tests in your own words and provide two examples of each type.
6. Use the data from the wishbird.net example to run a two-way ANOVA, including the factors (1) ease-of-use and (2) brand image, with sales as the dependent variable. To do so, go to Analyze ▶ General Linear Model ▶ Univariate and enter *sales* in the Dependent Variables box and *image* and *ease* in the Fixed Factor(s) box. Interpret the results.

Further Readings

Field, A. (2013). *Discovering statistics using SPSS* (4th ed.). London: Sage.
An excellent reference for advanced types of ANOVA.
Hubbard, R., & Bayarri, M. J. (2003). Confusion over measure of evidence (p's) versus errors (α's) in classical statistical testing. *The American Statistician, 57(3),* 171–178.
The authors discuss the distinction between p-value and α and argue that there is general confusion about these measures' nature among researchers and practitioners. A very interesting read!
Kanji, G. K. (2006). *100 statistical tests* (3rd ed.). London: Sage.
If you are interested in learning more about different tests, we recommend this best-selling book in which the author introduces various tests with information on how to calculate and interpret their results using simple datasets.
Sawyer, A. G., & Peter, J. P. (1983). The significance of statistical significance tests in marketing research. *Journal of Marketing Research, 20(2),* 122–133.
Interesting article in which the authors discuss the interpretation and value of classical statistical significance tests and offer recommendations regarding their use.

References

Boneau, C. A. (1960). The effects of violations of assumptions underlying the t test. *Psychological Bulletin, 57*(1), 49–64.
Brown, M. B., & Forsythe, A. B. (1974). Robust tests for the equality of variances. *Journal of the American Statistical Association, 69*(346), 364–367.
Cho, H. C., & Abe, S. (2012). Is two-tailed testing for directional research hypotheses tests legitimate? *Journal of Business Research, 66*(9), 1261–1266.
Cohen, J. (1992). A power primer. *Psychological Bulletin, 112*(1), 155–159.
Field, A. (2013). *Discovering statistics using SPSS* (4th ed.). London: Sage.
Hubbard, R., & Bayarri, M. J. (2003). Confusion over measure of evidence (p's) versus errors (α's) in classical statistical testing. *The American Statistician, 57*(3), 171–178.

Lilliefors, H. W. (1967). On the Kolmogorov–Smirnov test for normality with mean and variance unknown. *Journal of the American Statistical Association, 62*(318), 399–402.

Welch, B. L. (1951). On the comparison of several mean values: An alternative approach. *Biometrika, 38*(3/4), 330–336.

Regression Analysis

7

Learning Objectives

After reading this chapter, you should understand:
- What regression analysis is and what it can be used for.
- How to specify a regression analysis model.
- How to interpret basic regression analysis results.
- What the issues with, and assumptions of regression analysis are.
- How to validate regression analysis results.
- How to conduct regression analysis in SPSS.
- How to interpret regression analysis output produced by SPSS.

Keywords

Adjusted R^2 • Autocorrelation • Durbin-Watson test • Errors • F-test • Heteroskedasticity • Linearity • Moderation • (Multi)collinearity • Ordinary least squares • Outliers • Regression analysis • Residuals • R^2 • Sample size • Stepwise methods • Tolerance • Variance inflation factor • Weighted least squares

Agripro is a US-based firm in the business of selling seeds to farmers and distributors. Regression analysis can help them understand what drives customers to buy their products, helps explain their customer's satisfaction, and informs how Agripro measures up against their competitors. Regression analysis provides precise quantitative information on which managers can base their decisions.

M. Sarstedt and E. Mooi, *A Concise Guide to Market Research*,
Springer Texts in Business and Economics, DOI 10.1007/978-3-642-53965-7_7,
© Springer-Verlag Berlin Heidelberg 2014

7.1   Introduction

Regression analysis is one of the most frequently used tools in market research. In its simplest form, regression analysis allows market researchers to analyze relationships between one independent and one dependent variable. In marketing applications, the dependent variable is usually the outcome we care about (e.g., sales), while the independent variables are the instruments we have to achieve those outcomes with (e.g., pricing or advertising). Regression analysis can provide insights that few other techniques can. The key benefits of using regression analysis are that it can:

1. Indicate if independent variables have a significant relationship with a dependent variable.
2. Indicate the relative strength of different independent variables' effects on a dependent variable.
3. Make predictions.

Knowing about the effects of independent variables on dependent variables can help market researchers in many different ways. For example, it can help direct spending if we know promotional activities significantly increases sales.

Knowing about the relative strength of effects is useful for marketers because it may help answer questions such as whether sales depend more on price or on promotions. Regression analysis also allows us to compare the effects of variables measured on different scales such as the effect of price changes (e.g., measured in $) and the number of promotional activities.

Regression analysis can also help to make predictions. For example, if we have estimated a regression model using data on sales, prices, and promotional activities, the results from this regression analysis could provide a precise answer to what would happen to sales if prices were to increase by 5% and promotional activities were to increase by 10%. Such precise answers can help (marketing) managers make sound decisions. Furthermore, by providing various scenarios, such as calculating the sales effects of price increases of 5%, 10%, and 15%, managers can evaluate marketing plans and create marketing strategies.

7.2   Understanding Regression Analysis

In the previous paragraph, we briefly discussed what regression can do and why it is a useful market research tool. But what is regression analysis all about? To answer this question, consider Figure 7.1 which plots a dependent (y) variable (weekly sales in $) against an independent (x) variable (an index of promotional activities). Regression analysis is a way of fitting a "best" line through a series of observations. With "best" line we mean that it is fitted in such a way that it minimizes the sum of squared differences between the observations and the line itself. It is important to know that the best line fitted with regression analysis is not necessarily the true line (i.e., the line that holds in the population). Specifically, if we have data issues, or fail to meet the regression assumptions (discussed later), the estimated line may be biased.

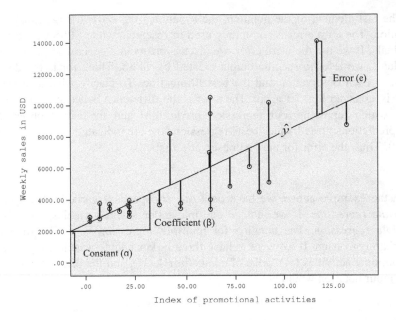

Fig. 7.1 A visual explanation of regression analysis

Before we introduce regression analysis further, we should discuss regression notation. *Regression models* are generally noted as follows:

$$y = \alpha + \beta_1 x_1 + e$$

What does this mean? The y represents the dependent variable, which is the variable you are trying to explain. In Fig. 7.1, we plot the dependent variable on the vertical axis. The α represents the *constant* (sometimes called *intercept*) of the regression model, and indicates what your dependent variable would be if all of the independent variables were zero. In Fig. 7.1, you can see the constant indicated on the y-axis. If the index of promotional activities is zero, we expect sales of around $2,500. It may of course not always be realistic to assume that independent variables are zero (just think of prices, these are rarely zero) but the constant should always be included to make sure that the regression model has the best possible fit with the data.

The independent variable is indicated by x_1. β_1 (pronounced as *beta*) indicates the (regression) coefficient of the independent variable x. This coefficient represents the gradient of the line and is also referred to as the *slope* and is shown in Fig. 7.1. A positive β_1 coefficient indicates an upward sloping regression line while a negative β_1 indicates a downward sloping line. In our example, the gradient slopes upward. This makes sense since sales tend to increase as promotional activities increase. In our example, we estimate β_1 as 55.968, meaning that if we increase promotional activities by one unit, sales will go up by $55.968 on average. In regression analysis, we can calculate whether this value (the β_1 parameter) differs significantly from zero by using a t-test.

The last element of the notation, the e denotes the *error* (or *residual*) of the equation. The term error is commonly used in research, while SPSS uses the term residuals. If we use the word error, we discuss errors in a general sense. If we use residuals, we refer to specific output created by SPSS. The error is the distance between each observation and the best fitting line. To clarify what a regression error is, consider Fig. 7.1 again. The error is the difference between the regression line (which represents our regression prediction) and the actual observation. The predictions made by the "best" regression line are indicated by $\hat{y}$ (pronounced *y-hat*). Thus, the error for the first observation is:[1]

$$e_1 = y_1 - \hat{y}_1$$

In the example above, we have only one independent variable. We call this *bivariate regression*. If we include multiple independent variables, we call this *multiple regression*. The notation for multiple regression is similar to that of bivariate regression. If we were to have three independent variables, say index of promotional activities (x_1), price of competitor 1 (x_2), and the price of competitor 2 (x_3), our notation would be:

$$y = \alpha + \beta_1 x_1 + \beta_2 x_2 + \beta_3 x_3 + e$$

We need one regression coefficient for each independent variable (i.e., β_1, β_2, and β_3). Technically the βs indicate how a change in an independent variable influences the dependent variable if all other independent variables are held constant.[2]

Now that we have introduced some basics of regression analysis, it is time to discuss how to execute a regression analysis. We outline the key steps in Fig. 7.2. We first introduce the data requirements for regression analysis that determine if regression analysis can be used. After this first step, we specify and estimate the regression model. Next, we discuss the basics, such as which independent variables to select. Thereafter, we discuss the assumptions of regression analysis, followed by how to interpret and validate the regression results. The last step is to use the regression model, for example to make predictions.

7.3   Conducting a Regression Analysis

7.3.1   Consider Data Requirements for Regression Analysis

Several data requirements have to be considered before we undertake a regression analysis. These include the following:
- Sample size,
- Variables need to vary,
- Scale type of the dependent variable, and
- Collinearity.

---

[1] Strictly speaking, the difference between predicted and observed y-values is $\hat{e}$.
[2] This only applies to the standardized βs.

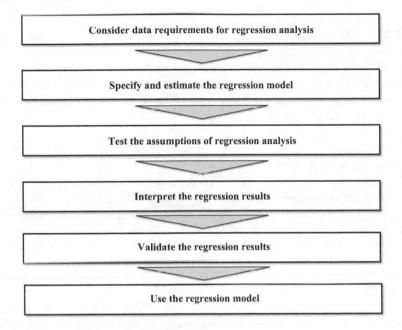

Fig. 7.2 Steps to conduct a regression analysis

7.3.1.1 Sample Size

The first data requirement is that we need a sufficiently large sample size. Acceptable sample sizes relate to a minimum sample size where you have a good chance of finding significant results if they are actually present, and not finding significant results if these are not present. There are two ways to calculate "acceptable" sample sizes.

- The first, formal, approach is a power analysis. As mentioned in Chap. 6 (Box 6.2), these calculations are difficult and require you to specify several parameters, such as the expected effect size or the maximum type I error you want to allow for to calculate the resulting level of power. By convention, 0.80 is an acceptable level of power. Kelley and Maxwell (2003) discuss sample size requirements.
- The second approach is through rules of thumb. These rules are not specific to a situation but are easy to apply. Green (1991) proposes a rule of thumb for sample sizes in regression analysis. Specifically, he proposes that if you want to test for individual parameters' effect (i.e., if one coefficient is significant or not), you need a sample size of $104 + k$. Thus, if you have ten independent variables, you need $104 + 10 = 114$ observations.[3]

---

[3] Rules of thumb are almost never without issues. For Green's formula, these are that you need a larger sample size than he proposes if you expect small effects (an expected R^2 of 0.10 or smaller). In addition, if the variables are poorly measured, or if you want to use a stepwise method, you need a larger sample size. With "larger" we mean around three times the required sample size if the expected R^2 is low, and about twice the required sample size in case of measurement errors or if stepwise methods are used.

7.3.1.2 Variables Need to Vary

A regression model cannot be estimated if the variables have no variation. Specifically, if there is no variation in the dependent variable (i.e., it is constant), we also do not need regression, as we already know what the dependent variable's value is. Likewise, if an independent variable has no variation, it cannot explain any variation in the dependent variable.

> No variation can lead to epic fails! Consider the admission tests set by the University of Liberia. Not a single student passed the entry exams. Clearly in such situations, a regression analysis will make no difference!
> http://www.independent.co.uk/student/news/epic-fail-all-25000-students-fail-university-entrance-exam-in-liberia-8785707.html

7.3.1.3 Scale Type of the Dependent Variable

The third data requirement is that the dependent variable needs to be interval or ratio scaled (scaling is discussed in Chap. 2). If the data are not interval or ratio scaled, alternative types of regression need to be used. You should use *binary logistic regression* if the dependent variable is binary and only takes on two values (e.g., zero and one). If the dependent variable consists of a nominal variable with more than two levels, you should use *multinomial logistic regression*. This should, for example, be used if you want to explain why people prefer product A over B or C. We do not discuss these different methods in this chapter, but they are intuitively similar to regression. For an introductory discussion of regression methods with dependent variables measured on a nominal scale, see Field (2013).

7.3.1.4 Collinearity

The last data requirement is that no or little *collinearity* is present. Collinearity is a data issue that arises if two independent variables are highly correlated. *Multicollinearity* occurs if more than two independent variables are highly correlated. *Perfect (multi)collinearity* occurs if we enter two (or more) independent variables with exactly the same information in them (i.e., they are perfectly correlated).

> Perfect collinearity may happen because you entered the same independent variable twice, or because one variable is a linear combination of another (e.g., one variable is a multiple of another variable such as sales in units and sales in thousands of units). If this occurs, regression analysis cannot estimate one of the two coefficients and SPSS will automatically drop one of the independent variables.

In practice, however, weaker forms of collinearity are common. For example, if we study how much customers are wiling to pay in a restaurant, satisfaction with the waiter/waitress and satisfaction with the speed of service may be highly related. If this is so, there is little uniqueness in each variable, since both provide much the same information. The problem with having substantial collinearity is that it tends to disguise significant parameters as insignificant.

Fortunately, collinearity is relatively easy to detect by calculating the *tolerance* or *VIF (Variance Inflation Factor)*. A tolerance of below 0.10 indicates that (multi) collinearity is a problem.[4] The VIF is just the reciprocal value of the tolerance. Thus, VIF values above ten indicate collinearity issues. We can produce these statistics in SPSS by clicking on **Collinearity diagnostics** under the **Options** button found in the main regression dialog box of SPSS.

You can remedy collinearity in several ways. If perfect collinearity occurs, SPSS will automatically delete one of the perfectly overlapping variables. SPSS indicates this through an additional table in the output with the title "Excluded Variables". If weaker forms of collinearity occur, it is up to you to decide what to do.

- The first option is to use factor analysis (see Chap. 8). Using factor analysis, you create a small number of factors that have most of the original variables' information in them but which are mutually uncorrelated. For example, through factor analysis you may find that satisfaction with the waiter/waitress and satisfaction with the speed of service fall under a factor called *service satisfaction*. If you use factors, collinearity between the original variables is no longer an issue.
- The second option is to re-specify the regression model by removing highly correlated variables. Which variables should you remove? If you create a correlation matrix (see Chap. 5) of all the independent variables entered in the regression model, you should focus first on the variables that are most strongly correlated. Initially, try removing one of the two most strongly correlated variables. Which one you should remove is a matter of taste and depends on your analysis set-up.

7.3.2 Specify and Estimate the Regression Model

To conduct a regression analysis, we need to select the variables we want to include and decide on how the model is estimated. In the following, we will discuss each step in detail.

7.3.2.1 Model Specification

Let's first show the main regression dialog box in SPSS to provide some idea of what we need to specify for a basic regression analysis. First open the dataset called

---

[4] The tolerance is calculated using a completely separate regression analysis. In this regression analysis, the variable for which the tolerance is calculated is taken as a dependent variable and all other independent variables are entered as independents. The R^2 that results from this model is deducted from 1, thus indicating how much is *not explained* by the regression model. If very little is not explained by the other variables, (multi) collinearity is a problem.

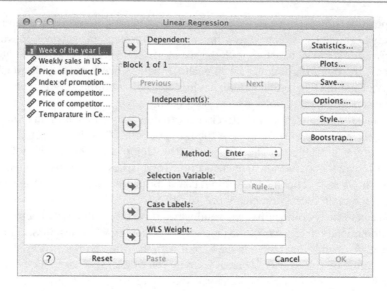

Fig. 7.3 The main regression dialog box in SPSS

Sales data.sav (🖰 Web Appendix → Chap. 7). These data contain information on supermarket sales per week in $ (*sales*), the (average) price level (*price*), and an index of promotional activities (*promotion*), amongst other variables. After opening the dataset, click on ▶ Analyze ▶ Regression ▶ Linear. This opens a box similar to Fig. 7.3.

For a basic regression model, we need to specify the **Dependent** variable and choose the **Independent(s)**. As discussed before, the dependent variable is the variable we care about as the outcome.

How do we select independent variables? Market researchers usually select independent variables on the basis of what the client wants to know and on prior research findings. For example, typical independent variables explaining the super-market sales of a particular product include the price, promotional activities, level of in-store advertising, the availability of special price promotions, packaging type, and variables indicating the store and week. Market researchers may, of course, select different independent variables for other applications. A few practical suggestions to help you select variables:

– Never enter all the available variables at the same time. Carefully consider which independent variables may be relevant. Irrelevant independent variables may be significant due to chance (remember the discussion on hypothesis testing in Chap. 6) or can reduce the likelihood of determining relevant variables' significance.
– If you have a large number of variables that overlap in terms of how they are defined, such as satisfaction with the waiter/waitress and satisfaction with the speed of service, try to pick the variable that is most distinct or relevant to the client. Alternatively, you could conduct a factor analysis first and use the factor scores as input for the regression analysis (factor analysis is discussed in Chap. 8).

- Take the sample size rules of thumb into account. If practical issues limit the sample size to below the threshold recommended by the rules of thumb, use as few independent variables as possible. With larger sample sizes, you have more freedom to add independent variables, although they still need to be relevant.

As an example, we use *sales* as the dependent variable and *price* as well as the *index of promotional activities* as independent variables.

7.3.2.2 Model Estimation

Once we know which variables we want to include, we need to specify if all of them should be used, or if – based on the significance of the findings – the analysis procedure can further select variables from this set. There are two general options to select variables under **Method** in Fig. 7.3. Either you choose the independent variables to be in the model yourself (the *enter* method) or you let a process select the best subset of variables available to you (a *stepwise* method). There are many different types of stepwise methods such as the *forward* and *backward* methods, which we explain in Box 7.1.

Choosing between the enter and stepwise methods means making a choice between letting the researcher or a procedure choose the best independent variables. We recommend using the enter method. Why? Because stepwise methods often result in adding variables that are only significant "by chance," rather than truly interesting or useful. Another problem with forward and backward methods is related to how regression deals with missing values. Regression can only estimate models when it has complete information on all the variables. If a substantial number of missing values are present, using backward or forward methods may result in adding variables that are only relevant for a subset of the data for which

Box 7.1 Forward or backward methods

Forward and backward methods are often used for data mining purposes. How do these work? Starting with the constant (α) only, the forward method runs a very large number of separate regression models. Then it tries to find the best model by adding just one independent variable from the remaining variables. Subsequently it compares the results between these two models. If adding an independent variable produces a significantly better model, it proceeds by adding a second variable from the variables that remain. The resulting model (which includes the two independent variables) is then compared to the previous model (which includes one independent variable). This process is repeated until adding another variable does not improve the model significantly. The backward method does something similar but initially enters all variables that it may use and removes the least contributing independent variable until removing another makes the model significantly worse.

complete information is present. If data are missing, backward or forward methods often result in finding highly significant models that only use a small number of observations from the total number of available observations. In this case, the regression model fits a small set of the data well but not the entire data or population. Finally, as a market researcher, you want to select variables that are meaningful for the decision-making process. You also need to think about the actual research problem, rather than choosing the variables that produce the "best model." Does this mean that the forward and backward methods are completely useless? Certainly not! Market researchers commonly use stepwise methods to find their way around the data quickly and to develop a feel for relationships in the data.

After deciding on the variable selection process, we need to choose an estimation procedure. *Estimation* refers to how the "best line" we discussed earlier is calculated. SPSS estimates regression models by default, using *ordinary least squares (OLS)*. As indicated before, OLS estimates a regression line so that it minimizes the squared differences between each observation and the regression line. By squaring distances, OLS avoids negative and positive deviations from the regression line cancelling each other out. Moreover, by squaring the distances, OLS also puts greater weight on observations that are far away from the regression line. The sum of all these squared distances is called the *sum of squares* and is indicated in

A practical issue related to specifying and estimating the regression model is if we conduct just one regression analysis, or if we run multiple models. Market researchers typically run many different models. A standard approach is to start with relatively simple models, such as with one, two, or three independent variables. These independent variables should be those variables you believe are the most important ones. You should start with just a few variables because adding further variables may cause the already entered variables to lose significance. If important decisions are made with a regression model, we need to be aware that sometimes variables that are significant in one model may no longer be significant if we add (or remove) variables. As discussed earlier, this is often due to collinearity. Once you have determined a number of key basic variables, you could (depending on the research purpose) add further independent variables until you have a model that satisfies your needs and does a good job of explaining the dependent variable. Generally, regression models have between 3 and 10 independent variables but bivariate regression models are also common. In specific applications, such as regression models that try to explain economic growth, regression models can have dozens of independent variables.

the SPSS output. While minimizing the sum of squares, OLS also ensures that the mean of all errors is always zero. Because the error is zero on average, researchers sometimes omit the *e* from the regression notation. Nevertheless, errors do occur in respect of individual observations (but not *on average*). Figure 7.1

illustrates this. Almost all observations fall above or below the regression line. However, if we calculate the mean of all the squared distances of regression points above and below the line, the result is exactly zero. In Box 7.2 we discuss estimation methods other than OLS.

7.3.3   Test the Assumptions of Regression Analysis

We have already discussed several issues that determine if it is useful to run a regression analysis. We now turn to discussing the assumptions of regression analysis. If a regression analysis fails to meet the assumptions, regression analysis can provide invalid results. Four regression analysis assumptions are required to provide valid results:

Box 7.2 Different problems, different estimators

OLS is a very robust estimator. However, there are alternatives that work better and are best used in specific situations. Typically these situations occur if we violate on of the regression assumptions. For example, if the regression residuals are heteroskedastic, we need to use alternative procedures such as *weighted least squares (WLS)*. We briefly discuss when WLS should be used in this chapter. If the expected mean error of the regression model is not zero, estimators such as *two-staged least squares (2SLS)* can be used in specific situations. If the errors are not independent, estimators such as random-effects estimators may be used. Such estimators are beyond the scope of this book. Greene's (2007) work discusses these, and other estimation procedures in detail.

---

1. The regression model can be expressed in a linear way,
2. The expected mean error of the regression model is zero,
3. The variance of the errors is constant (homoskedasticity), and
4. The errors are independent (no autocorrelation).

The fifth assumption is optional. If we meet this assumption, we have information on how the regression parameters are distributed, thus allowing straightforward conclusions on their significance. If we fail to meet this assumption, the regression model will still be accurate but it becomes more difficult to determine the regression parameters' significance.

5. The errors need to be approximately normally distributed.

We next discuss these assumptions and how we can test each of them.

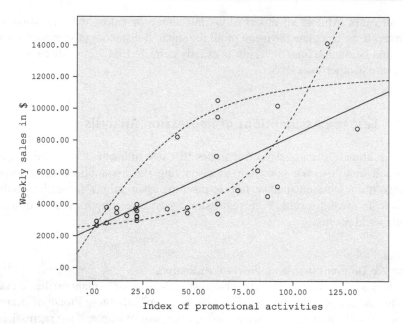

Fig. 7.4 Different relationships between promotional activities and weekly sales

7.3.3.1 First Assumption: Linearity

The *first assumption* means that we can write the regression model as $y = \alpha + \beta_1 x_1 + e$. Thus, relationships such as $\beta_1^2 x_1$ are not permissible. On the other hand, expressions such as x_1^2 or $\log(x_1)$ are possible as the regression model is still specified in a linear way. As long as you can write a model where the regression parameters (the βs) are linear, you satisfy this assumption. A separate issue is if the relationship between an independent variable x and the dependent variable y, is linear. Checking the linearity between x and y variables can be done by plotting the independent variables against the dependent variable. Using a scatter plot, we can then assess whether there is some type of non-linear pattern. Figure 7.4 shows such a plot. The straight line indicates a linear relationship. For illustration purposes, we have also added an upward sloping and downward sloping line. The upward sloping line corresponds to an x_1^2 transformation, while the downward sloping line corresponds to a $\log(x_1)$ transformation. For this particular data, it appears however that a linear line fits the data best. It is important to correctly specify the relationship, because if we specify a relationship as linear when it is in fact non-linear, the regression analysis results do not fit the data in the best possible way. After transforming x_1 by squaring it or taking the log, you still satisfy the assumption of specifying the regression model in a linear way, despite that the relationship between x and y is nonlinear.

7.3.3.2 Second Assumption: Expected Mean Error is Zero

The *second assumption* is that the expected (not the estimated!) mean error is zero. If we do not expect the sum of the errors to be zero, we obtain a line that is biased. That is, we have a line that consistently over- or under-estimates the true relationship. This assumption is not testable by means of statistics, as OLS always renders a best line where the mean error is exactly zero. If this assumption is challenged, this is done on theoretical grounds. Imagine that we want to explain the weekly sales in \$ of all US supermarkets. If we were to collect our data only in downtown areas, we would mostly sample smaller supermarkets. Thus, a regression model fitted using the available data would differ from those models obtained if we were to include all supermarkets. Our error in the regression model (estimated as zero) therefore differs from the population as a whole (where the estimate should be truly zero). Furthermore, omitting important independent variables could cause the expected mean not to be zero. Simply put, if we were to omit a relevant variable x_2 from a regression model that only includes x_1, we induce a bias in the regression model. More precisely, β_1 is likely to be inflated, which means that the estimated value is higher than it should actually be. Thus, β_1 itself is biased because we omit x_2!

7.3.3.3 Third Assumption: Homoskedasticity

The *third assumption* is that the errors' variance is constant, a situation we call *homoskedasticity*. Imagine that we want to explain the weekly sales of various supermarkets in \$. Clearly, large stores have a much larger spread in sales than small supermarkets. For example, if you have average weekly sales of \$50,000, you might see a sudden jump to \$60,000 or a fall to \$40,000. However, a very large supermarket could see sales move from an average of \$5,000,000–\$7,000,000. This issue causes weekly sales' error variance to be much larger for large supermarkets than for small supermarkets. We call this non-constant variance *heteroskedasticity*. We visualize the increasing error variance of supermarket sales in Fig. 7.5, in which we can see that the errors increase as weekly sales increase.

If we estimate regression models on data in which the variance is not constant, they will still result in errors that are zero on average (i.e., our predictions are still correct), but this may cause some βs not to be significant, whereas, in reality, they are.

Unfortunately, there is no easy (menu-driven) way to test for heteroskedasticity in SPSS. Thus, understanding whether heteroskedasticity is present, is (if you use the SPSS menu functions) only possible on theoretical grounds and by creating graphs. On theoretical grounds, try to understand whether it is likely that the errors increase as the value of the dependent variable increases or decreases. If you want to visualize heteroskedasticity, it is best to plot the errors against the dependent variable, as in Fig. 7.5. As the dependent variable increases or decreases, the variance should appear as constant. If heteroskedasticity is an issue, the points are often funnel shaped, becoming more, or less, spread out across the graph. This funnel shape is typical of heteroskedasticity and indicates increasing variance across the errors.

If you think heteroskedasticity is an issue, SPSS can deal with it by using weighted least squares (WLS). Simply use the variable that you think causes the error variance not to be constant (e.g., store size) and "weight" the results by this variable. In Fig. 7.3 you see a box labelled **WLS Weight** at the bottom to which you can add the variable that causes the increase in error variance. Only use WLS if

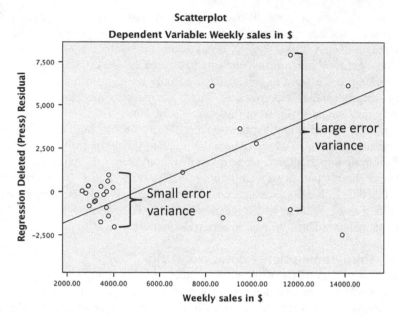

Fig. 7.5 An example of heteroskedasticity

heteroskedasticity is a real concern. If WLS is used, and heteroskedasticity is no problem, or the weight variable has not been chosen correctly, the regression results may be invalid.

7.3.3.4 Fourth Assumption: No Autocorrelation

The *fourth assumption* is that the regression model errors are independent; that is, the error terms are uncorrelated for any two observations. Imagine that you want to explain the sales of a particular supermarket using that supermarket's previous week sales. It is very likely that if sales increased last week, they will also increase this week. This may be due to, for example, a growing economy, or other reasons that underlie supermarket sales growth. This issue is called *autocorrelation* and means that regression errors are correlated positively, or negatively, over time. Fortunately, we can identify this issue using the Durbin–Watson test. The *Durbin–Watson test* assesses whether there is autocorrelation by testing a null hypothesis of no autocorrelation, which is tested against a lower and upper bound for negative autocorrelation and against a lower and upper bound for postive autocorrelation. Thus there are four critical values. If we reject the null hypothesis of no autocorrelation, we find support for an alternative hypothesis that there is some degree of autocorrelation. To carry out this test, first sort the data on the variable that indicates the time dimension in your data, if you have this included in your data. Otherwise, the test should not be carried out. With time dimension, we mean that you have at least two observations collected from a single respondent or object at different points in time. Do this by going to ▶ Data ▶ Sort Cases. Then enter your time variable under **Sort by:** and click on **OK**. To carry out the actual test, you need to check **Durbin–Watson** under the **Statistics** option of the main regression dialog box in SPSS. SPSS calculates a Durbin–Watson statistic, but does not indicate if the

test is significant or not. This requires comparing the calculated Durbin–Watson value with the critical Durbin–Watson value. These Durbin–Watson values lie between 0 and 4. Essentially, there are four situations. First, the errors may be positively related (called *positive autocorrelation*). This means that if we take observations ordered according to time, we observe that positive errors are typically followed by positive errors and that negative errors are typically followed by negative errors. For example, supermarket sales usually increase over certain periods in time (e.g., before Christmas) and decrease in other periods (e.g., the summer holidays). Second, if positive errors are commonly followed by negative errors and vice-versa, we have *negative autocorrelation*. Negative autocorrelation is less common than positive autocorrelation, but also occurs. If we study, for example, how much time salespeople spend on shoppers, we may see that if they spend much time on one shopper, they spend less time on the next, allowing the salesperson to stick to his/her schedule or simply go home on time. Third, if no systematic pattern of errors occurs, we have *no autocorrelation*. Fourthly, the Durbin–Watson values may fall in between the lower and upper critical value. In this case, the test is *inconclusive*. We indicate these four situations in Fig. 7.6. Which situation occurs, depends on the interplay between the Durbin-Watson test statistic (d) and the lower (d_L) and upper (d^U) critical value.
– If the test statistic is lower than the lower critical value ($d < d_L$) we have positive autocorrelation.
– If the test statistic is higher than 4 minus the lower critical value ($d > 4\text{-}d_L$) we have negative autocorrelation
– If the test statistic falls between the upper critical value and 4 minus the upper critical value ($d^U < d < 4\text{-}d^U$) we have no autocorrelation.
– If the test statistic falls in-between the lower and upper critical value ($dl < d < d^U$) or it falls in-between 4 minus the upper critical value and 4 minus the lower critical value ($4\text{-}d^U < d < 4\text{-}d_L$) we cannot make a decision on the presence of autocorrelation.

The critical values can be found on the website accompanying this book (🖰 Web Appendix → Chap. 7). From this table, you can see that the lower critical value of a model with five independent variables and 200 observations is 1.718 and the upper critical value is 1.820. Figure 7.6 shows the intervals for the above example and if the Durbin–Watson test concludes that there is no autocorrelation, you can proceed with the regression model. If the Durbin–Watson test indicates autocorrelation, you may have to use models that account for this problem, such as panel and time-series

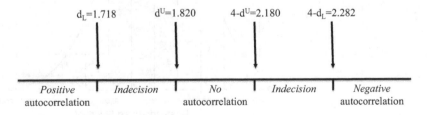

Fig. 7.6 Durbin-Watson test values ($n = 200$, $k = 5$)

models. We do not discuss these in this book, but a useful source of further information is Hill et al. (2008).

7.3.3.5 Fifth (Optional) Assumption: Error Distribution

The *fifth*, *optional*, *assumption* is that the regression model errors are approximately normally distributed. If this is not the case, the t-values may be incorrect. However, even if the errors of the regression model are not normally distributed, the regression model still provides good estimates of the coefficients. Therefore, we consider this assumption as optional. Potential reasons for non-normality include outliers (discussed in Chap. 5) and a non-linear relationship between an independent and a dependent variable.

There are two main ways of checking for normally distributed errors, either you use plots or you can perform a formal test. The plots are easily explained and interpreted and may suggest the source of non-normality (if present). The formal test may indicate non-normality and provide absolute standards. However, the formal test results reveal little about the source of non-normality.

To test for non-normality using plots, first save the unstandardized errors by going to the **Save** dialog box in the regression menu. Then, create a histogram of these errors and plot a normal curve in it to understand if any deviations from normality are present. We can make histograms by going to ▶ Graphs ▶ Legacy Dialogs ▶ Histogram. Make sure to check **Display normal curve**. The result may look something like Fig. 7.7. How do we interpret this figure? If we want the errors to be approximately normally distributed, the bars should end very "close" to the normal curve, which is the black bell-shaped curve. What "close" means exactly is

Fig. 7.7 Histogram of the errors

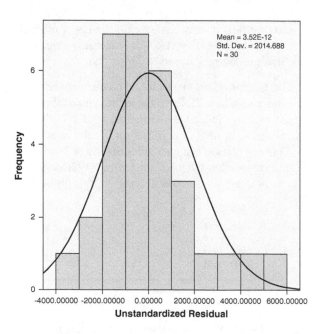

open to different interpretations, but Fig. 7.7 suggests that the errors produced by the estimated regression model are almost normally distributed.

In addition to the normal curve, SPSS produces a table, showing the results of two formal tests of normality (i.e., Kolmogorov-Smirnov and Shapiro-Wilk). Since we have only 30 observations in our dataset, we should use the Shapiro–Wilk test (see Chap. 6) as a formal test of normality. As we can easily see, the Shapiro–Wilk test result indicates that the errors are normally distributed as we cannot reject the null hypothesis at a significance level of 5% (p-value $= 0.084$) (Table 7.1).

7.3.4 Interpret the Regression Results

In the previous sections, we discussed how to specify a basic regression model and how to test regression assumptions. We now turn to discussing the fit of the regression model, followed by the interpretation of the effects of individual variables.

Table 7.1 Output produced by the Shapiro–Wilk test

Tests of Normality

	Kolmogorov-Smirnov[a]			Shapiro-Wilk		
	Statistic	df	Sig.	Statistic	df	Sig.
Unstandardized Residual	.101	30	.200*	.939	30	.084

a. Lilliefors Significance Correction

*. This is a lower bound of the true significance.

7.3.4.1 Overall Model Fit

We can assess the overall model fit using the (adjusted) R^2 and significance of the F-value.

The R^2 (or *coefficient of determination*) indicates the degree to which the model explains the observed variation in the dependent variable, relative to the mean. In Fig. 7.8, we explain this graphically with a scatter plot. The y-axis relates to the dependent variable (weekly sales in $) and the x-axis to the independent variable (*price*). In the scatter plot, we see 30 observations of sales and price (note that we use a small sample size for illustration purposes). The horizontal line (at about $5,000 sales per week) refers to the average sales of all 30 observations. This is also our benchmark. After all, if we were to have no regression line, our best estimate of the weekly sales is also the average. The sum of all squared differences between each observation and the average is the total variation or total sum of the squares (usually referred to as SS_T). We indicate the total variation for only one observation on the right of the scatter plot.

The upward sloping line (starting at the y-axis at about $2,500 sales per week when there are no promotional activities) is the regression line that is estimated

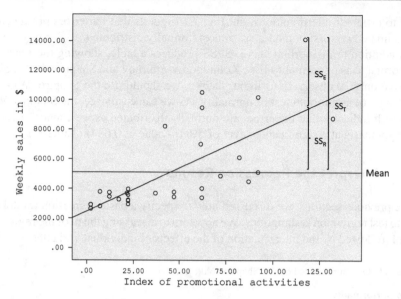

Fig. 7.8 Explanation of the R^2

using OLS. If we want to understand what the regression model adds beyond the average (the benchmark), we can calculate the difference between the regression line and the average. We call this the regression sum of the squares (usually abbreviated SS_R) as it is the variation in the data that is explained by the regression analysis. The final point we need to understand regarding how well a regression line fits the available data, is the unexplained sum of squares. This refers to the regression error that we discussed previously and which is consequently denoted as SS_E. In more formal terms, we can describe these types of variation as follows:

$$SS_T = SS_R + SS_E$$

This is the same as:

$$\sum_{i=1}^{n} (y_i - \bar{y})^2 = \sum_{i=1}^{n} (\hat{y}_i - \bar{y})^2 + \sum_{i=1}^{n} (y_i - \hat{y}_i)^2$$

Here, n describes the number of observations, y_i is the value of the independent variable for observation i, $\hat{y}_i$ is the predicted value of observation i and $\bar{y}$ is the mean value of y. As you can see, this description is very similar to the one-way ANOVA, discussed in Chap. 6. A good regression line should explain a substantial amount of variation (have a high SS_R) relative to the total variation (SS_T). This is the R^2 and we can calculate this as:

$$R^2 = \frac{SS_R}{SS_T}$$

The R^2 always lies between 0 and 1, where a higher R^2 indicates a better model fit. When interpreting the R^2, higher values indicate that more of the variation in y is explained by variation in x, and therefore that the SS_E is low relative to the SS_R.

It is difficult to provide rules of thumb regarding what R^2 is appropriate, as this varies from research area to research area. For example, in longitudinal studies R^2s of 0.90 and higher are common. In cross-sectional designs, values of around 0.30 are common while for exploratory research, using cross-sectional data, values of 0.10 are typical. In scholarly research that focuses on marketing issues, R^2 values of 0.75, 0.50, or 0.25 can, as a rough rule of thumb, be respectively described as substantial, moderate, or weak.

If we use the R^2 to compare different regression models (but with the same dependent variable), we run into problems. If we add irrelevant variables that are slightly correlated with the dependent variable, the R^2 will increase. Thus, if we use the R^2 as the only basis for understanding regression model fit, we are biased towards selecting regression models with many independent variables. Selecting a model only based on the R^2 is plainly not a good strategy, as we want regression models that do a good job of explaining the data (thus a low SS_F), but which also have few independent variables (these are called *parsimonious models*). We do not want too many independent variables because this makes using the regression model more difficult. It is easier to recommend that management changes a few key variables to improve an outcome than to recommend a long list of somewhat related variables. Of course, relevant variables should always be included. To quote Albert Einstein: "Everything should be made as simple as possible, but not simpler!"

To avoid a bias towards complex models, we can use the *adjusted R^2* to select regression models. The adjusted R^2 only increases if the addition of another independent variable explains a substantial amount of variance. We calculate the adjusted R^2 as follows:

$$\text{Adjusted } R^2 = 1 - \left(1 - R^2\right) \cdot \frac{(n-1)}{n-k-1}$$

Here, n describes the number of observations and k the number of independent variables (not counting the constant α). This adjusted R^2 is a relative measure and should be used to compare different regression models with the same dependent variable. You should pick the model with the highest adjusted R^2 when comparing regression models.

However, do not blindly use the adjusted R^2 as a guide, but also look at each individual variable and see if it is relevant (practically) for the problem you are researching. Furthermore, it is important to note that we cannot interpret the adjusted R^2 as the percentage of explained variance in the sample used for regression analysis. The adjusted R^2 is only a measure of how much the model explains while controlling for model complexity.

Besides the (adjusted) R^2, the F-test is an important determinant of model fit. The test statistic's F-value is the result of a one-way ANOVA (see Chap. 6) that tests the null hypothesis that all regression coefficients together are equal to zero. Thus, the following null hypothesis is tested:

$$H_0 : \beta_1 = \beta_2 = \beta_3 = \ldots = 0$$

The alternative hypothesis is that at least one β differs from zero. If the regression coefficients were all equal to zero, then the effect of all the independent variables on the dependent variable is zero. In other words, there is no (zero) relationship between the dependent variable and the independent variables. If we do not reject the null hypothesis, we need to change the regression model or, if this is not possible, report that the regression model is insignificant.

The test statistic's F-value closely resembles the F-statistic, as discussed in Chap. 6 and is also directly related to the R^2 we discussed previously. We can calculate the F-value as follows:

$$F = \frac{SS_{R/K}}{SS_{E/(n-k-1)}} = \frac{R^2}{(1-R^2)} \cdot \frac{(n-k-1)}{k}$$

The test statistic follows an F-distribution with k and $(n-k-1)$ degrees of freedom. Finding that the p-value of the F-test is below 0.05 (i.e., a significant model), does not, however, automatically mean that all of our regression coefficients are significant or even that one of them is significant, when considered in isolation. However, if the F-value is significant, it is highly likely that at least one or more regression coefficients are significant.

When we interpret the model fit, the F-test is the most critical, as it determines if the overall model is significant. If the model is insignificant, we do not interpret the model further. If the model is significant, we proceed by interpreting individual variables.

7.3.4.2 Effects of Individual Variables

After having established that the overall model is significant and that the R^2 is satisfactory, we need to interpret the effects of the various independent variables used to explain the dependent variable. First, we need to look at the t-values reported for each individual parameter. These t-values are similar to those discussed in Chap. 6 in the context of hypothesis testing. If a regression coefficient's p-value (indicated in SPSS by the column headed by **Sig.**) is below 0.05, we generally say that that particular independent variable relates significantly to the dependent variable.

To be precise, the null and alternative hypotheses tested for an individual parameter (e.g., β_1) are:

$$H_0 : \beta_1 = 0$$

$$H_1 : \beta_1 \neq 0$$

If a coefficient is significant (meaning we reject the null hypothesis), we also need to look at the unstandardized and standardized β coefficients. The *unstandardized β coefficient* indicates the effect of a 1-unit increase in the independent variable (on the scale in which the original independent variable is measured) on the dependent variable. Thus it is the partial relationship between a single independent variable and the dependent variable. At the very beginning of this chapter, we learned that there is a positive relationship between promotional activities and the weekly sales in \$ with a β_1 coefficient of 55.968. This means that if we increase promotional activities by one unit, weekly sales are expected to go up by \$55.968. In other variables, the effect could of course be negative (e.g., increasing prices reduces sales). Importantly, if we have multiple independent variables, the unstandardized β_1 coefficient is the effect of an increase of that independent variable by one unit, keeping the other independent variables constant.

While this is a very simple example, we might run a multiple regression in which the independent variables are measured on different scales, such as in \$, units sold, or on Likert scales. Consequently, the independent variables' effects cannot be directly compared with one another as their influence also depends on the type of scale used. Comparing the (unstandardized) β coefficients would in any case amount to comparing apples with oranges!

Fortunately, the *standardized βs* allow us to compare the relative effect of differently measured independent variables. This is achieved by expressing β as standard deviations with a mean of zero. The standardized βs coefficient expresses the effect of a single standardized deviation change of the independent variable on the dependent variable. All we need to do is to look at the highest absolute value. This value indicates which variable has the strongest effect on the dependent variable. The second highest absolute value indicates the second strongest effect, etc. Only consider the significant βs in this respect, as insignificant βs do not (statistically) differ from zero! Practically, the standardized β is important, because it allows us to ask questions on what, for example, the relative effect of promotional activities is relative to decreasing prices. It can therefore guide management decisions.

While the standardized βs are helpful from a practical point of view, there are two issues. First, standardized βs allow comparing the coefficients only within and not between models! Even if you add just a single variable to your regression model, standardized βs may change substantially. Second, standardized βs are not meaningful when the independent variable is binary.

When interpreting (standardized) β coefficients, you should always keep the effect size in mind. If a β coefficient is significant, it indicates merely an effect that differs from zero. This does not necessarily mean that the effect is managerially relevant. For example, we may find a \$0.01 sales effect of spending \$1 more on promotional activities that is statistically significant. Statistically, we could conclude that the effect of a \$1 increase in promotional activities increases sales by an average of \$0.01 (just one dollar cent). While this effect differs significantly from zero, in practice we would probably not recommend increasing promotional activities (we would lose money at the margin) as the effect size is just too small.[5]

There are also situations in which an effect is not constant for all observations but depends on the values of another variable. To disclose such effects, researchers can run a *moderation analysis*, which we discuss in Box 7.3.

Box 7.3 Moderation
The discussion on the effects of individual variables assumes that there is only *one* effect. That is, there is only one β parameter that represents all observations well. Often, this is not true. For example, the link between customer satisfaction and loyalty has been shown to be stronger for people with low income than for people with high income. In other words, there is *heterogeneity* in the effect between satisfaction and loyalty.

Moderation analysis is one way to test if such heterogeneity is present. A moderator variable, usually denoted with m, is a variable that changes the strength (or even direction) of the relationship between the independent variable (x) and the dependent variable (y). This moderation variable is frequently called an *interaction variable*. The moderating variable can weaken or strengthen the effect of x on y. Potentially, the m variable could even reverse the effect of x on y.

Moderation is easy to test if the moderator variable m is binary, ordinal, or interval scaled. All that is required is to create a new variable that is the multiplication of $x \cdot m$. This can be done in SPSS using ▶ Transform ▶ Compute. The regression model then takes the following form:

$$y = \alpha + \beta x + \beta m + \beta x \cdot m + e$$

In words, conducting a moderator analysis requires entering the independent variable x, the moderator variable m and the product $x \cdot m$. After estimating this

(continued)

---

[5] An interesting perspective on significance and effect sizes is offered by Cohen's (1994) classical article "The Earth is Round (p $<.05$).

Box 7.3 (continued)

regression model, you can interpret the significance and sign of the β_3 parameter. A significant effect suggests that:

– The effect of x increases as m increases (when the sign of β_3 is positive),
– The effect of x decreases as m increases (when the sign of β_3 is negative).

Finding a significant moderator effect suggests heterogeneity in the effect of x on y, where the effect of x of y may increase as m increases or may decrease as m decreases.

For a further discussion on moderation analyses, please see David Kenny's discussion on moderation (http://www.davidakenny.net/cm/moderation.htm) or the advanced discussion of Aiken and West (1991). Jeremy Dawson's website (http://www.jeremydawson.co.uk/slopes.htm) offers a tool to visualize moderation effects. An example of a moderation analysis is for example found in (Mooi and Frambach 2009).

7.3.5 Validate the Regression Model

After we have checked for the assumptions of regression analysis and interpreted the results, we need to check for the *stability* of the regression model. Stability means that the results are stable over time, do not vary across different situations, and do not depend heavily on the model's specification. We can check for the stability of a regression model in several ways.

1. We could validate the regression results by splitting our data into two parts (called *split-sample validation*) and run the regression model again on each subset of data. 70% of the randomly chosen data are often used to estimate the regression model and the remaining 30% are used for comparison purposes. We can only split the data if the remaining 30% still meets the sample size rules of thumb discussed earlier. If the use of the two samples results in similar effects, we can conclude that the model is stable.
2. We can also cross-validate our findings on a new dataset and see if those findings are similar to the original findings. Again, similarity in the findings indicates stability and that our regression model is properly specified. This, naturally, assumes that we have a second dataset.
3. We could add a number of alternative variables to the model. But we would need to have more variables available than included in the regression model to do so. For example, if we try to explain weekly supermarket sales, we could use a number of "key" variables (e.g., the breadth of the assortment or downtown/non-downtown location) in our regression model to help us. Once we have a suitable regression model, we could use these variables. If the basic findings of, for example, promotional activities are the same for stores with a differing assortment width or store location (i.e., the assortment width and location are not

significant), we conclude that the effects are stable. However, it might also be the opposite, but whatever the case, we want to know.

Note that not all regression models need to be identical when you try to validate the results. The signs of the individual parameters should at least be consistent and significant variables should remain so, except if they are marginally significant, in which case changes are expected (e.g., p = 0.045 becomes p = 0.051).

7.3.6   Use the Regression Model

When we have found a useful regression model that satisfies the assumptions of regression analysis, it is time to use the regression model. A key use of regression models is *prediction*. Essentially, prediction entails calculating the values of the dependent variable based on assumed values of the independent variables and their related but previously calculated unstandardized β coefficients. Let us illustrate this by returning to our opening example. Imagine that we are trying to predict weekly supermarket sales (in $) (y) and have estimated a regression model with two independent variables: the average price (x_1) and an index of promotional activities (x_2). The regression model for this is as follows:

$$y = \alpha + \beta_1 x_1 + \beta_2 x_2 + e$$

If we estimate this model on a dataset, the estimated coefficients using regression analysis could be similar to those in Table 7.2.

Table 7.2 Table containing sample regression coefficients[a]

Coefficients[a]

Model		Unstandardized Coefficients		Standardized Coefficients	t	Sig.
		B	Std. Error	Beta		
1	(Constant)	29011.585	18448.456		1.573	.127
	Price of product	−24003.037	16694.676	−.241	−1.438	.162
	Index of promotional activities	44.227	13.567	.547	3.260	.003

a. Dependent Variable: Weekly sales in USD

We can also use these coefficients to make predictions of sales in different situations. Imagine, for example, that we have set the price at $1.10 and promotional activities at 50. Our expectation of the weekly sales would then be:

$\hat{y}$ = 29,011.585 - 24,003.037 × $1.10 + 44.227 × 50 promotional activities
   = $4,819.594 sales per week.

We could also build several scenarios to plan for different situations, by, for example, increasing the price to $1.20 and reducing promotional activities to 40. Regression models can be used like this to, for example, automate stocking and logistical planning or develop strategic marketing plans.

Another way in which regression can help is by providing insight into variables' specific effects. For example, if the effect of price is not significant, it may tell managers that the supermarket's sales are relatively insensitive to pricing decisions. Alternatively, the strength of promotional activities' effect may help managers understand whether promotional activities are useful.

Table 7.3 summarizes (on the left side) the major theoretical decisions we need to make if we want to run a regression model. On the right side, these decisions are then "translated" into SPSS actions, which are related to these theoretical decisions.

Table 7.3 Key steps involved in carrying out a regression analysis

Theory	Execution in SPSS
Issues with regression analysis	
Is the sample size sufficient?	Conduct a power analysis. Alternatively, check if sample size is 104 + k, where k indicates the number of independent variables.
Do the dependent and independent variables show variation?	Calculate the standard deviation of the variables by going to ▶ Analyze ▶ Descriptive Statistics ▶ Descriptives ▶ Options (check **Std. Deviation**). At the very least, the standard deviation should be a positive value.
Is the dependent variable interval or ratio scaled?	Use Chap. 2 to determine the measurement level.
Is (multi)collinearity present?	Check for tolerance and VIF. Do this with ▶ Analyze ▶ Regression ▶ Linear ▶ Statistics (check **Collinearity diagnostics**). The tolerance should be above 0.10. The VIF should be below 10.
Specifying and estimating the regression model	
Select variables based on theory or based on strength of effects	Preferably use the enter method. If stepwise methods are used (such as the forward method), only add variables that could have a relationship with the dependent variable.
Testing the assumptions of regression analysis	
Is the relationship between the independent and dependent variables linear?	Consider whether you can write the regression model as $y = \alpha + \beta_1 x_1 + \ldots + \beta_k x_k + e$.
	To understand if the independent variables are linearly related to the dependent variable, plot the y variables separately against the dependent variable of

(continued)

Table 7.3 (continued)

Theory	Execution in SPSS
	the regression model. Create scatter plots using ▶ Graphs ▶ Legacy Dialogs ▶ Scatter/Dot (choose **Simple Scatter**). If you see a non-linear pattern showing up, non-linearity is an issue. To specify a different relationship, see the *transform variables* section in Chap. 5.
Is the expected mean error of the regression model zero?	No actions in SPSS. Choice made on theoretical grounds.
Are the errors constant (homoskedastic)?	Plot the residual of the regression model on the y-axis and the dependent variable on the x-axis, using a scatter plot under ▶ Graphs ▶ Legacy Dialogs ▶ Scatter/Dot (choose **Simple Scatter**). If you see that the errors in/decrease as the dependent variable increases, the variance of the errors is not constant. You can use WLS to remedy this.
Are the errors correlated (autocorrelation)?	First assess if there is a time component to the data (i.e., multiple observations, across time, from one respondent/object). If there is, sort the data according to the time variable and conduct the Durbin–Watson test. Compare the calculated Durbin–Watson test statistic with the critical lower and upper values. If positive or negative autocorrelation is present, panel or time-series models need to be used:
	▶ Analyze ▶ Regression ▶ Linear ▶ Statistics and check the **Durbin–Watson** box.
Are the errors normally distributed?	Create a histogram of the errors with a standard normal curve in it: ▶ Graphs ▶ Legacy Dialogs ▶ Histogram and enter the saved errors. Also check Display normal curve.
	Calculate the Kolmogorov-Smirnov test (for $n \geq 50$) or Shapiro–Wilk test (for $n < 50$). ▶ Analyze ▶ Descriptive Statistics ▶ Explore ▶ Plots and check the **Normality plots with tests** box.
Interpret the regression model	
Consider the overall model fit.	Check the R^2 and significance of the F-value. For model comparisons, use the adjusted R^2.
Consider the effects of the independent variables separately.	Check the (standardized) β. Also check the sign of the β. Consider significance of the t-value.
Validate the model	
Are the results robust?	Split the file into subsets or run the regression model against another sample to check for robustness. Add additional variables that may be useful and check if a similar regression model results.

7.4   Example

In the example, we take a closer look at the American Customer Satisfaction Index (*ACSI Data.sav*, ⏚ Web Appendix → Chap. 7). Every year, the American Customer Satisfaction Index (ACSI) surveys about 80,000 Americans about their level of satisfaction with a number of products and services. These satisfaction scores are used to benchmark competitors and to rate industries. For example, towards the beginning of 2014, the Quaker (PepsiCo), the H.J. Heinz Company, and General Mills were rated as the three food manufacturers with the highest scores. If you go to http://www.theacsi.org, you will find the current scores for various industries.[6] The ACSI data contain several variables, but we only focus on the following (variable names in parentheses):

- *Overall Customer Satisfaction* (*lvsat*) is measured by statements put to consumers about their overall satisfaction, expectancy disconfirmation (degree to which performance falls short of, or exceeds, expectations) and performance versus the customer's ideal product or service in the category.
- *Customer Expectations* (*lvexpect*) is measured by statements put to consumers about their overall expectations of quality (prior to purchase), their expectation regarding to how well the product fits the customer's personal requirements (prior to purchase), and expectation regarding reliability, or how often things will go wrong (prior to purchase).
- *Perceived Value* (*lvvalue*) is the consumers' rating of quality given price, and price given quality.
- *Customer Complaints* (*lvcomp*) captures whether or not the customer has complained formally or informally about the product or service (1 = yes, 0 = no).

The data includes 1,640 responses from customers, but due to item non-response, the actual number of responses for each variable is lower.

7.4.1   Consider Data Requirements for Regression Analysis

First we need to check if our sample size is sufficient. By calculating descriptive statistics (▶ Analyze ▶ Descriptive Statistics ▶ Descriptives; see Chap. 5) of the four above mentioned variables we can see that we have 1,640 valid listwise observations. This means that we have complete information for 1,640 observations. This is far above the minimum sample sizes as recommended by Green (1991). The sampling process has been documented by Fornell, Johnson, Anderson, Cha, and Bryant (1996) and we assume this is done correctly. Looking at the dependent and independent variables' variance, we can also see that all variables show variation. Finally, as our dependent variable is also ratio scaled, we can proceed with regression analysis. Multicollinearity might be an issue, but

---

[6] For an application of the ACSI, see, for example, Ringle et al. (2010).

we can only check this thoroughly after running a regression analysis. We will therefore discuss this aspect later.

7.4.2   Specify and Estimate the Regression Model in SPSS

Although it is useful to know who comes out on top, from a marketing perspective, it is more useful to know how organizations can increase their satisfaction. We can use regression for this and explain how a number of independent variables relate to satisfaction. Simply click on ▶ Analyze ▶ Regression ▶ Linear and then enter *Overall Customer Satisfaction* into the **Dependent** box and *Customer Expectations, Perceived Value*, and *Customer Complaints* into the **Independent(s)** box. Figure 7.9 shows the regression dialog box in SPSS.

SPSS provides us with a number of options. Under **Method** choose **Enter**. The enter option includes all variables added into the **Independent(s)** box and does not

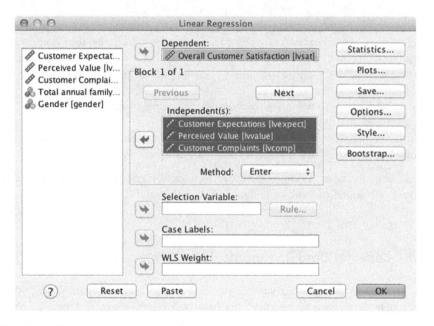

Fig. 7.9 The Linear Regression dialog box

remove any of the variables on statistical grounds (as opposed to the stepwise methods). Under **Statistics** in the main regression dialog box (see Fig. 7.10), SPSS offers several options on the output that you may want to see. The **Estimates** and **Model fit** options are checked by default and are essential. The **Confidence intervals** and **Covariance matrix** options are not necessary for standard analysis

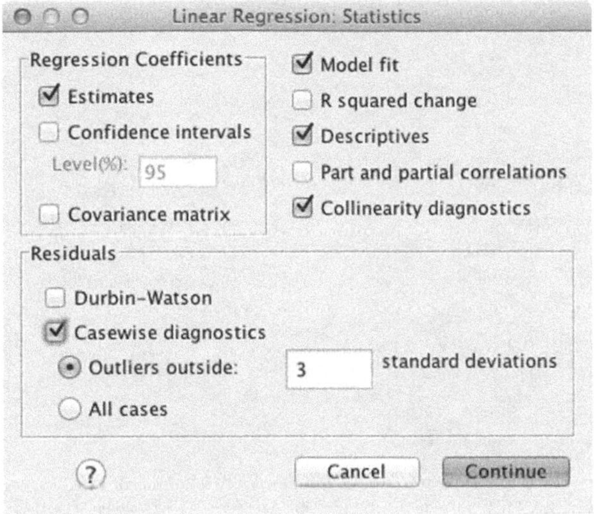

Fig. 7.10 The statistics dialog box

purposes, so we skip these. The **R squared change** option is only useful if you select any of the stepwise methods but is irrelevant if you use the (recommended) enter option. The **Descriptives** option does what it says and provides the mean, standard deviation, and number of observations for the dependent and independent variables. The **Part and partial correlations** option produces a correlation matrix, while the **Collinearity diagnostics** option checks for (multi)collinearity. The **Durbin–Watson** option checks for autocorrelation, while **Casewise diagnostics** provides outlier diagnostics. In this case, there is no time component to our data and thus the Durbin–Watson test is not applicable.

Next, make sure the **Estimates, Model fit, Descriptives, Collinearity diagnostics**, and **Casewise diagnostic** options are checked. Then click on **Continue**. In the main regression dialog box, click on **Save**. This displays a dialog box similar to Fig. 7.11. Here, you can save predicted values and residuals.

Check the boxes **Unstandardized** under **Predicted Values** and **Residuals**. After clicking on **Continue** in the **Linear Regression: Save** dialog box and **OK** in the **Linear Regression** dialog box, SPSS runs a regression analysis and saves the residuals as a new variable in your dataset. We will discuss all the output in detail below.

Fig. 7.11 The Save options for regression analysis

7.4.3 Test the Assumptions of Regression Analysis Using SPSS

To test the assumptions, we need to run three separate analyses.

The first assumption, the regression model can be expressed in a linear way, is implied if you can write the regression model linearly as $y = \alpha + \beta_1 x_1 + \beta_2 x_2 + \beta_3 x_3 + e$. This is easy to do! While not needed, we also check for linearity of the relationships between the independent and dependent variables. If we create a scatter plot of *Overall Customer Satisfaction* against *Customer Expectations*, SPSS produces Fig. 7.12. This plot seems to suggest a linear relationship between the two variables. For a full analysis, we should plot every separate independent variable against the dependent variable. Try this yourself and you will see that the other independent variables are also linearly related to *Overall Customer Satisfaction*. Note that *Perceived Value* includes a clear outlier but with or without this outlier the relationship is still linear. Also note that if we include variables that take on only few different values, such as *Customer Complaints* (values of 0 and 1), we cannot use graphs to see if these relationships are linear.

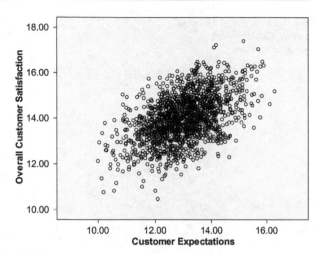

Fig. 7.12 Overall customer satisfaction against customer expectations

Next, we have to check if the regression model's expected mean error is zero (second assumption). Remember, this choice is made on theoretical grounds. We have a randomly drawn sample from the population and the model is similar in specification to other models explaining customer satisfaction. This makes it highly likely that the regression model's expected mean error is zero.

The third assumption is that of homoskedasticity. To test for this, we plot the errors against the dependent variable. Do this by going to ▶ Graphs ▶ Legacy Dialogs ▶ Scatter/Dot (choose **Simple Scatter**). Enter the *Overall Customer Satisfaction* to the **Y-axis** and put *Unstandardized Residual* to the **X-axis**. Then click on **OK**. SPSS then produces a plot similar to Fig. 7.13. The results do not suggest heteroskedasticity. Note that it clearly seems that there is an outlier present. By looking at the **Casewise Diagnostics** in Table 7.4, we can further investigate this issue (note that we have set Casewise diagnostics to "Outliers outside: 3 standard deviations" to be conservative).

Cases where the errors are high indicate that those cases influence the results. SPSS assumes by default (see Fig. 7.10 under **Outliers outside: 3 standard deviations**) that observations that are three standard deviations away from the mean are potential outliers. The results in Table 7.4 suggest that there are four potential outliers. Case 257 has the strongest influence on the results (the standardized error is the highest). Should we delete these four cases? Case 257 seems to be very far away from the other observations (also see Fig. 7.13) and is likely an entry error or mistake, meaning the observation should be deleted. The other potential outliers appear to be simply part of the data, and should be retained.

If we delete a case from the initial dataset, we have to re-run the model. When doing so, we have to re-consider the assumptions we just discussed based on the newly estimated unstandardized residuals. However, we refrain from displaying the results twice – just try it yourself! Let's instead continue by discussing the remaining two (partly optional) assumptions using the dataset <u>without the outlier</u>.[7]

---

[7] You can download the reduced dataset *ACSI Data_without outlier.sav* in the 🔗 Web Appendix (Chap. 7)

Fig. 7.13 A plot of the errors against the dependent variable's values

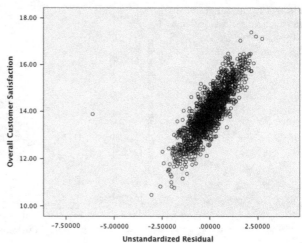

Table 7.4 Casewise diagnostics

Casewise Diagnostics[a]

Case Number	Std. Residual	Overall Customer Satisfaction	Predicted Value	Residual
257	-7.212	13.89	20.0091	-6.12239
600	-3.594	10.46	13.5149	-3.05122
655	3.200	17.12	14.3997	2.71669
1044	-3.053	10.82	13.4133	-2.59206

a. Dependent Variable: Overall Customer Satisfaction

If we had data with a time component, we would also perform the Durbin–Watson test to test for potential autocorrelation (fourth assumption). However, since the data do not include any time component, we should not conduct this test.

Lastly, we should explore how the errors are distributed. Do this by going to ▶ Graphs ▶ Legacy Dialogs ▶ Histogram. Enter the *Unstandardized Residual* under **Variable**. Also make sure that you check **Display normal curve.** In Fig. 7.14, we show a histogram of the errors.

Figure 7.13 suggest that our data are normally distributed as the bars indicating the frequency of the errors generally follow the normal curve. However, we can check this further by conducting the Kolmogorov-Smirnov test (with Lilliefors correction) by going to ▶ Analyze ▶ Descriptive Statistics ▶ Explore. Table 7.5 shows the output.

The results of this test (Table 7.5) suggest that the errors are normally distributed as we do not reject the test's null hypothesis. Thus, we can assume that the errors are normally distributed.

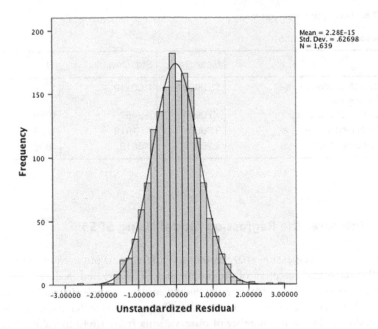

Fig. 7.14 Histogram of the errors with a standard normal curve

Table 7.5 Output produced by the Kolmogorov–Smirnov test

Tests of Normality

	Kolmogorov-Smirnov[a]			Shapiro-Wilk		
	Statistic	df	Sig.	Statistic	df	Sig.
Unstandardized Residual	.016	1639	.200[*]	.998	1639	.041

a. Lilliefors Significance Correction

*. This is a lower bound of the true significance.

Now we turn to testing for multicollinearity. There are two tables in which SPSS indicates if multicollinearity issues are present. The first table is Table 7.11, in which the regression coefficient estimates are displayed. This table output also shows each variable's **Tolerance** in the second to last column and **VIF** in the last column. In this example, the tolerance values clearly lie above 0.10, and VIF values below 10, indicating that multicollinearity is of no concern.

Table 7.6 Descriptive statistics table

Descriptive Statistics

	Mean	Std. Deviation	N
Overall Customer Satisfaction	13.9999	1.00219	1639
Customer Expectations	13.0009	.99957	1639
Perceived Value	9.9990	1.01018	1639
Customer Complaints	.2288	.42019	1639

7.4.4   Interpret the Regression Model Using SPSS

The results of the regression analysis that we just carried out are presented below. We will discuss each element of the output that SPSS created in detail.

Tables 7.6 and 7.7 describe the dependent and independent variables in detail and provide several descriptives discussed in Chap. 5. Notice that the deletion of the outlier reduced the overall number of observations from 1,640 to 1,639. These are the observations for which we have complete information for the dependent and independent variables. Table 7.7 shows the correlation matrix and gives an idea how the different variables are related to each other.

SPSS also produces Table 7.8, which indicates the variables used as dependent and independent variables and how they were entered in the model. It confirms that we use the **Enter** option (indicated under **Method**). All independent variables included in the model are mentioned under **Variables Entered** and under **b.** Furthermore, under **Dependent Variable**, the name of the dependent variable is indicated.

We interpret Tables 7.9 and 7.10 jointly, as they provide information on the model fit; that is, how well the independent variables relate to the dependent variable. The R^2 provided in Table 7.9 seems satisfactory and is above the value of 0.30 that is common for cross-sectional research. Usually, as is the case in our analysis, the R^2 and adjusted R^2 are similar. If the adjusted R^2 is substantially lower, this could indicate that you have used too many independent variables and that some could possibly be removed. Next, consider the significance of the F-test. The result in Table 7.10 indicates that the regression model is significant (**Sig.** <0.5).

After assessing the overall model fit, it is time to look at the individual coefficients. We find these in Table 7.11. First, you should look at the individual parameters' t-values, which test if the regression coefficients are individually equal to zero. If this is the case, the parameter is insignificant. In the model above, we find

Table 7.7 Correlation matrix

Correlations

		Overall Customer Satisfaction	Customer Expectations	Perceived Value	Customer Complaints
Pearson Correlation	Overall Customer Satisfaction	1.000	.492	.766	−.144
	Customer Expectations	.492	1.000	.478	−.073
	Perceived Value	.766	.478	1.000	−.137
	Customer Complaints	−.144	−.073	−.137	1.000
Sig. (1-tailed)	Overall Customer Satisfaction	.	.000	.000	.000
	Customer Expectations	.000	.	.000	.001
	Perceived Value	.000	.000	.	.000
	Customer Complaints	.000	.001	.000	.
N	Overall Customer Satisfaction	1639	1639	1639	1639
	Customer Expectations	1639	1639	1639	1639
	Perceived Value	1639	1639	1639	1639
	Customer Complaints	1639	1639	1639	1639

three significant coefficients, those with p-values (under **Sig.** in Table 7.11) are below the commonly used level of 0.05. Although the constant is also significant, this is not a variable and is usually excluded from further interpretation. The significant variables require further interpretation.

First look at the sign (plus or minus) in the **Standardized Coefficients** column. Here, we find that *Customer Expectations* and *Perceived Value* are significantly and positively related to *Overall Customer Satisfaction*. *Customer Complaints* is significant and negatively related to *Overall Customer Satisfaction*. This means that if people complain, their customer satisfaction is significantly lower on average. By looking at the standardized coefficients' values you can assess if *Customer Expectations*, *Perceived Value*, or *Customer Complaints* is most strongly related to *Overall Customer Satisfaction*. You only look at the absolute value (without the minus or plus sign therefore) and choose the highest value. In this case, *Perceived Value* (0.677) has clearly the strongest relationship with overall customer satisfaction. Therefore, this might be the first variable you want to focus on through marketing activities if you aim to increase customer satisfaction. Although standardized βs cannot be fully compared when an independent variable is binary (as it is the case with *Customer Complaints*) the comparison gives us a rough idea regarding the relative strengths of the independent variables' effects on the dependent variable.

Table 7.8 Variables used and regression method

Variables Entered/Removed[b]

Model	Variables Entered	Variables Removed	Method
1	Customer Complaints, Customer Expectations, Perceived Value[a]	.	Enter

a. All requested variables entered.

b. Dependent Variable: Overall Customer Satisfaction

Table 7.9 The model summary[a]

Model Summary[b]

Model	R	R Square	Adjusted R Square	Std. Error of the Estimate
1	.780[a]	.609	.608	.62756

a. Predictors: (Constant), Customer Complaints, Customer Expectations, Perceived Value

b. Dependent Variable: Overall Customer Satisfaction

Table 7.10 ANOVA[a]

ANOVA[b]

Model		Sum of Squares	df	Mean Square	F	Sig.
1	Regression	1001.261	3	333.754	847.453	.000[a]
	Residual	643.914	1635	.394		
	Total	1645.175	1638			

a. Predictors: (Constant), Customer Complaints, Customer Expectations, Perceived Value

b. Dependent Variable: Overall Customer Satisfaction

Table 7.11 The estimated coefficients

Coefficients[a]

Model	Unstandardized Coefficients		Standardized Coefficients			Collinearity Statistics	
	B	Std. Error	Beta	t	Sig.	Tolerance	VIF
1 (Constant)	5.124	.215		23.863	.000		
Customer Expectations	.164	.018	.163	9.257	.000	.771	1.296
Perceived Value	.677	.018	.683	38.484	.000	.761	1.314
Customer Complaints	−.092	.037	−.038	−2.458	.014	.981	1.019

a. Dependent Variable: Overall Customer Satisfaction

The **Unstandardized Coefficients** column gives you an indication of what would happen if you were to increase one of the independent variables by exactly one unit. For example, if *Customer Expectations* were to increase by one unit, we would expect *Overall Customer Satisfaction* to increase by 0.164 units. The standard errors are used to calculate the t-values. If we take the unstandardized coefficient of *Customer Expectations* (0.164) and divide this by its standard error (0.018), we obtain a value that is approximately the t-value of the 9.257 indicated in the table (see Chap. 6 for a description of the t-test statistic). The slight differences are due to rounding. As indicated before, *Customer Complaints* is a binary variable which can only take the value of 0 or 1. More precisely, for those customers who have not complained thus far, *Customer Complaints* takes the value 0. On the contrary, if a customer has already complained, the variable's value is 1 for this observation. Thus, the corresponding coefficient (-0.092) is the difference in satisfaction for customers who complained compared to those who have not complained. Overall, the results indicate that we have found a useful model that satisfies the assumptions of regression analysis.

7.4.5 Validate the Regression Model Using SPSS

Next, we need to validate the model. Let's first split-validate our model. Do this by going to ▶ Data ▶ Select Cases. This displays a dialog box similar to Fig. 7.15.

In this dialog box, go to **Select Cases: Range**. This displays a dialog box similar to Fig. 7.16.

Select the first 1,150 cases, which is approximately 70% of the data. Then run the regression analysis again. Afterwards, return to **Select Cases: Range** and select observations 1,151–1,639. Compare the results of this model to those of the previous model. This approach is simple to execute but *only* works if the ordering of the data are random.

Next, we can add a few key additional variables to our model and see if the basic results change. Key variables with which to check the stability (the so-called *covariates*) could be the total annual family income and the respondent's gender. Then interpret the basic model again to see if the regression results change.

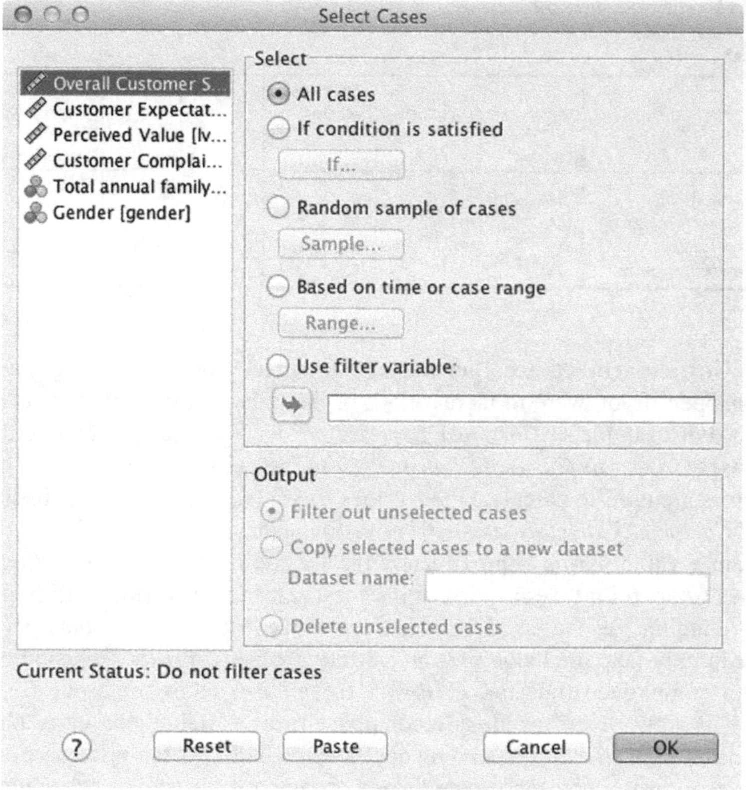

Fig. 7.15 The select cases dialog box

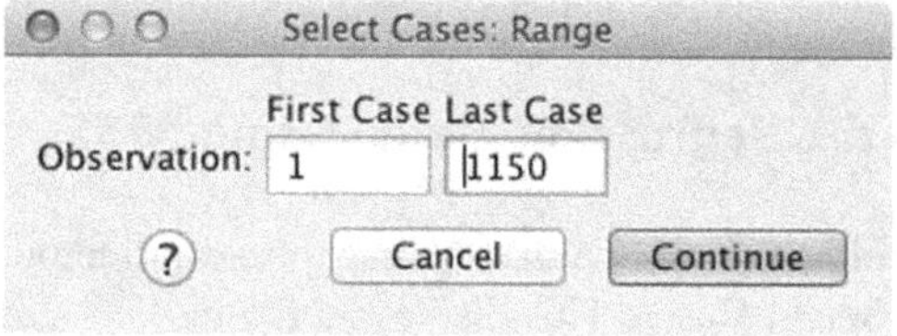

Fig. 7.16 The select cases: range dialog box

7.5 Farming with AgriPro (Case Study)

AgriPro is a firm based in Colorado, USA, which does research on and produces genetically modified wheat seed. Every year AgriPro conducts thousands of experiments on different varieties of wheat seeds in different locations of the USA. In these experiments, the agricultural and economic characteristics, regional adaptation, and yield potential of different varieties of wheat seeds are investigated. In addition, the benefits of the wheat produced, including the milling and baking quality, are examined. If a new variety of wheat seed with superior characteristics is identified, AgriPro produces and markets it throughout the USA and parts of Canada.

AgriPro's product is sold to farmers through their distributors, known in the industry as growers. Growers buy wheat seed from AgriPro, grow wheat, harvest the seeds, and sell the seed to local farmers, who plant them in their fields. These growers also provide the farmers who buy their seeds with expert local knowledge on management and the environment.

AgriPro sells its products to these growers in several geographically defined markets. These markets are geographically defined because different local conditions (soil, weather, and local plant diseases) force AgriPro to produce different products. One of these markets, the heartland region of the USA is an important market for AgriPro, but the company has been performing below management expectations in these markets. The heartland region includes the states of Ohio, Indiana, Missouri, Illinois, and Kentucky.

To help AgriPro understand more about farming in the heartland region, they commissioned a marketing research project among farmers in these states. AgriPro, together with a marketing research firm, designed a survey, which included questions on what farmers who decide to plant wheat find important, how they obtain information on growing and planting wheat, what is important in their purchasing decision, and their loyalty to and satisfaction with the top five wheat suppliers (including AgriPro). In addition, questions were asked about how many acres of farmland the respondents possessed, how much wheat they planted, how old they were, and their level of education.

http://www.agriprowheat.com

This survey was mailed to 650 farmers selected from a commercial list that includes nearly all farmers in the heartland region. In all, 150 responses were received, resulting in a 23% response rate. The marketing research firm also assisted AgriPro to assign variable names and labels. They did not delete any questions or observations due to nonresponse to items.

Your task is to analyze the dataset further and provide the management of AgriPro with advice based on the dataset. This dataset is labeled *Agripro.sav* and is available in the ⫟ Web Appendix (→ Chap. 7). Note that the dataset (under

Variable View at the bottom of the SPSS screen) contains the variable names and labels and these match those in the survey. In the ⌁ Web Appendix (→ Chap. 7), we also include the original survey.[8]

To help you with this task, a number of questions have been prepared by AgriPro that they would like to see answered:

1. Produce appropriate descriptive statistics for each item in the dataset. Consider descriptive statistics that provide useful information in a succinct way. In addition, produce several descriptive statistics on the demographic variables in the dataset, using appropriate charts and/or graphs.
2. Are there any outliers in the data? What (if any) observations do you consider to be outliers and what would you do with these?
3. What are the most common reasons for farmers to plant wheat? From which source are farmers most likely to seek information on wheat? Is this source also the most reliable one?
4. Consider the five brands included in the dataset. Describe how these brands compare on quality, advice provided, and farmer loyalty.
5. How satisfied are the farmers with the brand's distributors?
6. AgriPro expects that farmers who are more satisfied with their products devote a greater percentage of the total number of acres available to them to wheat. Please test this assumption by using regression analysis. In addition, check the assumptions of regression analysis.
7. Is there a relationship between farmers' satisfaction with AgriPro and the respondent's educational level, age, and number of acres of farmland? Conduct a regression analysis with all these four variables. How do these results relate to question 6?
8. Are all assumptions satisfied? If not, is there anything we can do about it or should we ignore the assumptions if they are not satisfied?
9. What is the relationship between the quality of AgriPro seed and the satisfaction with AgriPro?
10. As AgriPro's consultant, and based on the empirical findings of this study, what marketing advice would you have for AgriPro's marketing team? Provide four or five carefully thought through suggestions as bullet points.

Review Questions

1. Try to explain what regression analysis is in your own words.
2. Imagine you are asked to use regression analysis to explain the profitability of new supermarket products, such as the introduction of a new type of jam or yoghurt, in the first year of the launch. What independent variables would you use to explain the profitability of these new products?

---

[8] We would like to thank Dr. D.I. Gilliland and AgriPro for making the data and case study available.

3. Imagine you are going to a client to present the findings of a regression model. The client believes that the regression model is a "black box" and that anything can be made significant. What would your reaction be?
4. I do not care about the assumptions – just give me the results! Please evaluate this statement. Do you agree?
5. Are all regression assumptions equally important? Please discuss.
6. Using standardized βs, we can compare effects between different variables. Can we really compare apples and oranges after all? Please discuss.
7. Run the ACSI example without deleting the outlier observation (i.e. using the full dataset with 1,640 observations) and compare the results with those presented above. Explain why deviations occur.

Further Readings

American Customer Satisfaction index at http://www.theacsi.org
This website contains scores of the American Satisfaction Index.
Hair, J. F., Black, W. C., Babin, B. J., & Anderson, R. E. (2010). *Multivariate data analysis. A global perspective* (7th ed.). Upper Saddle River, NJ: Pearson Prentice Hall.
This is an excellent book, which discusses many statistical terms from a theoretical perspective in a highly accessible manner.
Nielsen at http://www.nielsen.com
This is the website for Nielsen, one of the world's biggest market research companies. They publish many reports that use regression analysis.
The Food Marketing Institute at http://www.fmi.org
This website contains data, some of which can be used for regression analysis.

References

Aiken, L. S., & West, S. G. (1991). *Multiple regression: Testing and interpreting interactions.* Thousand Oaks, CA: Sage.
Cohen, J. (1994). The Earth is round (P < .05). *The American Psychologist, 49*(912), 997–1003.
Field, A. (2013). *Discovering statistics using SPSS* (4th ed.). London: Sage.
Fornell, C., Johnson, M. D., Anderson, E. W., Cha, J., & Johnson, B. E. (1996). The American customer satisfaction index: Nature, purpose, and findings. *Journal of Marketing, 60*(4), 7–18.
Green, S. B. (1991). How many subjects does it take to do a regression analysis? *Multivariate Behavioral Research, 26*(3), 499–510.
Greene, W. H. (2007). *Econometric analysis* (6th ed.). Upper Saddle River, NJ: Prentice Hall.
Hill, C., Griffiths, W., & Lim, G. C. (2008). *Principles of econometrics* (3rd ed.). Hoboken, NJ: Wiley.
Kelley, K., & Maxwell, S. E. (2003). Sample size for multiple regression: Obtaining regression coefficients that are accurate, not simply significant. *Psychological Methods, 8*(3), 305–321.
Mooi, E. A., & Frambach, R. T. (2009). A stakeholder perspective on buyer–supplier conflict. *Journal of Marketing Channels, 16*(4), 291–307.
Rigdon, E. E., Ringle, C. M., Sarstedt, M., & Gudergan, S. P. (2011). Assessing heterogeneity in customer satisfaction studies: Across industry similarities and within industry differences. *Advances in International Marketing, 22*, 169–194.
Ringle, C. M., Sarstedt, M., & Mooi, E. A. (2010). Response-based segmentation using FIMIX-PLS. Theoretical foundations and an application to ACSI data. *Annals of Information Systems, 8*, 19–49.

Factor Analysis

8

Learning Objectives

After reading this chapter, you should understand:
- The principles of exploratory and confirmatory factor analysis.
- The difference between principal components analysis and principal axis factoring.
- Key terms such as Eigenvalues, communality, factor loadings, and factor scores.
- How to determine whether data are suitable for carrying out an exploratory factor analysis.
- How to interpret SPSS factor analysis output.
- The principles of reliability analysis and how to carry it out in SPSS.
- The basic idea behind structural equation modeling.

Keywords

Anti-image • Bartlett's test of sphericity • Communality • Cronbach's Alpha • Eigenvalue • Exploratory and confirmatory factor analysis • Factor loadings • Factor scores • Kaiser criterion • Kaiser–Meyer–Olkin (KMO) criterion • Measure of sampling adequacy (MSA) • Orthogonal and oblique rotation • Partial least squares • Principal axis factoring • Principal components analysis • Reliability analysis • Scree plot • Structural equation modeling • Varimax and direct oblimin rotation

M. Sarstedt and E. Mooi, *A Concise Guide to Market Research*,
Springer Texts in Business and Economics, DOI 10.1007/978-3-642-53965-7_8,
© Springer-Verlag Berlin Heidelberg 2014

Soccer clubs no longer just compete on the sport field, but also compete for revenues from broadcasting and sponsoring rights, tickets, and merchandise. Running professional sporting clubs means managing corporate businesses and creating memorable experiences for fans. Therefore, managing fan satisfaction is of great importance to sport organizations. Based on a thorough literature review and an empirical study of soccer fans, Sarstedt et al. (2014) develop an index for measuring fan satisfaction. In the initial development stage, the authors use the results from a factor analysis to establish a preliminary measurement model which they subsequently revise using qualitative interviews. Using data from a second soccer fan sample, the proposed fan satisfaction (FANSAT) index is assessed and applied to predict fan attendance. The results of structural equation modeling analysis imply that aspects of the stadium, club management, and the fan-based support for the club are the most important determinants of fan satisfaction and therefore affect their leisure experiences.

8.1   Introduction

Factor analysis identifies unobserved (i.e., latent) variables that explain patterns of correlations within a set of observed variables. It is often used to identify a small number of latent variables that explain most of the variance embedded in a larger number of observed variables. Thus, factor analysis is about data reduction. It can also be used to generate hypotheses regarding the composition of factors. Furthermore, factor analysis is often used to screen variables for subsequent analysis (e.g., to identify collinearity prior to performing a linear regression analysis as discussed in Chap. 7).

There are three types of factor analyses we discuss, namely *exploratory factor analysis, confirmatory factor analysis*, and *structural equation modeling*. The first two techniques are identical from a statistical point of view; however, they are used in different ways. Exploratory factor analysis is used to reveal the number of factors and the variables that belong to specific factors. When we conduct a confirmatory factor analysis, we have clear expectations regarding the factor structure (e.g., because we make use of a previously used survey) and we want to test if the expected structure is indeed present. Structural equation modeling differs from those two techniques, both statistically and practically. It is used to evaluate how well observed variables relate to factors and what the relationships between the factors are. This technique will be briefly discussed at the end of this chapter.

In this chapter, we primarily deal with exploratory factor analysis, as it conveys the principles that underlie all factor analytic procedures. Two exploratory factor analytic procedures are commonly used in market research: *Principal components analysis* and *principal axis factoring*. Principal components and principal axis factoring essentially require the same analysis steps and involve the same interpretation but differ in their assumptions regarding the nature of the variables used in the analysis (we will discuss the differences between the two procedures later in this chapter). As the concept of principal components analysis is easier to understand, we focus on this approach.

8.2 Understanding Principal Components Analysis

In many situations, researchers face the problem of working with large questionnaires that comprise many *items*. For example, in a survey of a major German soccer club's marketing department, the management was particularly interested in identifying and evaluating performance features that relate to soccer fans' satisfaction (Sarstedt et al. 2014). Features that could be of importance include the stadium, the composition of the team and their success, the trainer, and the management. The marketing department therefore commissioned a questionnaire comprising 99 items that had been previously identified using literature databases and focus groups with various fans. All the items were measured on scales ranging from 1 ("very dissatisfied") to 7 ("very satisfied"). Table 8.1 shows an overview of selected items considered in the study.

Imagine you were a market researcher and were asked to identify features that relate to soccer fans' satisfaction. What would be the first thing to do? A first step would likely be to compute descriptive statistics to gain an overview of the dataset. You could compute the mean values of each item and rank these. You could then identify features with which fans are very dissatisfied and take measures to address these deficiencies. A problem with this approach is that the differences in the fans' satisfaction with features might only be marginal. Moreover, carrying out pairwise t-tests to evaluate whether these differences are significant is problematic considering the large number of items involved. In our example, comprising 99 items, we would have to carry out exactly 4,851 pairwise t-tests![1]

Furthermore, this approach does not help explain which features contribute most to the respondents' overall satisfaction. In order to address the latter question, you may use the item "Overall, how satisfied are you with your soccer club?" as a dependent variable and regress it on all items. However, this is likely to create the collinearity problem discussed in Chap. 7. Just by looking at the formulation of the items, we expect that many items are highly correlated. For example, satisfaction with the condition of the stadium (x_1), outer appearance of the stadium (x_2), and interior design of the stadium (x_3) cover similar aspects relating to the respondents' satisfaction with the stadium. If a soccer fan is generally very satisfied with the stadium, he/she will most likely answer all three items positively. Conversely, if a respondent is generally dissatisfied with the stadium, he/she is most likely to be rather dissatisfied with all the performance aspects of the stadium, such as the outer appearance and interior design. Consequently, these three items are most likely to

---

[1] This number is calculated as $k \cdot (k-1)/2$, with k being the number of items to compare.

Table 8.1 Items in the soccer fan satisfaction study

Satisfaction with...	
Condition of the stadium	Public appearances of the players
Interior design of the stadium	Number of stars in the team
Outer appearance of the stadium	Interaction of players with fans
Signposting outside the stadium	Volume of the loudspeakers in the stadium
Signposting inside the stadium	Choice of music in the stadium
Roofing inside the stadium	Entertainment program in the stadium
Comfort of the seats	Stadium speaker
Video score boards in the stadium	Newsmagazine of the stadium
Condition of the restrooms	Price of annual season ticket
Tidiness within the stadium	Entry fees
Size of the stadium	Offers of reduced tickets
View onto the playing field	Design of the home jersey
Number of restrooms	Design of the away jersey
Sponsors' advertisements in the stadium	Assortment of merchandise
Location of the stadium	Quality of merchandise
Name of the stadium	Prices of merchandise
Determination and commitment of the players	Pre-sale of tickets
Current success regarding matches	Online-shop
Identification of the players with the club	Opening times of the fan-shops
Quality of the team composition	Accessibility of the fan-shops
Presence of a player with whom fans can identify	Behavior of the sales persons in the fan shops

be highly correlated, as they cover related aspects of the respondents' overall satisfaction with the stadium. In other words, these items overlap considerably. This is where principal components analysis comes into play.

The basic idea of principal components analysis is to make use of these correlations to summarize sets of items using latent variables. As the name already suggests, these latent variables are not directly observable but each is inferred and based on several items. A latent variable is also called a *factor* or *component*. Technically, components and factors/latent variables refer to two different things but the more general term factor is most commonly used in the context of principal components analysis. Figure 8.1 displays the coherence between two factors and a set of items.

The upper part of the figure suggests that there is one factor (indicated by an oval) that relates directly to the three items x_1, x_2, and x_3 (indicated by boxes). These three items are likely to be highly correlated, as indicated by the arrows between them. We assume that these correlations are caused by an underlying factor, which is indicated by the arrows pointing from the factor to the items. Specifically, the items are reflecting the factor. Consequently, the items can be interpreted as manifestations of the factor with the factor capturing the "joint meaning" of the items related to it. In our example, the "joint meaning" of the three items could be described as *satisfaction with the stadium*, since the items represent somewhat different, yet related, aspects of this issue. Likewise, we can think of another factor that relates to another set of items as described in Fig. 8.1. This factor relates to two

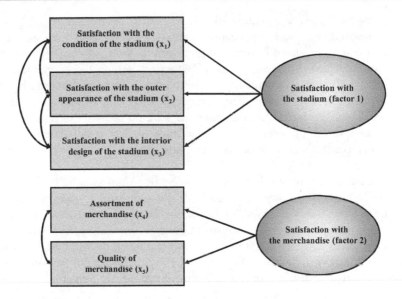

Fig. 8.1 Example of a factor model

items (x_4 and x_5), which, similarly to the first factor, share a common meaning. This common meaning is captured by the factor which we could label *satisfaction with the merchandise.* Such labeling is subjective and the researcher needs to find a term that captures the overlap in the items, which, according to the principal components analysis, belong together.

The basic idea of principal components analysis is to use clusters of large correlations between the items to compute factors that best represent the items in our dataset. Therefore, a certain amount of correlation is necessary to conduct a principal components analysis. Often, many items in a dataset are correlated with one another. Figure 8.1 therefore only indicates that there are high correlations between x_1, x_2, and x_3 on the one hand and x_4 and x_5 on the other. Other items, such as x_1 and x_4, are most likely somewhat correlated but to a lesser degree than the group of items x_1, x_2, and x_3 and the pair of x_4 and x_5.

Principal components analysis strives to reduce the correlation matrix down to underlying factors by looking at which variables cluster together in terms of increased correlations. Specifically, using the correlations between sets of items, principal components analysis extracts a number of factors, which can be considered latent variables capturing communalities of the complete item set. That's why we also talk about *factor extraction.* Initially, these factors are, by definition, uncorrelated so that each factor covers distinct and unrelated aspects.[2] This is a very important feature, as it means that factors are uncorrelated and thus, if we use

---

[2] Note that this changes when oblique rotation is used. We will discuss factor rotation later in this chapter.

them in regression analysis, collinearity is not an issue. Instead of using many highly correlated items as independent variables in a regression analysis, we can use only a few uncorrelated factors that represent the original item set. However, using only a few factors reduces accuracy. Naturally, these factors cannot represent all the information included in the items. Consequently, there is a trade-off between simplicity and accuracy. In order to make the analysis as simple as possible, we want to extract only a few factors. At the same time, we do not want to lose too much information by having too few factors. This trade-off has to be addressed in any principal components analysis when deciding how many factors should be extracted from the data.

In the example above, we do not have much prior knowledge of how the items relate to a factor or how many factors underlie the items (that's the basic idea of an exploratory factor analysis). We simply use all the items related to our research question and include them in the analysis. In practice, we usually have expectations of what the factor structure might look like and can test if the fit of a factor model with expectations is reasonable. We can do this by fixing the number of expected factors (e.g., two or five factors) and letting the principal components analysis determine which items belong to each factor.

After having decided on the number of factors to retain from the data, we can proceed with the interpretation of the factor solution. This requires us to come up with a label for each factor that best characterizes the joint meaning of all the variables associated with it. Often, this step is challenging but there are means that can facilitate the interpretation of the factor solution. Lastly, we have to assess how well the factors reproduce the data, which is done by examining the solution's goodness-of-fit. Figure 8.2 illustrates the steps involved in a principal components analysis; we will discuss these in more detail in the following sections.

Fig. 8.2 Steps involved in conducting a principal components analysis

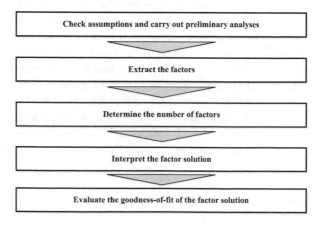

8.3   Conducting a Principal Components Analysis

8.3.1   Check Assumptions and Carry Out Preliminary Analyses

Before carrying out a principal components analysis, we have to consider several assumptions. Testing these assumptions requires answering the following questions:
- Are the measurement scales appropriate?
- Is the sample size sufficiently large?
- Are the observations independent?
- Are the variables sufficiently correlated?

Are the measurement scales appropriate?
To conduct a principal components analysis, it is best to have data measured on an interval or ratio scale. In practical applications, however, it has become common to also use items measured on an ordinal scale level. Ordinal scales can be used if:
- The scale points are equidistant, which means that the difference in the wording between scale steps is the same (see Chap. 3), *and*
- There are five or more response categories.

Is the sample size sufficiently large?
Another point of concern is the sample size. As a rule of thumb, the number of (valid) observations should be at least ten times the number of items used for analysis. This also includes a missing value analysis. Since it is generally recommended that cases with missing values should be excluded, this can greatly reduce the number of valid observable variables in our analysis.

Obviously, this rule of thumb provides only a rough indication regarding the necessary sample size. Fortunately, researchers have conducted studies to determine minimum sample size requirements dependent on other aspects of the study. MacCallum et al. (1999) suggest the following:
- When all communalities (we will discuss this term later) are above 0.60, small sample sizes of below 100 are adequate.
- With communalities around 0.50, sample sizes between 100 and 200 are sufficient.
- When communalities are consistently low, with many or all under 0.50, a sample size between 100 and 200 is adequate, provided that there is a small number of factors, each measured with six or more indicators.
- When communalities are consistently low and there is a high number of factors or the factors are measured with only few indicators (i.e., 3 or less), 300 observations are recommended.

Are the observations independent?
We have to ensure that the observations are independent. This means that the observations need to be completely unrelated (see Chap. 3). If we use dependent observations, we would introduce "artificial" correlations, which do not occur because of an underlying factor structure but because the same respondents answered the same questions multiple times.

Are the variables sufficiently correlated?

As indicated before, principal components analysis is based on correlations between items. Consequently, carrying out a principal components analysis only makes sense if the items are sufficiently correlated. The problem is how to decide what "sufficient" actually means.

An obvious step is to examine the *correlation matrix*. Naturally, we want correlations between different items to be as high as possible.[3] However, this will not always be the case. Regarding our previous example, we expect high correlations between x_1, x_2, and x_3, on the one hand, and x_4 and x_5 on the other. Conversely, we might expect lower correlations between, for example, x_1 and x_4 and between x_3 and x_5. Thus, not all elements of the correlation matrix necessarily have to have high values. The principal components analysis depends on the relative size of the correlations. Therefore, if single correlations are very low, this is not necessarily problematic. Only when all the correlations are around 0 principal components analysis stops being useful. In addition, the statistical significance of each correlation coefficient (indicated in the output produced by SPSS) helps decide whether it differs significantly from zero.

There are additional measures to determine whether the items are sufficiently correlated. One is the *anti-image*. The anti-image describes the portion of an item's variance that is independent of another item in the analysis. Obviously, we want all items to be highly correlated, so that an item's anti-images are as small as possible. This issue is captured in the anti-image matrices. Initially, we do not interpret these matrices directly but, instead, revert to two measures based on the concept of anti-image: *The Kaiser–Meyer–Olkin (KMO)* statistic and the *Bartlett's test of sphericity*. The KMO statistic, also called the *measure of sampling adequacy (MSA)*, indicates whether the correlations between variables can be explained by the other variables in the dataset. Kaiser (1974), who introduced the statistic, recommends a set of (very vividly labeled) threshold values for KMO and MSA, as presented in Table 8.2.

Table 8.2 Threshold values for KMO and MSA

KMO/MSA value	Adequacy of the correlations
Below 0.50	Unacceptable
0.50–0.59	Miserable
0.60–0.69	Mediocre
0.70–0.79	Middling
0.80–0.89	Meritorious
0.90 and higher	Marvelous

---

[3] When variables are perfectly correlated (the correlation is −1 or 1), factor analysis is not needed.

The *Bartlett's test of sphericity* can be used to test the null hypothesis that the correlation matrix is a diagonal matrix (i.e., all non-diagonal elements are zero) in the population. Since we need high correlations for principal components analysis, we want to reject the null hypothesis. A large test statistic value and corresponding a small p-value will favor the rejection of the hypothesis. In practical applications, it is virtually impossible not to reject this null hypothesis, as typically there are some correlations, particularly in larger sets of items. In addition, principal components analysis is typically used with large samples, a situation, which favors the rejection of the null hypothesis. Thus, Bartlett's test is of rather limited value for assessing whether the variables are sufficiently correlated. Moreover, since low test statistic values always go hand in hand with poor KMO values, one should rather rely on the latter criterion.

To summarize, the final decision of whether the data are appropriate for principal components analysis should be primarily based on the KMO statistic. Likewise, the correlation matrix with the associated significance levels provides a first insight into the correlation structures. If these measures indicate sufficiently correlated variables, we can continue the analysis of the results. If not, we should try to identify items that are only weakly correlated with the remaining items and remove them. In Box 8.1, we discuss how to do this.

Box 8.1 Identifying problematic items

Items that are only weakly correlated with the remaining items can be identified by examining the correlation matrix and the significance levels of correlations. A better approach, however, is to take another look at the anti-image correlation matrix. The diagonal elements of this matrix describe the *variable-specific MSA values*, which are interpreted like the overall KMO statistic (see Table 8.2). In fact, the KMO statistic is nothing but the overall mean of all item-specific MSA values. Consequently, all MSA values on the anti-image correlation matrix's diagonal should also lie above the threshold level of 0.50. If this is not the case, we should consider removing this item from the analysis. An item's *communality* (see next section) can also serve as a useful indicator of how well an item is represented by the factors extracted. However, communalities are more often considered when evaluating the solution's goodness-of-fit.

8.3.2 Extract the Factors

In a principal components analysis, factors are extracted in such a way that the variables' initial correlation matrix is reproduced in the best possible way. This means that the discrepancy between the initial and reproduced correlation matrix should be as small as possible. Operationally, the principal components analysis extracts factors step-by-step.

Fig. 8.3 Factor extraction

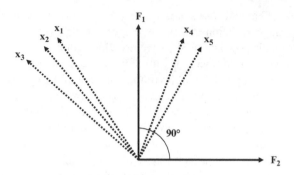

Specifically, the first factor is extracted in such a way that it maximizes the variance accounted for in the variables. We can easily visualize this by looking at the vector space illustrated in Fig. 8.3. In this example, we have five variables $(x_1, \ldots, x_5)$ that are represented by five vectors starting at the zero point (with each vector's length standardized to one). To maximize the variance accounted for, the first factor F_1 is fitted into this vector space in such a way that the sum of all the angles between this factor and the five variables in the vector space is minimized. This is done because we can interpret the angle between two vectors as correlations. For example, if the factor's vector and a variable's vector are congruent, the angle between these two is zero, indicating that the factor and the variable are perfectly correlated. On the other hand, if the factor and the variable are uncorrelated, the angle between these two is 90°. This correlation between factor and variables is referred to as the *factor loading*.

After the extraction of F_1, a second factor (F_2) is extracted which maximizes the remaining variance accounted for. The second factor is – by definition – independent from the first factor and, thus, is fitted into the vector space at a 90° angle (Fig. 8.3). If we extract a third factor, it would explain the maximum amount of the variance that has hitherto not been accounted for by factors 1 and 2. This one would also be fitted in a 90° angle from the first two factors. We don't illustrate this third factor in Fig. 8.3, as we would be looking at a three-dimensional space.[4] This procedure continues until as many factors as there are items (i.e., five) are extracted.

One important feature of the principal components analysis is that it works with standardized variables (see Chap. 5 for an explanation of what standardized variables are). The standardization of the variables is done automatically by SPSS, which means we do not have to bother with this. However, this characteristic has important implications for our analysis, since it helps us assess how much information a factor captures. This information is incorporated in a factor's *Eigenvalue*. An Eigenvalue describes how much variance is accounted for by a certain factor.

---

[4] Note that in Fig. 8.3, we consider a special case as the five variables are scaled down into a two-dimensional space. Actually, in this set-up, it would be possible to explain all five items by means of the two factors. However, in real-life, the five items span a five-dimensional vector space.

Likewise, the standardization of variables allows assessing how much of each variable's variance is captured or reproduced by the factors extracted. This is referred to as *communality*.

How can we interpret these two measures adequately? To answer this question, think of the soccer fan satisfaction study (Fig. 8.1). In the example, there are five variables. As all variables are standardized prior to the analysis, each has a variance of 1. In a simplified way, we could say that the overall information (i.e., variance) that we want to reproduce by means of factor extraction is 5 units. Let's assume that we extract the two factors presented above.

The first factor's Eigenvalue indicates how much variance of the total variance (i.e., 5 units) this factor accounts for. If this factor has an Eigenvalue of, let's say 2.10, it covers the information of 2.10 variables or, put differently, accounts for $2.10/5.00 = 42\%$ of the overall variance (Fig. 8.4).

Extracting a second factor will allow us to explain another part of the remaining variance (i.e., $5.00 - 2.10 = 2.90$ units, Fig. 8.4). However, the Eigenvalue of the second factor will always be smaller than that of the first factor. Assume that the second factor has an Eigenvalue of 1.30 units. The second factor then accounts for $1.30/5.00 = 26\%$ of the overall variance. Together, these two factors explain $(2.10 + 1.30)/5.00 = 68\%$ of the overall variance.

Every additional factor extracted, increases the variance accounted for until we have extracted as many factors as there are variables. In this case, the overall variance accounted for by the factors is 100%, which means that the complete variance is reproduced by the factors (Fig. 8.4).

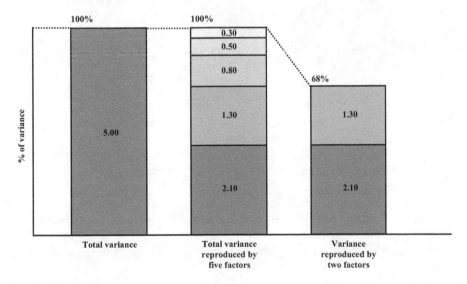

Fig. 8.4 Total variance explained by variables and factors

Following the principal components approach, we assume that each variable's entire variance can be reproduced by means of factor extraction. In other words, we assume that each variable's variance is common, that is, it is shared with other variables. As a consequence, variables do not have any unique variance. A different, but also popular, approach to factor analysis is *principal axis factoring* (also called *common factor analysis*). In Box 8.2, we contrast the two approaches to factor analysis and offer recommendations for choosing between them.

Box 8.2 Principal components analysis vs. principal axis factoring
Principal components analysis assumes that each variable's variance is common variance (i.e., variance shared with all the other variables in the analysis), which can be fully explained by means of factor extraction. Different from this, in principal axis factoring, each variable also has some specific variance (i.e., variance associated with only one specific variable) as well as error variance (i.e., variance due to measurement error). However, only the common variance, also referred to as communality, can be reproduced by means of factor extraction. Therefore, principal axis factoring draws on less variance in the extraction of factors than principal components analysis does. Figure 8.5 illustrates these concepts graphically. The extraction of factors follows the same principles as in principal components analysis and the interpretation of statistical measures such as KMO, Eigenvalues, or factor loadings are analogous.

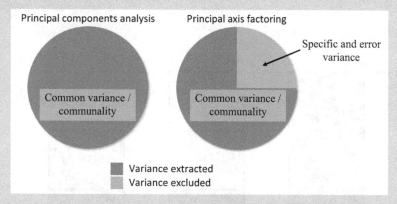

Fig. 8.5 Principal components analysis vs. principal axis factoring

From a theoretical perspective, the assumption that there is a unique variance, which cannot be fully accounted for by the factors is generally more realistic but, at the same time, more restrictive. Although theoretically sound, this restriction can sometimes lead to complications in the analysis

(continued)

Box 8.2 (continued)

which have contributed to the widespread use of principal components analysis, especially in market research practice.

Usually, researchers suggest using the principal components analysis when data reduction is the primary concern; that is, when the focus is to extract a minimum of factors that account for a maximum proportion of the variables' total variance. On the contrary, if the primary concern is to identify latent dimensions represented in the variables, principal axis factoring should be applied.[5] However, prior research has shown that both approaches arrive at essentially the same result when

- more than 30 variables are being used, *or*
- communalities exceed 0.60 for most variables.

With 20 or fewer variables and communalities below 0.40, differences are likely pronounced (Stevens 2009). As low communalities are undesirable and because of restrictive assumptions, we generally recommend using principal components analysis.

However, note that among researchers, feelings on the appropriateness of principal components analysis and principal axis factoring is strong. This is nicely summarized by Cliff (1987, p. 349) who notes that proponents of principal axis factoring "insist that components analysis is at best a common factor analysis with some error added and at worst an unrecognizable hodgepodge of things from which nothing can be determined."

Lastly, additional methods for carrying out factor analyses are available, such as the unweighted least squares, generalized least squares, or maximum likelihood approaches. However, these are statistically complex and inexperienced users should therefore not consider them. Mulaik (2009) provides an excellent (but rather technical) introduction to these advanced techniques.

Whereas the Eigenvalue tells us how much variance is accounted for by each factor, the *communality* indicates how much variance of each variable can be reproduced through factor extraction. There is no commonly agreed threshold for a variable's communality, as this depends strongly on the complexity of the analysis at hand. However, generally, at least 50% of a variable's variance should be accounted for through the extracted factors. Thus, the communalities should lie above 0.50. Every additional factor extracted will increase this variance and if we extract as many factors as there are items (in our example five), the communality of each variable would be 1.00. The variable will then be entirely explained by the

---

[5] Researchers often argue along the lines of measurement error when distinguishing between principal components analysis and principal axis factoring (e.g., Hair et al. 2010). However, as this distinction does not really have implications for market research studies, we omitted this argument.

factors extracted; that is, a certain amount of its variance will be explained by the first factor, another part by the second factor, and so on.

However, as our overall objective is to reduce the number of variables through factor extraction, we should rather extract only a few factors that account for a high degree of the overall variation. This raises the question of how to decide on the number of factors to extract from the data, which we discuss in the following section.

8.3.3   Determine the Number of Factors

The intuitive way to decide on the number of factors is to extract all factors with an Eigenvalue greater than one. The reason is that every factor with an Eigenvalue greater than one accounts for more variance than a single variable (remember, we are looking at standardized variables, which is why each variable's variance is exactly one). As the overall objective of principal components analysis is to reduce the overall number of variables, each factor should, of course, account for more variance than a single variable can. If this occurs, then this factor is useful for reducing the set of variables. Extracting all factors with an Eigenvalue greater than one is frequently called the *Kaiser criterion* or *latent root criterion* and is by far the most frequently used criterion to decide on the number of factors. However, the Kaiser criterion is well known to overspecify the number of factors; that is, the criterion suggests more factors than it should.

There are also alternative approaches to decide on the number of factors to extract. SPSS offers the possibility to plot each factor's Eigenvalue (y-axis) against the factor with which it is associated (x-axis). This results in a so-called *scree plot* that typically has a distinct break in it, thereby showing the "correct" number of factors. This distinct break is referred to as the "elbow" and it is generally recommended that all factors should be retained above this break, as they contribute most to the explanation of the variance in the dataset. Thus, we select one factor less than indicated by the elbow. In some situations, however, the distinct break is not clear-cut and we should instead rely on the Kaiser criterion.

In other situations, we might have a priori information regarding the number of factors we want to find, which might be the case in a situation in which we want to replicate a previous market research study. In this case, we should also be guided by the findings of this previous study. Thus, if we find four factors and a number of previous studies suggest that five are present, we should try to select five factors. Strictly speaking, this is a confirmatory approach to factor analysis. Ultimately however, we should not entirely rely on the data but keep in mind that the research results should be interpretable and actionable for market research practice. Whatever approach is used to determine the number of factors, the factors extracted should account for at least 50% of the total variance explained (75% or more is recommended).

There are also more advanced approaches such as *parallel analysis* and the *broken stick procedure*, which compare the Eigenvalues with those obtained from randomly generated data or the *minimum average partial test*. We discuss these approaches in the Web Appendix (⌂ Web Appendix → Chap. 8).

After having decided on the number of factors to retain from the data, we can proceed with the interpretation of the factor solution.

8.3.4   Interpret the Factor Solution

To interpret the solution of the principal components analysis, we have to determine which variables relate to each of the factors extracted. This is done by examining the *factor loadings*, which represent the correlations between the factors and the variables and, thus, can take values from -1 to $+1$. High factor loadings indicate that a variable is well represented by a certain factor. Subsequently, we look for high absolute values as the correlation between a variable and a factor can also be negative. Using the highest absolute factor loadings, we "assign" each variable to a certain factor and then try to come up with a label for each factor that best characterizes the joint meaning of all the variables associated with it. This labeling is subjective, but nevertheless a key step in principal components analysis. An example of a label is the respondents' satisfaction with the stadium that represents the items referring to its condition, outer appearance, and interior design.

To facilitate the interpretation of the factors, we can make use of *factor rotation*. We do not have to rotate the factor solution, but it will facilitate interpreting findings, particularly if we have a reasonably large number of items (say six or more). To understand what factor rotation is all about, reconsider the factor structure described in Fig. 8.3. Here, we see that both factors relate to the variables in the set. However, the first factor appears to be generally more strongly correlated with the variables, whereas the second factor is only weakly correlated with the variables (to clarify: we look for small angles between the factors and variables). This implies that we "assign" all variables to the first factor without taking the second one into consideration. This does not appear to be very meaningful, as we want both factors to represent certain facets of the variable set. This problem can be resolved by means of factor rotation. By rotating the factor axes, we can bring about a situation in which a set of variables is loaded highly on only one specific factor, whereas another set loads highly on another. Figure 8.6 illustrates the factor rotation graphically.

On the left hand side of the figure, we can see that both factors are rotated $49°$ orthogonally, meaning that a $90°$ angle between the factors is sustained during the rotation procedure. Consequently, the factors remain uncorrelated, which is in line with the initial objective of the principal components analysis. By rotating the first factor from F_1 to $F_{1'}$, it is now strongly related to variables x_1, x_2, and x_3 but weakly

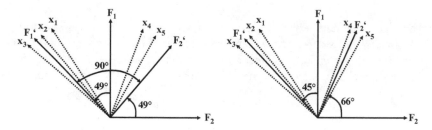

Fig. 8.6 Orthogonal and oblique factor rotation

related to x_4 and x_5. Conversely, by rotating the second factor from F_2 to $F_{2'}$, it is now strongly related to x_4 and x_5 but weakly related to the remaining variables. The assignment of the variables is now much clearer, which facilitates the interpretation of the factors significantly.

Various *orthogonal rotation* methods exist which differ with regard to their treatment of the loading structure. The *varimax* procedure is the most prominent one; this procedure aims at maximizing the dispersion of loadings within factors. Other orthogonal rotation methods include the quartimax or equamax procedures. See the SPSS help option for more information on these procedures' properties.

Alternatively, we can choose an *oblique rotation* technique. In this approach, the 90° angle between the factors is not maintained during rotation and the resulting factors are therefore correlated. Figure 8.6 (right hand side) illustrates an example of an oblique factor rotation. *Direct oblimin* is the most commonly used oblique rotation technique. Here, researchers have to specify a constant δ (pronounced as *delta*), which determines the level of correlation allowed between the factors. The default value of zero ensures that the factors are – if at all – only moderately correlated, which is acceptable for most analyses. For example, it is very likely that the respondents' satisfaction with the stadium is unrelated to their satisfaction with other aspects of a soccer club, such as the number of stars in the team or the quality of merchandise. However, giving up the initial objective of extracting uncorrelated factors can diminish the interpretability of the factors.

> We recommend using the varimax rotation to enhance the interpretability of the results. Only if the results are difficult to interpret, should an oblique rotation be applied.

After rotating the factors we need to interpret the factors. Interpreting factors is usually the most challenging step in a principal components analysis, as the assignment of variables is often not clear-cut. Sometimes it is reasonable to assign a variable to another factor even though it does not load highly on this specific factor. While this can help to increase the results' face validity, we should make sure that the variable's factor loading with the designated factor is above an acceptable level. With very few factors extracted, the loading should be at least 0.50, but with a high number of factors, lower loadings of above 0.30 are acceptable. In other situations, it might even be worthwhile simply ignore a certain variable as it does not nicely fit with the factor structure we found. In such a situation, we might re-run the analysis without variables that do not load highly on one specific factor. In the end, the results should be interpretable and actionable, but keep in mind that this technique is first and foremost exploratory!

Following the rotation and interpretation of the factors, we can consider another important element of the analysis, the *factor scores*. The factor scores are standardized to a mean of zero. This means that if a respondent has a value greater than 0 for a certain factor, he/she exhibits the characteristic described by the factor above the average. Conversely, if a factor score is below 0 then this respondent exhibits the characteristic below average. There are different procedures to produce factor scores but we suggest using the *regression method*, as this method is the most commonly used and easily understood approach.[6]

Factor scores are frequently used in subsequent analyses. For example, instead of calculating the average for x_1, x_2, and x_3 and using this as a construct value, we can use the factor scores of *satisfaction with the stadium*. The scores of the uncorrelated factors, instead of highly correlated predictor variables, can specifically be used if the objective of the principal components analysis is to overcome collinearity problems in an OLS regression.

8.3.5 Evaluate the Goodness-of-fit of the Factor Solution

The overall objective of principal components analysis is to extract factors in such a way that the factors and their loadings reproduce the correlations in the best possible way. Consequently, we can make use of the differences between the correlations in the data and those implied by the factors to assess the solution's goodness-of-fit. We require the absolute difference between the observed and reproduced correlation coefficients (the *residuals*) to be as small as possible. In practice, we check the proportion of the correlation matrices' residuals with an absolute value higher than 0.05. Even though there is no rule of thumb regarding the maximum proportion, a proportion of more than 50% should raise concern. However, low correlations and an unsatisfactory KMO measure usually go hand in hand with high residuals; consequently, this problem typically already surfaces when testing of assumptions.

Furthermore, we should consider each variable's communality, which should, of course, be as high as possible. However, if several communalities exhibit low values, we should consider removing these variables. To help make that decision,

---

[6] Alternative procedures include the *Bartlett method* and the *Anderson–Rubin method*, which are designed to overcome potential problems associated with the regression technique. However, these problems are of rather theoretical nature and of little importance to market research practice.

we could take the variable-specific MSA measures into account. There is no minimum value for a variable's communality, as the values usually depend on the number of variables considered. If there are more variables in your dataset, communalities usually become smaller, however, if your factor solution accounts for less than 30% of a variable's variance (i.e., the variable's communality is less than 0.30), it is worthwhile reconsidering your set-up. In Table 8.3 we summarize the main steps that need to be taken when conducting a factor analysis using SPSS.

Table 8.3 Steps involved in carrying out a factor analysis in SPSS

Theory	SPSS
Research problem	
Select variables that should be reduced to a set of underlying factors (principal factor analysis) or that should be used to identify underlying dimensions (principal axis factoring)	Enter the variables into the Variables box in the Factor Dialog Box: ▶ Analyze ▶ Dimension Reduction ▶ Factor.
Assumptions	
Are the variables interval or ratio scaled?	Determine the measurement level of your variables (see Chap. 3). If ordinal variables are used, make sure that the scale steps are equidistant.
Missing value analysis	Check descriptive statistics output for the number of valid cases out of the total number of cases: ▶ Analyze ▶ Dimension Reduction ▶ Factor ▶ Descriptives ▶ Univariate descriptives
Is the sample size sufficiently large?	Check that the number of valid observations is at least ten times the number of items.
Are the observations independent?	Determine whether the observations are dependent or independent (see Chap. 3).
Are the variables sufficiently correlated?	▶ Analyze ▶ Dimension Reduction ▶ Factor ▶ Descriptives ▶ Coefficients | Significance levels | KMO and Bartlett's test of sphericity | Anti-image. – Are correlation coefficients' p-values ≤ 0.05? – Is the KMO ≥ 0.50? – Is the p-value of the Bartlett's test ≤ 0.05? – Are the variable-specific MSA values ≥ 0.50?
Specification	
Handle missing values	Delete missing values listwise: ▶ Analyze ▶ Dimension Reduction ▶ Factor ▶ Options ▶ Exclude cases listwise

(continued)

Table 8.3 (continued)

Theory	SPSS
Choose the method of factor analysis	If the scope of the analysis is to reduce the number of variables: ▶ Analyze ▶ Dimension Reduction ▶ Factor ▶ Extraction ▶ Principal components.
	If the scope of the analysis is to identify underlying dimensions: ▶ Analyze ▶ Dimension Reduction ▶ Factor ▶ Extraction ▶
Determine the number of factors	Extract all factors with an Eigenvalue greater than one (default) and create a scree plot ▶ Analyze ▶ Dimension Reduction ▶ Factor ▶ Extraction ▶ Scree plot Alternatives: – Pre-specify the number of factors based on a priori information: ▶ Analyze ▶ Data Reduction ▶ Factor ▶ Extraction ▶ Factors to extract – Extract factors that jointly account for at least 50% (75% recommended) of the total variance: Examine the plot Total Variance Explained. – Split-half reliability: Split up the dataset in two halves of equal size and carry out separate factor analyses.
Rotate the factors	Use the varimax procedure or, if necessary, choose the direct oblimin procedure with $\delta = 0$: ▶ Analyze ▶ Dimension Reduction ▶ Factor ▶ Rotation
Assign variables to factors	Use the rotated solution to assign each variable to a certain factor based on the highest absolute loading. To facilitate interpretation, you may also assign a variable to a different factor but check that the loading lies at an acceptable level (0.50 if only few factors are extracted, 0.30 if many factors are extracted).
Compute factor scores	Save factor scores as new variables using the regression method: ▶ Analyze ▶ Dimension Reduction ▶ Factor ▶ Scores ▶ Save as variables: Regression
Checking results	
Determine the number of factors	Check the factors' Eigenvalues, the % of variance and the cumulative % explained: Examine the scree plot. Consider using more advanced approaches such as parallel analysis.
Interpret the factors	Consider the rotated component matrix and find an umbrella term for clusters of items assigned to each factor.
Checking goodness-of-fit	

(continued)

Table 8.3 (continued)

Theory	SPSS
Check the congruence of the initial and reproduced correlations	Create reproduced correlation matrix: ▶ Analyze ▶ Dimension Reduction ▶ Factor ▶ Descriptives ▶ Reproduced Is the proportion of residuals greater than $0.05 \leq 50\%$?
Check how much of each variable's variance is reproduced by means of factor extraction	Examine the communalities. Check if communalities are greater than 0.50.

8.4   Confirmatory Factor Analysis and Reliability Analysis

Many researchers and practitioners acknowledge the prominent role that factor analysis plays in exploring data structures. Data can be analyzed without preconceived ideas regarding the number of factors or how they relate to the variables under consideration. Whereas this approach is exploratory in nature, the *confirmatory factor analysis* (often simply referred to as *CFA*) allows for testing hypothesized structures underlying a set of variables.

Consequently, in a confirmatory factor analysis, the researcher needs to first specify the factors and their associations with variables, which should be based on previous measurements or theoretical considerations. Instead of allowing the procedure to determine the number of factors, as is done in an exploratory factor analysis, the confirmatory factor analysis tells us how well the actual data fit the pre-specified structure. Reverting to our introductory example, we could, for example, assume that the construct *satisfaction with the stadium* can be measured using the three items x_1, x_2, and x_3 (without having carried out an exploratory factor analysis beforehand!). Likewise, we could hypothesize that *satisfaction with the merchandise* can be adequately measured using the items x_4 and x_5. In a confirmatory factor analysis, we set up a theoretical model (also referred to as measurement model) linking the items with the respective construct.

> In confirmatory factor analysis, researchers generally use the term construct rather than factor.

This process is also called operationalization (see Chap. 3) and usually involves drawing a visual representation (called a *path diagram*) indicating the expected relationships. This path diagram is very similar to the model presented in Fig. 8.1. In a confirmatory factor analysis, constructs (e.g., Y_1, satisfaction with the stadium) are presented as circles or ovals, and measured variables (*xs*) are presented as boxes. Other elements include the relationships between the constructs and respective items (i.e., the loadings *l*), the error terms (i.e., *e*) that capture the extent to which a construct does not explain the item, and the correlations between the constructs of interest (i.e., *r*). Figure 8.7 shows the expected relationship between the measured variables and constructs.

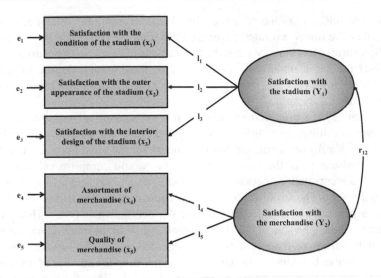

Fig. 8.7 Example of a path diagram

Having defined the individual constructs and developed the overall measurement model, the researcher needs to gather data. This allows the model parameters to be estimated. In this respect, the relationships between the constructs and items (i.e., the loadings) and the item correlations are of particular interest as they indicate whether the construct has been reliably and validly measured.

An important element of a confirmatory factor analysis, which is crucial when working with scales, is the reliability analysis. Unlike the confirmatory factor analysis, which requires special software such as AMOS, LISREL or EQS, a reliability analysis (see Chap. 3 for a discussion of reliability) can easily be carried out using SPSS. The preferred way to evaluate reliability is to make two independent measurements (using the same subjects) and to compare the measurements through correlations. This is also referred to as test-retest reliability (see Chap. 3). However, practicalities often stop researchers from surveying their subjects for a second time.

An alternative is to use the *split-half approach*. In the split-half approach, scale items are divided into halves and the scores of the halves are correlated to obtain an estimate of reliability. As all items should be consistent in what they indicate about the construct, the halves can be considered approximations of alternative forms of the same scale. Consequently, instead of looking at the scale's test-retest reliability, researchers consider the scale's equivalence, showing to which extent two measures of the same general trait agree. We call this type of reliability the *internal consistency reliability*.

In the example of "satisfaction with the stadium," we could compute this scale's split-half reliability manually by, for example, splitting up the scale into

x_1 on the one side, and x_2 and x_3 on the other. We then compute the sum of x_2 and x_3 (or calculate the items' average) to form a total score and correlate this score with x_1. A high correlation indicates that the two subsets of items are measuring related aspects of the same underlying construct and, thus, a high degree of internal consistency. However, this example suggests that the results strongly depend on how the items are split.

Cronbach (1951) proposed calculating the average of all possible split-half coefficients resulting from different ways of splitting the sample's scale items. The *Cronbach's Alpha* coefficient has become by far the most popular measure of internal consistency. In the example above, this would comprise calculating the average of the correlations between (1) x_1 and x_2+x_3, (2) x_2 and x_1+x_3, as well as (3) x_3 and x_1+x_2. The Cronbach's Alpha coefficient generally varies from 0 to 1, whereas a generally agreed lower limit for the coefficient is 0.70.[7] However, in exploratory studies, a value of 0.60 is acceptable, while in the more advanced stages of research, values of 0.80 or higher are regarded as satisfactory. One issue of assessing Cronbach's Alpha is its tendency to increase as the number of items in the scale increases. Consequently, researchers have to impose more stringent requirements (i.e., higher threshold values for Cronbach's Alpha) for scales with a large number of items. In particular, scales with more than ten items, should have a Cronbach's Alpha of least 0.80. In Box 8.3, we provide some further advice on the use of Cronbach's Alpha. We will illustrate a reliability analysis using the standard SPSS module in the example at the end of this chapter.

Box 8.3 Calculating Cronbach's Alpha

When calculating Cronbach's Alpha, ensure that all items are formulated in the same direction (positively or negatively worded). For example, in psychological measurement, it is common to use both negatively and positively worded items in a questionnaire. These need to be reversed prior to the reliability analysis. In SPSS, this can be achieved using the **Recode** option discussed in Chap. 5. Furthermore, we have to be aware of potential subscales in our item set. Some multi-item scales comprise subsets of items that measure different facets of a multidimensional construct. For example, soccer fan satisfaction is a multidimensional construct that includes aspects such as satisfaction with the stadium, the merchandise (as described above), the team, and the coach. Each of these dimensions is measured by means of different sets of items, which have to be evaluated separately with regard to internal consistency. Calculating one Cronbach's Alpha value of all 99 items would certainly be inappropriate. Cronbach's Alpha is always calculated over the items belonging to one construct and not all items in the dataset!

---

[7] Note that in extreme cases, Alpha can also take on negative values.

8.5   Structural Equation Modeling

Whereas a confirmatory factor analysis involves testing if and how items relate to specific constructs, structural equation modeling (SEM) involves the estimation of relations between these constructs. It has become one of the most important methods in the social sciences, including marketing research.

There are two approaches for estimating structural models. Covariance-based SEM (CB-SEM), also referred to as linear structural relations (LISREL) owing to its corresponding software application, and partial least squares SEM (PLS-SEM). Both estimation methods are based on the idea of an underlying model that allows the researcher to model, verify, and measure causal relationships between multiple items and constructs.

Figure 8.8 shows an example path model with four constructs and their respective items (note that we omitted the error terms for clarity's sake). A path model incorporates two types of constructs (1) Exogenous constructs (here: satisfaction with the stadium (Y_1) and satisfaction with the merchandise (Y_2)) that do not depend on other constructs and (2) endogenous constructs (here: fan loyalty (Y_3)) that depend on one or more exogenous (or other endogenous) constructs. The relations between the constructs (indicated with p) are called inner relations, while the relations between the constructs and their respective items (indicated with l) are called outer relations. One can distinguish between the structural model (also inner model) that incorporates the relations between the constructs and the (exogenous and endogenous) measurement models (also outer models) that represent the relations between the constructs and their related items. Items that measure constructs are labeled x. For reasons of clarity and comprehensiveness, we omitted the error terms of the items in Fig. 8.8. In this model, we assume that the two exogenous constructs *satisfaction with the stadium* and *satisfaction with the merchandise* relate to the endogenous construct *fan loyalty*. Depending on the research question, we could, of course, incorporate additional exogenous and endogenous constructs. Using data from an empirical survey, we could test this model and, thus, evaluate the exogenous constructs' influence on the endogenous construct. By doing so, we could assess which of the two constructs, Y_1 or Y_2, exerts the greater influence on Y_3. This could guide us in developing marketing plans in order to increase fan loyalty by answering the research question whether we should rather concentrate on increasing the fans' satisfaction with the stadium or with the merchandise.

The results evaluation of a path model analysis requires several steps that include the assessment of both measurement models and the structural model. Diamantopoulos and Siguaw (2000) and Hair et al. (2010) provide a thorough description of this approach and its application. Hair et al. (2014) provide a step-by-step introduction on how to set up and test path models using PLS-SEM. Hair et al. (2011, 2012a, 2012b) and Ringle et al. (2012) provide insights into the principles of PLS-SEM and its use in a variety of disciplines.

Lastly, it should be noted that confirmatory factor analysis and structural equation modeling primarily involve the testing of a hypothesized model based on theoretical

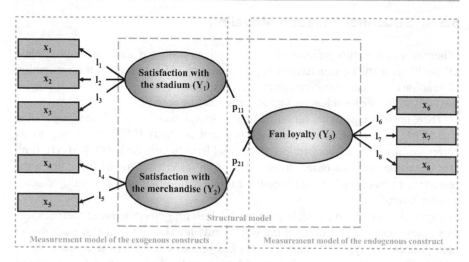

Fig. 8.8 Path model (structural equation modeling)

reasoning, which is more the domain of academic research than business practice. Consequently, these procedures currently play a limited role in market research practice, although this is expected to grow as the investigation of complex model set-ups becomes increasingly important to gain consumer insights and competitive advantages.

8.6   Example

In this example, we take a closer look at some of the items from our soccer fan satisfaction study (*soccer_fan_satisfaction.sav*, ⊕ Web Appendix → Chap. 8). For each of the following items, the respondents had to rate their degree of satisfaction from 1 ("very unsatisfied") to 7 ("very satisfied"). The performance features comprise the respondents' satisfaction with the following features (variable names in parentheses):

– Condition of the stadium (x_1),
– Outer appearance of the stadium (x_2),
– Interior design of the stadium (x_3),
– Quality of the team composition (x_4),
– Number of stars in the team (x_5),
– Price of annual season ticket (x_6), and
– Entry fees (x_7).

The complete item set was presented to various clubs' soccer fans. The selection of the respondents comprised fans of several German soccer clubs. Invitations to participate in the study were posted on various Internet fan forums. Of the 953 people who participated in the study, 495 completed the survey. Since the link to the survey appeared in several club-affiliated Internet forums, the database had to be reduced further to avoid having too many fans from the same clubs. In total, the market research agency selected 251 observations for further analysis. Let us use that dataset to run a principal components analysis.

8.6.1 Principal Components Analysis

To run the principal components analysis, simply click on ▶ Analyze ▶ Dimension Reduction ▶ Factor, which will open a dialog box similar to Fig. 8.9. Next, enter all seven variables into the **Variables** box.

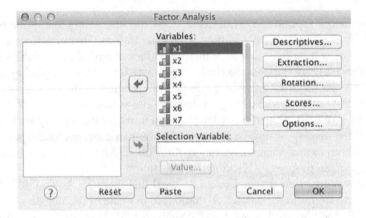

Fig. 8.9 Factor analysis dialog box

SPSS provides several options that directly relate to Table 8.3. Under **Descriptives**, you can choose to display univariate descriptive statistics (menu function: **Univariate descriptives**), which is a useful way of gaining an overview of the extent of the missing values in your dataset. Furthermore, you can choose from several outputs and statistical measures that relate to the correlation matrix and help assess the data's appropriateness for the analysis. Be sure to check the **Coefficients**, **Significance levels**, **Reproduced** (which refers to the reproduced correlation matrix), **Anti-image**, as well as the **KMO and Bartlett's test of sphericity** boxes to check the assumptions. All other options are of minor importance, so skip these and click **Continue**.

The **Extraction** option allows you to specify the analysis method. By default, SPSS selects **Principal components**; however, you can also set it to different types in the **Method** drop-down menu. Under **Extract**, you can determine the rule for factor extraction: By default, all factors with an Eigenvalue greater than one will be extracted. This default option is acceptable – except when you have previous information on the factor structure. If so, you should specify the number of factors manually. Under **Display**, you should check the scree plot option, which provides additional help in determining the number of factors to extract.[8] Now click **Continue** to access the main menu again.

Under **Rotation**, you can choose between several orthogonal and oblique rotation methods. Always use the **Varimax** procedure – unless your initial solution is difficult to interpret and you have strong theoretical grounds for assuming (moderately) correlated factors. Click **Continue**.

> If you wish to use factor scores in subsequent analyses, you can save these in the **Scores** option. Since we strongly recommend using the regression method, choose **Save as variables** and **Regression**, followed by **Continue**.

Lastly, under **Options**, you can decide how missing values should be handled and specify the display format of the coefficients in the component matrix. In this analysis, we exclude cases that have missing values in any of the variables used in any of the analyses (Option: **Exclude cases listwise**). Avoid replacing missing values with the mean as this will diminish the variation in the data, especially if there are many missing values in your dataset. You should always check the menu **Sorted by size** (under **Coefficient Display Format**), as this greatly increases the clarity of the display of results. If you wish, you can suppress loadings less than 0.10; however, in this example, we ignore this option. After having specified all the options, you can proceed by clicking the **OK** button.

The descriptive statistics in Table 8.4 reveal that there are several observations with missing values in the dataset. According to our rule of thumb, we would need $7 \cdot 10 = 70$ observations. Likewise, as the analysis will show, all communalities are uniformly high (i.e., above 0.60), which suggests that 100 observations are sufficient to run the analysis. As there are 195 observations without any missing values in the dataset (last column on the right in Table 8.4), we can proceed with checking the variables' correlations. The correlation matrix in Table 8.5 indicates that there are several pairs of variables that are highly correlated. For example, condition of the stadium (x_1) is highly correlated with the outer appearance (x_2, correlation $= 0.783$), as well as the interior design (x_3, correlation $= 0.754$) of the stadium. Likewise, x_2 and x_3 are highly correlated (correlation $= 0.762$). As these variables' correlations with the remaining ones are less pronounced, we may suspect that these three variables constitute one factor. As you can see, by just looking at the correlation matrix, we can already see what factor structure might result.

However, at this point of the analysis, we are more interested in checking whether the variables are sufficiently correlated to conduct a principal components analysis. When we look at the lower part of Table 8.5, we see that the p-values are extremely low. These results indicate that the variables are sufficiently correlated. However, for a concluding evaluation, we need to take the anti-image and related statistical measures into account. These are presented in Tables 8.6 and 8.7.

---

[8] Check the ⌀ Web Appendix (→ Chapter 8) for an application of more advanced methods for determining the number of factors.

Table 8.4 Descriptive statistics

Descriptive Statistics

	Mean	Std. Deviation	Analysis N
x1	5.39	1.962	195
x2	5.50	1.795	195
x3	5.02	1.905	195
x4	4.65	1.718	195
x5	4.56	1.864	195
x6	4.43	1.614	195
x7	4.22	1.509	195

Table 8.5 Correlation matrix

Correlation Matrix

		x1	x2	x3	x4	x5	x6	x7
Correlation	x1	1.000	.783	.754	.395	.338	.246	.172
	x2	.783	1.000	.762	.445	.350	.238	.224
	x3	.754	.762	1.000	.445	.329	.287	.235
	x4	.395	.445	.445	1.000	.829	.311	.241
	x5	.338	.350	.329	.829	1.000	.304	.214
	x6	.246	.238	.287	.311	.004	1.000	.696
	x7	.172	.224	.235	.241	.214	.696	1.000
Sig. (1-tailed)	x1		.000	.000	.000	.000	.000	.008
	x2	.000		.000	.000	.000	.000	.001
	x3	.000	.000		.000	.000	.000	.000
	x4	.000	.000	.000		.000	.000	.000
	x5	.000	.000	.000	.000		.000	.001
	x6	.000	.000	.000	.000	.000		.000
	x7	.008	.001	.000	.000	.001	.000	

The analysis results in Table 8.6 reveal that the KMO value is 0.721, which is middling (see Table 8.2) but still satisfactory. Likewise, the variable-specific MSA values (Table 8.7) on the diagonal of the anti-image correlation matrix are all above the threshold value of 0.50. Not surprisingly the Bartlett's test is significant ($p < 0.05$), which means that we can reject the null hypothesis that, in the population, all variables are uncorrelated. Consequently, we know that the data are appropriate for principal components analysis.

We can now take a look at the factor extraction process table.

Table 8.6 KMO and Bartlett's test measures

KMO and Bartlett's Test		
Kaiser-Meyer-Olkin Measure of Sampling Adequacy.		.721
Bartlett's Test of Sphericity	Approx. Chi-Square	809.353
	df	21
	Sig.	.000

Table 8.7 Anti-image matrices

Anti-image Matrices								
		x1	x2	x3	x4	x5	x6	x7
Anti-image Covariance	x1	.321	-.153	-.127	.023	-.032	-.032	.039
	x2	-.153	.308	-.120	-.033	.007	.033	-.042
	x3	-.127	-.120	.337	-.054	.038	-.031	-.008
	x4	.023	-.033	-.054	.275	-.229	-.007	-.011
	x5	-.032	.007	.038	-.229	.304	-.036	.012
	x6	-.032	.033	-.031	-.007	-.036	.479	-.329
	x7	.039	-.042	-.008	-.011	.012	-.329	.507
Anti-image Correlation	x1	.787[a]	-.488	-.385	.077	-.101	-.082	.096
	x2	-.488	.798[a]	-.373	-.113	.024	.086	-.105
	x3	-.385	-.373	.824[a]	-.177	.119	-.076	-.018
	x4	.077	-.113	-.177	.672[a]	-.793	-.018	-.028
	x5	-.101	.024	.119	-.793	.638[a]	-.094	.031
	x6	-.082	.086	-.076	-.018	-.094	.647[a]	-.668
	x7	.096	-.105	-.018	-.028	.031	-.668	.607[a]

a. Measures of Sampling Adequacy(MSA)

Table 8.8 lists the Eigenvalues associated with each factor before extraction, after extraction, and after rotation. In the columns labeled **Initial Eigenvalues,** we see the results before extraction. SPSS lists all seven factors (we know that there are potentially as many factors as there are variables) in this column. Most of these factors are of course only of minor importance. This is reflected in each factor's Eigenvalue, which is displayed in the table's second column. Here, we see that the first factor has an Eigenvalue of 3.520. As there are seven variables in our dataset, this factor accounts for $3.520/7.00 = 50.290\%$ of the overall variance, which is indicated in the third column. It is quite remarkable that by using only one factor instead of seven variables, we can account for over 50% of the overall variance! The second factor has an Eigenvalue of 1.415 and, thus, still covers more variance than a single variable (remember: Since we are looking at standardized variables, each variable has a variance of 1). The same holds for the third factor whose Eigenvalue lies at 1.135. Factors 4–7, however, only marginally account for the total variance explained, as their Eigenvalues are considerably smaller than 1.

Table 8.8 Results of factor extraction

Total Variance Explained

Component	Initial Eigenvalues			Extraction Sums of Squared Loadings			Rotation Sums of Squared Loadings		
	Total	% of Variance	Cumulative %	Total	% of Variance	Cumulative %	Total	% of Variance	Cumulative %
1	3.520	50.290	50.290	3.520	50.290	50.290	2.527	36.096	36.096
2	1.415	20.217	70.507	1.415	20.217	70.507	1.831	26.162	62.258
3	1.135	16.220	86.727	1.135	16.220	86.727	1.713	24.469	86.727
4	.312	4.450	91.177						
5	.257	3.666	94.844						
6	.208	2.969	97.812						
7	.153	2.188	100.000						

Extraction Method: Principal Component Analysis.

The second set of columns, labeled **Extraction Sums of Squared Loadings**, contains the factor solutions after extraction. Since we chose the default option, SPSS extracts all factors with an Eigenvalue greater than 1 (the Kaiser criterion discussed previously). This leads to a solution in which three factors are extracted, which account for 86.727% of the overall variance. The final part of the table, labeled **Rotation Sums of Squared Loadings**, displays the factors after rotation. Rotation is carried out to optimize the factor structure in order to facilitate the interpretation of the factor solution. Rotation usually alters the factors' Eigenvalues, but will not change the total variance explained. For example, the third factor accounted for 16.220% of the overall variance before rotation; however, after rotation, it accounts for 24.469%.

Whereas the Kaiser criterion offers one possibility to determine the number of factors to extract, we can also use the scree plot (Fig. 8.10) to help making that decision. In the scree plot the curve steeply slopes downward, then levels off for four factors. Since we always extract one factor less than indicated by the elbow, a three-factor solution is deemed appropriate.[9] As this is in accordance with the Kaiser criterion, we can continue evaluating the results by interpreting the factors.

To do so, take a look at the initial component matrix (Table 8.9), that is, the loadings matrix before factor rotation. In order to interpret the factors, we first "assign" each variable to a certain factor based on its maximum absolute factor loading. After that, we have to find an umbrella term for each factor that best describes the set of variables associated with that factor. Looking at Table 8.9, we see that x_1 through x_5 show the highest loadings for the first factor, whereas the other variables load highly on the second factor. However, what about the third factor? Should it be excluded? It probably should not, as this is a typical example of how an unrotated solution can be misleading. If you take a look at the rotated solution (Table 8.10), a different picture emerges. In this case, only x_1, x_2, and x_3 load highly on the first factor, whereas x_4 and x_5 load on the second, and x_6 and x_7 on the third factor. Comparing the loadings in the unrotated and rotated solution

---

[9] In the ⌀ Web Appendix (→ Chapter 8), we illustrate the use of the parallel analysis, the broken stick method, and the minimum average partial test for determining the number of factors using this dataset.

Fig. 8.10 Scree plot

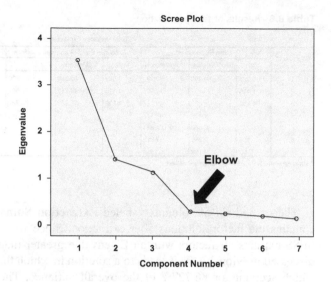

Table 8.9 Unrotated factor loadings matrix

Component Matrix[a]

	Component		
	1	2	3
x2	.814	−.369	.230
x3	.813	−.326	.256
x1	.792	−.398	.253
x4	.750	.078	−.586
x5	.680	.135	−.665
x7	.485	.718	.326
x6	.555	.688	.248

Extraction Method: Principal Component
Analysis.
a. 3 components extracted.

reveals that the differences in the loadings are quite remarkable. As you can see, the
rotation greatly facilitates the results interpretation. The unrotated solution is only
used to determine the number of factors to extract from the dataset. Since the
rotation changes the factors' Eigenvalues, the unrotated solution might indicate
another number of factors to retain from the data than those indicated by the rotated
solution. You see this by comparing the first two and the third set of columns in
Table 8.8 (**Initial Eigenvalues** and **Extraction Sums of Squared Loadings** rather
than **Rotation Sums of Squared Loadings**).

Table 8.10 Rotated factor loadings matrix

Rotated Component Matrix[a]

	Component		
	1	2	3
x1	.903	.167	.083
x2	.895	.201	.107
x3	.880	.185	.152
x5	.166	.937	.132
x4	.280	.902	.142
x7	.102	.077	.917
x6	.139	.177	.890

Extraction Method: Principal Component
Analysis.
Rotation Method: Varimax with Kaiser
Normalization.
a. Rotation converged in 4 iterations.

Having identified which variables load highly on which factor in the rotated solution, we should now try to identify labels for each factor. Variables condition of the stadium (x_1), outer appearance of the stadium (x_2), and interior design of the stadium (x_3) clearly relate to the stadium as such. This seems to be the factor that we mentioned in the introduction of this chapter. Therefore, we could label this *satisfaction with the stadium*. Quality of the team composition (x_4) and number of stars in the team (x_5) describe traits of the soccer team that the respondents evaluated. Even though there are certainly more facets to it, we could label this factor *satisfaction with the team*. The remaining variables, that is, price of annual season ticket (x_6), and entry fees (x_7) relate to ticket prices. Consequently, we could label the third factor *satisfaction with ticket prices*. Of course, the labeling of factors is subjective and you could provide different descriptions.

The last step involves assessing the analysis's goodness-of-fit. To do so, we first look at the residuals (i.e., the differences between observed and reproduced correlations) in the reproduced correlation matrix (Table 8.11). If we examine the lower part of the table, we see that there are several residuals with absolute values larger than 0.05. Nevertheless, we do not have to count every single value in the matrix (this could be quite exhausting if there are over 100 variables in the dataset!). Instead, SPSS counts the proportion of residuals with high residuals, which is reported in the first part of the table. As we can see in point **b.** beneath the table, 23.0% of the residuals have absolute values greater than 0.05. Therefore, we can presume a good model fit. This is also illustrated by the variables' communalities, which are displayed in Table 8.12. Finally, over 80% of each variable's variance is explained by the three factors (Table 8.8), which is a good result.

At this point, we have completed the principal components analysis. However, if we wish to continue using the results for further analyses, we should calculate factor scores. We can save factor scores using the **Scores** option; SPSS creates three new variables, one for each factor in the final solution (Fig. 8.11). Using these variables,

Table 8.11 Reproduced correlations and residual matrices

Reproduced Correlations

		x1	x2	x3	x4	x5	x6	x7
Reproduced Correlation	x1	.850[a]	.850	.838	.415	.317	.229	.181
	x2	.850	.852[a]	.841	.447	.351	.255	.205
	x3	.838	.841	.832[a]	.434	.339	.290	.243
	x4	.415	.447	.434	.912[a]	.910	.325	.229
	x5	.317	.351	.339	.910	.923[a]	.306	.210
	x6	.229	.255	.290	.325	.306	.843[a]	.845
	x7	.181	.205	.243	.229	.210	.845	.858[a]
Residual[b]	x1		−.067	-.085	−.020	.021	.017	−.009
	x2	−.067		−.080	−.002	−.001	−.017	.019
	x3	−.085	−.080		.010	−.010	−.003	−.008
	x4	−.020	−.002	.010		−.081	−.014	.012
	x5	.021	−.001	−.010	−.081		−.003	.004
	x6	.017	−.017	−.003	−.014	−.003		−.149
	x7	−.009	.019	−.008	.012	.004	−.149	

Extraction Method: Principal Component Analysis.
a. Reproduced communalities
b. Residuals are computed between observed and reproduced correlations. There are 5 (23.0%) nonredundant residuals with absolute values greater than 0.05.

Table 8.12 Communalities

Communalities

	Initial	Extraction
x1	1.000	.850
x2	1.000	.852
x3	1.000	.832
x4	1.000	.912
x5	1.000	.923
x6	1.000	.843
x7	1.000	.858

Extraction Method: Principal
Component Analysis.

we could, for example, evaluate whether male and female fans differ significantly with regard to their satisfaction with the stadium (first factor), the team (second factor), or the ticket prices (third factor). SPSS can only calculate these scores if it has information on all the variables included in the factor analysis. If SPSS does not have all the information, it only shows a "." (dot) in the data view window, indicating system-missing values for a certain observation (as it is the case with observations 2, 3, and 4; Fig. 8.11).

	x6	x7	FAC1_1	FAC2_1	FAC3_1
1	5	5	-.34006	.55138	.45799
2	8	1	.	.	.
3	8	6	.	.	.
4	8	6	.	.	.
5	4	5	.84722	.61924	-.04384
6	4	6	-1.18989	-1.46760	.89205
7	4	4	.83536	.08754	-.35509
8	8	7	.	.	.
9	8	4	.	.	.
10	4	3	-.00081	.34037	-.67535
11	8	4	.	.	.
12	6	4	.73211	.04437	.33035
13	6	6	.64652	1.14657	.95279

Fig. 8.11 SPSS data view window

Instead of using the factor scores in subsequent analyses, we could use an average score, calculated as the mean of the variables related to the respective factor. This is usually done in cases where the researcher already has an idea which variables relate to which factors.

A typical application would be to conduct a follow-up study of fan satisfaction. To ensure the comparability of the results, we could replicate the factor structure from the initial analysis, using summated scores obtained from the follow-up study. However, before doing so, we have to carry out a reliability analysis to assess whether the scale's items are internally consistent.

8.6.2 Reliability Analysis

To illustrate its usage, let's carry out a reliability analysis of the factor *satisfaction with the stadium* by calculating Cronbach's Alpha as a function of the variables satisfaction with the condition of the stadium, satisfaction with the outer appearance of the stadium, and satisfaction with the interior design of the stadium. To run the reliability analysis, click on ▶ Analyze ▶ Scale ▶ Reliability Analysis. Next, enter variables x_1, x_2, and x_3 into the **Items** box and type in the scale's name, namely *satisfaction with the stadium*. Check that **Alpha** is selected in the **Model** drop-down list (Fig. 8.12).

Next, click on **Statistics** and choose **Scale if item deleted** (under **Descriptives for**). If you want, you could also request descriptive statistics for each item and the entire scale or item correlations (submenu **Inter-item**). However, for the sake of simplicity, we will work with the default settings.

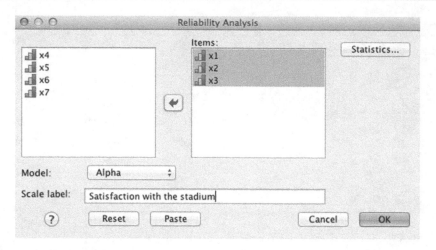

Fig. 8.12 Reliability analysis dialog box

The **Reliability Statistics** (Table 8.13) show that the scale exhibits a high degree of reliability. With a value of 0.902, the Cronbach's Alpha coefficient lies well above the commonly suggested threshold of 0.70. This result is not surprising, since we are simply testing a scale that has previously been established by means of item correlations. Keep in mind that we usually carry out a reliability analysis to test a scale using a different sample—this example is only for illustration purposes!

Table 8.13 Reliability statistics

Reliability Statistics	
Cronbach's Alpha	N of Items
.902	3

The rightmost column of Table 8.14 indicates what the Cronbach Alpha would be if we would delete the item indicated on that row. When we compare each of the values with the overall Alpha value, we can see that any change in the scale's set-up would reduce the Alpha value. For example, by removing x_1 from the scale, the

Table 8.14 Item-total statistics

Item-Total Statistics

	Scale Mean if Item Deleted	Scale Variance if Item Deleted	Corrected Item-Total Correction	Cronbach's Alpha if them Deleted
x1	10.60	11.082	.808	.860
x2	10.53	11.951	.817	.853
x3	11.00	11.421	.796	.869

Cronbach's Alpha of the new scale comprising only x_2 and x_3 would be reduced to 0.860. Deleting this item therefore makes little sense.

> Only if the initial Cronbach's Alpha is below acceptable standards (i.e., below 0.70), we should try to increase it by removing one or more items from the scale. If it is acceptable, we should not attempt to improve it by changing the scale's set-up.

8.7 Customer Satisfaction at Haver & Boecker (Case Study)

Haver & Boecker (http://www.haverboecker.com) is one of the world's leading providers of complete solutions in the fields of mineral processing as well as the storing, conveying, packing, and loading of bulk material. The German, family-owned group operates through a global network of own facilities, with manufacturing units in Germany, UK, Belgium, US, Canada, Brazil, China, and India to mention a few. Haver & Boecker is a recognized specialist in the fields of weighing, filling, and material handling technology. The company develops, designs, produces, and markets technologies and systems for storing, conveying, filling, and processing loose bulk materials of any type and, thus, solely operates in industrial markets.

The company's relationships with its customers are usually long-term oriented, and complex. Since the company's philosophy is to assist customers and business partners in jointly solving their challenges or problems, their products and services are often customized to the buyers' needs. Therefore, the customer is no longer a passive buyer, but an active partner. Given this background, the customers' satisfaction plays an important role in establishing, developing, and maintaining successful customer relationships.

Very early on, the company's management realized the importance of customer satisfaction and decided to commission a market research project to identify marketing activities that can positively contribute to the business' overall success. Based on a thorough literature review as well as interviews with experts, the company developed a short survey to explore their customers' satisfaction with specific performance features and their overall satisfaction. All items were measured on 7-point scales with higher scores denoting higher levels of satisfaction. A standardized survey was mailed to customers in 12 countries worldwide, which yielded 281 fully completed questionnaires. The following items (names in parentheses) were listed in the survey:
- Reliability of the machines and systems (s_1)
- Life-time of the machines and systems (s_2)
- Functionality and user-friendliness operation of the machines and systems (s_3)
- Appearance of the machines and systems (s_4)
- Accuracy of the machines and systems (s_5)
- Timely availability of the after-sales service (s_6)
- Local availability of the after-sales service (s_7)
- Fast processing of complaints (s_8)
- Composition of quotations (s_9)
- Transparency of quotations (s_{10})
- Fixed product prize for the machines and systems (s_{11})
- Cost/performance ratio of the machines and systems (s_{12})
- Overall, how satisfied are you with the supplier (*overall*)?

Your task is to analyze the dataset to provide the management of Haver & Boecker with advice for effective customer satisfaction management. The dataset is labeled *haver_and_boecker.sav* (⏴ Web Appendix → Chap. 8).

1. Using regression analysis, locate those variables that best explain the customers' overall satisfaction (*overall*). Evaluate the model fit and assess the impact of each variable on the criterion variable. Remember to consider collinearity diagnostics.
2. Determine the factors that characterize the respondents by means a factor analysis. Use items s_1–s_{12} for this. Run a principal axis factoring with varimax rotation to facilitate interpretation. Consider the following issues:
   (a) Are all assumptions for carrying out a factor analysis met? Pay special attention to the question whether the data are sufficiently correlated.
   (b) How many factors would you extract?
   (c) Try to find suitable labels for the extracted factors.
   (d) Evaluate the solution's goodness-of-fit.
3. Use the factor scores and regress the customers' overall satisfaction (*overall*) on these. Evaluate the strength of the model and compare it with the initial regression. What should Haver & Boecker's management do to increase their customers' satisfaction?
4. Calculate Cronbach's Alpha over items s_1–s_5 and interpret the results.

For further information on the dataset and the study, see Festge and Schwaiger (2007) as well as Sarstedt et al. (2009).

Review Questions

1. What is factor analysis? Try to explain what factor analysis is in your own words.
2. Describe the terms Eigenvalue, communality, and factor loading. How do these concepts relate to one another?
3. What is the difference between principal components analysis and principal axis factoring?
4. Describe three approaches used to determine the number of factors.
5. What are the purpose and the characteristic of a varimax rotation? Does a rotation alter Eigenvalues, factor loadings or communalities?
6. Re-run the analysis on soccer fan satisfaction by carrying out principal axis factoring and compare the results with our example analysis.
7. Explain the similarities and differences between exploratory factor analysis and confirmatory factor analysis.
8. Explain the basic principle of structural equation modeling.

Further Readings

Fornell, C., & Bookstein, F. L. (1982). Two structural equation models: LISREL and PLS applied to consumer exit-voice theory. *Journal of Marketing Research*, *19*(4), 440–452.

In this seminal article, the authors compare the statistical principles of covariance- and variance-based structural equation modeling. The illustrations are rather technical and more suited for readers with a strong background in statistics and research methodology.

Nunnally, J. C., & Bernstein, I. H. (1993). *Psychometric theory* (3rd ed.). New York: McGraw-Hill.

Psychometric theory is a classic text and the most comprehensive introduction to the fundamental principles of measurement. Chapter 7 provides an in-depth discussion of the nature of reliability and its assessment.

Stewart, D. W., (1981). The application and misapplication of factor analysis in marketing research. *Journal of Marketing Research, 18*(1), 51–62.

David Stewart discusses procedures for determining when data are appropriate for factor analysis, as well as guidelines for determining the number of factors to extract, and for rotation.

References

Cliff, N. (1987). *Analyzing multivariate data*. New York: Harcourt Brace Jovanovich.

Cronbach, L. J. (1951). Coefficient alpha and the internal structure of tests. *Psychometrika, 16*(3), 297–334.

Diamantopoulos, A., & Siguaw, J. A. (2000). *Introducing LISREL: A guide for the uninitiated*. London: Sage.

Festge, F., & Schwaiger, M. (2007). The drivers of customer satisfaction with industrial goods: An international study. *Advances in International Marketing, 18*, 179–207.

Hair, J. F., Black, W. C., Babin, B. J., & Anderson, R. E. (2010). *Multivariate data analysis. A global perspective* (7th ed.). Upper Saddle River, NJ: Pearson Prentice Hall.

Hair, J. F., Ringle, C. M., & Sarstedt, M. (2011). PLS-SEM: Indeed a silver bullet. *Journal of Marketing Theory and Practice, 19*(2), 139–151.

Hair, J. F., Sarstedt, M., Pieper, T. M., & Ringle, C. M. (2012a). The use of partial least squares structural equation modeling in strategic management research: a review of past practices and recommendations for future applications. *Long Range Planning, 45*(5–6), 320–340.

Hair, J. F., Sarstedt, M., Ringle, C. M., & Mena, J. (2012b). An assessment of the use of partial least squares structural equation modeling in marketing research. *Journal of the Academy of Marketing Science, 40*(3), 414–433.

Hair, J. F., Hult, G. T. M., Ringle, C. M., & Sarstedt, M. (2014). *A primer on partial least squares structural equation modeling (PLS-SEM)*. Thousand Oaks, CA: Sage.

Kaiser, H. F. (1974). An index of factorial simplicity. *Psychometrika, 39*(1), 31–36.

MacCallum, R. C., Widaman, K. F., Zhang, S., & Hong, S. (1999). Sample size in factor analysis. *Psychological Methods, 4*(1), 84–99.

Mulaik, S. A. (2009). *Foundations of factor analysis* (2nd ed.). London: Chapman & Hall.

Ringle, C. M., Sarstedt, M., & Straub, D. W. (2012). A critical look at the use of PLS-SEM in MIS Quarterly. *MIS Quarterly, 36*(1), iii–xiv.

Sarstedt, M., Schwaiger, M., & Ringle, C. M. (2009). Do we fully understand the critical success factors of customer satisfaction with industrial goods? Extending Festge and Schwaiger's model to account for unobserved heterogeneity. *Journal of Business Market Management, 3*(3), 185–206.

Sarstedt, M., Ringle, C.M., Raithel, S., & Gudergan, S. (2014). In pursuit of understanding what drives fan satisfaction. *Journal of Leisure Research, 46*(4), 419–447.

Stevens, J. P. (2009). *Applied multivariate statistics for the social sciences* (5th ed.). Hillsdale: Erlbaum.

Cluster Analysis

9

Learning Objectives

After reading this chapter you should understand:
- The basic concepts of cluster analysis.
- How basic cluster algorithms work.
- How to compute simple clustering results manually.
- The different types of clustering procedures.
- The SPSS clustering outputs.

Keywords

Agglomerative and divisive clustering • Chebychev distance • City-block distance • Clustering variables • Dendrogram • Distance matrix • Euclidean distance • Hierarchical and partitioning methods • Icicle diagram • k-means • Matching coefficients • Profiling clusters • Two-step clustering

Thaltegos (http://www.thaltegos.com) is a German management consulting company, focusing on analytical approaches for marketing, sales and after sales challenges in the automotive industry. Due to their industry experience, a major US car manufacturer commissioned Thaltegos to develop a segmentation concept of the European car market. Using cluster analysis, Thaltegos identified three distinct segments comprising light-weight compact cars, sports cars, and limousines. Using this segmentation concept, the automotive manufacturer can derive concrete steps on how to position their new electric car in the market.

M. Sarstedt and E. Mooi, *A Concise Guide to Market Research*,
Springer Texts in Business and Economics, DOI 10.1007/978-3-642-53965-7_9,
© Springer-Verlag Berlin Heidelberg 2014

9.1   Introduction

One of the most fundamental marketing activities is in *market segmentation*. As companies cannot connect with all their potential customers, they have to divide markets into groups (segments) of consumers, customers, or clients with similar needs and wants. Firms can then target each of these segments by positioning themselves in a unique segment (such as Ferrari in the high-end sports car market). While market researchers often form market segments based on practical grounds, industry practice and wisdom, cluster analysis allows segments to be formed that are based on data that are less dependent on subjectivity.

The segmentation of customers is a standard application of cluster analysis, but it can also be used in different contexts such as evaluating typical supermarket shopping paths (Larson et al. 2005) or deriving employers' branding strategies (Moroko and Uncles 2009).

9.2   Understanding Cluster Analysis

Cluster analysis is a convenient method for identifying homogenous groups of objects called *clusters*. Objects (or cases, observations) in a specific cluster share many characteristics, but are very dissimilar to objects not belonging to that cluster.

Let's try to gain a basic understanding of the cluster analysis procedure by looking at a simple example. Imagine that you are interested in segmenting your customer base in order to better target them through, for example, pricing strategies.

The first step is to decide on the characteristics that you will use to segment your customers. In other words, you have to decide which *clustering variables* will be included in the analysis. For example, you may want to segment a market based on customers' price consciousness (x) and brand loyalty (y). These two variables can be measured on a 7-point scale with higher values denoting a higher degree of price consciousness and brand loyalty. The values of seven respondents are shown in Table 9.1 and the scatter plot in Fig. 9.1.

The objective of cluster analysis is to identify groups of objects (in this case, customers) that are very similar with regard to their price consciousness and brand loyalty and assign them into clusters. After having decided on the clustering variables (brand loyalty and price consciousness), we need to decide on the clustering procedure to form our groups of objects. This step is crucial for the analysis, as different procedures require different decisions prior to analysis. There is an abundance of different approaches and little guidance on which one to use in

Table 9.1 Data

Customer	A	B	C	D	E	F	G
x	3	6	5	3	6	4	1
y	7	7	6	5	5	3	2

Fig. 9.1 Scatter plot

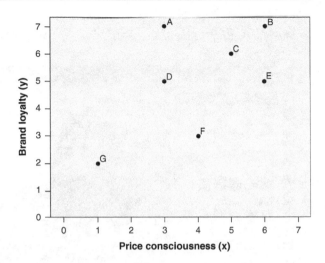

practice. We are going to discuss the most popular approaches in market research, as they can be easily computed using SPSS. These approaches are the following:

– *Hierarchical methods*,
– *Partitioning methods* (more precisely, *k-means*), and
– *Two-step clustering*.

Each of these procedures follows a different approach to grouping the most similar objects into clusters. Specifically, whereas an object in a certain cluster should be as similar as possible to all the other objects in the same cluster, it should likewise be as distinct as possible from objects in different clusters.

But how do we measure similarity? Most methods calculate measures of (dis) similarity by estimating the distance between pairs of objects. Objects with smaller distances between one another are more similar, whereas objects with larger distances are more dissimilar.

An important problem in the application of cluster analysis is the decision regarding how many clusters should be derived from the data. This question is explored in the next step of the analysis. Sometimes, we already know the number of segments that have to be derived from the data. For example, if we were asked to ascertain what characteristics distinguish frequent shoppers from infrequent ones, we need to find two different clusters. However, we do not usually know the exact number of clusters and then we face a trade-off. On the one hand, you want as few clusters as possible to make clusters easy to understand and actionable. On the other hand, having many clusters allows you to identify more segments and more subtle differences between segments. In an extreme case, you can address each individual separately (called *micromarketing*) to meet consumers' specific needs in the best possible way.

However, the costs associated with such a strategy may be prohibitively high in many business contexts. Thus, we have to ensure that the segments are large enough

Micromarketing in Practice

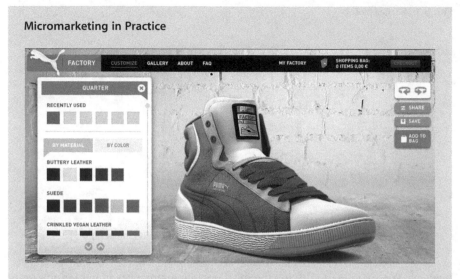

In the PUMA Factory, customers can fully customize a pair of shoes in a hands-on, tactile, and interactive shoe-making experience. This customization by the customers allows PUMA to target each customer individually with promotions or special offerings, allowing for a one-to-one interaction.

to make marketing programs profitable. As a result, we create some within-cluster heterogeneity, which makes targeted marketing programs less effective.

In the final step, we need to interpret the solution by defining and labeling the obtained clusters. This can be done by examining the clustering variables' mean values or by identifying explanatory variables to profile the clusters. Ultimately, managers should be able to identify customers in each segment on the basis of easily measurable variables. This final step also requires us to assess the clustering solution's stability and validity. Figure 9.2 illustrates the steps associated with a cluster analysis; we will discuss these steps in more detail in the following sections.

9.3   Conducting a Cluster Analysis

9.3.1   Decide on the Clustering Variables

At the beginning of the clustering process, we have to select appropriate variables for clustering. Even though this choice is of utmost importance, it is rarely treated as such and, instead, a mixture of intuition and data availability guide most analyses in marketing practice. However, faulty assumptions may lead to improper market segments and, consequently, to deficient marketing strategies. Thus, great care should be taken when selecting the clustering variables!

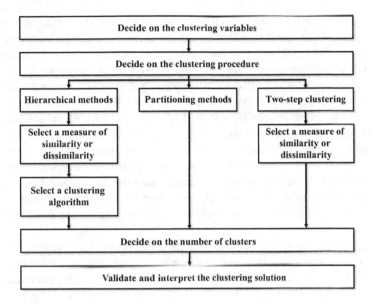

Fig. 9.2 Steps in a cluster analysis

There are several types of clustering variables and these can be classified as follows:
– *General* vs. *specific*, and
– *Observable* vs. *unobservable*.

General clustering variables are independent of products, services or circumstances whereas specific variables relate to both the customer and the product, service and/or particular circumstance. Furthermore, observable clustering variables can be measured directly while unobservable ones are inferred, for example, through observation or respondents' self-assessments. Table 9.2 provides several types and examples of clustering variables.

Table 9.2 Types and examples of clustering variables

	General	Specific
Observable	– Cultural – Demographic – Geographic – Socio-economic – …	– Brand loyalty – Store loyalty – User status – Usage frequency – …
Unobservable	– Lifestyle – Personality – Psychographics – Values – …	– Attitudes – Intentions – Perceptions – Preferences – …

The types of variables used for cluster analysis provide different segments and, thereby, influence segment-targeting strategies. Over the last decades, attention has shifted from more traditional general clustering variables towards product-specific unobservable variables. The latter generally provide better guidance for decisions on marketing instruments' effective specification. Generally, segments identified by means of specific unobservable variables are more homogenous and their consumers respond more consistent to marketing actions (see Wedel and Kamakura 2000). However, consumers in these segments are also frequently hard to identify from variables that are easily measured, such as demographics. Conversely, segments determined by means of observable variables usually stand out due to their identifiability but often lack a unique response structure.[1] Consequently, researchers frequently combine different variables (e.g., multiple lifestyle characteristics combined with demographic variables), benefiting from each one's strengths.

In some cases, the choice of clustering variables is apparent because of the task at hand. For example, a managerial problem regarding corporate communications will have a fairly well defined set of clustering variables, including contenders such as awareness, attitudes, perceptions, and media habits. However, this is not always the case and researchers have to choose from a set of candidate variables. But how do we make this decision? To facilitate the choice of clustering variables, you should consider the following guiding questions:
– Do the variables sufficiently differentiate the segments?
– Are the clustering variables highly correlated?
– Is the relation between sample size and number of clustering variables reasonable?
– Are the data underlying the clustering variables of high quality?

Do the variables sufficiently differentiate the segments?
It is important to select those clustering variables that provide a clear-cut differentiation between the segments regarding a specific managerial objective.[2] More precisely, criterion validity is of special interest; that is, the extent to which the "independent" clustering variables are associated with one or more "dependent" variables not included in the analysis. Such "dependent" variables typically relate to some aspect of behavior, such as purchase intention or willingness-to-pay. Given this relationship, there should be significant differences between the "dependent" variable(s) across the clusters (e.g., consumers in one cluster exhibit a significantly higher willingness-to-pay than those in other clusters). These associations may or may not be causal, but it is essential that the clustering variables distinguish the variable(s) of interest significantly.

---

[1] See Wedel and Kamakura (2000).

[2] Tonks (2009) provides a discussion of segment design and the choice of clustering variables in consumer markets.

Are the clustering variables highly correlated?
If there is strong correlation between the variables, they are not sufficiently unique to identify distinct market segments. If highly correlated variables are used for cluster analysis, specific aspects covered by these variables will be overrepresented in the clustering solution. In this regard, absolute correlations above 0.90 are always problematic. For example, if we were to add another variable called *brand preference* to our analysis, it would virtually cover the same aspect as *brand loyalty*. Thus, the concept of being attached to a brand would be overrepresented in the analysis because the clustering procedure does not differentiate between the clustering variables in a conceptual sense. Researchers frequently handle such correlation problems by applying cluster analysis to the observations' factor scores derived from a previously carried out factor analysis. However, this so called *factor-cluster segmentation* approach is subject to several limitations which we discuss in Box 9.1.

Box 9.1 Issues with factor-cluster segmentation
Dolnicar and Grün (2009) identify several problems of the factor-cluster segmentation approach:

1. The data are pre-processed and the clusters are identified on the basis of transformed values, not on the original information, which leads to different results.
2. In factor analysis, the factor solution does not explain a certain amount of variance; thus, information is discarded before segments have been identified or constructed.
3. Eliminating variables with low loadings on all the extracted factors means that, potentially, the most important pieces of information for the identification of niche segments are discarded, making it impossible to ever identify such groups.
4. The interpretations of clusters based on the original variables become questionable given that the segments have been constructed using factor scores.

Several studies have shown that the factor-cluster segmentation significantly reduces the success of finding useable segments.[3] Consequently, you should rather reduce the number of items in the questionnaire's pre-testing phase, retaining a reasonable number of relevant, non-redundant questions that you believe differentiate the segments well. However, if you have your doubts about the data structure, factor-clustering segmentation may still be a better option than discarding items that may conceptually be necessary.

---

[3] See the studies by Arabie and Hubert (1994), Sheppard (1996), or Dolnicar and Grün (2009).

Is the relation between sample size and number of clustering variables reasonable?
When choosing clustering variables, sample size is a point of concern. First and
foremost, this relates to issues of managerial relevance as segment sizes need to be
substantial to ensure that targeted marketing programs are profitable. From a
statistical perspective, every additional variable requires an over-proportional
increase in observations to ensure valid results. Unfortunately, there is no generally
accepted rule of thumb regarding minimum sample sizes or the relationship
between the objects and the number of clustering variables used. Formann (1984)
recommends a minimum sample size of 2^m, where m equals the number of
clustering variables. This rule-of-thumb can only provide rough guidance; nevertheless, we should pay attention to the relationship between the sample size and the
number of clustering variables. It does not, for example, appear logical to cluster
ten objects using ten variables. Keep in mind that no matter how many variables are
used and no matter how small the sample size, cluster analysis will always render a
result!

Are the data underlying the clustering variables of high quality?
Ultimately, the choice of clustering variables always depends on contextual
influences such as data availability or resources to acquire additional data.
Market researchers often overlook the fact that the choice of clustering variables
is closely connected to data quality. Only those variables that ensure that high
quality data can be used should be included in the analysis (Dolnicar and
Lazarevski 2009). Data are of high quality if...
– ... the questions asked have a strong theoretical basis,
– ... are not contaminated by respondent fatigue or response styles, and
– ... reflect the current market situation (i.e., they are recent).

> The requirements of other functions in the organization often play a major role
> in the choice of clustering variables. For example, sales may wish to have
> segments that they can send the same salespeople to. Consequently, we have to
> be aware that the choice of clustering variables should lead to segments
> acceptable to the different functions in the organization.

9.3.2   Decide on the Clustering Procedure

By choosing a specific clustering procedure, we determine how clusters are to be
formed. This always involves optimizing some kind of criterion, such as
minimizing the within-cluster variance (i.e., the clustering variables' overall variance of objects in a specific cluster), or maximizing the distance between the

objects or clusters. The procedure could also address the question of how to determine the (dis)similarity between objects in a newly formed cluster and the remaining objects in the dataset.

There are many different clustering procedures and also many ways of classifying these (e.g., overlapping versus non-overlapping, unimodal versus multimodal, exhaustive versus non-exhaustive).[4] A practical distinction is the differentiation between *hierarchical* and *partitioning methods* (most notably the *k-means* procedure), which we will discuss in the next sections. We also introduce *two-step clustering*, which combines the principles of hierarchical and partitioning methods and which has recently gained increasing attention from market research practice.

9.3.2.1 Hierarchical Methods
Understanding Hierarchical Clustering
Hierarchical clustering procedures are characterized by the tree-like structure established in the course of the analysis. Most hierarchical techniques fall into a category called *agglomerative clustering*. In this category, clusters are consecutively formed from objects. Initially, this type of procedure starts with each object representing an individual cluster. These clusters are then sequentially merged according to their similarity. First, the two most similar clusters are merged to form a new cluster at the bottom of the hierarchy. In the next step, another pair of clusters is merged and linked to a higher level of the hierarchy, and so on. This allows a hierarchy of clusters to be established from the bottom up. In Fig. 9.3 (left-hand side), we show how agglomerative clustering assigns additional objects to clusters step-by-step.

A cluster hierarchy can also be generated top-down. In this *divisive clustering*, all objects are initially merged into a single cluster, which is then gradually split up. Figure 9.3 illustrates this concept (right-hand side). As we can see, in both agglomerative and divisive clustering, a cluster on a higher level of the hierarchy always encompasses all clusters from a lower level. This means that if an object is assigned to a certain cluster, there is no possibility of reassigning this object to another cluster. This is an important distinction between these types of clustering and partitioning methods such as k-means, which we will explore in the next section.

Divisive procedures are quite rarely used in market research. We therefore concentrate on the agglomerative clustering procedures. There are various types of agglomerative procedures. However, before we discuss these, we need to define how similarities or dissimilarities are measured between pairs of objects.

---

[4] See Wedel and Kamakura (2000), Dolnicar (2003), and Kaufman and Rousseeuw (2005) for a review of clustering techniques.

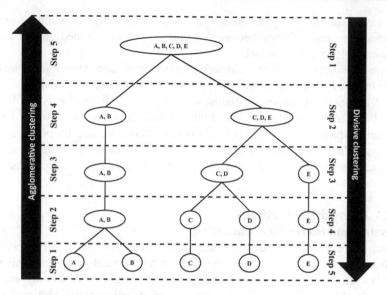

Fig. 9.3 Agglomerative and divisive clustering

Select a Measure of Similarity or Dissimilarity
Metric and Ordinal Variables

There are various measures to express (dis)similarity between pairs of objects. A straightforward way to assess two objects' proximity is by drawing a straight line between them. For example, when we look at the scatter plot in Fig. 9.1, we can easily see that the length of the line connecting observations B and C is much shorter than the line connecting B and G. This type of distance is also referred to as *Euclidean distance* (or *straight-line distance*) and is the most commonly used type when it comes to analyzing ratio or interval-scaled variables.[5] In our example, we have ordinal variables, but market researchers usually treat ordinal variables as metric data to calculate distance metrics by assuming that the scale steps are equidistant (very much like in factor analysis, which we discussed in Chap. 8).

To use a hierarchical clustering procedure, we need to express these distances mathematically. Using the data from Table 9.1, we can compute the Euclidean distance between customer B and customer C (generally referred to as d(B,C)) using variables x and y by with the following formula:

$$d_{Euclidean}(B, C) = \sqrt{(x_B - x_C)^2 + (y_B - y_C)^2}$$

---

[5] Note that researchers also often use the squared Euclidean distance.

The Euclidean distance is the square root of the sum of the squared differences in the variables' values. Using the data from Table 9.1, we obtain the following:

$$d_{Euclidean}(B,C) = \sqrt{(6-5)^2 + (7-6)^2} = \sqrt{2} = 1.414$$

This distance corresponds to the length of the line that connects objects B and C. In this case, we only used two variables but we can easily add more under the root sign in the formula. However, each additional variable will add a dimension to our research problem (e.g., with six clustering variables, we have to deal with six dimensions), making it impossible to represent the solution graphically. Similarly, we can compute the distance between customer B and G, which yields the following:

$$d_{Euclidean}(B,G) = \sqrt{(6-1)^2 + (7-2)^2} = \sqrt{50} = 7.071$$

Likewise, we can compute the distance between all other pairs of objects. All these distances are usually expressed by means of a *distance matrix*. In this distance matrix, the non-diagonal elements express the distances between pairs of objects and zeros on the diagonal (the distance from each object to itself is, of course, 0). In our example, the distance matrix is an 8×8 table with the lines and rows representing the objects (i.e., customers) under consideration (see Table 9.3). As the distance between objects B and C (in this case 1.414 units) is the same as between C and B, the distance matrix is symmetrical. Furthermore, since the distance between an object and itself is 0, you only need to loot at either the lower or upper non-diagonal elements.

An important feature of distance (and similarity) matrices are *ties*, which are, identical distances between two or more objects. For example, in Table 9.3, there are three pairs of objects with distances of 2.236. In fact, in the 21 cells, there are only 13 unique distance values. In practical applications (which usually rely on much more clustering variables and objects), ties are more the exception than the rule and generally don't have a pronounced impact on the results.

Table 9.3 Euclidean distance matrix

Objects	A	B	C	D	E	F	G
A	0						
B	3	0					
C	2.236	1.414	0				
D	2	3.606	2.236	0			
E	3.606	2	1.414	3	0		
F	4.123	4.472	3.162	2.236	2.828	0	
G	5.385	7.071	5.657	3.606	5.831	3.162	0

There are also alternative distance measures: The *city-block distance* uses the sum of the variables' absolute differences. This distance measure is often called the *Manhattan metric* as it is akin to the walking distance between two points in a city like New York's Manhattan district, where the distance equals the number of blocks in the directions North-South and East-West. Using the city-block distance to compute the distance between customers B and C (or C and B) yields the following:

$$d_{City-block}(B,C) = |x_B - x_C| + |y_B - y_C| = |6 - 5| + |7 - 6| = 2$$

The resulting distance matrix is in Table 9.4.

Table 9.4   City-block distance matrix

Objects	A	B	C	D	E	F	G
A	0						
B	3	0					
C	3	2	0				
D	2	5	3	0			
E	5	2	2	3	0		
F	5	6	4	3	4	0	
G	7	10	8	5	8	4	0

Lastly, when working with metric (or ordinal) data, researchers frequently use the *Chebychev distance*, which is the maximum of the absolute difference in the clustering variables' values. In respect of customers B and C, this result is:

$$d_{Chebychec}(B,C) = \max(|x_B - x_C|, |y_B - y_C|) = \max(|6 - 5|, |7 - 6|) = 1$$

Figure 9.4 illustrates the interrelation between these three distance measures regarding two objects, C and G, from our example.

Fig. 9.4   Distance measures

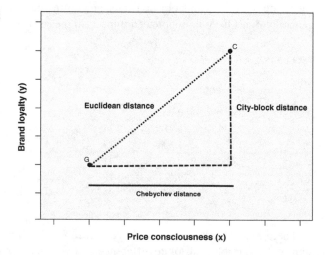

> There are other distance measures such as the *Angular*, *Canberra* or *Mahalanobis distances*. In many situations, the latter is desirable as it compensates for collinearity between the clustering variables. However, it is (unfortunately) not menu-accessible in SPSS.

In many analysis tasks, the variables under consideration have a different number of categories. This would be the case if we extended our set of clustering variables by adding another ordinal variable representing the customers' income measured by means of, for example, 15 categories. Since the absolute variation of the income variable would be much greater than the variation of the remaining two variables (remember, that x and y are measured on 7-point scales), this would clearly distort our analysis results. We can resolve this problem by standardizing the data prior to the analysis.

Different standardization methods are available, such as the simple z standardization, which rescales each variable to have a mean of 0 and a standard deviation of 1 (see Chap. 5). In most situations, however, standardization by range (e.g., to a range of 0 to 1 or −1 to 1) performs better.[6] We recommend standardizing the data in general, even though this procedure can reduce or inflate the variables' influence on the clustering solution.

Another way of (implicitly) standardizing the data is by using the correlation between the objects instead of distance measures. For example, suppose a respondent rated price consciousness 2 and brand loyalty 3. Now suppose a second respondent indicated 5 and 6, whereas a third rated these variables 3 and 3. Euclidean, city-block, and Chebychev distances would indicate that the first respondent is more similar to the third than to the second. Nevertheless, one could convincingly argue that the first respondent's ratings are more similar to the second's, as both rate brand loyalty higher than price consciousness. This can be accounted for by computing the correlation between two vectors of values as a measure of similarity (i.e., high correlation coefficients indicate a high degree of similarity). Consequently, similarity is no longer defined by means of the difference between the answer categories but by means of the similarity of the answering profiles. Using correlation is also a way of standardizing the data implicitly.

Whether you use correlation or one of the distance measures depends on whether you think the relative magnitude of the variables within an object (which favors correlation) matters more than the relative magnitude of each variable across objects (which favors distance). However, it is generally recommended that one uses correlations when applying clustering procedures that are susceptible to outliers, such as complete linkage, average linkage or centroid (see section "Select a Clustering Algorithm").

---

[6] See Milligan and Cooper (1988).

Nominal Variables

Whereas the distance measures presented thus far can be used for variables measured on a metric and, in general, ordinal scale, applying them to nominal variables is problematic. When nominal variables are involved you should rather select a similarity measure expressing the degree to which variables' values share the same category. These so-called *matching coefficients* can take different forms but rely on the same allocation scheme shown in Table 9.5. In this crosstab, cell a is the number of characteristics present in both objects, whereas cell d describes the number of characteristics absent in both objects. Cells b and c describe the number of features present in one but not the other object. This scheme applies to binary variables, that is, those with two categories. For variables with more than two categories, you need to convert the categorical variable into a set of binary variables in order to use matching coefficients. For example, a variable with three categories needs to be transformed into three binary variables, one for each category (see the following example).

Table 9.5   Allocation scheme for matching coefficients

		Object 2	
		Presence of a characteristics (1)	Absence of a characteristic (0)
Object 1	Presence of a characteristic (1)	a	b
	Absence of a characteristic (0)	c	d

Based on the allocation scheme in Table 9.5, we can compute different matching coefficients, such as the *simple matching coefficient (SM)*:

$$SM = \frac{a+d}{a+b+c+d}$$

This coefficient takes into account both, the joint presence and the joint absence of a characteristic (as indicated by cells a and d in Table 9.5). This feature makes the simple matching coefficient particularly useful for symmetric variables, where the joint presence and absence of a characteristic carries an equal degree of information (e.g., gender). However, if used on non-symmetric variables, objects may appear very similar because they both lack the same characteristics (as expressed through cell d) rather than because they share common characteristics (as expressed through cell a).

In light of this issue, researchers have proposed the *Jaccard (JC)* and the *Russel and Rao (RR)* coefficients, which do not include missing observations in the calculation of similarity (i.e., they (partially) omit the d cell from Table 9.5 in the calculation). Like the simple matching coefficient, they range from 0 to 1 with higher values indicating a greater degree of similarity.[7] They are defined as follows:

$$JC = \frac{a}{a+b+c}$$

$$RR = \frac{a}{a+b+c+d}$$

To provide a brief example comparing the three coefficients, consider the following three variables:
- *Gender*: male, female
- *Product use*: light, medium, and heavy
- *Income*: low, medium, high

We consider the following two objects:
- *Object #1*: male customer, light user with low income and
- *Object #2*: female customer, medium user with a low income

We first transform the measurement data into binary data by recoding the original three variables into eight binary variables (i.e., two for gender and three for product use as well as income). The resulting binary data matrix is displayed in Table 9.6.

Table 9.6 Recoded measurement data

	Gender (binary code)		Product use (binary code)			Income (binary code)		
	Male	Female	Light	Medium	Heavy	Low	Medium	High
Object #1	1	0	1	0	0	1	0	0
Object #2	0	1	0	1	0	1	0	0

Using the allocation scheme from Table 9.5 yields the following results for the cells: $a=1$, $b=2$, $c=2$, and $d=3$.

This means that the two objects have only one shared characteristic ($a=1$), but three characteristics, which are absent from both objects ($d=3$). Using this information, we can now compute the three coefficients described earlier:

---

[7] There are many other matching coefficients such as *Yule's Q, Kulczynski* or *Ochiai*, but since most applications of cluster analysis rely on metric or ordinal data, we will not discuss these in greater detail. Check Wedel and Kamakura (2000) for more information on alternative matching coefficients.

$$SM = \frac{1+3}{1+2+2+3} = 0.5,$$

$$JC = \frac{1}{1+2+2} = 0.2, \text{ and}$$

$$RR = \frac{1}{1+2+2+3} = 0.125$$

As can be seen, the simple matching coefficient suggests that the two objects are reasonably similar. On the contrary, the Jaccard coefficient and in particular the Russel Rao coefficient suggests that they are not.

Combinations of Metric, Ordinal, and Nominal Variables

Most datasets contain variables that are measured on multiple scales. For example, a market research questionnaire may ask about the respondent's income, product ratings, and last brand purchased. Thus, we have to consider variables measured on a ratio, ordinal, and nominal scale. How can we simultaneously incorporate these variables into one analysis? Unfortunately, this problem cannot be easily resolved. Often research use the distance measures discussed in the context of metric (and ordinal) data. Even though this approach may slightly change the results compared to using matching coefficients, it should not be rejected. Cluster analysis is mostly an exploratory technique whose results only provide a rough guidance for managerial decisions.

An alternative is to dichotomize all variables and apply the matching coefficients discussed above. For metric variables, this involves specifying categories (e.g., low, medium, and high income) and converting these into sets of binary variables. In most cases the specification of categories is somewhat arbitrary. Furthermore, this procedure leads to a severe loss in precision as we disregard more detailed information on each object. For example, we would lose precise information on each respondent's income, when scaling this variable down into income categories. In the light of these issues, you should avoid combining metric and nominal variables in a single cluster analysis. If this is not feasible, the *two-step clustering procedure* provides a valuable alternative, which we will discuss later. Lastly, the choice of the (dis)similarity measure is not very critical for the cluster structure. The choice of the clustering algorithm is far more important. We therefore deal with this first.

Select a Clustering Algorithm

After having chosen the distance or similarity measure, we need to decide which clustering algorithm to apply. There are several agglomerative procedures and they can be distinguished by the way they define the distance from a newly formed cluster to a certain object, or to other clusters in the solution. The most popular agglomerative clustering procedures include the following:

- *Single linkage* (*nearest neighbor*): The distance between two clusters corresponds to the shortest distance between any two members in the two clusters.
- *Complete linkage* (*furthest neighbor*): The oppositional approach to single linkage assumes that the distance between two clusters is based on the longest distance between any two members in the two clusters.
- *Average linkage*: The distance between two clusters is defined as the average distance between all pairs of the two clusters' members.
- *Centroid*: In this approach, the geometric center (centroid) of each cluster is computed first. This is done by computing the clustering variables' average values of all the objects in a certain cluster. The distance between the two clusters equals the distance between the two centroids.

Figures 9.5–9.8 illustrate these linkage procedures for two clusters.

Fig. 9.5 Single linkage

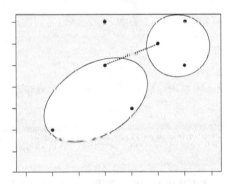

Fig. 9.6 Complete linkage

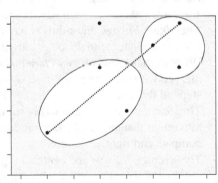

Fig. 9.7 Average linkage

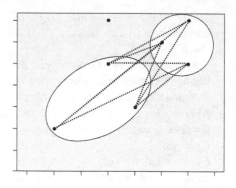

Fig. 9.8 Centroid

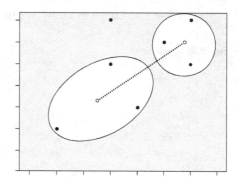

Each of these linkage algorithms can yield totally different results when used on the same dataset, as each has its specific properties:

- The *single linkage* algorithm is based on minimum distances, it tends to form one large cluster with the other clusters containing only one or few objects each. We can make use of this *chaining effect* to detect outliers, as these will be merged with the remaining objects—usually at very large distances—in the last steps of the analysis. Single linkage is considered the most versatile algorithm.
- The *complete linkage* method is strongly affected by outliers, as it is based on maximum distances. Clusters produced by this method are likely to be rather compact and tightly clustered.
- The *average linkage* and *centroid* algorithms tend to produce clusters with low within-cluster variance and with similar sizes. Complete and average linkage are affected by outliers but less than the complete linkage method.

Another commonly used approach in hierarchical clustering is *Ward's method*. This approach does not combine the two most similar objects successively. Instead, those objects whose merger increases the overall within-cluster variance to the smallest possible degree, are combined. If you expect somewhat equally sized clusters and the dataset does not include outliers, you should always use Ward's method.

To better understand how a clustering algorithm works, let's manually examine some of the single linkage procedure's calculation steps. We start off by looking at the initial (Euclidean) distance matrix in Table 9.3. In the very first step, the two objects exhibiting the smallest distance in the matrix are merged. Note that we always merge those objects with the smallest distance, regardless of the clustering procedure (e.g., single or complete linkage). As we can see, this happens to two pairs of objects, namely B and C (d(B, C) = 1.414), as well as C and E (d(C, E) = 1.414). Depending on the clustering procedure used, this tie can lead to different clustering results. In this example we simply proceed by forming a new cluster using objects B and C.[8]

Having made this decision, we then form a new distance matrix by considering the single linkage decision rule as discussed above. According to this rule, the distance from, for example, object A to the newly formed cluster is the minimum of d(A, B) and d(A, C). As d(A, C)=2.236 is smaller than d(A, B)=3, the distance from A to the newly formed cluster is equal to d(A, C); that is, 2.236. We also compute the distances from cluster [B,C] (clusters are indicated by means of squared brackets) to all other objects (i.e. D, E, F, G) and simply copy the remaining distances—such as d(E, F)—that the previous clustering step has not affected. This yields the distance matrix shown in Table 9.7.

Table 9.7 Distance matrix after first clustering step (single linkage)

Objects	A	B, C	D	E	F	G
A	0					
B, C	2.236	0				
D	2	2.236	0			
E	3.606	1.414	3	0		
F	4.123	3.162	2.236	2.828	0	
G	5.385	5.657	3.606	5.831	3.162	0

[8] Note that because of ties, the final results may depend on the order of objects in the input file. Against this background, van der Kloot et al. (2005) recommend re-running the analysis with different input order of the data. At the same time, however, ties are more the exception than the rule in practical applications and generally don't have a pronounced impact on the results.

Continuing the clustering procedure, we simply repeat the last step by merging the objects in the new distance matrix that exhibit the smallest distance (in this case, the newly formed cluster [B, C] and object E) and calculate the distance from this new cluster to all other objects. The result of this step is described in Table 9.8.

Table 9.8 Distance matrix after second clustering step (single linkage)

Objects	A	B, C, E	D	F	G
A	0				
B, C, E	2.236	0			
D	2	2.236	0		
F	4.123	2.828	2.236	0	
G	5.385	5.657	3.606	3.162	0

Try to calculate the remaining steps yourself and compare your solution with the distance matrices in the following Tables 9.9–9.11.

Table 9.9 Distance matrix after third clustering step (single linkage)

Objects	A, D	B, C, E	F	G
A, D	0			
B, C, E	2.236	0		
F	2.236	2.828	0	
G	3.606	5.657	3.162	0

Table 9.10 Distance matrix after fourth clustering step (single linkage)

Objects	A, B, C, D, E	F	G
A, B, C, D, E	0		
F	2.236	0	
G	3.606	3.162	0

Table 9.11 Distance matrix after fifth clustering step (single linkage)

Objects	A, B, C, D, E, F	G
A, B, C, D, E, F	0	
G	3.162	0

By following the single linkage procedure, the last steps involve the merger of cluster [A,B,C,D,E,F] and object G at a distance of 3.162. Do you get the same results? As you can see, conducting a basic cluster analysis manually is not that hard at all – not if there are only a few objects in the dataset.

A common way to visualize the cluster analysis's progress is by drawing a *dendrogram*, which displays the distance level at which there is a merger of objects and clusters (Fig. 9.9).

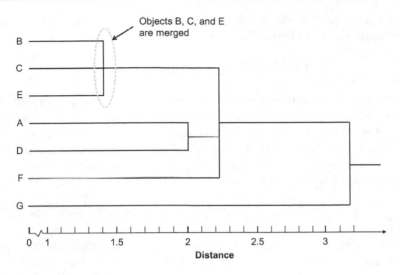

Fig. 9.9 Dendrogram

We read the dendrogram from left to right. The vertical lines indicate the distances at which objects have been combined. For example, according to our calculations above, objects B, C, and E are merged at a distance of 1.414.

Decide on the Number of Clusters

An important question we haven't yet addressed is how to decide on the number of clusters. Unfortunately, hierarchical methods provide only very limited guidance for making this decision. The only meaningful indicator relates to the distances at which the objects are combined. Similar to the scree plot in factor analysis, we can seek a solution in which an additional combination of clusters or objects would occur at a greatly increased distance. This raises the issue of what a great distance is.

One potential way to solve this problem is to plot the number of clusters on the x-axis (starting with the one-cluster solution at the very left) against the distance at which objects or clusters are combined on the y-axis. Using this plot, we then search for the distinctive break (*elbow*).

Alternatively, we can make use of the dendrogram which essentially carries the same information. SPSS provides a dendrogram; however, it differs slightly from the one presented in Fig. 9.9 as SPSS rescales the distances to a range of 0–25 (i.e., the last merging step to a one-cluster solution takes place at a rescaled distance of 25). The rescaling often lengthens the merging steps, thus making breaks occurring at a greatly increased distance level more obvious.

However, this distance-based decision rule does not work very well in all cases. It is often difficult to identify where the break actually occurs. This is also the case in our example above. By looking at the dendrogram, we could justify a two-cluster solution ([A,B,C,D,E,F] and [G]), as well as a five-cluster solution ([B,C,E], [A], [D], [F], [G]).

Research has suggested several other procedures for determining the number of clusters in a dataset. Most notably, the *variance ratio criterion* (VRC) by Calinski and Harabasz (1974) works well in many situations.[9] For a solution with n objects and k segments, the VRC is as follows:

$$VRC_k = (SS_B/(k-1))/(SS_W/(n-k)),$$

where SS_B is the sum of the squares between the segments and SS_W is the sum of the squares within the segments. The criterion should seem familiar, as this is similar to the F-value of a one-way ANOVA. Consequently, the VRC can easily be computed using SPSS, even though it is not readily available in the clustering procedures' outputs. To finally determine the appropriate number of segments, we compute ω_k for each segment solution as follows:

$$\omega_k = (VRC_{k+1} - VRC_k) - (VRC_k - VRC_{k-1}).$$

In the next step, we choose the number of segments k that minimizes the value in ω_k. Owing to the term VRC_{k-1}, the minimum number of clusters that can be selected is three, which is a clear disadvantage of the criterion, thus limiting its application in practice.

Overall, the data can often only provide rough guidance regarding the number of clusters you should select; consequently, you should rather revert to practical considerations. Occasionally, you might have a priori knowledge, or a theory on which you can base your choice. However, first and foremost, you should ensure that your results are interpretable and meaningful. Not only must the number of clusters be small enough to ensure manageability, but each segment should also be large enough to warrant strategic attention.

9.3.2.2 Partitioning Methods: k-means
Understanding k-means Clustering
Another important group of clustering procedures are partitioning methods. As with hierarchical clustering, there is a wide array of different algorithms; of these, the *k-means procedure* is the most important one for market research.[10] The k-means algorithm follows an entirely different concept than the hierarchical methods discussed before. This algorithm is not based on distance measures such as Euclidean distance or city-block distance, but uses the within-cluster variation as a

---

[9] Milligan and Cooper (1985) compare various criteria.

[10] Note that the k-means algorithm is one of the simplest non-hierarchical clustering methods. Several extensions, such as *k-medoids* (Kaufman and Rousseeuw 2005) have been proposed to handle limitations of the procedure. More advanced methods include finite mixture models (McLachlan and Peel 2000), neural networks (Bishop 2006), and self-organizing maps (Kohonen 1982). Andrews and Currim (2003) discuss the validity of some of these approaches.

measure to form homogenous clusters. Specifically, the procedure aims at partitioning the data in such a way that the within-cluster variation is minimized.

The clustering process starts by randomly assigning objects to a (pre-specified) number of clusters. The objects are then successively reassigned to other clusters to minimize the within-cluster variation, which is basically the (squared) distance from each observation to the center of the associated cluster. If the reallocation of an object to another cluster decreases the within-cluster variation, this object is reassigned to that cluster.

With the hierarchical methods, an object remains in a cluster once it is assigned to it, but with k-means, cluster affiliations can change in the course of the clustering process. Consequently, k-means does not build a hierarchy as described before (Fig. 9.3), which is why the approach is also frequently labeled as non-hierarchical. Another important property of k-means clustering is that we have to pre-specify the number of clusters prior to running the analysis. We discuss this issue later in this chapter.

For a better understanding of the approach, let's take a look at how it works in practice. Figs. 9.10–9.13 illustrate the four steps of the k-means clustering process:

– **Step 1:** Using the pre-specified number of clusters as input, the algorithm randomly selects a center for each cluster. In our example, two cluster centers are randomly initiated, which CC1 (first cluster) and CC2 (second cluster) in Fig. 9.10 represent.[11]

– **Step 2:** Euclidean distances are computed from the cluster centers to every single object. Each object is then assigned to the cluster center with the shortest distance to it. In our example (Fig. 9.11), objects A, B, and C are assigned to the first cluster, whereas objects D, E, F, and G are assigned to the second. We now have our initial partitioning of the objects into two clusters.

Fig. 9.10 k-means procedure (step 1)

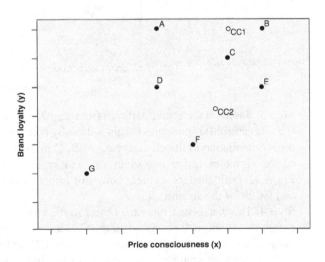

[11] Conversely, SPSS always sets one observation as the cluster center instead of picking some random point in the dataset.

Fig. 9.11 k-means
procedure (step 2)

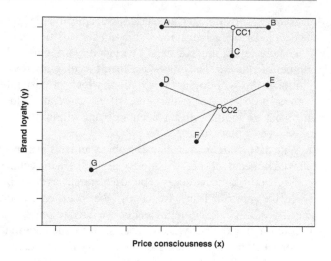

Fig. 9.12 k-means
procedure (step 3)

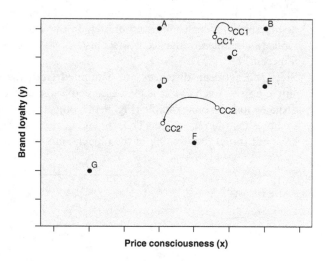

- **Step 3:** Based on the initial partition from step 2, each cluster's geometric center
  (i.e., its centroid) is computed. This is done by computing the mean values of the
  objects contained in the cluster (e.g., A, B, C in the first cluster) regarding each
  of the variables (price consciousness and brand loyalty). As we can see in
  Fig. 9.12, both clusters' centers now shift into new positions (CC1' for the first
  and CC2' for the second cluster).
- **Step 4:** The distances from each object to the newly located cluster centers are
  computed and objects are again assigned to a certain cluster on the basis of their
  minimum distance to other cluster centers (CC1' and CC2'). Since the cluster
  centers' position changed with respect to the initial situation in the first step,
  this could lead to a different cluster solution. This is also true of our example,
  as object E is now – unlike in the initial partition – closer to the first cluster
  center (CC1') than to the second (CC2'). Consequently, this object is now assigned
  to the first cluster (Fig. 9.13).

Fig. 9.13 k-means
procedure (step 4)

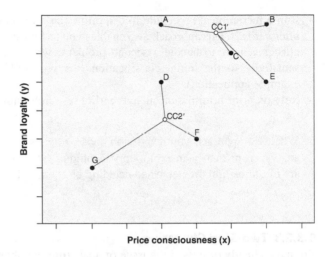

The k-means procedure now repeats until a predetermined number of iterations are reached, or convergence is achieved (i.e., there is no change in the cluster affiliations).

Hierarchical or k-means clustering?

Generally, k-means is superior to hierarchical methods as it is less affected by outliers and the presence of irrelevant clustering variables. Furthermore, k-means can be applied to very large datasets, as the procedure is less computationally demanding than hierarchical methods. In fact, we suggest k-means for sample sizes above 500, especially if many clustering variables are used. However, k-means should only be used on interval or ratio-scaled data as the procedure relies on Euclidean distances. Nevertheless, the procedure is routinely used on ordinal data as well, even though there might be some distortions. Finally, in k-means clustering, we have to pre-specify the number of clusters, which means we need to have some idea of the expected cluster solution before we start.

Decide on the Number of Clusters

When running k-means clustering, the researcher has to pre-specify the number of clusters to retain from the data. This makes k-means somewhat less attractive to some researchers and hinders its routine application in practice. Nevertheless, there are different ways to make this decision:

- Apply the VRC (discussed in the context of hierarchical clustering) on different number of clusters and chose the number that minimizes ω_k. See the ⊕ Web Appendix ($\rightarrow$ Chap. 9) for an application of the VRC.

- Run a hierarchical procedure to determine the number of clusters and k-means afterwards.[12] This approach also enables you to find starting values for the initial cluster centers to handle a second problem, which relates to the procedure's sensitivity to the initial classification (we will follow this approach in the example application).
- Rely on prior information such as earlier research findings.

> Whatever approach you decide to choose, always keep in mind that cluster analysis is primarily an exploratory technique. Thus, practical considerations are of utmost importance when deciding on the number of clusters.

9.3.2.3 Two-Step Clustering

We have already discussed the issue of analyzing variables measured on different scale levels in this chapter. The *two-step cluster analysis* developed by Chiu et al. (2001) has been specifically designed to handle this problem. Like k-means, the procedure can also effectively cope with very large datasets.

The name two-step clustering is already an indication that the algorithm is based on a two-stage approach: In the first stage, the algorithm undertakes a procedure that is very similar to the k-means algorithm. Based on these results, the procedure conducts a modified hierarchical agglomerative clustering procedure that combines the objects sequentially to form homogenous clusters. This is done by building a so-called *cluster feature tree* whose "leaves" represent distinct objects in the dataset.

The procedure can handle categorical and continuous variables simultaneously and offers the user the flexibility to specify the cluster numbers as well as the maximum number of clusters, or to allow the technique to automatically choose the number of clusters on the basis of statistical evaluation criteria. Likewise, the procedure guides the decision of how many clusters to retain from the data by calculating measures of fit such as *Akaike's Information Criterion (AIC)* or *Bayes Information Criterion (BIC)*. These are relative measures of goodness-of-fit and are used to compare different solutions with different numbers of segments. "Relative" means that these criteria are not scaled on a range of, for example, 0 to 1 but can generally take any value. Compared to an alternative solution with a different number of segments, smaller values in AIC or BIC indicate a better fit. SPSS computes solutions for different segment numbers (up to the maximum number of segments specified before) and chooses the appropriate solution by looking for the smallest value in the chosen criterion.

---

[12] See Punji and Stewart (1983) for additional information on this sequential approach.

However, which criterion should we choose? AIC is well-known for overestimating the "correct" number of segments, while BIC has a slight tendency to underestimate this number. Thus, it is worthwhile comparing the clustering outcomes of both criteria and selecting a smaller number of segments than actually indicated by AIC. Nevertheless, when running two separate analyses, one based on AIC and the other based on BIC, SPSS usually renders the same results. But what do we do if the two criteria indicate different numbers of clusters? In such a situation, we should evaluate each solution on practical grounds as well as in light of the solution's interpretability. Do not solely rely on the automatic model selection, especially when there is a combination of continuous and categorical variables, as this does not always work well. Examine the results very carefully!

Two-step clustering also offers an overall goodness-of-fit measure called *silhouette measure of cohesion and separation*. It is essentially based on the average distances between the objects and can vary between −1 and +1. Specifically, a silhouette measure of less than 0.20 indicates a poor solution quality, a measure between 0.20 and 0.50 a fair solution, whereas values of more than 0.50 indicate a good solution. Furthermore, the procedure indicates each variable's importance for the construction of a specific cluster.

These desirable features make the somewhat less popular two-step clustering a viable alternative to the traditional methods. You can find a more detailed discussion of the two-step clustering procedure in the ⌁ Web Appendix (→ Chap. 9), but we will also apply this method to the subsequent example.

9.3.3 Validate and Interpret the Cluster Solution

Before *interpreting the cluster solution*, we need to assess the *stability* of the results. Stability means that the cluster membership of individuals does not change, or only changes little when different clustering methods are used to cluster the objects. Thus, when different methods produce similar results, we claim stability.

The aim of any cluster analysis is to differentiate well between the objects. Thus, the identified clusters should substantially *differ* from each other and members of different clusters should respond differently to different marketing-mix elements and programs.

Lastly, we need to *profile* the cluster solution by using observable variables. This step ensures that we can easily assign new objects to clusters based on observable traits. For example, we could identify clusters based on loyalty to a product, but to use these different clusters, their membership should be identifiable according to tangible variables, such as income, location, or family size in order to be actionable.

The key to successful segmentation is to critically revisit the results of different cluster analysis set-ups (e.g., by using different algorithms on the same data) in terms of managerial relevance. The following criteria help identify a clustering solution (Kotler and Keller 2011; Tonks 2009).

- *Substantial*: The segments are large and profitable enough to serve.
- *Reliability*: Only segments that are stable over time can provide the necessary grounds for a successful marketing strategy. If segments change their composition quickly, or their members' behavior, targeting strategies are not likely to succeed. Therefore, a certain degree of stability is necessary to ensure that marketing strategies can be implemented and produce adequate results. Reliability can be evaluated by critically revisiting and replicating the clustering results at a later date.
- *Accessible*: The segments can be effectively reached and served, which requires them to be characterized by means of observable variables.
- *Actionable*: Effective programs can be formulated to attract and serve the segments.
- *Parsimonious*: To be managerially meaningful, only a small set of substantial clusters should be identified.
- *Familiar*: To ensure management acceptance, the segments composition should be comprehensible.
- *Relevant*: Segments should be relevant in respect of the company's competencies and objectives.
- *Compatibility*: Segmentation results meet other managerial functions' requirements.

9.3.3.1 Stability

Stability is evaluated by using different clustering procedures on the same data and considering the differences that occur. For example, you may first run a hierarchical clustering procedure, followed by k-means clustering to check whether the cluster affiliations of the objects change. Alternatively, in hierarchical clustering, you can use different distance measures and evaluate their effect on the stability of the results. However, note that it is common for results to change even when your solution is adequate. As a rule of thumb, if more than 20% of the cluster affiliations change from one technique to the other, you should reconsider the set-up and use, for example, a different set of clustering variables, or reconsider the number of clusters. Note, however, that this percentage is likely to increase with the number of clusters used.

Another common approach is to split the dataset into two halves and to analyze each separately using the same settings (i.e., the same clustering variables, procedure, number of segments, etc.). You then compare the two solutions' cluster centroids using, for example, t-tests of an ANOVA (see Chap. 6). If these do not differ significantly, you can presume that the overall solution has a high degree of stability.

When using hierarchical clustering, it is also worthwhile changing the order of the objects in your dataset and re-running the analysis to check the results' stability. As discussed earlier, due to ties in the distance matrix, hierarchical clustering can suffer from a non-uniqueness problem. If changing the order of the objects drastically changes the segment compositions (e.g., in terms of segment sizes), you should reconsider the set-up of the analysis and, for example, re-run it with different clustering variables.

9.3.3.2 Differentiation of the Data

To examine whether the final partition differentiates the data well, we need to examine the cluster centroids. This step is highly important, as the analysis sheds light on whether the segments are truly distinct. Only if objects across two (or more) clusters exhibit significantly different means in the clustering variables (or any other relevant variable) can they be distinguished from each other. This can easily be ascertained by comparing the means of the clustering variables across the clusters with independent t-tests or ANOVA (see Chap. 6).

Furthermore, we need to assess the solution's criterion validity. We do this by focusing on the criterion variables that have a theoretical relationship with the clustering variables, but were not included in the analysis. In market research, criterion variables are usually managerial outcomes, such as the sales per person, or willingness-to-pay. If these criterion variables differ significantly, we can conclude that the clusters are distinct groups with criterion validity.

9.3.3.3 Profiling

As indicated at the beginning of the chapter, cluster analysis usually builds on unobservable clustering variables. This creates an important problem when working with the final solution: How can we decide to which segment a new object should be assigned if its unobservable characteristics, such as personality traits, personal values, or lifestyles, are unknown? We could survey these attributes and make a decision based on the clustering variables. However, this is costly and researchers therefore usually try to identify observable variables (e.g., demographics) that best mirror the partition of the objects. More precisely, these observable variables should partition the data into similar groups as the clustering variables do. Using these observable variables, it is then easy to assign a new object (whose cluster membership is unknown) to a certain segment. For example, assume that we used a set of items to assess the respondents' values and learned that a certain segment comprises respondents who appreciate self-fulfillment, enjoyment of life, and a sense of accomplishment, whereas this is not the case in another segment. If we were able to identify explanatory variables such as gender or age, which distinguish these segments adequately, then we could assign a new person to a specific segment on the basis of these observable variables whose value traits may still be unknown.

9.3.3.4 Interpret the Clustering Solution

The interpretation of the solution requires characterizing each segment by using the criterion or other variables (in most cases, demographics). This characterization should focus on criterion variables that convey why the cluster solution is relevant.

For example, you could highlight that customers in one segment have a lower willingness to pay and are satisfied with lower service levels, whereas customers in another segment are willing to pay more for a superior service. By using this information, we can also try to come up with a meaningful name or label for each cluster; that is, one that adequately reflects the objects in the cluster. This is usually a challenging task, especially when unobservable variables are involved.

> While companies develop their own market segments, they frequently use standardized segments, based on established buying trends, habits, and customers' needs to position their products in different markets. The PRIZM lifestyle by Nielsen is one of the most popular segmentation databases. It combines demographic, consumer behavior, and geographic data to help marketers identify, understand, and reach their customers and prospective customers. PRIZM defines every US household in terms of 66 distinct segments to help marketers discern these consumers' likes, dislikes, lifestyles, and purchase behaviors.
>
> An example is segment #51, called "Shotguns & Pickups," which comprises lower to middle-class families in rural areas in the US with a low to mid-level income (http://www.MyBestSegments.com).

Table 9.12 summarizes the steps involved in a hierarchical and k-means clustering. We also describe steps related to two-step clustering, which we will further introduce in the subsequent example.

Table 9.12 Steps involved in carrying out a cluster analysis in SPSS

Theory	Action
Research problem	
Identification of homogenous groups of objects in a population	
Select clustering variables that should be used to form segments	Select relevant variables that potentially exhibit high degrees of criterion validity with regard to a specific managerial objective.
Requirements	
Sufficient sample size	Make sure that the relationship between objects and clustering variables is reasonable (rule of thumb: Number of observations should be at least 2^m, where m is the number of clustering variables). Ensure that the sample size is large enough to guarantee substantial segments.
Low levels of collinearity among the variables	▶ Analyze ▶ Correlate ▶ Bivariate Eliminate or replace highly correlated variables (correlation coefficients > 0.90).

(continued)

Table 9.12 (continued)

Theory	Action
Specification	
Choose the clustering procedure	If there is a limited number of objects in your dataset or you do not know the number of clusters: ▶ Analyze ▶ Classify ▶ Hierarchical Cluster
	If there are many observations (> 500) in your dataset and you have a priori knowledge regarding the number of clusters: ▶ Analyze ▶ Classify ▶ K-Means Cluster
	If there are many observations in your dataset and the clustering variables are measured on different scale levels: ▶ Analyze ▶ Classify ▶ Two-Step Cluster
Select a measure of similarity or dissimilarity (only hierarchical and two-step clustering)	*Hierarchical methods*: ▶ Analyze ▶ Classify ▶ Hierarchical Cluster ▶ Method ▶ Measure
	Depending on the scale level, select the measure; convert variables with multiple categories into a set of binary variables and use matching coefficients; standardize variables if necessary (on a range of 0 to 1 or −1 to 1).
	Two-step clustering: ▶ Analyze ▶ Classify ▶ Two-Step Cluster ▶ Distance Measure
	Use Euclidean distances when all variables are continuous; for mixed variables, use log-likelihood.
Choose clustering algorithm (only hierarchical clustering)	▶ Analyze ▶ Classify ▶ Hierarchical Cluster ▶ Method ▶ Cluster Method
	Use Ward's method if equally sized clusters are expected and no outliers are present. Preferably use single linkage, also to detect outliers.
Decide on the number of clusters	*Hierarchical clustering:* Examine the dendrogram: ▶ Analyze ▶ Classify ▶ Hierarchical Cluster ▶ Plots ▶ Dendrogram
	Draw a scree plot (e.g., using Microsoft Excel) based on the coefficients in the agglomeration schedule.
	Compute the VRC using the ANOVA procedure: ▶ Analyze ▶ Compare Means ▶ One-Way ANOVA
	Move the cluster membership variable in the **Factor** box and the clustering variables in the **Dependent List** box.
	Compute VRC for each segment solution and compare values.
	k-means: Run a hierarchical cluster analysis and decide on the number of segments based on a dendrogram or scree plot; use this information to run k-means with k clusters.

(continued)

Table 9.12 (continued)

Theory	Action
	Compute the VRC using the ANOVA procedure: ▶ Analyze ▶ Classify ▶ K-Means Cluster ▶ Options ▶ ANOVA table; Compute VRC for each segment solution and compare values.
	Two-step clustering: Specify the maximum number of clusters: ▶ Analyze ▶ Classify ▶ Two-Step Cluster ▶ Number of Clusters
	Run separate analyses using AIC and, alternatively, BIC as clustering criterion: ▶ Analyze ▶ Classify ▶ Two-Step Cluster ▶ Clustering Criterion
	Examine the auto-clustering output.
Validate and interpret the cluster solution	
Stability	Re-run the analysis using different clustering procedures, algorithms or distance measures.
	Split the datasets into two halves and compute the clustering variables' centroids; compare centroids for significant differences (e.g., independent-samples t-test or one-way ANOVA).
	Change the ordering of objects in the dataset (hierarchical clustering only).
Differentiation of the data	Compare the cluster centroids across the different clusters for significant differences. Assess the solution's criterion validity.
Profiling	Identify observable variables (e.g., demographics) that best mirror the partition of the objects based on the clustering variables.
Interpretation of the cluster solution	Identify names or labels for each cluster and characterize each cluster by means of observable variables.

9.4   Example

Thaltegos (http://www.thaltegos.com) is a German management consulting company focusing on analytical approaches for marketing, sales, and after sales in the automotive industry. A major US car manufacturer commissioned Thaltegos to support the launch of an innovative electric car. To better position the car in the market, the manufacturer asked Thaltegos to provide transparency concerning the

European car market. In cooperation with a market research firm, Thaltegos gathered data from major automotive manufacturers to develop a segmentation concept. The database consists of the following vehicle characteristics, all of which have been measured on a ratio scale (variable names in parentheses):
- Engine displacement (*displacement*)
- Turning moment in Nm (*moment*)
- Horsepower (*horsepower*)
- Length in mm (*length*)
- Width in mm (*width*)
- Net weight in kg (*weight*)
- Trunk volume in liters (*trunk*)
- Maximum speed in km/h (*speed*)
- Acceleration 0–100 km/h in seconds (*acceleration*)

The pretest sample of 15, randomly taken, cars is shown in Fig. 9.14. In practice, clustering is done on much larger samples but we use a small sample size to illustrate the clustering process. Keep in mind that in this example, the ratio between the objects and clustering variables is much too small. The dataset used is *thaltegos.sav* (🖰 Web Appendix → Chap. 9).

	Name	displacement	moment	horsepower	length	width	weight	trunk	speed	acceleration
1	Kia Picanto 1.1 Start	1086	97	65	3535	1595	929	127	154	15.10
2	Suzuki Splash 1.0	996	90	65	3715	1680	1050	178	160	14.70
3	Renault Clio 1.2	1149	105	75	3986	1719	1155	288	167	13.40
4	Dacia Sandero 1.6	1598	128	87	4020	1746	1111	320	174	11.50
5	Fiat Grande Punto 1.4	1598	140	88	3986	1719	1215	288	177	11.90
6	Peugot 207 1.4	1360	133	88	4030	1748	1214	270	180	12.70
7	Renault Clio 1.6	1368	125	95	4030	1687	1135	275	178	11.40
8	Porsche Cayman	3386	340	295	4341	1801	1340	410	275	5.40
9	Nissan 350Z	3498	353	301	4315	1815	1610	235	250	5.80
10	Mercedes C 200 CDI	2148	270	136	4595	1770	1605	485	208	10.80
11	VWPassat Variant 2.0	1968	320	140	4774	1820	1596	588	201	10.50
12	Skoda Octavia 2.0	1968	320	140	4572	1769	1425	580	207	9.70
13	Mercedes E 280	2996	300	231	4852	1822	1660	540	250	7.30
14	Audi A6 2.4	2393	230	177	4916	1855	1525	546	231	8.90
15	BMW 525i	2497	250	218	4841	1846	1550	520	245	7.50

Fig. 9.14 Data

In the next step, we will run several different clustering procedures on the data. We first apply a hierarchical cluster analysis based on Euclidean distances, using the single linkage method. This will help us determine a suitable number of segments, which we will use as input for a subsequent k-means clustering. Finally, we will run a two-step cluster analysis using SPSS.

9.4.1 Pre-analysis: Collinearity Assessment

Before we start with the clustering process, we have to examine the variables for substantial collinearity. Just by looking at the variable set, we suspect that there are some highly correlated variables in our dataset. For example, we expect rather high correlations between *speed* and *acceleration*. To determine this, we run a bivariate correlation analysis by clicking ▶ Analyze ▶ Correlate ▶ Bivariate, which will open a dialog box similar to that in Fig. 9.15. Enter all variables into the **Variables** box and select the box **Pearson** (under **Correlation Coefficients**) because these are continuous variables.

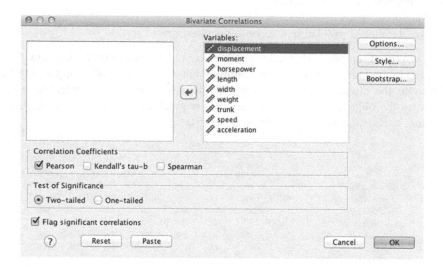

Fig. 9.15 Bivariate correlations dialog box

The correlation matrix in Table 9.13 supports our expectations – there are several variables that have high correlations. *Displacement* exhibits high (absolute) correlation coefficients with *horsepower*, *speed*, and *acceleration*, with values well above 0.90, indicating possible collinearity issues. Similarly, *horsepower* is highly correlated with *speed* and *acceleration*. Likewise, *length* shows a high degree of correlation with *width*, *weight*, and *trunk*.

A potential solution to this problem would be to run a factor analysis and perform a cluster analysis on the resulting factor scores. Since the factors obtained are, by definition, independent, this would allow for an effective handling of the collinearity issue. However, as this approach is associated with several problems (see Box 9.1), we should reduce the variables, for example, by omitting *displacement*, *horsepower*, and *length* from the subsequent analyses. The remaining variables still provide a sound basis for carrying out cluster analysis.

Table 9.13 Correlation matrix

Correlations

		displacement	moment	horsepower	length	width	weight	trunk	speed	acceleration
displacement	Pearson Correlation	1	.875**	.983**	.657**	.764**	.768**	.470	.967**	-.969**
	Sig. (2-tailed)		.000	.000	.008	.001	.001	.077	.000	.000
	N	15	15	15	15	15	15	15	15	15
moment	Pearson Correlation	.875**	1	.847**	.767**	.766**	.862**	.691**	.859**	-.861**
	Sig. (2-tailed)	.000		.000	.001	.001	.000	.004	.000	.000
	N	15	15	15	15	15	15	15	15	15
horsepower	Pearson Correlation	.983**	.847**	1	.608*	.732**	.714**	.408	.968**	-.961**
	Sig. (2-tailed)	.000	.000		.016	.002	.003	.131	.000	.000
	N	15	15	15	15	15	15	15	15	15
length	Pearson Correlation	.657**	.767**	.608*	1	.912**	.921**	.934**	.741**	-.714**
	Sig. (2-tailed)	.008	.001	.016		.000	.000	.000	.002	.003
	N	15	15	15	15	15	15	15	15	15
width	Pearson Correlation	.764**	.766**	.732**	.912**	1	.884**	.783**	.819**	-.818**
	Sig. (2-tailed)	.001	.001	.002	.000		.000	.001	.000	.000
	N	15	15	15	15	15	15	15	15	15
weight	Pearson Correlation	.768**	.862**	.714**	.921**	.884**	1	.785**	.778**	-.763**
	Sig. (2-tailed)	.001	.000	.003	.000	.000		.001	.001	.001
	N	15	15	15	15	15	15	15	15	15
trunk	Pearson Correlation	.470	.691**	.408	.934**	.733**	.785**	1	.579*	-.552*
	Sig. (2-tailed)	.077	.004	.131	.000	.001	.001		.024	.033
	N	15	15	15	15	15	15	15	15	15
speed	Pearson Correlation	.967**	.859**	.968**	.741**	.819**	.778**	.579*	1	-.971**
	Sig. (2-tailed)	.000	.000	.000	.002	.000	.001	.024		.000
	N	15	15	15	15	15	15	15	15	15
acceleration	Pearson Correlation	-.969**	-.861**	-.961**	-.714**	-.818**	-.763**	-.552*	-.971**	1
	Sig. (2-tailed)	.000	.000	.000	.003	.000	.001	.033	.000	
	N	15	15	15	15	15	15	15	15	15

**. Correlation is significant at the 0.01 level (2-tailed).

*. Correlation is significant at the 0.05 level (2-tailed).

9.4.2   Hierarchical Clustering

To run the hierarchical clustering procedure, click on ▶ Analyze ▶ Classify ▶
Hierarchical Cluster, which opens a dialog box similar to Fig. 9.16.

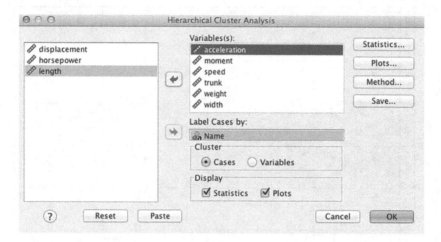

Fig. 9.16 Hierarchical cluster analysis dialog box

Move the variables *acceleration*, *moment*, *speed*, *trunk*, *weight*, and *width* into
the **Variable(s)** box and specify *name* as the labeling variable (box **Label Cases
by**). The **Statistics** option gives us the opportunity to request the distance matrix
(labeled proximity matrix in this case) and the agglomeration schedule, which
provides information on the objects being combined at each stage of the clustering
process. Furthermore, we can specify the number or range of clusters to retain from
the data. As we do not yet know how many clusters to retain, just check the box
Agglomeration schedule and continue.

Under **Plots**, check the box **Dendrogram** to graphically display the distances at
which objects and clusters are joined. Also ensure you select the **Icicle** diagram (**All
clusters**), which is yet another graph for displaying clustering solutions.

The option **Method** allows us to specify the cluster method (e.g., single linkage
or Ward's method), the distance measure (e.g., Chebychev distance or the Jaccard
coefficient), and the type of standardization of values. In this example, we use the
single linkage method (**Nearest neighbor**) based on **Euclidean distances**. Since
the variables are measured on different levels (e.g., speed versus weight), make sure
to standardize the variables, using the **Range −1 to 1 (by variable)** in the
Transform Values drop-down list.

Lastly, the **Save** option enables us to save cluster memberships for a single
solution or a range of solutions. Saved variables can then be used in subsequent

analyses to explore differences between groups. As a start, we will skip this option, so continue and click on **OK** in the main menu.

First, we take a closer look at the agglomeration schedule (Table 9.14), which displays the objects or clusters combined at each stage (second and third column) and the distances at which this merger takes place. For example, in the first stage, objects 5 and 6 are merged at a distance of 0.149. From here onward, the resulting cluster is labeled as indicated by the first object involved in this merger, which is object 5. The last column on the very right tells you in which stage of the algorithm this cluster will appear next. In this case, this happens in the second step, where it is merged with object 7 at a distance of 0.184. The resulting cluster is still labeled 5, and so on. Similar information is provided by the *icicle diagram* shown in Fig. 9.17. Its name stems from the analogy to rows of icicles hanging from the eaves of a house. The diagram is read from the bottom to the top; the columns correspond to the objects being clustered, and the rows represent the number of clusters.

Table 9.14 Agglomeration schedule

Agglomeration Schedule

Stage	Cluster Combined		Coefficients	Stage Cluster First Appears		Next Stage
	Cluster 1	Cluster 2		Cluster 1	Cluster 2	
1	5	6	.149	0	0	2
2	5	7	.184	1	0	3
3	4	5	.201	0	2	5
4	14	15	.213	0	0	6
5	3	4	.220	0	3	8
6	13	14	.267	0	4	11
7	11	12	.321	0	0	9
8	2	3	.353	0	5	10
9	10	11	.357	0	7	11
10	1	2	.389	0	8	14
11	10	13	.484	9	6	13
12	8	9	.575	0	0	13
13	8	10	.618	12	11	14
14	1	8	.910	10	13	0

As described earlier, we can use the agglomeration schedule to determine the number of segments to retain from the data. Next, we generate a *Scree Plot* by plotting the distances (**Coefficients** column in Table 9.14) against the number of clusters. The distinct break (elbow) indicates the solution regarding where an additional combination of two objects or clusters would occur at a greatly increased distance.

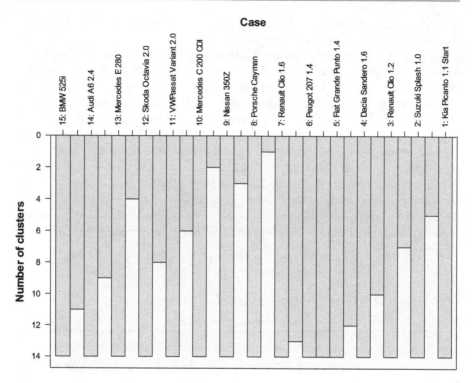

Fig. 9.17   Icicle diagram

Thus, the number of clusters prior to this merger is the most probable solution. SPSS does not automatically provide this plot. To generate a scree plot we have to double-click the **Agglomeration Schedule** in the output window. Next, we select all coefficients and right-click the mouse button. In the menu that opens up, we have to select   **Create Graph ▶ Line** (Fig. 9.18). SPSS will add a line chart to the output which represents a scree plot. Note that in this plot, the *x*-axis represents the merging steps which means that, for example, the step from stage 13 to 14 represents the step from the two-cluster to the one-cluster solution. Note that – unlike in the factor analysis – we do not pick the solution with one cluster less than indicated by the elbow. The sharp increase in distance when switching from a one to a two-cluster solution occurs in almost all analyses and must not be viewed as a reliable indicator for the decision regarding the number of segments.

The scree plot in Fig. 9.19 shows that there is no clear elbow indicating a suitable number of clusters to retain. Based on the results, one could argue for a five-segment or six-segment solution. However, considering that there are merely 15 objects in the dataset, this seems too many, as we then have very small (and, most probably, meaningless) clusters. Consequently, a two, three or four-segment solution seems more appropriate.

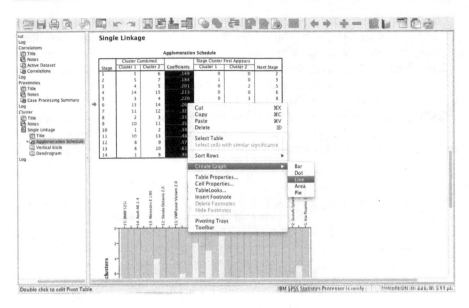

Fig. 9.18 Generating a scree plot

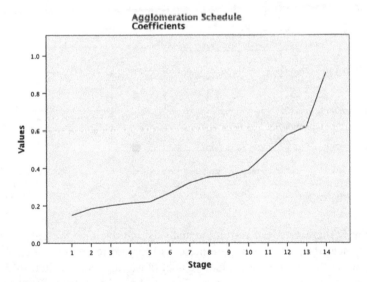

Fig. 9.19 Scree plot

Let's take a look at the dendrogram shown in Fig. 9.20. We read the dendrogram from the left to the right. Vertical lines are objects and clusters joined together – their position indicates the distance at which this merger takes place. When creating a dendrogram, SPSS rescales the distances to a range of 0–25; that is, the last merging step to a one-cluster solution takes place at a (rescaled) distance of 25. Note that this differs from our manual calculation shown in Fig. 9.9, where we did not do any rescaling! Again, the analysis only provides a rough guidance regarding the number of segments to retain. The change in distances between the mergers indicates that (besides a two-segment solution) both a three and four-segment solution are appropriate.

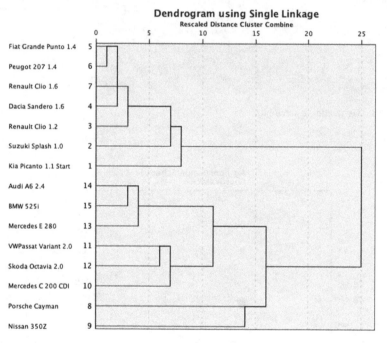

Fig. 9.20 Dendrogram

To clarify this issue, let's re-run the analysis, but this time we pre-specify different segment numbers to compare these with regard to content validity. To do so, just re-run the analysis using hierarchical clustering. Now switch to the **Save** option, specify a range of solutions from 2 to 4 and run the analysis. SPSS generates the same output but also adds three additional variables to your dataset (*CLU4_1*, *CLU3_1*, and *CLU2_1*), which reflect each object's cluster membership for the respective analysis. SPSS automatically places *CLU* in front, followed by the number of clusters (4, 3, or 2), to identify each object's cluster membership. Table 9.15 illustrates the results. SPSS does not produce this table for us, so we need to enter these cluster memberships ourselves in a table or spreadsheet.

Table 9.15 Cluster memberships

Name	Observation member of cluster (four clusters)	Observation member of cluster (three clusters)	Observation member of cluster (two clusters)
Kia Picanto 1.1 Start	1	1	1
Suzuki Splash 1.0	1	1	1
Renault Clio 1.2	1	1	1
Dacia Sandero 1.6	1	1	1
Fiat Grande Punto 1.4	1	1	1
Peugot 207 1.4	1	1	1
Renault Clio 1.6	1	1	1
Porsche Cayman	2	2	2
Nissan 350Z	3	2	2
Mercedes C 200 CDI	4	3	2
VW Passat Variant 2.0	4	3	2
Skoda Octavia 2.0	4	3	2
Mercedes E 280	4	3	2
Audi A6 2.4	4	3	2
BMW 525i	4	3	2

When we view the results, a three-segment solution appears promising. In this solution, the first segment comprises compact cars, whereas the second segment contains sports cars, and the third limousines. Increasing the solution by one segment would further split up the sports cars segment into two sub-segments. This does not appear to be very helpful, as now two of the four segments comprise only one object. This underlines the single linkage method's tendency to identify outlier objects—in this case the Nissan 350Z and Porsche Cayman. In this specific example, the Nissan 350Z and Porsche Cayman should not be regarded as outliers in a classical sense but rather as those cars which may be key competitors in the sports car market. In contrast, the two-segment solution appears to be rather imprecise considering the vast differences in the mix of sports and middle-sized cars in this solution.

To get a better overview of the results, let's examine the cluster centroids; that is, the mean values of the objects contained in the cluster on selected variables. To do so, we split up the dataset using the **Split File** command (▶ Data ▶ Split File) (see Chap. 5). This enables us to analyze the data on the basis of a grouping variable's values. In this case, we choose *CLU3_1* as the grouping variable and select the option **Compare groups**. Subsequently, we calculate descriptive statistics (▶ Analyze ▶ Descriptive Statistics ▶ Descriptives, also see Chap. 5) and calculate the mean, minimum and maximum values, as well as the standard deviations of the clustering variables. Table 9.16 shows the results for the variables *weight*, *speed*, and *acceleration*.

Table 9.16 Cluster centroids

Descriptive Statistics

CLU3_1		N	Minimum	Maximum	Mean	Std. Deviation
1	weight	7	929	1215	1115.57	100.528
	speed	7	154	180	170.00	9.950
	acceleration	7	11.40	15.10	12.9571	1.50317
	Valid N (listwise)	7				
2	weight	2	1340	1610	1475.00	190.919
	speed	2	250	275	262.50	17.678
	acceleration	2	5.40	5.80	5.6000	.28284
	Valid N (listwise)	2				
3	weight	6	1425	1660	1560.17	81.081
	speed	6	201	250	223.67	21.163
	acceleration	6	7.30	10.80	9.1167	1.48649
	Valid N (listwise)	6				

From the descriptive statistics, it seems that the first segment contains light-weight compact cars (with a lower maximum speed and acceleration). In contrast, the second segment comprises two sports cars with greater speed and acceleration, whereas the third segment contains limousines with an increased weight and intermediate speed and acceleration. Since the descriptives do not tell us if these differences are significant, we could use a one-way ANOVA (▶ Analyze ▶ Compare Means ▶ One-Way ANOVA) to calculate the cluster centroids and compare the differences formally.

9.4.3 k-means Clustering

In the next step, we want to use the *k-means* method on the data. We have previously seen that we need to specify the number of segments when conducting k-means clustering. SPSS then initiates cluster centers and assigns objects to the clusters based on their minimum distance to these centers. Instead of letting SPSS choose the centers, we can also save the centroids (cluster centers) from our previous analysis as input for the k-means procedure. To do this, we need to do some data management in SPSS, as the cluster centers have to be supplied in a specific format. Consequently, we need to aggregate the data first (briefly introduced in Chap. 5). By selecting ▶ Data ▶ Aggregate, a dialog box similar to Fig. 9.21 opens up. Note that we choose **Display Variable Names** instead of **Display Variable Labels** by clicking the right mouse button on the left box showing the variables in the dataset. Now we proceed by choosing the cluster membership variable (*CLU3_1*) as a break variable and move the *moment, width, weight, trunk, speed,* and *acceleration* variables into the **Summaries of Variable(s)** box. When using the default settings, SPSS computes the variables' mean values along the lines of the break variable (indicated by the postfix *_mean*, which is added to

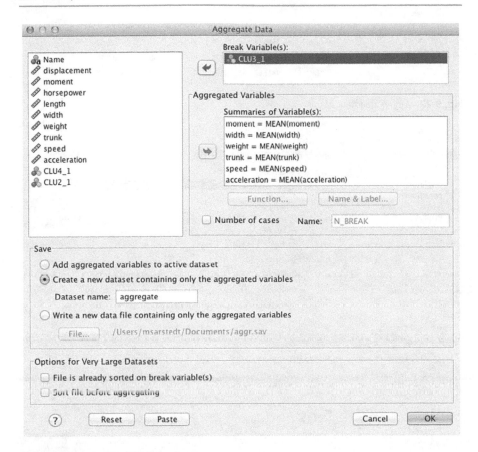

Fig. 9.21 Aggregate data dialog box

each aggregate variable's name), which corresponds to the cluster centers that we need for the k-means analysis. You can change each aggregate variable's name from the original one by removing the postfix _mean – using the **Name & Label** option – if you want to. Lastly, we do not want to add the aggregated variables to the active dataset, but rather need to create a new dataset comprising only the aggregated variables. You must therefore check this under **Save** and specify a dataset label such as *aggregate*. When clicking on **OK**, a new dataset labeled *aggregate* is created and opened automatically.

The new dataset is almost in the right format – but we still need to change the break variable's name from *CLU3_1* to *cluster_* (SPSS will issue a warning but this can be safely ignored). The final dataset should have the form shown in Fig. 9.22.

Now let's proceed by using k-means clustering. Make sure that you open the original dataset and go to Analyze ▶ Classify ▶ K-Means Cluster, which brings up a new dialog box (Fig. 9.23).

	cluster_	moment	width	weight	trunk	speed	acceleration
1	1	116.86	1699.14	1115.57	249.43	170.00	12.96
2	2	346.50	1808.00	1475.00	322.50	262.50	5.60
3	3	281.67	1813.67	1560.17	543.17	223.67	9.12

Fig. 9.22 Aggregated data file

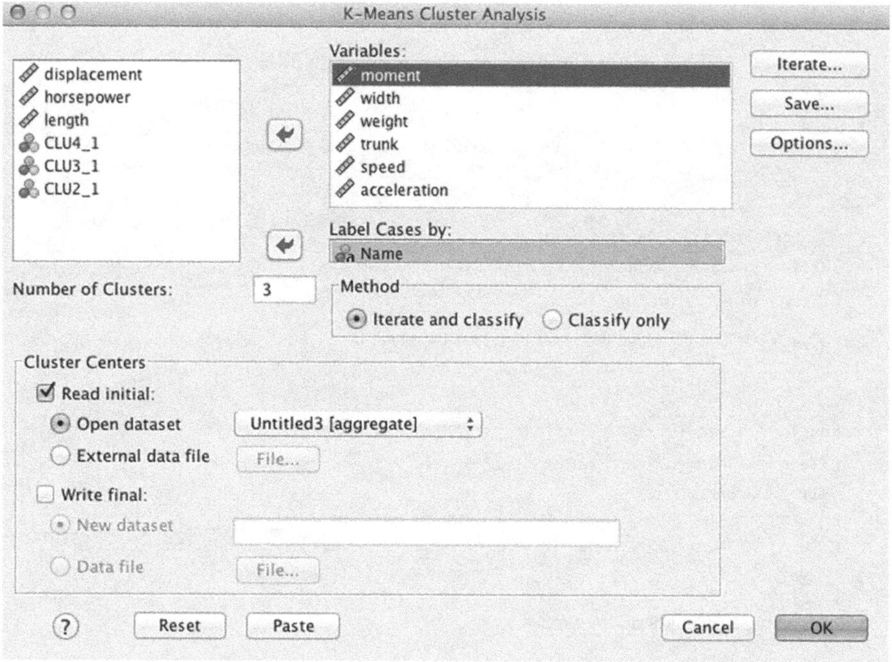

Fig. 9.23 K-means cluster analysis dialog box

As you did in the hierarchical clustering analysis, move the six clustering variables to the **Variables** box and specify the case labels (variable *name*). To use the cluster centers from our previous analysis, check the box **Read initial** and click on **Open dataset**. You can now choose the dataset labeled *aggregate*. Specify 3, which corresponds to the result of the hierarchical clustering analysis, in the **Number of Clusters** box. The **Iterate** option is of less interest to us. Instead, click on **Save** and check the box **Cluster Membership**. This creates a new variable indicating each object's final cluster membership. SPSS indicates whether each observation is a member of cluster 1, 2, or 3. Under **Options**, you can request several statistics and specify how missing values should be treated. Ensure that you request the **Initial cluster centers** as well as the **ANOVA table** and that you exclude the missing values listwise (default). Now start the analysis.

The k-means procedure generates Tables 9.17 and 9.18, which show the initial and final cluster centers. As you can see, these are identical (also compare Fig. 9.22), which indicates that the initial partitioning of the objects in the first step of the k-means procedure was retained during the analysis. This means that it was not possible to reduce the overall within-cluster variation by re-assigning objects to different clusters.

Table 9.17 Initial cluster centers

Initial Cluster Centers

	Cluster		
	1	2	3
moment	117	347	282
width	1699	1808	1814
weight	1116	1475	1560
trunk	249	323	543
speed	170	263	224
acceleration	12.96	5.60	9.12

Input from FILE Subcommand

Table 9.18 Final cluster centers

Final Cluster Centers

	Cluster		
	1	2	3
moment	117	347	282
width	1699	1808	1814
weight	1116	1475	1560
trunk	249	323	543
speed	170	263	224
acceleration	12.96	5.60	9.12

Likewise, the output **Iteration History** shows that there is no change in the cluster centers. Similarly, if you compare the partitioning of objects into the three clusters by examining the newly generated variable QCL_1, you see that there is no change in the clusters' composition. At first sight, this does not look like a very exciting result, but this in fact signals that the initial clustering solution is stable.

In other words, the fact that two different clustering methods yield the same outcomes provides some evidence of the results' stability.

In contrast to hierarchical clustering, the k-means outputs provide us with an ANOVA of the cluster centers (Table 9.19). As you can see, all the clustering variables' means differ significantly across at least two of the three segments, because the null hypothesis is rejected in every case (**Sig.** ≤ 0.05).

Table 9.19 ANOVA output

ANOVA

	Cluster		Error			
	Mean Square	df	Mean Square	df	F	Sig.
moment	64318.455	2	784.224	12	82.015	.000
width	23904.771	2	1966.183	12	12.158	.001
weight	339920.393	2	10829.712	12	31.388	.000
trunk	142764.143	2	4311.754	12	33.110	.000
speed	8628.283	2	262.153	12	32.913	.000
acceleration	50.855	2	2.057	12	24.722	.000

Since we used the prior analysis results from hierarchical clustering as an input for the k-means procedure, the problem of selecting the "correct" number of segments is not problematic in this example. As discussed above, we could have also used the VRC to make that decision. In the ⌂ Web Appendix (→ Chap. 9), we present a VRC application to this example.

9.4.4   Two-step Clustering

As a last step of the analysis, we conduct a two-step clustering approach. First, go to Analyze ▶ Classify ▶ Two-Step Cluster. A new dialog box opens, similar to that shown in Fig. 9.24. First, move the variables we used in the previous analyses to the **Continuous Variables** box.

The **Distance Measure** box determines how the distance between two objects or clusters is computed. While **Log-likelihood** can be used for categorical and continuous variables, the **Euclidean** distance can only be applied when all of the variables are continuous. Unless your dataset contains categorical variables (e.g., gender) you should choose the Euclidean distance measure, as this generally provides better results. If you use ordinal variables and therefore use the **Log-likelihood** procedure, check that the answer categories are equidistant. In our dataset, all variables are continuous, therefore select the second option, namely **Euclidean**.

Under **Number of Clusters**, you can specify a fixed number or a maximum number of segments to retain from the data. One of two-step clustering's major

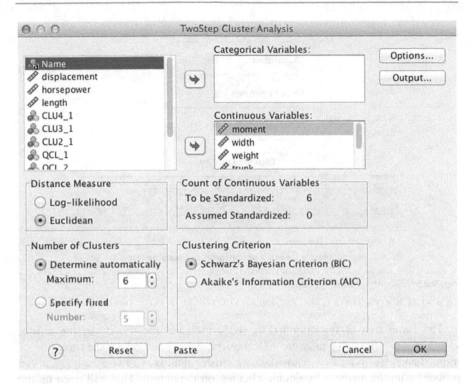

Fig. 9.24 Two-step cluster analysis dialog box

advantages is that it allows the automatic selection of the number of clusters. To make use of this advantage, you should specify a maximum number of clusters, for example, 6. Next to this box, in which the number of clusters is specified, you can choose between two criteria (also referred to as model selection or information criteria) which SPSS can use to pick an appropriate number of segments. Select Schwarz's Bayesian Criterion (BIC) but – as discussed above – you should re-run the analysis using AIC.

Under **Options**, you can specify issues related to outlier treatment, memory allocation, and variable standardization. Variables that are already standardized have to be assigned as such, but since this is not the case in our analysis, you can simply proceed.

Lastly, under the option **Output**, we can specify additional variables for describing the obtained clusters. However, let's stick to the default option for now. Make sure that you click the box **Create cluster membership variable** before clicking **Continue**.

SPSS produces a very simple output, as shown in Fig. 9.25. The upper part of the output describes the algorithm applied, the number of variables used (labeled input features) and the final number of clusters retained from the data. In our case, the number of clusters is chosen according to BIC, which indicates a two-segment solution (the same holds when using AIC instead of BIC). Note that this result differs from our previous analysis where we used a three-cluster solution!

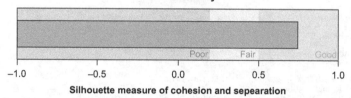

Model Summary

Algorithm	TwoStep
Input Features	6
Clusters	2

Cluster Quality

Silhouette measure of cohesion and sepearation

Fig. 9.25 Two-step clustering output

The lower part of the output (Fig. 9.25) indicates the quality of the cluster solution. The silhouette measure of cohesion and separation reaches a value of more than 0.50, indicating a satisfactory cluster quality. Consequently, you can proceed with the analysis by double-clicking on the output. This will open up the model viewer (Fig. 9.26), an evaluation tool that graphically presents the structure of the revealed clusters.

The model viewer provides us with two windows: The main view, which initially shows a model summary (left-hand side), and an auxiliary view, which initially features the cluster sizes (right-hand side). At the bottom of each window (option: **View**), you can request different information on each of the clusters. To further analyze the clusters, select **Clusters** in the main view and **Predictor Importance** in the auxiliary view (Fig. 9.26).

In the main view, we can now see a description of the two clusters, including their (relative) sizes. Furthermore, the output shows each clustering variables' mean values across the two clusters as well as their relative importance. Darker shades (i.e., higher values in feature importance) denote the variable's greater importance for the clustering solution (in terms of predicting each observation's cluster membership). Comparing the results, we can see that *moment* is the most important variable for each of the clusters, followed by *weight*, *speed*, *width*, *acceleration*, and *trunk*. Clicking on one of the boxes will show a graph with the frequency distribution of each cluster.

The auxiliary view on the right-hand side shows an overview of the variables' overall importance for predicting the clustering solution, which provides the same result as the cluster-specific analysis. The model viewer provides us with additional options for visualizing the results or comparing clustering solutions. It is

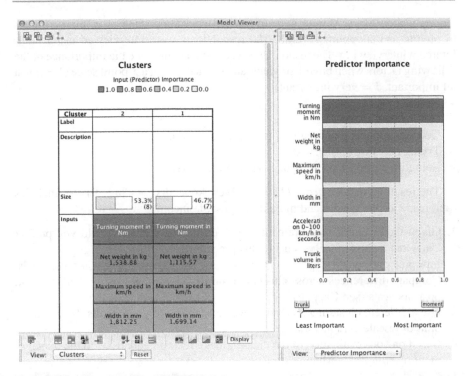

Fig. 9.26 Additional options in the model viewer

worthwhile to simply play around with the different self-explanatory options. So go ahead and explore the model viewer's features yourself!

9.5 Shopping at Projekt 2 (Case Study)

Facing dramatically declining sales and decreased turnover, retailers such as H&M and Zara are rethinking their pricing strategies, scaling back inventories, and improving the fashion content. Men's accessories are one of the bright spots and Projekt 2, an apparel retailer, has jumped on the trend with three recently opened shops prominently featuring this category. The largest men's store opened in Munich in 2011 and stocks top brands in jewelry, watches, sunglasses, and leather goods. By providing a better showcase for men's accessories, Projekt 2 aims at strengthening its position in a market that is often neglected in the larger department stores. This is because the men's accessories business generally requires expertise in buying since this typically involves small, artisan vendors – an investment many department stores are not willing to make.

Projekt 2's strategy seemed to be successful. However, before opening accessories shops in any other existing stores, the company wanted to gain further insights into their customers' preferences. Consequently, a survey was conducted among visitors of the Munich store to gain a deeper understanding of their attitudes to buying and shopping. Overall, 180 respondents were interviewed using mall-intercept interviewing. The respondents were asked to indicate the importance of the following factors when buying products and services using a 5-point scale (1 = not at all important, 5 = very important):

- Saving time (x_1),
- Getting bargains (x_2),
- Getting products that aren't on the high street (x_3),
- Trying new things (x_4), and
- Being aware of what companies have to offer (x_5).

The resulting dataset *projekt2.sav* (⬙ Web Appendix → Chap. 9) also includes each respondent's gender and monthly disposable income.

1. Given the levels of measurement, which clustering method would you prefer? Carry out a cluster analysis using this procedure.
2. Interpret and profile the obtained clusters by examining cluster centroids. Compare differences across clusters on observed variables using ANOVA and post-hoc tests (see Chap. 6).
3. Use a different clustering method to test the stability of your results. If necessary, omit or rescale certain variables.
4. Based on your evaluation of the dataset, make recommendations to the management of Projekt 2's Munich store.

Review Questions

1. In your own words, explain the objective and basic concept of cluster analysis.
2. What are the differences between hierarchical and partitioning methods? When do we use hierarchical or partitioning methods?
3. Run the k-means analysis again from the example application (*thaltegos.sav*, ⬙ Web Appendix → Chap. 9). Compute a three-segment solution and compare the results with those obtained by the initial hierarchical clustering.
4. Run the k-means analysis again from the example application (*thaltegos.sav*, ⬙ Web Appendix → Chap. 9). Use a factor analysis considering all nine variables and perform a cluster analysis on the resulting factor scores (factor-cluster segmentation). Interpret the results and compare these with the initial analysis.
5. Repeat the manual calculations of the hierarchical clustering procedure from the beginning of the chapter, but use complete or average linkage as clustering method. Compare the results with those of the single linkage method.
6. What clustering variables could be used to segment:
   - The market for smartphones?
   - The market for chocolate?
   - The market for car insurances?

Further Readings

Bottomley, P., & Nairn, A. (2004). Blinded by science: The managerial consequences of inadequately validated cluster analysis solutions. *International Journal of Market Research* 46(2):171–187

In this article, the authors investigate if managers could distinguish between cluster analysis outputs derived from real-world and random data. They show that some managers feel able to assign meaning to random data devoid of a meaningful structure, and even feel confident formulating entire marketing strategies from cluster analysis solutions generated from such data. As such, the authors provide a reminder of the importance of validating clustering solutions with caution.

Everitt, B. S., Landau, S., & Leese, M. (2001). *Cluster analysis*, (4th edn). London: Arnold.

This book is comprehensive yet relatively non-mathematical, focusing on the practical aspects of cluster analysis. The authors discuss classical approaches as well as more recent methods such as finite mixture modeling and neural networks.

Journal of Classification. New York, NY: Springer, available at: http://www.springer.com/statistics/statistical+theory+and+methods/journal/357

If you are interested in the most recent advances in clustering techniques and have a strong background in statistics, you should check out this journal. Among the disciplines represented are statistics, psychology, biology, anthropology, archeology, astronomy, business, marketing, and linguistics.

Punj, G., & Stewart, D. W. (1983). Cluster analysis in marketing research: Review and suggestions for application. *Journal of Marketing Research* 20(2):134–148

In this seminal article, the authors discuss several issues in applications of cluster analysis and provide further theoretical discussion of the concepts and rules of thumb that we included in this chapter.

Romesburg, C. (2004). *Cluster analysis for researchers*. Morrisville: Lulu Press.

Charles Romesburg nicely illustrates the most frequently used methods of hierarchical cluster analysis for readers with limited backgrounds in mathematics and statistics.

Wedel, M., & Kamakura, W. A. (2000). *Market segmentation: Conceptual and methodological foundations* (2nd ed.). Boston: Kluwer Academic.

This book is a clear, readable, and interesting presentation of applied market segmentation techniques. The authors explain the theoretical concepts of recent analysis techniques and provide sample applications. Probably the most comprehensive text in the market.

References

Andrews, R. L., & Currim, I. S. (2003). Recovering and profiling the true segmentation structure in markets: An empirical investigation. *International Journal of Research in Marketing, 20*(2), 177–192.

Arabie, P., & Hubert, L. (1994). Cluster analysis in marketing research. In R. P. Bagozzi (Ed.), *Advanced methods in marketing research* (pp. 160–189). Cambridge: Basil Blackwell & Mott, Ltd.

Bishop, C. M. (2006). *Pattern recognition and machine learning*. Berlin: Springer.

Caliński, T., & Harabasz, J. (1974). A dendrite method for cluster analysis. *Communications in Statistics—Theory and Methods, 3*(1), 1–27.

Chiu, T., Fang, D., Chen, J., Wang, Y., & Jeris, C. (2001). A robust and scalable clustering algorithm for mixed type attributes in large database environment. In *Proceedings of the 7th ACM SIGKDD international conference in knowledge discovery and data mining* (pp. 263–268). San Francisco, CA: Association for Computing Machinery.

Dolnicar, S. (2003). Using cluster analysis for market segmentation—typical misconceptions, established methodological weaknesses and some recommendations for improvement. *Australasian Journal of Market Research, 11*(2), 5–12.

Dolnicar, S., & Grun, B. (2009). Challenging "factor-cluster segmentation". *Journal of Travel Research, 47*(1), 63–71.

Dolnicar, S., & Lazarevski, K. (2009). Methodological reasons for the theory/practice divide in market segmentation. *Journal of Marketing Management, 25*(3–4), 357–373.

Formann, A. K. (1984). *Die Latent-Class-Analyse: Einführung in die Theorie und Anwendung*. Beltz: Weinheim.

Kaufman, L., & Rousseeuw, P. J. (2005). *Finding groups in data. An introduction to cluster analysis*. Hoboken, NY: Wiley.

Kohonen, T. (1982). Self-organized formation of topologically correct feature maps. *Biological Cybernetics, 43*(1), 59–69.

Kotler, P., & Keller, K. L. (2011). *Marketing management* (14th ed.). Upper Saddle River, NJ: Prentice Hall.

Larson, J. S., Bradlow, E. T., & Fader, P. S. (2005). An exploratory look at supermarket shopping paths. *International Journal of Research in Marketing, 22*(4), 395–414.

McLachlan, G. J., & Peel, D. (2000). *Finite mixture models*. New York: Wiley.

Milligan, G. W., & Cooper, M. (1985). An examination of procedures for determining the number of clusters in a data set. *Psychometrika, 50*(2), 159–179.

Milligan, G. W., & Cooper, M. (1988). A study of variable standardization. *Journal of Classification, 5*(2), 181–204.

Moroko, L., & Uncles, M. D. (2009). Employer branding and market segmentation. *Journal of Brand Management, 17*(3), 181–196.

Okazaki, S. (2006). What do we know about mobile internet adopters? A cluster analysis. *Information Management, 43*(2), 127–141.

Punji, G., & Stewart, D. W. (1983). Cluster analysis in marketing research: Review and suggestions for application. *Journal of Marketing Research, 20*(2), 134–148.

Sheppard, A. (1996). The sequence of factor analysis and cluster analysis: Differences in segmentation and dimensionality through the use of raw and factor scores. *Tourism Analysis, 1*, 49–57.

Tonks, D. G. (2009). Validity and the design of market segments. *Journal of Marketing Management, 25*(3/4), 341–356.

Wedel, M., & Kamakura, W. A. (2000). *Market segmentation: Conceptual and methodological foundations* (2nd ed.). Boston, NE: Kluwer Academic.

van der Kloot, W. A., Spaans, A. M. J., & Heinser, W. J. (2005). Instability of hierarchical cluster analysis due to input order of the data: The PermuCLUSTER solution. *Psychological Methods, 10*(4), 468–476.

Communicating the Results

10

Learning Objectives

After reading this chapter you should understand:

- Why communicating the results is a crucial element of every market research study.
- Which elements should be included in a written research report and how these elements can be structured.
- How to communicate the findings in an oral presentation.
- Ethical issues regarding the communication of the report findings to the client.

Keywords

Ethics • Follow-up • Identify and understand the audience • Minto principle • Oral presentation • Pyramid structure for presentations • Report structure • Visual aids • Written report

To discuss the significance and future development of information and communication technologies (ICT), TNS Infratest published the International Delphi Study 2030 in May 2010. 551 international experts from business, academia and politics assessed 144 future scenarios in two consecutive survey waves by mid 2009. The development and use of ICT and media up to 2030 were assessed under four focal issues:

- Social implications of ICT development,
- ICT innovation policy,
- Infrastructure development and key technologies, and
- ICT drivers of innovation in central areas of application.

The final 300-page report provides a comprehensive overview over the survey method, survey period, sample structure, study's results and includes recommendations for public policy and companies. The authors also included an executive summary which highlights the main findings by means of five core messages.

M. Sarstedt and E. Mooi, *A Concise Guide to Market Research*,
Springer Texts in Business and Economics, DOI 10.1007/978-3-642-53965-7_10,
© Springer-Verlag Berlin Heidelberg 2014

10.1 Introduction

Communicating results is a critical step in a market research project. This includes giving clear answers to the research questions and recommending a course of action, where appropriate. The importance of communicating marketing research results should not be underestimated. Even if the research has been carefully conducted, spending too little time and energy on communication makes it difficult for recipients to understand the implications of the results and to appreciate the study's quality. Clear communication may also set the stage for follow-up research. To communicate the findings effectively, these need to be understandable to clients who may know little about market research and who may even be unfamiliar with the specific market research project. Hence, the communication must provide a clear picture of the whole project and should be relevant for the audience.

Usually, market researchers provide a written report summarizing the key findings. This report is the written evidence of the research effort and is often the only record of the full results. In addition, market researchers frequently present their findings orally, which requires specific communication skills. Identifying the audience is critical, as this determines how the findings are best communicated.

In this chapter, we discuss guidelines on how to communicate research findings effectively in written and oral form. We first discuss written reports before listing some basics of oral presentations. We also provide some hints for research follow-up. At the end of the chapter, ethical issues related to market research are briefly reviewed.

10.2 Identify the Audience

When providing reports and presentations, you should keep the audience's characteristics and needs in mind and should tailor the report to their objectives. In market research, we have two audiences who need to be treated differently: Academics and practitioners. In this chapter, we focus on practitioners.

Imagine the marketing department of a company planning to launch a new product and therefore needing to learn more about potential customers' buying behavior. The knowledge and level of interest in the study might greatly differ within the department. While managers who commissioned the study generally know its objective and design, others who are unfamiliar with its background (e.g., the marketing director or the sales staff) must be made familiar with the research so that they can understand the research findings. When preparing the report, you should consider the following questions:
- Who will read the report?
- Why will they read the report?
- Which parts of the report are of specific interest to them?
- What do they already know about the study?
- What information will be new to them?
- What is the most important point for them to know after having read the report?

These questions help you determine the level of detail that has to be included in your report. Furthermore, they reveal information that requires specific focus during the project. Remember that a successful report is one that meets its audience's needs! However, not everything that you consider appropriate for your audience might actually be. Nothing is worse than suggesting an idea that is unpalatable to the audience (e.g., saying that a specific behavior or attitude of the senior management is a major obstacle to success), or to propose a course of action that has been attempted before. Thus, informal talks with the client before results are presented are vital—never formally present findings without discussing them with the client first!

Further, ask clients early in the project what their expectations are and what recommendations they think will be made. A good market research company can then go beyond these anticipated findings and offer recommendations that clients do not expect. It increases the chances of obtaining truly new insights. Furthermore, this avoids presenting research findings that clients already know. Essentially, why spend, say, $50,000 if the answers are at hand? Asking clients what they anticipate can avoid this issue.

10.3 Guidelines for Written Reports

As already mentioned, you should always keep in mind who is being addressed in the report. Decision makers are typically less familiar with statistical details, but they wish to know how the findings relate to practice. Research jargon should be avoided, while keeping to the point, stating points clearly and not omitting any important facts. There are several major rules to consider when writing a report (Armstrong 2010; Churchill and Iacobucci 2009):

1. The report must be *complete*, that is, it must contain all information that the reader needs to fully understand and appreciate the research. This also means that technical or ambiguous terms should be defined and illustrated. Not all readers understand terms like heteroskedasticity or Eigenvalue.

2. The report must be *accurate*. The readers will base their assessment of the entire research project's quality on the report. Consequently, the report must be well written. For example, the grammar must be correct, no slang should be used, tables must be labeled correctly, and page numbers should be included. Readers may think small errors are due to a lack of care and generalize about your analysis! Therefore, proofread multiple times (preferrably by someone else) to eliminate obvious errors. Lastly, objectivity is an important attribute of any report. This means that personal beliefs or feelings should influence the interpretation of the findings to the smallest possible degree.

3. The report must be *clear*. The art of writing a research report is to keep the language simple and concise. Consider the following points:
   - Short sentences instead of a complex sentence structure.

- Simple and unambiguous words.
- Concrete examples to illustrate aspects of the research (e.g., unexpected findings). These can also be helpful when the audience has strong beliefs that are not consistent with your proposals.
- Active instead of passive voice to bring life to the report and to facilitate understanding.
- Do not use negative words as they reduce clarity.
- Use business language. Avoid exclamation marks and do not use all caps. Avoid bolding that extends more than several words.
- Depending on your audience, try to present statistical data in a way that is easy to follow: For example, instead of saying "53% of the respondents are familiar with the brand," you could say "more than half of the respondents know the brand."

4. Follow the *KISS principle: Keep it short and simple!* This requires the report to be *concise*. As the report should be action-driven, the reader must immediately understand its purpose as well as its results. This means that you should not describe all the details, but should select important and interesting points. This rule also applies to the appendix, which should not be overloaded with irrelevant material. In addition, keep in mind that the first sentences of each section are the most important ones: They should summarize the main idea you want to express in this section.

5. The report must be *structured* in a logical manner. This applies to the general structure of the report (see Table 10.1) as well as the line of argumentation within each of the sections. Make sure to avoid style elements that may disctract the reader:
   - Avoid cross-references. Going elsewhere to see important results is disruptive. For example, do not put important tables in the appendix.
   - Use footnotes instead of endnotes.
   - Use as few footnotes as possible.

10.4 Structure the Written Report

When preparing a written report—besides the difficulty of satisfying several audiences—you also face the trade-off between discussing the study in too much detail and providing too little information. Whereas providing too much detail might bore the audience and perhaps even hide the message, providing too little information might leave the reader unsure of the research quality. A clear structure can help readers navigate through the report to quickly and easily find those elements in which they are interested.

Although reports differ regarding the researcher, the client, the topic, and the nature of the project itself (just think of the introductory example on the International Delphi Study 2030), the outline presented in Table 10.1 is a suggested structure for writing a research report.

Some general recommendations in case you need to adjust the structure above:

Table 10.1 Suggested structure for a written research report

TITLE PAGE

EXECUTIVE SUMMARY

TABLE OF CONTENTS

1. INTRODUCTION

  1.1 Problem definition

  1.2 Research objectives

  1.3 Research questions and/or hypotheses[a]

2. METHODOLOGY

  2.1 Population, sampling method and sample description

  2.2 Quantitative and qualitative methods used for data analysis

3. RESULTS

4. CONCLUSIONS AND RECOMMENDATIONS

5. LIMITATIONS

6. APPENDIX

[a]In practice, the word hypotheses may not be used but terms such as research question(s) or proposition(s)

- The structure should adequately reflect the central theme of the report.
- The structure should not be too detailed. As a rule of thumb, you should avoid using more than four levels.
- A new level must include at least two sections. For example, if there is 3.1.1, there must also be 3.1.2.

10.4.1 Title Page

The title page should state the title of the report, the name of the client who commissioned the report, the organization or researcher submitting it, and the date of release. The heading should clearly state the nature of the report. It may simply describe the research (e.g., "Survey of Mobile Phone Usage") or may outline the objectives of the study in the form of an action title (e.g., "How to Increase the Adoption of Wireless Internet").

10.4.2 Executive Summary

The executive summary is the heart and core of the report because it is often the only part that executives read. But even those who read more will be influenced in their expectations by the summary. Hence, this section must be short enough so that busy executives are willing to read it and should enable them to grasp the essence of the research. As a rule of thumb, the executive summary should not exceed 150 words. The executive summary should contain key findings and recommendations and should stimulate interest in the full study. Furthermore, it should help the readers remember the key points of the entire report by providing the necessary background information on the study (research problem, approach, and design).

Since the executive summary is very important, you should pay special attention to its structure. A common way of doing this is to tell a story. Begin with a description of the situation, then introduce a complication, which gives rise to a number of questions; lead the reader through your line of reasoning to the answer:

- *Situation*: Background information that the reader already knows.
- *Complication*: A change from a formerly stable situation or a new business opportunity (i.e., the reason for your research study).
- *Question*: The scope and goal of your research study.
- *Answer*: Your findings, conclusions, and recommendations.

10.4.3 Table of Contents

The table of contents helps the reader locate specific aspects of the report. Listings in the table of contents should correspond to the main headings of the report. It should also include lists of tables and figures with page references.

10.4.4 Introduction

This section must provide the reader with the project context. Questions to be answered include:

- Why was the study undertaken?
- What were the objectives and key questions?
- Is the study related to other studies and, if so, what findings did they produce?
- How is the remainder of the report structured?

Besides introducing the background and purpose of the research, this part should also shortly explain how the problem was addressed. In particular, theoretical foundations or analytical models on which the study was based are presented in this section. Hypotheses or propositions that will be tested during the research should be mentioned. Furthermore, unfamiliar terms used in the report have to be defined. For example, in the airline industry, terms such as CASM (cost per available seat mile) are used, which need explanation. As a rule, the following three questions regarding the research should be answered in the introduction, but should be neither too detailed nor too technical:

- What was done?
- How was it done?
- Why was it done?

Keep in mind that the introduction should set the stage for the body of the report and presentation of the results, but no more than that. A detailed description of how the data were collected and analyzed is provided in the next section of the report. Lastly, at the end of the introduction, you should provide a brief summary of how the report is organized.

10.4.5 Methodology

In this section, you should describe the procedure of the research and the different statistical methods used for the data analysis. Although not everyone will be interested in the details, these must be presented precisely and coherently, allowing the reader to understand the process and basic principles of the analyses. Always consider your audience! If the audience has a strong interest in research methodology, you should describe the procedures in detail, but skip the basics. If the client has little knowledge of the analyses, you could introduce the methodology briefly. Consider moving selected contents in the appendix.

If not already stated in the previous section, you should define whether the study is exploratory, descriptive or causal in nature and whether the results are based on secondary or primary data. If primary data are used, their source should be specified (observation vs. questionnaire). If a questionnaire was used, you should state whether it was administered through face-to-face interviews, telephone interviews or web or mailed surveys. Explain why this particular method was chosen.

The reader should also know the demographic or other relevant characteristics of the target population. This includes the geographical area, age group, and gender. While it is usually sufficient to describe the population in a few sentences, the sampling method needs more explanation: How was the sample selected? Which sampling units were chosen? In addition, information on the sample size, response rate, and sample characteristics are essential as they indicate the results' reliability and validity.

A copy of the actual instruments used, such as the questionnaire or the interview guide, as well as detailed statistical analyses of the results should be included in the appendix or even as a separate report. Although these are important to fully understand the characteristics of the research project, including them in the main text would make reading the report more difficult.

10.4.6 Results

This section is usually the longest in the report. Here, the researcher presents the findings and describes how these relate to a possible solution to the research problem and to the recommendations. There are several ways to logically present the results. You could, for instance, use the different research objectives as a guideline to structure this section and then analyze them one by one.

Another way is to first summarize the overall findings and then analyze them according to the relevant subgroups, such as gender or geographical regions. If several research methods were used, it is also possible to classify the findings correspondingly. For example, you could first present the conclusions of the secondary data collection and then those derived from an analysis of the questionnaire.

When presenting statistical data, tables and graphs should be used to bring life to the report and make it more interesting. Furthermore, tables and graphs structure information, thereby facilitating its understanding. Both allow the researcher to visually represent very complex data in a way which is not fully feasible when using tables. However, graphs can also be misleading as they can be adjusted to favor a specific viewpoint (see Box 10.1 for examples).

Box 10.1 Window-dressing with graphs

While graphs have the obvious advantage of presenting complex information in an accessible manner, they can be used to mislead the reader by promoting an idea or favoring a specific viewpoint. Experience in generating and interpreting graphs will help you spot these issues. In this box, examples are shown of how graphs can be presented in a misleading way.

By simply shortening the x-axis in Fig. 10.1 (i.e., removing the years 2003–2007), we convey a potentially misleading idea of the growth in units sold (Fig. 10.2). Likewise, we can "adjust" the y-axis by modifying the scale range (Fig. 10.3 vs. Fig. 10.4). By simply reducing the axis to a range from 98 to 114 units, the situation is made to look much more positive. Another typical example is the "floating" y-axis (Fig. 10.5 vs. Fig. 10.6) which increases the scale range along the y-axis, thus making the drop in number of units sold less pronounced visually.

Data are often presented using three-dimensional figures such as in Fig. 10.7. While these can be visually appealing, they are also subject to window-dressing. In this example, the lengths of all the edges were doubled to correspond to the 100% increase in turnover. However, the resulting area is not twice but four times as large as the original image, thus presenting a false picture of the increase.

These are just some common examples; Huff's (1993) classical text offers more on this topic.

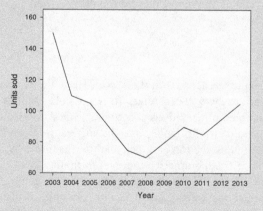

Fig. 10.1 Where does the curve start? (I)

(continued)

Box 10.1 (continued)

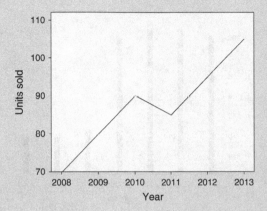

Fig. 10.2 Where does the curve start? (II)

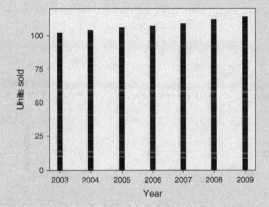

Fig. 10.3 Stretching the y-axis (I)

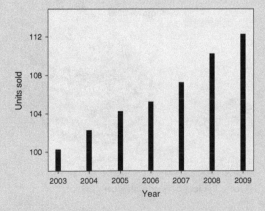

Fig. 10.4 Stretching the y-axis (II)

(continued)

Box 10.1 (continued)

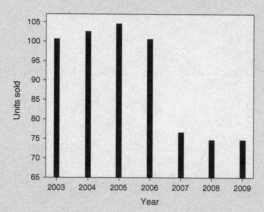

Fig. 10.5 The "floating" y-axis (I)

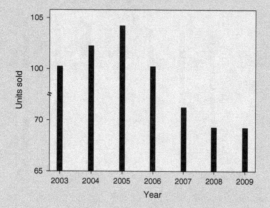

Fig. 10.6 The "floating" y-axis (II)

Fig. 10.7 Doubling the edge length quadruples the area

Tables are generally less susceptible to manipulation as they contain more detail. Tables present exact figures and thus enable the reader to accurately retrieve specific facts. As a rule of thumb, every table or graph in the report should be numbered sequentially and have a meaningful title, which briefly describes the information provided. Alternatively, you could use a representative quote from an interview as the title, giving the graph or table a personal touch.

Note that readers need to grasp the message presented in the table or graph at a glance, because most first turn their attention to these before reading the accompanying text. Therefore, you should organize data so that the conclusion is obvious. You should:

- Put data to be compared in columns, not rows,
- Round data, typically to three digits,
- Highlight data to reinforce conclusions (e.g., boldface key numbers), and
- Clearly state the units of measurement.

There are many different kinds of graphs and each type has its advantages and disadvantages. Please review Chap. 5 where we discussed the most commonly used graphs in market research studies.

10.4.7 Conclusion and Recommendations

Having presented the findings, the next step is to summarize the most relevant points and interpret them in light of the research objectives. You should write the conclusions in such a way that they present information relevant to managerial decision-making. Keep in mind that, for the client, the quality of the marketing research depends heavily on how well decision makers can use the information! The research must provide the client with clear benefits, which could lead to further research assignments.

Researchers are increasingly asked to go beyond merely stating facts and interpreting them, but to also provide recommendations or to advise on management decisions. Whereas conclusions that are purely based on the research have to be unbiased and impersonal, specific recommendations are grounded in a personal and (at least partially) subjective opinion on how the results can be most favorably used in the clients' interest. Thus, you have to make sure that recommendations are recognizable as such. The extent to which a research report should include recommendations is determined by the client during negotiations prior to the start of the project. This will also depend on the researcher's expertise in the area of concern. In this respect, the researcher should be aware of all factors that influence the marketing issue. Researchers may provide logical recommendations based upon the findings of their work, yet these might be unrealistic or impossible for the client to implement due to issues such as insufficient budgets, fixed operation methods, or specific policies, regulations, and politics. To avoid such issues, make sure that you or another member of your research team is familiar with the overall context, including regulatory and legal issues. Furthermore, before making recommendations, review them with the client to determine whether these are acceptable and actionable (see Box 10.2 for an example).

> **Box 10.2 An example of BAD recommendations**
> A candy producing company wishes to know how it can increase sales and has commissioned a research organization to gain insights into its different customer segments. The researchers find that teenagers are the most important target for the given brand and suggest that vending machines within schools would increase the company's revenue. Although this could indeed boost sales, the recommendation does not help the company if vending machines are not allowed in schools.

10.4.8 Limitations

Finally, you should explain the extent to which the findings can be generalized. All research studies have limitations due to time, budget, and other constraints. Furthermore, errors might have occurred during the data collection. Not mentioning potential weaknesses (e.g., the use of a convenience sample, or a small sample size), for whatever reason, reduces the credibility of the research. Not disclosing important facts also violates common codes of industry conduct, such as those drafted by ESOMAR. Taking all factors into regard, the results of the research should always be discussed in a balanced and objective way. You should neither overly diminish the importance and validity of the research, nor try to conceal sources of errors and, hence, potentially mislead managers regarding the results you present.

10.4.9 Appendix

All material not directly necessary for an understanding of the project, but still related to the study should be included in the appendix. This includes questionnaires, interview guides, detailed data analyses or other types of data or material.

10.5   Guidelines for Oral Presentations

Most clients want a presentation in addition to the written report. This could be given during the research in the form of an interim report or at the end to explain the findings to the management. Often, members of the client staff present research findings to the management and not the market research company. By letting a member of the client staff such as an internal market researcher or business analyst deliver the presentation of the report, acceptance may increase as the client can provide content.

If asked to deliver an oral presentation, you should keep the principles of a written report in mind. It is especially important to identify and understand your audience and to prepare the presentation thoroughly. A professional and interesting presentation might increase interest in the written report! Furthermore, since the oral presentation allows for interaction, interesting points can be highlighted and discussed in more detail. However, if you are not well prepared for the presentation nor understand the expectations, needs, and wants of your audience, you could face an unpleasant situation. You should always keep the following golden rule in mind: *Never deliver a presentation you wouldn't want to sit through*!

10.6 Visual Aids in Oral Presentations

It is useful to provide the audience with a written summary or a handout so that they do not have to take notes of everything but can focus on the presentation. If focus group interviews were conducted, for example, you could show excerpts from the recordings to provide concrete examples in support of a finding. The saying "a picture says more than a thousand words" is also true of the oral presentation. Visual aids such as overhead transparencies, flip charts or computer slide shows (e.g., Powerpoint or Prezi at http://www.prezi.com) not only help emphasize important points, but also facilitate the communication of difficult ideas. In the following, we summarize some hints concerning slide shows (see Armstrong 2010).

Use of visual aids:

- Use a simple master slide and avoid fancy animations.
- Use a sufficiently large font size (as a rule of thumb, 16pt. or higher and never less than 12pt.) so that everyone attending the presentation can read the slides.
- Use high contrasts for text. Use black and white. Do not write on illustrations or wallpapers.
- Use contrasting colors to emphasize specific points, but not too many.
- Use simple graphs, diagrams or short sentences rather than tables.

Arranging visual aids:

- Do not have too much information on one slide (as a general rule, one key issue per slide). Never put a block of text on a page.
- Organize the material so that the different modes reinforce one another. For example, you do not want people running ahead of you, so either roll out each point as you discuss it on a slide of use many simple slides.
- Use a small number of slides relative to the time available for the presentation. The focus should be on the presenter and not on the slides. Having more slides than minutes available is not a good idea. Good presenters often use between 3 and 5 minutes to discuss a slide.
- Prepare (color) handouts for all members of the audience.
- If you intend to use media elements in your presentation, make sure the equipment to be used supports them (e.g., that the sound equipment is working or that your video formats are supported).

10.7 Structure the Oral Presentation

Be aware that an oral presentation cannot cover the same amount of information as a written report. You must be selective and structure the presentation content clearly and logically. A good way of starting your presentation is by structuring the introduction in the classic narrative pattern of story-telling (situation → complication → question → answer) introduced earlier in the context of written reports. Limit the introduction to what the audience can accept. Nothing would be worse than triggering resistance of what is presented right at the beginning of your oral presentation.

Next, move on to the main part of your presentation. Based on a brief description of your major findings, capture the audience's attention by presenting answers to the logical questions that arise from the project, such as "How were these results achieved?" or "How did we reach this conclusion?"

Essentially, you follow a pyramid structure: At any point you raise a question in the audience's mind that has to be answered in this pyramid's subsequently lower level. Figure 10.8 illustrates this concept using an example of a mobile phone study which found that a novel smartphone should be introduced in white.

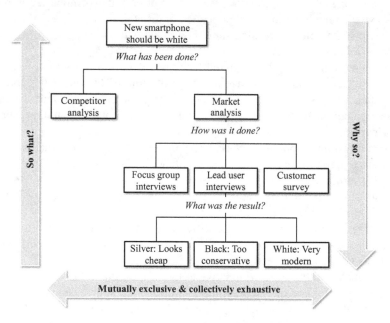

Fig. 10.8 Pyramid structure for presentations

You begin by introducing the result of the study (i.e., the smartphone should be introduced in white) and then work your way down. Begin by explaining that a comprehensive market analysis was carried out, after which you discuss the elements of the analysis (i.e., focus group interviews, lead user interviews, and a customer survey). Finally, present the results of each element of the analysis (e.g., that lead users perceived the black color as too conservative, silver as too cheap, while white was perceived as modern). Once at the bottom of the pyramid, it is time to pause and to provide a summary, before moving from the first key line which you have just presented to the next key line, and so on.

This process forces you to only provide the information relevant to the question under consideration. Moving from top to bottom and then bottom to top, helps you answer the questions: "Why so?" and "So what?," while being collectively exhaustive and mutually exclusive regarding the results and concepts you have presented. Ensure you never provide findings that do not lead to specific conclusions and do not offer conclusions that are not based on findings. Ultimately, this pyramid approach helps the audience grasp the line of reasoning better. This technique is also frequently called the *Minto principle* or *Minto pyramid*, called after its founder Barbara Minto. To learn more about this principle, we recommend reading Minto (2008).

10.8 Follow-Up

After having delivered the written report and oral presentation, two tasks remain: First, you need to help the client in implementing the findings. This includes answering questions that may arise from the written report and oral presentation, providing assistance in selecting a product, advertising agency, marketing actions etc., or incorporating information from the report into the firm's marketing information system or decision support system (see Chap. 3). This provides an opportunity for discussing further research projects. For example, you might agree on repeating the study after one year to see whether the marketing actions were effective. Second, you need to evaluate the market research project, both internally, and with the client. Only (critical) feedback can help disclosing potential problems that may have occurred and, thus, provide the necessary grounds for improving your work. Using uniform questionnaires for the evaluation of different projects helps to compare the feedback across different projects conducted simultaneously or different points in time.

10.9 Ethics in Research Reports

Ethics is an important topic in marketing research, because research interacts with human beings at several stages (e.g., data collection and the communication of findings). There are two "problematic" relations that can ultimately lead to ethical dilemmas. First, ethical issues arise when the researcher's interests conflict with those of the participants. For instance, the researcher's interest is to gather as much information as possible from respondents but respondents often request confidentiality and privacy. Second, in addition to the legal and professional responsibilities that researchers have regarding their respondents, they also have reporting responsi-bilities. The Council of American Research Organizations (CASRO) sets clear guidelines in its "Code of Standards and Ethics for Survey Research":

> *It is the obligation of the Research Organization to insure that the findings they release are an accurate portrayal of the survey data, and careful checks on the accuracy of all figures are mandatory. (CASRO 2011, p. 17)*

Similarly, the European Society for Opinion and Marketing Research (ESOMAR) has established a code which sets minimum standards of ethical conduct to be followed by all researchers:

> 1. *Market researchers shall conform to all relevant national and international laws.*
> 2. *Market researchers shall behave ethically and shall not do anything which might damage the reputation of market research.*
> 3. *Market researchers shall take special care when carrying out research among children and young people.*
> 4. *Respondents' cooperation is voluntary and must be based on adequate, and not misleading, information about the general purpose and nature of the project when their agreement to participate is being obtained and all such statements shall be honoured.*
> 5. *The rights of respondents as private individuals shall be respected by market researchers and they shall not be harmed or adversely affected as the direct result of cooperating in a market research project.*
> 6. *Market researchers shall never allow personal data they collect in a market research project to be used for any purpose other than market research.*
> 7. *Market researchers shall ensure that projects and activities are designed, carried out, reported and documented accurately, transparently and objectively.*
> 8. *Market researchers shall conform to the accepted principles of fair com-petition. (ESOMAR 2007, p. 4)*

In practice, researchers face an ethical dilemma. They are paid by the client and feel forced to deliver "good" results. In this sense, they might be tempted to interpret results in a way that fits the client's perspective or the client's presumed interests. For instance, researchers might ignore data because they would reveal an inconvenient truth (e.g., the client's brand has low awareness or customers do not like the product design).

Remember that researchers should never mislead the audience! For instance, it would be ethically questionable to modify the scales of a graph so that the results look more impressive, as shown in Fig. 10.1–10.4. Furthermore, researchers have a duty to treat information and research results confidentially, to store data securely and to use data only for the research purpose agreed upon. Above all, you should keep in mind that marketing research is based on trust. Thus, when writing the report, you should respect the profession's ethical standards in order to maintain this trust.

Review Questions

1. What are the basic elements of any written research report?
2. Revisit the case study on Haver & Boecker in Chap. 8 and prepare an outline for a written research report.
3. Consider the following situations. Do you think they confront the market researcher with ethical issues?
   (a) The client asks the researcher to make a list of respondents available to target selling activities at these people.
   (b) The client asks the researcher not to disclose part of the research to his organization.
   (c) The client asks the researcher to present other recommendations.
   (d) The client asks the researcher to re-consider the analysis because the findings seem implausible to him/her.
   (e) The client wishes to know the name of a particular customer who was very negative about the quality of service provided.

Further Readings

Huff D. (1993). *How to lie with statistics.* New York: Norton & Company.
   First published in 1954, this book remains relevant as a wake-up call for people unaccustomed to the slippery world of means, correlations, and graphs. Although many of the examples used in the book are dated, the conclusions are timeless.
Durate N. (2008). *Slideology. The art and science of crafting great presentations.* Sebastopol: O'Reilly Media.
   In this book, the author presents a rich source for effective visual expression in presentations. It is full of practical approaches to visual story development that can be used to connect with your audience. The text provides good hints to fulfill the golden rule to never deliver a presentation you wouldn't want to sit through.
Market Research Society at http://www.mrs.org.uk/standards/guidelines.htm

Under this link you find the (ethical) guidelines of the Market Research Society. The guidelines discuss for example the ethical issues surrounding research using children or elderly as participants.

References

Armstrong, J. S. (2010). *Persuasive advertising: Evidence-based principles*. New York: Palgrave Macmillan.

Churchill, G. A., Jr., & Iacobucci, D. (2009). *Marketing research: Methodological foundations* (10th ed.). Mason, OH: South-Western College Publishers.

Council of American Survey Research Organizations (CASRO) (2011). Codes of standards and ethics for survey research. www.casro.org/resource/resmgr/casro_code_of_standards.pdf

European Society for Opinion and Marketing Research (ESOMAR) (2007). ICC/ESOMAR International Code On Market And Social Research. http://www.esomar.org/uploads/public/knowledge-and-standards/codes-and-guidelines/ICCESOMAR_Code_English_.pdf

Huff, D. (1993). *How to lie with statistics*. New York: W. W. Norton & Company.

Minto, B. (2008). *The pyramid principle: Logic in writing and thinking* (3rd ed.). Harlow: Pearson.

Index

M. Sarstedt and E. Mooi, *A Concise Guide to Market Research*,
Springer Texts in Business and Economics, DOI 10.1007/978-3-642-53965-7,
© Springer-Verlag Berlin Heidelberg 2014